DICTIONARY OF
POLITICS AND GOVERNMENT

THIRD EDITION

P.H. Collin

D0726344

BLOOMSBURY

A BLOOMSBURY REFERENCE BOOK DICT.

www.bloomsbury.com/reference

Originally published by Peter Collin Publishing

First published 1988
Second edition published 1997, 2001
Third edition published 2004

Bloomsbury Publishing Plc
38 Soho Square, London W1D 3HB

British Library Cataloguing-in-Publication Data
A catalogue record for this book is available from the British Library

ISBN 0 7475 7220 8

Editor
Peter Holmes
Head of Political and Social Sciences
Hills Road Sixth Form College, Cambridge, UK

Text Production and Proofreading
Katy McAdam, Heather Bateman, Emma Harris

All papers used by Bloomsbury Publishing are natural, recyclable
products made from wood grown in well-managed forests.
The manufacturing processes conform to the
environmental regulations of the country of origin.

Text processing and computer typesetting by Bloomsbury
Printed and bound in Italy by Legoprint

Contents

Introduction
Preface
Pronunciation Guide
The Dictionary
Supplements
    Legislative Procedure in the United Kingdom
    Legislative Procedure in the European Union
    Legislative Procedure in the United States of America
    United Kingdom Court Structure
    United States of America Court Structure
    The United Kingdom: Members of the Cabinet
    Prime Ministers of Great Britain
    Structure of a British Government Department:
      The Department of Trade and Industry
    Kings and Queens of England
    The United States of America: Members of the Cabinet
                Presidents of the United States of America

Introduction

When we are constantly told that there is widespread disillusionment with the political system, it is gratifying to observe that it remains a subject of intense study. There is much to examine. Constitutional change is in the air. Politicians are seeking new ways to combat voter apathy. This third edition of the Dictionary comes at a highly relevant time.

The democratic structure of the United Kingdom has changed and is changing. Devolved legislatures and Assemblies are in place in Scotland and Wales. A devolved Assembly in Northern Ireland remains in abeyance until political dialogue is resumed. The devolution process is still evolving. The dividing line between what is devolved and what is reserved will inevitably be subject to ongoing debate. Questions will continue to be raised about the role of MPs at Westminster who represent parts of the United Kingdom which control their own domestic affairs.

Devolution does not necessarily stop at the borders of England. The English regions are expected to have the opportunity of deciding whether they too would prefer a new unit of devolved government. If agreed, this would have a knock-on effect on the existing structure of local government both in metropolitan and shire areas. What is already a non-uniform pattern of provision looks set to become more varied still.

The present Government has re-lit the blue touch paper of House of Lords reform, starting with the partial abolition of the hereditary peers in 1999. It has continued to burn slowly. In a democracy, there should arguably be no contest between the legitimacy of an elected and an appointed second chamber. However, in the United Kingdom the issue is clouded with unresolved questions over powers, systems of election and scope of prime ministerial patronage. Hybrid solutions abound, all with their champions. But when given an opportunity in early 2003, the House of Commons could not resolve the matter of Lords' composition. The end of what was begun is not yet in sight.

The evolution of the European Union also has an impact on internal democratic structures. Whether it is through the pressure of European integration or the wider process of globalisation, there are complaints from people that more is happening which is outwith their control. National parliaments across Europe are stirring as they sense that they are losing ownership of legislation. The much talked about democratic deficit has yet to be addressed to the satisfaction of many parliamentarians and people.

It is perhaps the growing perception that ordinary people have less and less influence in important decisions affecting their lives, which has increased voter alienation and has affected participation in elections. This has prompted debate about ways to make elections more user friendly. E-voting and non-traditional polling stations are under active consideration, but the highest profile experiment to date has been the introduction of all postal ballot elections. Early evidence suggests that turn-out increases, but so allegedly does the risk of fraud. The jury (in this case the Electoral Commission) is still out. If eventually information technology is fully harnessed to the electoral process, a distant prospect is held out of almost instant elections in which voters will have at their fingertips comprehensive information about parties and candidates. The ramifications for all concerned would be profound.

By a variety of means, contact between the elected and their electors may be increasing, but the quality as well as quantity of those exchanges needs to be addressed. For a democratic system to work properly there has to be dialogue. But can dialogue adequately be achieved by electronic means or paper surveys? Electors and elected need to debate together so that the comparative strengths of various propositions can be tested. Through better two-way communication, it is important to ensure that disappointment does not automatically lead to feelings of rejection. The true test of a democracy is how it deals with minorities. Everyone cannot be in the majority on every issue.

The media might be expected to provide the channels through which information and ideas can flow. Yet too often there is an emphasis on entertainment or controversy for its own sake in reporting parliamentary and political events. Opinion has priority over fact. Parliament is more often sketched than reported.

Members of the public are often candid in admitting that there is much they do not know. A great deal can be picked up from this Dictionary to improve people's confidence in negotiating their way through the system.

But politics and Parliament can only be brought alive through debate, the injection of ideas, the clash of personality and a degree of passion. The political system is not a private club; it is a broad public network which anyone can enter. The more people do so, the healthier democracy will be whether at village, town, city, national and, even international levels. If this Dictionary encourages participation as well as study, it will be doubly welcome.

Rt Hon Sir Alan Haselhurst MP

Chairman, Ways and Means and Deputy Speaker
House of Commons

Preface

This dictionary provides the user with the basic vocabulary used in the fields of government and politics, especially in the United Kingdom, the European Union and the United States, and also contains some more informal terms used in the media. The subject matter covers national legislatures, elections, local government, parliamentary and council procedure, international affairs and political parties and theories.

Each entry is explained in clear straightforward English. Examples are given to show how the words and phrases are used in normal contexts. Many words also have comments of a more general nature, giving encyclopedic information about procedures and institutions. At the back of the book there are supplements giving information about the political and legislative systems in the United Kingdom, the European Union and the United States.

Pronunciation Guide

The following symbols have been used to show the pronunciation of the main words in the dictionary.

Stress is indicated by a main stress mark (') and a secondary stress mark (,). Note that these are only guides, as the stress of the word changes according to its position in the sentence.

Vowels		*Consonants*	
æ	back	b	buck
ɑː	harm	d	dead
ɒ	stop	ð	other
aɪ	type	dʒ	jump
aʊ	how	f	fare
aɪə	hire	g	gold
aʊə	hour	h	head
ɔː	course	j	yellow
ɔɪ	annoy	k	cab
e	head	l	leave
eə	fair	m	mix
eɪ	make	n	nil
eʊ	go	ŋ	sing
ɜː	word	p	print
iː	keep	r	rest
i	happy	s	save
ə	about	ʃ	shop
ɪ	fit	t	take
ɪə	near	tʃ	change
u	annual	θ	theft
uː	pool	v	value
ʊ	book	w	work
ʊə	tour	x	loch
ʌ	shut	ʒ	measure
		z	zone

A

AAFC *abbreviation* Agriculture and Agri-Food Canada

abandon /əˈbændən/ *verb* to give up or not to continue something □ **to abandon a Bill, an action** to give up trying to promote a Bill

abdicate /ˈæbdɪkeɪt/ *verb* to give up the position of king or queen of a country

abdication /ˌæbdɪˈkeɪʃ(ə)n/ *noun* the act of giving up the position of king or queen of a country

abide by /əˈbaɪd baɪ/ *verb* to obey something such as an order or a rule ○ *The government promised to abide by the decision of the High Court.* ○ *The rebels did not abide by the terms of the agreement.*

abjuration /ˌæbdʒʊəˈreɪʃ(ə)n/ *noun* the act of giving up something

abjure /əbˈdʒʊə/ *verb* **1.** to give up something **2.** *US* to swear not to bear allegiance to another country

abode /əˈbəʊd/ *noun* the place where someone lives (*formal*) ◊ **right of abode**

abolish /əˈbɒlɪʃ/ *verb* to put an end to an institution or practice ○ *The Chancellor of the Exchequer refused to ask Parliament to abolish the tax on alcohol.* ○ *The Senate voted to abolish the death penalty.*

abolition /ˌæbəˈlɪʃ(ə)n/ *noun* an act of putting an end to an institution or practice ○ *to campaign for the abolition of the death penalty* ○ *Anarchists advocate the abolition of the state.*

abrogate /ˈæbrəgeɪt/ *verb* to overturn a treaty or law

abrogation /ˌæbrəˈgeɪʃ(ə)n/ *noun* the act of overturning a treaty or law

absence /ˈæbsəns/ *noun* the fact of not being where you usually are or where you are expected to be. ◊ **leave of absence** □ **in the absence of** when someone is not present ○ *In the absence of the chairman, his deputy took the chair.* □ **apologies for absence** the list of members of a committee or other group who have apologised for not being able to attend a meeting, read out at the beginning of the meeting

absent /ˈæbsənt/ *adjective* not present

absentee /ˌæbsənˈtiː/ *noun* a person who does not attend a meeting or event when they are expected

absentee ballot /ˌæbsenˈtiː ˌbælət/ *noun* same as **postal vote**

absolute government /ˌæbsəluːt ˈgʌvəmənt/ *noun* government by a person or group of people who exercise total power and where the ordinary population has no vote and no say in the government of the state

absolute majority /ˌæbsəluːt məˈdʒɒrɪti/ *noun* the situation of having more votes than all other candidates or parties combined ○ *In the alternative vote system, if no candidate has an absolute majority at the first count, the second preferences are counted.*

absolute privilege /ˌæbsəluːt ˈprɪvɪlɪdʒ/ *noun* a privilege which protects an MP speaking in the House of Commons from being sued for defamation or libel

absolutism /ˈæbsəluːˌtɪz(ə)m/ *noun* the political theory that a government should have total power

absolutist /ˌæbsəˈluːtɪst/ *adjective, noun* a person who believes the government should have total power

abstain /əb'steɪn/ *verb* not to do something deliberately, especially not to vote ○ *Sixty MPs abstained in the vote on capital punishment.*

abstention /əb'stenʃən/ *noun* the act of deliberately not doing something, especially voting ○ *The motion was carried by 200 votes to 150, with 60 abstentions.*

abstract /'æbstrækt/ *verb* to make a summary of a document or speech

abuse *noun* /ə'bjuːs/ **1.** the wrong use of something ○ *The Chancellor of the Exchequer has introduced a Bill to correct some of the abuses in the present tax system.* □ **abuse of Parliament** something that is breaks accepted parliamentary rules of conduct □ **abuse of power** the use of legal powers in an illegal or harmful way □ **abuse of rules** the use of rules to achieve a purpose which is open to criticism, e.g. the use of the right to introduce a motion into the House of Commons to prevent a debate from continuing **2.** rude or insulting words **3.** bad treatment of a person, often of a sexual nature (NOTE: no plural for (2) or (3)) ■ *verb* /ə'bjuːz/ **1.** to use something wrongly ○ *It was claimed that the government whips had abused the rules of the House of Commons by preventing full discussion of the Private Members Bill.* □ **to abuse your authority** to use your authority in an illegal or harmful way **2.** to say rude words to someone ○ *He abused the police before being taken to the cells.* **3.** to treat someone badly, often in a sexual way

ACAS /'eɪkæs/ *abbreviation* Advisory Conciliation and Arbitration Service

ACC /ˌeɪ siː 'siː/ *abbreviation* Association of County Councils

accede /ək'siːd/ *verb* **1.** to sign an international treaty or agreement ○ *In 1972 Britain acceded to the European Economic Community.* **2.** to take up an official position, especially as king or queen ○ *accede to the throne* **3.** to accept or agree with something □ **to ac-**cede to a request** or **demand** to do what someone wants

access /'ækses/ *noun* **1.** the opportunity to use or do something ○ *access to education and healthcare* **2.** the opportunity to meet someone important ○ *They have access to the Prime Minister and are said to influence the decisions he takes.* ■ permission to obtain or see private or secret information ○ *to have access to personal records* ■ *noun* **1.** a way of getting to a place ○ *level access to the seating areas* ○ *wheelchair access* **2.** the right of the owner of a piece of land to use a public road which is next to the land ○ *She complained that she was being denied access to the main road.* (NOTE: no plural) ■ *verb* **1.** to get information, e.g. to be able to obtain data from a computer ○ *The staff in the Housing Department can access records on all properties and tenants.* **2.** to get to a place

accession /ək'seʃ(ə)n/ *noun* **1.** the act of signing an international treaty or agreement **2.** the occasion of taking up an official position □ **accession to the throne** the occasion of becoming King or Queen

accession country /ək'seʃ(ə)n ˌkʌntri/ *noun* a country that will become or has recently become a Member State of the European Union

Accession Treaties /ək'seʃ(ə)n ˌtriːtiz/ *plural noun* the international agreements establishing the conditions under which countries become Member States of the European Union

accommodation centre /əˌkɒmə 'deɪʃ(ə)n ˌsentə/ *noun* a place where people live while their request to enter and remain in a country is considered

account /ə'kaʊnt/ *noun* **1.** a description of, or explanation for, some event or situation ○ *The minister gave a full account to Parliament of the accident.* **2.** a financial statement (NOTE: Often used in the plural.) ■ *verb* to give an explanation of some event or situation, especially a bad one ○ *They will have to account to their constituents for this failure.* ◊ to consider something carefully as part of doing something else ○ *The Committee will take account of the report of the Royal Commission* or *will take the Royal Commission's report into account when drafting the Bill.*

accountability /əˌkaʊntəˈbɪlɪti/ *noun* the situation of being required to explain what has happened and take responsibility for it ○ *the accountability of elected representatives to their electors* ○ *There have been demands for increased accountability for ministers.*

accountable /əˈkaʊntəb(ə)l/ *adjective* being required to explain what has happened and take responsibility for it ○ *Ministers are accountable to Parliament.*

accredit /əˈkredɪt/ *verb* to appoint somebody as an envoy or ambassador to represent their country abroad

accredited /əˈkredɪtɪd/ *adjective* **1.** chosen and officially appointed to represent an organisation ○ *an accredited agent* **2.** chosen and appointed by one country to represent it in an official capacity in another country ○ *She is accredited as her country's ambassador to the United Nations.*

acculturation /əˌkʌltjʊˈreɪʃ(ə)n/ *noun* the assimilation of parts of a different culture

acknowledge /əkˈnɒlɪdʒ/ *verb* **1.** to accept that something is true or necessary ○ *We acknowledge there were mistakes made in the past and we must learn from them.* **2.** to confirm that something has been received, such as a letter ○ *The office of the Ombudsman has acknowledged receipt of the letter.* **3.** to thank someone publicly or officially for something they have done ○ *I'd like to take this opportunity to acknowledge all the hard work that has gone into making this campaign such a success.* **4.** to recognise rights or authority officially ○ *They refused to acknowledge the new regime.*

acknowledgement /əkˈnɒlɪdʒmənt/ *noun* **1.** acceptance that something is true or necessary ○ *There* is almost universal acknowledgment of the need to take global warming seriously. **2.** a letter or card to say that something has been received ○ *She wrote to her MP and received an acknowledgement immediately.* **3.** thanks for something that has been done ○ *acknowledgement of her role in the achievement*

acquis communautaire *French words meaning* 'established community rights': the contents of the various treaties agreed to by the Member States of the European Union, which have gradually built up a body of law under which the EU operates

act /ækt/ *noun* a law which has been approved by a law-making body. See Comment at **bill** (NOTE: In the United Kingdom, laws are approved by Parliament and in the USA by Congress.)

COMMENT: Before an Act becomes law, it is presented to Parliament in the form of a Bill. See notes at BILL.

active citizenship /ˌæktɪv ˈsɪtɪzənʃɪp/ *noun* the full involvement of people in a variety of forms of politics, including voting, joining a party or pressure group, campaigning or standing for election ○ *It is important for the survival of democracy that active citizenship should be encouraged.*

activism /ˈæktɪvɪz(ə)m/ *noun* energetic and sometimes aggressive support for a social or political cause

activist /ˈæktɪvɪst/ *noun* **1.** a person who is very active in pursuing social or political change, sometimes by extreme means **2.** a person who works regularly for a political party, sometimes a person who is in disagreement with the main policies of their party or whose views are more extreme than those held by the majority of their party ○ *The meeting was disrupted by an argument between the chairman and left-wing activists.* ○ *Party activists have urged the central committee to adopt a more radical approach to the problems of unemployment.* Also called **party activist**

Act of Parliament /ˌækt əv ˈpɑːləmənt/ *noun* a decision which has been approved by Parliament and has received the Royal Assent and so becomes law

Act of Union /ˌækt əv ˈjuːnjən/ *noun* the act of 1801, by which the parliaments of Great Britain and Ireland were joined to form the United Kingdom

Act of Union with Scotland /ˌækt əv ˌjuːnjən wɪð ˈskɒtlənd/ *noun* the parliamentary act of 1707 which joined England and Scotland together to form Great Britain

actual possession /ˌæktʃuəl pəˈzeʃ(ə)n/ *noun* the occupation and control of land and buildings

actual value /ˌæktʃuəl ˈvæljuː/ *noun* the real value of something if sold on the open market

actuarial tables /ˌæktʃueəriəl ˈteɪb(ə)lz/ *plural noun* lists showing how long people are likely to live, used to calculate life assurance premiums

additional member system /ə ˌdɪʃ(ə)nəl ˈmembə ˌsɪstəm/ *noun* an electoral system used in elections for the Scottish Parliament, Welsh Assembly and Greater London Assembly, where a proportion of the representatives are elected by the first-past-the-post system, and the others by a party list system, giving additional members to ensure the result is more proportional (NOTE: Note: the system operates in some countries with the constituency representatives elected by a majoritarian system)

address /əˈdres/ *noun* **1.** a formal speech ○ *In his address to the meeting, the mayor spoke of the problems facing the town.* ○ *In his State of the Union address, the president spoke of the problems of terrorism.* ◊ **humble address** □ **address of thanks** a formal speech thanking someone such as a well-known person for doing something such as officially opening a new building □ the Queen's Speech at the State Opening of Parliament. ◊ **debate**

on the address **2.** the details of number, street and town where an office is or where a person lives ■ *verb* **1.** to speak to ○ *The Leader of the Opposition was asked to address the meeting.* **2.** to speak about or deal with a particular subject or problem ○ *He then addressed the question of government aid to universities.* □ **to address yourself to something** to deal with a particular problem ○ *the government will have to address itself to problems of international trade* **3.** to write on an envelope the details of the number, street and town where an office is or a person lives ○ *an incorrectly addressed package*

ad hoc /ˌæd ˈhɒk/ *Latin phrase meaning* 'for this particular purpose' □ **an ad hoc committee** a temporary committee set up to study a particular problem. ◊ **standing committee**

ad hoc Select Committee /ˌæd hɒk sɪˈlekt kəˌmɪti/ *noun* a committee of Congress set up to examine a special case or problem

adjourn /əˈdʒɜːn/ *verb* to stop a meeting for a period or to postpone a legal hearing to a later date ○ *They adjourned the meeting* or *the meeting was adjourned.* ○ *The chairman adjourned the tribunal until three o'clock.* ○ *The meeting adjourned at midday.* ○ *The appeal was adjourned while further evidence was being produced.* □ **the House stands adjourned** the sitting of the House of Commons is adjourned and will resume on the following day

'…the Commons adjourned until January 18 without taking a vote on the Government's resolution' [*Toronto Globe & Mail*]

adjournment /əˈdʒɜːnmənt/ *noun* **1.** an act of stopping a meeting for a period or postponing a legal hearing to a later date ○ *The adjournment lasted two hours.* **2.** the act of ending a sitting of the House of Commons or Lords, or of the House of Representatives or Senate, which will meet again on the following day □ **motion for adjournment of the debate** a motion to adjourn a debate which has the effect of killing the motion being debated □ **motion for the adjournment of the House** motion to adjourn a sitting until the following day □ **adjournment sine die** an adjournment without fixing a date for the next meeting, used in the US Congress to end a session □ **adjournment to a day certain** a motion to adjourn a sitting of Congress to another day

adjournment debate /ə ˌdʒɜːnmənt dɪˈbeɪt/ *noun* a debate in the House of Commons on a motion to adjourn a sitting, used by backbench MPs to raise points of particular interest to themselves. Also called **debate on the adjournment**

administer /ədˈmɪnɪstə/ *verb* **1.** to control, manage or govern something ○ *The state is administered directly from the capital.* **2.** to be responsible for making sure something happens in the correct way □ **to administer justice** to carry out the law □ **to administer an oath** to make someone swear an oath

administration /ədˌmɪnɪˈstreɪʃ(ə)n/ *noun* **1.** the organisation, control or management of a geographical area or of a specific aspect of government, especially by a bureaucracy or group of experts ○ *There has been a lack of effective administration in the province since the riots.* ○ *The administration of justice is in the hands of the government-appointed justices of the peace.* ○ *She took up a career in hospital administration.* **2.** especially in the USA, a particular government ○ *It was one of the main policies of the last administration.* ○ *The Bush administration took office in 2001.*

administrative /ədˈmɪnɪstrətɪv/ *adjective* concerned with the organisation, control or management of a geographical area or with a specific aspect of government

administrative court /əd ˌmɪnɪstrətɪv ˈkɔːt/ *noun* in some countries such as France, a court or tribunal which decides in cases where government action is thought to have

affected and harmed the lives or property of citizens. Also called **administrative tribunal**

administrative law /əd ˈmɪnɪstrətɪv lɔː/ *noun* the laws relating to the running of government, and the relationship between the government and the citizens

administrator /ədˈmɪnɪstreɪtə/ *noun* a person who works for a government, public body or business as a senior manager ○ *The governor of the province has to be a good administrator.* ○ *The council has appointed too many administrators and not enough ordinary clerical staff.* ○ *The best administrators come from the civil service training school.*

Admiralty /ˈædm(ə)rəlti/ *noun* formerly in the UK, the government office which was in charge of the Navy

Admiralty Board /ˈædmərəlti ˌbɔːd/ *noun* a committee which is responsible for the administration of the Royal Navy, forming part of the UK Ministry of Defence

Admiralty law /ˈædm(ə)rəlti lɔːw/ *noun* the law relating to ships and sailors, and actions at sea

admission /ədˈmɪʃ(ə)n/ *noun* **1.** the act of accepting someone into a group or organisation ○ *admission into the European Union* **2.** permission to go into a place ○ *Admission to the visitors' gallery is restricted.* **3.** the act of making a statement agreeing that particular facts are correct or saying that something really happened ○ *The Opposition called for an admission of error on the part of the Minister.*

admit /ədˈmɪt/ *verb* **1.** to allow someone to go in ○ *The public is not being admitted at present.* **2.** to agree that an allegation or accusation is correct or to say that something really happened ○ *He admitted his mistake* or *his liability.* ○ *She admitted that the department was at fault.* ○ *He admitted having connections with the company which had been awarded the contract.* (NOTE: **admitted – admitting**.)

adopt /ə'dɒpt/ *verb* **1.** to agree to something or accept something so that it becomes law ○ *The report of the subcommittee was received and the amendments adopted.* ○ *The meeting adopted the resolution.* ○ *The proposals were adopted unanimously.* ○ *The council has adopted a policy of positive discrimination.* **2.** to be adopted, to be chosen by a party as a candidate in an election ○ *The Labour Party adopted more women as candidates for the General Election than ever before.* □ **to be adopted** to be chosen by the party as a candidate for election to a parliamentary constituency

adoption /ə'dɒpʃən/ *noun* **1.** the act of agreeing to something so that it becomes legal or accepted ○ *She moved the adoption of the resolution.* **2.** the act of choosing someone as a candidate in an election

adoption meeting /ə'dɒpən ˌmiːtɪŋ/ *noun* the meeting at which a local party adopts someone as its candidate for an election

ad valorem /ˌæd və'lɔːrəm/ *Latin phrase meaning* 'according to value'

COMMENT: Most taxes are 'ad valorem'; VAT is calculated as a percentage of the charge made, income tax is a percentage of income earned, etc.

ad valorem duty /ˌæd və'lɔːrəm ˌdjuːti/, **ad valorem tax** /ˌæd və 'lɔːrəm tæks/ *noun* a tax calculated according to the value of the goods being taxed

adventurism /əd'ventʒʊrɪz(ə)m/ *noun* intervention by one government in the affairs of another

adversarial politics /ˌædvɜː ˌseəriəl 'pɒlɪtɪks/ *noun* a system of political activity where two sides oppose each other vigorously. This is said to create the right conditions for effective scrutiny of the government, and for genuine debate.

adversary /'ædvəs(ə)ri/ *noun* a person or organisation who is the opposing side in situation ○ *a powerful political adversary*

advice /əd'vaɪs/ *noun* information or suggestions given by one person to another on what has happened in the past or on what is the best course of action to follow in the future □ **to take advice** to ask an expert to give information and help about a problem ○ *We'll need to take legal advice before agreeing.*

advise /əd'vaɪz/ *verb* **1.** to suggest to someone what should be done □ **to advise against something** to suggest that something should not be done ○ *The Minister advised against raising the matter in the House.* ○ *The consultants advised against the proposed development plan.* **2.** to tell someone what has happened or what will happen soon ○ *We are advised that the report will be published next week.*

adviser /əd'vaɪzə/, **advisor** *noun* a person who suggests what should be done, by giving information on a specific area where he or she is an expert

advisory /əd'vaɪz(ə)ri/ *adjective* acting as a person who tells someone what to do or informs them about events ○ *He is acting in an advisory capacity.* ■ *noun US* an official warning

advisory board /əd'vaɪz(ə)ri ˌbɔːd/ *noun* a group of people who help others to decide what to do or keep them informed about what is happening

advocacy /'ædvəkəsi/ *noun* active support for a cause or point of view

advocate *noun* /'ædvəkət/ someone who actively supports a cause or point of view ○ *an advocate of relaxing the laws on cannabis* ■ *verb* /'ædvəkeɪt/ to speak or work to support a cause or point of view ○ *Anarchists advocate the abolition of the state.*

Advocate General /ˌædvəkət 'dʒen(ə)rəl/ *noun* **1.** one of the two Law Officers for Scotland **2.** in the European Court of Justice, the officer who presents a summary of a case to the judges to help them in coming to a decision

affair /ə'feə/ *noun* **1.** a situation or event ○ *Is she involved in the copyright* *affair?* **2.** something shocking that involves public figures ○ *the arms smuggling affair* ○ *the Watergate affair* ■ *plural noun* activities and events related to the government of a country or countries ○ *topics of current importance in world affairs* ◊ **foreign affairs**

affairs of state /əˌfeəz əv ˈsteɪt/ *plural noun* government business

affiliate /əˈfɪlieɪt/ *verb* to associate with a group or organisation ○ *The trade union was affiliated to the Labour Party*

affiliation /əˌfɪliˈeɪʃ(ə)n/ *noun* association with a group or organisation □ **the union has no political affiliation** the union is not linked to any particular political party

affirm /əˈfɜːm/ *verb* **1.** (*of a MP*) to promise allegiance to the monarch, when the Oath of Allegiance is considered inappropriate on religious or other grounds ○ *Some of the new MPs affirmed, instead of swearing the oath of allegiance.* **2.** to support or approve of something publicly ○ *The report affirms the contribution of many voluntary groups working for racial harmony.* **3.** to confirm that something is correct

affirmation /ˌæfəˈmeɪʃ(ə)n/ *noun* **1.** a statement by an MP showing allegiance to the monarch, when the Oath of Allegiance is considered inappropriate on religious or other grounds **2.** support or approval

affirmative action /əˌfɜːmətɪv ˈækʃən/ *noun US* a policy of preventing the unfair treatment of specific groups in society who have a disadvantage, or who have suffered unfair treatment in the past, such as people with disabilities, ethnic groups and women

affirmative instrument /ə ˌfɜːmətɪv ˈɪnstrʊmənt/ *noun* a form of Statutory Instrument, or order made by a government minister on the authority of a previous act of parliament, which must be approved by both Houses of Parliament

African National Congress /ˌæfrɪkən ˌnæʃ(ə)nəl ˈkɒŋgres/ *noun* a South African political party that fought against apartheid and formed South Africa's first multiracial, democratically elected government in 1994. Abbr **ANC**

African Union /ˌæfrɪkən ˈjuːnjən/ *noun* an organisation of African states established for mutual cooperation, superseding the Organisation of African Unity in 2002

agency /ˈeɪdʒənsi/ *noun* **1.** a government office or department which is to some extent independent ○ *The Benefits Agency has responsibility for making welfare payments.* (NOTE: In the United Kingdom, under reforms which started under the Thatcher government, a large number of areas were transferred from the direct control of the Civil Service to agencies.) **2.** an independent organisation that deals with social problems ○ *a register of voluntary agencies in the field of mental health*

agenda /əˈdʒendə/ *noun* **1.** a list of things to be discussed at a meeting ○ *the committee agenda* or *the agenda of the committee meeting* ○ *After two hours we were still discussing the first item on the agenda.* **2.** a list of priorities ○ *Education was at the top of the government's agenda.*

agent /ˈeɪdʒənt/ *noun* **1.** a person who represents a company or another person **2.** a party official who works to support a candidate in an election ○ *The party has six full-time election agents.* ○ *The series of meetings was organised by the local agent for the Liberal Democrats.* **3.** a person who works for a branch of government. ◊ **secret agent**

Agent-General /ˌeɪdʒ(ə)nt ˈdʒen(ə)rəl/ *noun* the official representative of a provincial government of a Commonwealth country in another Commonwealth country ○ *the Agent-General for Quebec in London* (NOTE: The plural is **agents-general** or **agent-generals**.)

agent provocateur /ˌæʒɒn prə
ˌvɒkə'tɜːr/ *French words meaning*
'an agent who provokes': a person
employed secretly by a government
who provokes others to commit a
crime, often by taking part in it personally, in order to find out who is not
reliable or in order to have his or her
associates arrested

age of consent /ˌeɪdʒ əv kən'sent/
noun the age at which someone can
legally agree to have sex

age of majority /ˌeɪdʒ əv mə
'dʒɒrɪti/ *noun* the age of legal responsibility, at which civil duties and rights
such as voting or being on a jury are
first undertaken

aggression /ə'greʃ(ə)n/ *noun* hostile action against another country, especially without provocation ○ *They
accused the neighbouring states of aggression.* ○ *Numerous acts of aggression have been reported to the United
Nations.* (NOTE: no plural. For the plural, use **acts of aggression**)

aggressor /ə'gresə/ *noun* a person
or country which attacks another, especially without provocation ○ *The
UN resolution condemns one of the
superpowers as the aggressor.*

agitate /'ædʒɪteɪt/ *verb* to encourage people to take political action possibly involving protesting, demonstrating or engaging in direct action ○
*The party is agitating for social re-
forms.*

agitation /ˌædʒɪ'teɪʃ(ə)n/ *noun* the
action of encouraging people to protest and demonstrate ○ *There has been
widespread agitation in the capital
and the northern provinces.* (NOTE: no
plural)

agitator /'ædʒɪteɪtə/ *noun* a person
who attempts to cause political unrest
○ *Agitators from the right of the party
have tried to disrupt the meetings of
the council.*

AGM /ˌeɪ dʒiː 'em/ *abbreviation* Annual General Meeting

agrarian /ə'greəriən/ *adjective* promoting the interests of farmers and encouraging a fair system of land owner-

ship ■ *noun* someone who believes in
the fair distribution of land and the redistribution of land owned by rich
people

agrarianism /ə'greəriənɪz(ə)m/
noun a political movement or philosophy that promotes the interests of
farmers, especially the redistribution
of land owned by rich people or by
government

**Agriculture and Agri-Food
Canada** /ˌægrɪkʌltʃə ənd ægri fuːd
'kænədə/ *noun* a department of the
Canadian federal government that
conducts research and develops policies and programs to ensure the security of the country's food system.
Abbr **AAFC**

Ahern /ə'hɜːn/, **Bertie** (*b.* 1951) the
leader of the Fianna Fáil party since
1994 and Taoiseach (prime minister)
of the Republic of Ireland since 1997

aid /eɪd/ *noun* help, especially money, food or other gifts given to people
living in difficult conditions ○ *The
government has set aside $20m for aid
to under-developed countries.* ○ *The
poorer countries depend on aid from
richer nations.* ○ *The government will
allocate 6% of the gross national
product for overseas aid.*

AID /ˌeɪ aɪ 'diː/ *abbreviation* Agency
for International Development

aid agency /'eɪd ˌeɪdʒənsi/ *noun* an
independent organisation that sends
financial or other help to a country
which is experiencing difficult conditions or a catastrophic event such as a
natural disaster or famine

aide /eɪd/ *noun* an assistant to someone such as a politician, who may also
offer advice ○ *a presidential aide*

aid worker /'eɪd ˌwɜːkə/ *noun* a
person who works for an aid agency

airspace /'eəspeɪs/ *noun* the sky
above an area of land or water over
which a state claims control ○ *British
airspace*

Albion /'ælbiən/ *noun* Great Britain

alderperson /'ɔːldəˌpɜːsən/ *noun*
in the United States and Canada, a

member of the legislative body of some towns or cities

alderwoman /'ɔːldə,wʊmən/ *noun* in the United States and Canada, a woman member of the legislative body of some towns or cities

Al Fatah /,æl 'fætə/ *noun* a political group, part of the Palestine Liberation Organisation, that wants to establish an independent Palestinian state

alien /'eɪliən/ *noun* **1.** *mainly US* a person living in a country of which he or she is not a citizen **2.** (*in the UK*) a person who is not a citizen of the UK, not a citizen of a Commonwealth country and not a citizen of the Republic of Ireland ■ *adjective* **1.** *mainly US* from a different country or culture ○ *alien workers* **2.** different from what is usual or familiar ○ *an alien concept*

alienate /'eɪliəneɪt/ *verb* to do something that makes someone stop being friendly towards you ○ *The government has alienated its main supporters.* ○ *The terrorist campaign has alienated the public.*

align /ə'laɪn/ *verb* to give support publicly to a political group or party □ **to align yourself with another country** to follow a policy similar to that of another country ○ *the three neighbouring states aligned themselves with the USA*

allegiance /ə'liːdʒ(ə)ns/ *noun* obedience to the State or the Head of State. ◊ **oath of allegiance**

alliance /ə'laɪəns/ *noun* **1.** a group of two or more countries, people or political parties, that are linked together by a formal agreement **2.** a formal relationship between two or more parties or countries ○ *The country has built up a series of alliances with its larger neighbours.* ◊ **ally**

Alliance /ə'laɪəns/ *noun* in New Zealand, a left-wing political party that has been in coalition government with the Labour Party since 1999

allied /'ælaɪd/ *adjective* **1.** relating to countries that have joined together to fight a common enemy ○ *the allied*

forces **2.** associated or related ○ *building and allied trades*

allowance /ə'laʊəns/ *noun* **1.** an amount of something which you are legally or officially allowed to have ○ *a travel allowance* ○ *a baggage allowance* ◊ **personal allowances 2.** a payment made for a specific purpose ○ *an allowance for unsociable hours* ○ *an expenses allowance*

all-party /,ɔːl 'pɑːti/ *adjective* including members of all political parties ○ *the report of the all-party committee on procedure* ○ *An all-party group visited the United Nations.*

all-party group /,ɔːl ,pɑːti 'gruːp/ *noun* a group of MPs from different parties who have an interest in a particular subject ○ *the all-party group on telecommunications*

ally /'ælaɪ/ *noun* a country, person, political party or group which is linked to another in a friendly way so that they can support one another ○ *As the invasion seemed likely, the President called on his allies for help.* ○ *The committee has been run by the mayor and his allies in the Workers' Party.* ■ *verb* to link one country, political party, group or person to another □ **to ally yourself with** to become linked to someone or another party or country, for protection ○ *He has allied himself to the left wing of the party.*

ALP *abbreviation* Australian Labor Party

al-Qaeda /,æl 'kaɪdə/ *noun* an international Islamic fundamentalist organisation, founded by Osama bin Laden, which has been associated with several terrorist incidents, including the attack on the World Trade Center, New York (2001)

alternative vote /ɔːl'tɜːnətɪv vəʊt/ *noun* a system of voting used in elections in some countries such as Australia, in which voters show their preferences on the ballot paper by marking candidates with the numbers 1, 2, 3, 4, etc. If a candidate does not get 50% of the first preference votes in the first round of counting, the votes for the candidates with the lowest number of votes are given to the candidates shown as second preferences on their ballot papers in a number of further rounds until a single candidate gets 50%. Abbr **AV**

Althing /ˈælθɪŋ/ *noun* the law-making assembly in Iceland

AM *abbreviation* Assembly Member

AMA *abbreviation* Association of Metropolitan Authorities

ambassador /æmˈbæsədə/ *noun* a diplomat of the highest level, representing his country in another country ○ *the Spanish ambassador* ○ *our ambassador in France* ○ *The government has recalled its ambassador for consultations.*

'...an ambassador is an honest man sent to lie abroad for his country' [*Sir Henry Wotton*]

ambassador at large /æm ˈbæsədə ət lɑːdʒ/ *noun* an ambassador whose role is not restricted to one specific country

Ambassador Extraordinary and Plenipotentiary /æmˌbæsədə ɪkˌstrɔːdɪn(ə)ri ən ˌplenɪpəˈtenʃəri/ *noun* the official title of an ambassador

ambassadorial /ˌæmbæsəˈdɔːriəl/ *adjective* referring to an ambassador ○ *ambassadorial duties*

ambassador plenipotentiary /æmˌbæsədə ˌplenɪpəˈtenʃəri/ *noun* an ambassador with full powers to negotiate and sign treaties on behalf of his or her country

amend /əˈmend/ *verb* **1.** to make changes to a document, plan or policy, in order to correct or improve it **2.** to make an official change to a motion, Bill, Act or constitution

amendment /əˈmendmənt/ *noun* **1.** a change made in a document, plan or policy ○ *to make amendments to the minutes* **2.** a change proposed to a motion or to a bill which is being discussed in Parliament or Congress, or to an existing Act ○ *The amendment was proposed and seconded and put to the vote.* ○ *The government whips per-*

suaded her to withdraw her amendment. (NOTE: Amendments are usually made in the Committee Stage and Report Stage of a bill going through the House of Commons. In the House of Lords they can also be made at Third Reading.) **3.** *US* a new clause added to a written constitution, changing it in some way

'...a constitutional amendment that would acknowledge the commonwealth's right to override the states on matters of economic development' [*The Age (Melbourne)*]

COMMENT: The first ten amendments to the American Constitution are known as the Bill of Rights. The most important are the First Amendment (which provides for freedom of speech and thought), and the Fifth Amendment (which protects anyone from giving evidence in court which might incriminate himself or herself).

American Revolution /əˌmerɪkən ˌrevəˈluːʃ(ə)n/ *noun* the War of Independence (1775–83) by which the American colonies of Britain became independent and became the United States of America

Amicus /əˈmaɪkəs/ *noun* the UK's largest technical trade union, with more than 1.2 million members. It was formed in 2001 by the merging of AEEU (Amalgamated Engineering and Electrical Union) and MSF (Manufacturing, Science and Finance Union).

amnesty /ˈæmnəsti/ *noun* a pardon, often for political crimes, given by the state to several people at the same time ■ *verb* to grant a pardon to several people at the same time, often for political crimes ○ *They were amnestied by the president.*

Amnesty International /ˌæmnəsti ˌɪntəˈnæʃ(ə)nəl/ *noun* an international pressure group which works for human rights, and against the cruel treatment of prisoners

anarchic /əˈnɑːkɪk/, **anarchical** /əˈnɑːkɪkl/ *adjective* with no law or order ○ *the anarchic state of the country districts after the coup*

anarchism /'ænəkɪz(ə)m/ *noun* the belief that there is no need for a system of government in a society

COMMENT: Anarchism flourished in the latter part of the 19th and early part of the 20th century. Anarchists believe that there should be no government, no army, no civil service, no courts, no laws, and that people should be free to live without anyone to rule them.

anarchist /'ænəkɪst/ *noun* **1.** a person who believes that there should be no system of government **2.** a person who tries to destroy a government by violent means, without planning to replace it in any way ■ *adjective* referring to anarchists and their aims

anarchy /'ænəki/ *noun* the absence of law and order, because a government has lost control or because there is no government ○ *When the president was assassinated, the country fell into anarchy.*

ANC *abbreviation* African National Congress

ancillary /æn'sɪləri/ *adjective* providing help or support ○ *nursing and ancillary services*

annex /ə'neks/ *verb* to incorporate territory into another country or state

annexation /ˌænek'seɪʃ(ə)n/ *noun* the act of one state taking possession of a territory claimed by another, and claiming it as its own

annexe, annex *noun* a document added or attached to another ■ *verb* **1.** to attach a document **2.** (*of a state*) to take possession of a territory claimed by another and claim it as its own ○ *The island was annexed by the neighbouring republic.* (NOTE: [all senses] The US spelling is **annex**.)

announce /ə'naʊns/ *verb* to tell something to the public or to a group of people ○ *The returning officer announced the result of the election.* ○ *The Foreign Secretary announced that he would be going to Nigeria shortly.*

announcement /ə'naʊnsmənt/ *noun* **1.** a public statement giving information ○ *An announcement about the date of the election is expected very soon.* □ **to make an announce-**

ment to give information about something publicly ○ *The Home Secretary will make an announcement later today.* **2.** the act of telling something publicly ○ *The chairman of the council made an announcement about the development plans.*

Annual General Meeting /ˌænjuəl ˌdʒen(ə)rəl 'miːtɪŋ/ *noun* a meeting of all the members of a society or shareholders of a company which takes place once a year to agree the accounts and decide general policy. Abbr **AGM**

Annual Meeting /ˌænjuəl 'miːtɪŋ/ *noun* a meeting of a local council, which takes place once a year, to approve the accounts and elect a mayor among other things

annulment of adjudication /ə ˌnʌlmənt əv əˌdʒuːdɪ'keɪʃ(ə)n/ *noun* the cancelling of a legal order such as one making someone bankrupt

another place /ə'nʌðə pleɪs/ ♦ **place**

answer /'ɑːnsə/ *noun* a reply, letter or conversation coming after someone else has written or spoken □ **written answer** a formal reply to a question put in writing to a Minister ■ *verb* **1.** to speak or write after someone has spoken or written to you **2.** to reply formally to an accusation

answerable /'ɑːns(ə)rəb(ə)l/ *adjective* responsible for explaining why actions have been taken ○ *He is answerable to Parliament for the conduct of the Armed Forces.*

anti- /ænti/ *prefix* against ○ *an anti-drug campaign* ○ *the anti-terrorist squad* ○ *Anti-government posters appeared in the streets.*

anticipation /ænˌtɪsɪ'peɪʃ(ə)n/ *noun* doing something before it is due to be done or before something expected happens (NOTE: It is out of order on grounds of anticipation for a motion to be mentioned or discussed in the House of Commons before the day on which it is scheduled for discussion.)

anti-trust /ˌænti ˈtrʌst/ *adjective* attacking monopolies and encouraging competition ○ *anti-trust laws* or *legislation*

AOB *abbreviation* any other business

apartheid /əˈpɑːtheɪt/ *noun* the racist policy, operating until 1993 in South Africa, by which different racial groups were kept apart in most circumstances, largely to benefit the white population

apolitical /ˌeɪpəˈlɪtɪk(ə)l/ *adjective* not interested in politics, or not concerned with politics

apologist /əˈpɒlədʒɪst/ *noun* someone who publicly defends a doctrine or ideology

a posteriori /ˌeɪ pɒsteriˈɔːri/ *Latin phrase meaning* 'from what comes after.' Compare **a priori** □ **a posteriori argument** an argument based on observation

apparat /ˈæpəræt/ *noun* the large group of state employees who ran a Communist country

apparatchik /ˌæpəˈrættʃɪk/ *noun* **1.** a government employee in a Communist country **2.** a civil servant who follows rules too closely and works slowly (*disapproving or humorous*; *used as criticism*) (NOTE: The plural is **apparatchiki** or **apparatchiks**.)

appeal /əˈpiːl/ *noun* **1.** a challenge to the ruling of the chairman of a meeting ○ *Senator Brown made an appeal against the ruling of the President of the Senate.* **2.** the process of asking a government department to change a decision ○ *The appeal against the planning decision will be heard next month.* **3.** the process of asking a higher court to change a decision of a lower court ○ *an appeal to the House of Lords* ■ *verb* to ask someone to change a decision ○ *The company appealed against the decision of the planning officers.* ○ *She has appealed to the Supreme Court.* (NOTE: you appeal **to** a court or **against** a decision; an appeal is **heard** and **allowed** or **dismissed**)

Appeal Committee /əˈpiːl kəˌmɪti/ *noun* a committee set up by the House of Lords to consider petitions to appeal to the House of Lords from the Court of Appeal

Appeal Court /əˈpiːl kɔːt/ *noun* the civil or criminal court to which a person may go to ask for a decision made by a lower court to be changed, and the decisions of which are binding on the High Court and lower courts. Also called **Court of Appeal, Court of Appeals**

COMMENT: In English law, in the majority of cases decisions of lower courts and of the High Court can be appealed to the Court of Appeal. The Court of Appeal is divided into the Civil Division and the Criminal Division. The Civil Division hears appeals from the County Court and the High Court; the Criminal Division hears appeals from the Crown Court. From the Court of Appeal, appeal lies at present to the House of Lords. In 2004 parliament was debating legislation to replace the House of Lords with another final court of appeal to be called the Supreme Court. Appeals from some Commonwealth countries may be heard from the highest court of these countries by the Judicial Committee of the Privy Council, which is at present in effect made up of the same judges as the House of Lords.

appease /əˈpiːz/ *verb* to make concessions to another person, group or country in order to avoid conflict

appeasement /əˈpiːzmənt/ *noun* the policy of avoiding conflict by making concessions

appellate /əˈpelət/ *adjective* relating to a legal or formal appeal □ **appellate jurisdiction** the jurisdiction of the House of Lords to hear appeals

Appellate Committee /əˈpelət kəˌmɪti/ *noun* the committee of the House of Lords which considers appeals and reports on them to the House

appendix /əˈpendɪks/ *noun* additional text at the end of a document ○ *The map showing the properties covered by the proposal is attached as an Appendix.* ○ *See Appendix B for the list of county councils.* (NOTE: The plural is **appendices**.)

appoint /ə'pɔɪnt/ *verb* to choose someone for a job ○ *The government has appointed a QC to head the inquiry.* ○ *The council has appointed a race relations adviser.*

appointee /əpɔɪn'tiː/ *noun* a person who is appointed to a job

appointment /ə'pɔɪntmənt/ *noun* **1.** an arrangement to meet □ **by appointment** by arrangement in advance **2.** the fact of being given a new job ○ *his recent appointment as an EU Commissioner* □ **by royal appointment** requested by a king or queen as a supplier of goods or services **3.** a job ○ *applied for a government appointment*

apportionment /ə'pɔːʃ(ə)nmənt/ *noun* the distribution of seats in the US House of Representatives or a state legislature in proportion to the population of states or electoral districts

appropriation /ə,prəʊpri'eɪʃ(ə)n/ *noun* the granting of money for a particular purpose, especially allocating money to be spent by a particular government department

appropriation bill /ə,prəʊpri'eɪʃ(ə)n bɪl/ *noun* in the US Congress, a bill which grants money to the government to be used in a way which has been approved in an authorisation bill

appropriations committee /ə,prəʊpri'eɪʃ(ə)nz kə,mɪti/ *noun* especially in the US Congress, a committee which examines government spending

a priori /,eɪ praɪ'ɔːri/ *Latin phrase meaning* 'from what came before.' Compare **a posteriori** □ **a priori argument** reasoning based on principles or assumptions, not on real examples

Arabism /'ærəbɪz(ə)m/ *noun* support for Arab causes or viewpoints

Arab League /'ærəb liːg/ *noun* a political and economic association of Arab states

arbitrate /'ɑːbɪtreɪt/ *verb* to settle a legal dispute between parties by referring it to an outside person instead of going to court, e.g. in a building, ship-ping or employment dispute ○ *to arbitrate in a dispute*

arbitration /,ɑːbɪ'treɪʃ(ə)n/ *noun* the settling of a dispute by an outside person, chosen by both sides ○ *to submit a dispute to arbitration* ○ *to refer a question to arbitration* ○ *to take a dispute to arbitration* ○ *to go to arbitration*

arbitration agreement /,ɑːbɪ'treɪʃ(ə)n ə,griːmənt/ *noun* the agreement by two parties to allow an independent person to try to settle the dispute between them

arbitration award /,ɑːbɪ'treɪʃ(ə)n ə,wɔːd/ *noun* the ruling given by an independent person who has been asked to settle a dispute

arbitration board /,ɑːbɪ'treɪʃ(ə)n bɔːd/, **arbitration tribunal** /,ɑːbɪ'treɪʃ(ə)n traɪ,bjuːn(ə)l/ *noun* an independent group of people involved in settling a legal dispute

arbitrator /'ɑːbɪtreɪtə/ *noun* an independent person who is chosen by both sides in a dispute to try to settle it ○ *an industrial arbitrator* ○ *to accept or reject the arbitrator's ruling*

archives /'ɑːkaɪvz/ *plural noun* historical records ○ *18th century archives of borough council meetings*

archivist /'ɑːkɪvɪst/ *noun* a person who is responsible for the official records of a government department, local authority or other group

aristocracy /,ærɪ'stɒkrəsi/ *noun* the class in society composed of families who are landowners and who have inherited titles such as Lord or Duke

aristocrat /'ærɪstəkræt/ *noun* a member of the aristocracy ○ *Many aristocrats were killed during the revolution.*

aristocratic /,ærɪstə'krætɪk/ *adjective* relating to the aristocracy ○ *aristocratic families*

Aristotle /'ærɪstɒt(ə)l/ *noun* the Ancient Greek philosopher (384–322 BC) who began the study of political constitutions in his book *The Politics* (NOTE: Aristotle claimed that 'man was a political animal', meaning that living in political society was natural for human beings.)

arm /ɑːm/ *verb* to provide with weapons

armaments /'ɑːməmənts/ *plural noun* heavy weapons

armed /ɑːmd/ *adjective* provided with weapons ○ *It's now common to see armed guards at airports.*

armed conflict /ˌɑːmd kən'flɪkt/ *noun* war

armed forces /ˌɑːmd 'fɔːsɪz/ *plural noun* the army, navy and air force

armed neutrality /ˌɑːmd njuː'trælɪti/ *noun* the condition of a country which is not directly involved in a war between other countries, but is ready to defend itself in case it cannot avoid becoming involved

armistice /'ɑːmɪstɪs/ *noun* the agreement to stop fighting at the end of a war

armoury /'ɑːməri/ *noun* the arms of a country ○ *a country's nuclear armoury* (NOTE: The US spelling is **armory**.)

arms control /'ɑːmz kənˌtrəʊl/ *noun* the control of the sale of weapons by one country to another

arms race /'ɑːmz reɪs/ *noun* competition between countries to buy more and better weapons

army /'ɑːmi/ *noun* the part of a country's armed forces which fights mainly on land

article /'ɑːtɪk(ə)l/ *noun* 1. a section of a legal agreement ○ *See article 8 of the constitution.* 2. □ **articles of association, articles of incorporation** *US* a document which regulates the way in which a company's affairs are managed

ASEAN *abbreviation* Association of Southeast Asian Nations

Asquith /'æskwɪθ/, **Herbert Henry** (1852–1928) His 1908–16 government introduced retirement pensions and national insurance, and passed the Parliament Act (1911) that restricted the power of the House of Lords to veto bills

assembly /ə'sembli/ *noun* 1. a group of elected people who have the power to pass laws 2. a group of elected or appointed people who come together to discuss political issues and make decisions, especially for a specific region ○ *the assembly of the Organization of American States* □ **the General Assembly of the United Nations** the meeting of all the members of the United Nations to discuss international problems, where each member state has one vote 3. the action of coming together in a group for a meeting ○ *the right of assembly*

assemblyman /ə'semblimən/ *noun* in some countries, a member of a group of people who come together to discuss political problems or pass laws

assembly member /ə'sembli ˌmembə/, **Assembly Member** *noun* a member of an elected or appointed group of people who come together to discuss political problems or pass laws ○ *a Welsh Assembly Member* ◊ **Member of the Welsh Assembly**

Assembly of Deputies /əˌsembli əv 'depjʊtiz/ *noun* the lower house of the legislature in Romania

Assembly of the Republic /əˌsembli əv θə rɪ'pʌblɪk/ *noun* the legislature in Portugal

assemblywoman /ə'sembli ˌwʊmən/ *noun* in some countries, a woman who is a member of a group of people who come together to discuss political problems or pass laws

assistant /ə'sɪst(ə)nt/ *noun* a person who helps someone else, especially a superior employee ○ *The assistant librarian is away on holiday.*

associate of the Crown Office /əˌsəʊsieɪt əv ðɪ kraʊn 'ɒfɪs/ *noun* an official who is responsible for the administrative work of a court

Association of First Division Civil Servants /əˌsəʊsieɪʃ(ə)n əv ˌfɜːst dɪ'vɪʒ(ə)n ˌsɪv(ə)l 'sɜːvənts/ *noun* a trade union representing the most important British civil servants. Also called **First Division Association**. Abbr **FDA**. ◊ Civil and Public Services Association, Public Services, Tax and Commerce Union

ASSR *abbreviation* Autonomous Soviet Socialist Republic

assumption /əˈsʌmpʃən/ *noun* **1.** something that is believed to be true without proof ○ *The assumption that such people have a genuine choice of schools for their children is false.* □ **on the assumption that** taking something as generally accepted ○ *Such cases have usually been decided on the assumption that it is better for young children to live with their mother.* **2.** the process of beginning to take responsibility for something □ **assumption of office** the time when someone starts a job ○ *On his assumption of office, the premier arrested several of the ministers in the former government.*

asylum /əˈsaɪləm/ *noun* the right of someone to stay in a country that is not their own when their own country has treated them badly for political reasons □ **to ask for (political) asylum** to ask to be allowed to remain in a foreign country because it would be dangerous to return to the home country for political reasons

asylum seeker /əˈsaɪləm ˌsiːkə/ *noun* someone who has left their own country because they are in danger for political reasons and asks to be allowed to stay in another country □ **bogus asylum seeker** someone who comes to and asks to stay in another country because economic conditions are better rather than because of bad treatment at home. ◊ **economic migrant**

Atlanticism /ətˈlæntɪsɪz(ə)m/ *noun* a belief that western Europe and the United States can gain political and economic benefits from cooperation, especially in military matters

attaché /əˈtæʃeɪ/ *noun* a senior official in an embassy ○ *a military attaché* ○ *a cultural attaché* ○ *The government ordered the commercial attaché to return home.*

attack /əˈtæk/ *verb* **1.** to try to hurt or harm someone ○ *The security guard was attacked by three men carrying guns.* **2.** to criticise someone or something ○ *MPs attacked the government for not spending enough money on the police.* ■ *noun* **1.** the act of trying to hurt or harm someone ○ *There has been an increase in attacks on police* or *in terrorist attacks on planes.* **2.** criticism ○ *The newspaper published an attack on the government.*

attack dog /əˈtæk dɒg/ *noun* an aggressive supporter or spokesperson for a politician or political party

attainder /əˈteɪndə/ *noun* formerly, the method used to convict people of treason by an act of parliament rather than holding a trial

Attlee /ˈætli/, **Clement, 1st Earl Attlee** (1883–1967) His postwar government (1945–51) was the first majority Labour government and it introduced the welfare state and granted independence to India (1947)

attorney general /əˌtɜːni ˈdʒen(ə)rəl/ *noun* the chief law officer of the Australian Commonwealth or one of its states or territories

Attorney-General /əˌtɜːni ˈdʒen(ə)rəl/ *noun* **1.** in the United Kingdom, one of the Law Officers, a Member of Parliament and member of the government, who advises government departments on legal problems and decides if major criminal offences should be tried **2.** in a US state or in the federal government, the head of legal affairs (NOTE: In the US Federal Government, the Attorney-General is in charge of the Justice Department.)

COMMENT: In the US Federal Government, the Attorney-General is in charge of the Department of Justice.

attributable /əˈtrɪbjʊtəb(ə)l/ *adjective* able to be reported as an official statement of government policy with the source of the report named

Atty. Gen. *abbreviation* Attorney General

audience /'ɔːdiəns/ *noun* an interview or discussion with an important person ○ *The Prime Minister has a weekly audience of the Queen.*

Audit Commission /ˌɔːdɪt kə'mɪʃ(ə)n/ *noun* an independent body in the UK which examines the accounts of local authorities and checks for possible fraud and corruption

auditor-general /'ɔːdɪtə 'dʒen(ə)rəl/ *noun* an officer of the Australian government who makes sure government expenditure is approved by law

Australian ballot /ɒˌstreɪliən 'bælət/ *noun* same as **secret ballot**

Australian Capital Territory /ɒˌstreɪliən 'kæpɪt(ə)l 'terətri/ *noun* the region round the capital, Canberra, which is not part of any of the states. Abbr **ACT**

Australian Democrats /ɒˌstreɪliən 'deməkræts/ *noun* in Australia, a political party that has held power in the Australian upper house for most of the time since 1977

Australian Labor Party /ɒˌstreɪliən 'leɪbə ˌpɑːti/ *noun* in Australia, the principal political party of the left and one of the two main political parties. Abbr **ALP**

autarchy /'ɔːtɑːki/ *noun* the situation where a state has total power over itself, and rules itself without outside interference

autarky /'ɔːtɑːki/ *noun* the situation where a state can provide all it needs without outside help

authorisation bill /ˌɔːθəraɪ'zeɪʃn bɪl/ *noun US* in the US Congress, a bill which permits the spending of money on a project. It may also limit the amount of money which can be spent.

authoritarian /ɔːˌθɒrɪ'teəriən/ *adjective* exercising strict control □ **authoritarian regime** a government which rules its people strictly and does not allow anyone to oppose its decisions

authoritarianism /ɔːˌθɒrɪ'teəriənɪz(ə)m/ *noun* the theory that a government must rule its people strictly

authority /ɔː'θɒrɪti/ *noun* **1.** the official power given to someone to do something, the legal right to do something ○ *He has no authority to act on our behalf.* ○ *She was acting on the authority of the Borough Treasurer.* ○ *On whose authority were these computers ordered?* **2.** the person or book which has the best information ○ *She is an authority on the benefit system.* ○ *Erskine May is the authority on parliamentary procedure.* **3.** □ **the authorities** the government or people who have legal power over something ○ *The authorities are trying to put down the riots.* ○ *The prison authorities have complained about the lack of funding.*

autocracy /ɔː'tɒkrəsi/ *noun* **1.** rule by a dictator **2.** a country ruled by a dictator

autocrat /'ɔːtəkræt/ *noun* (*often as criticism*) a dictator, a ruler with total personal power over the people he or she rules

autocratic /ˌɔːtə'krætɪk/ *adjective* ruled by a dictator ○ *The regime became too autocratic and was overthrown by a military coup.*

autocratically /ˌɔːtə'krætɪk(ə)li/ *adverb* like a dictator

autonomous /ɔː'tɒnəməs/ *adjective* a region which governs itself within a larger political unit ○ *an autonomous regional government* ○ *The federation is formed of several autonomous republics.*

autonomy /ɔː'tɒnəmi/ *noun* the power of a region to govern itself within a larger political unit ○ *The separatists are demanding full autonomy for their state.* ○ *The government has granted the region a limited autonomy.*

AV *abbreviation* alternative vote

axis /'æksɪs/ *noun* an association between several people, organisations, or countries that is regarded as a centre of power or influence

Axis /'æksɪs/ *noun* the military and political alliance of Germany, Italy, and, later, Japan that fought the Allies in World War II

ayatollah /ˌaɪə'tɒlə/ *noun* a Muslim leader, especially in Iran

aye /aɪ/ *noun* in the House of Commons, a vote for a motion. ◊ **content** □

the Aye lobby, **the Ayes lobby** a room in the House of Commons, through which MPs pass if they are voting for a motion □ **the Ayes have it** an announcement that a motion has been passed

Azapo /ə'zæpəʊ/ *noun* a Socialist political movement in South Africa

B

Baath /bɑːθ/ *noun* a Socialist party in several Arab countries, including Iraq and Syria

Baathism /ˈbɑːθɪz(ə)m/ *noun* the beliefs of the Baath party, combining the elements of pan-Arabism, state control, anti-Semitism and the cult of an authoritarian ruler. Baathism was found in Iraq until the overthrow of Saddam Hussein in 2003, and still exists in Syria.

back /bæk/ *verb* to support someone or something □ **to back a bill** to support a Bill in Parliament

back bench /ˌbæk ˈbentʃ/ *adjective* referring to the seats behind the front row in the House of Commons and the MPs who occupy them ○ *backbench MPs*

backbencher /ˌbækˈbentʃə/ *noun* an ordinary Member of Parliament who does not sit on the front seats in the House of Commons, and is not a government minister or an Opposition shadow minister. Also called **backbench MP**

back benches /ˈbæk ˌbentʃɪz/ *plural noun* the rows of seats in the House of Commons, behind the front row, where the Members of Parliament who are not government ministers and not Opposition shadow ministers sit

back channel /ˈbæk ˌtʃæn(ə)l/ *noun* a way of passing sensitive information in politics or diplomacy that avoids the usual procedures ○ *They denied the existence of back-channel contacts between the two countries* ○ *They uncovered an apparent back channel (or attempted back channel) using a businessman who had a rela-tionship with a minister in their government.*

background /ˈbækɡraʊnd/ *noun* **1.** past work or experience or family connections ○ *Can you tell us something of the candidate's family background?* **2.** past details ○ *She explained the background to the claim.* ○ *The House asked for details of the background to the case.* ○ *I know the contractual situation as it stands now, but can you fill in the background details?*

backwoodsman /ˈbækwʊdzmən/ *noun* formerly, a hereditary peer in the House of Lords who lived in the country, appeared only rarely in the House and was regarded as having reactionary or eccentric opinions (*informal*)

balance of payments /ˌbæləns əv ˈpeɪmənts/ *noun* the international financial position of a country, measured according to the level of imports and exports

balance of power /ˌbæləns əv ˈpaʊə/ *noun* **1.** a situation where two powerful states, or groups of states, are equal in power ○ *The superpowers have achieved a balance of power for the last twenty years.* ○ *The rise of the military government has threatened the balance of power in the region.* **2.** □ **to hold the balance of power** (*of a small group*) to be in a position where no group has a majority and so effectively able to hold power by acting with another small group ○ *The balance of power is held by the small Democratic Party.* ○ *Although the Liberals only have two seats on the council, they hold the balance of power because the other two parties have twenty seats each.*

Balkanisation /ˌbɔːlkənaɪˈzeɪʃ(ə)n/ *noun* the division of an area into small political units that are often opposed to each other

ballot /ˈbælət/ *noun* **1.** an election where people vote for someone by marking a cross on a paper with a list of names **2.** an act of choosing someone by putting names in a box and then taking one name out at random ○ *In the House of Commons, private members Bills are placed in order of precedence by ballot.* ■ *verb* **1.** to take a vote by ballot ○ *The company is balloting for the post of president.* **2.** to choose by ballot ○ *MPs balloted for Private Member's Bills.*

ballot box /ˈbælət bɒks/ *noun* the box into which voting papers are put

ballot paper /ˈbælət ˌpeɪpə/ *noun* a paper on which the voter marks a cross to show for whom he or she wants to vote

ballot-rigging /ˈbælət ˌrɪɡɪŋ/ *noun* **1.** an illegal attempt to manipulate the votes in an election so that a specific candidate or party wins ○ *The electoral commission accused the government party of ballot-rigging.* **2.** an illegal attempt to miscount or lose voting papers, so that a particular candidate or party wins

bamboo curtain /bæmˈbuː ˌkɜːt(ə)n/ *noun* the imaginary barrier that isolated China on ideological grounds from Western countries after the Communist revolution of 1949 until 1979

banana republic /bəˌnɑːnə rɪˈpʌblɪk/ *noun* a small country with an economy that depends on the export of a single product

bandwagon effect /ˈbændwæɡən ɪˌfekt/ *noun* an increase in votes in an election for a political party or candidate who has been ahead in the opinion polls. Compare **boomerang effect**

banishment /ˈbænɪʃmənt/ *noun* the fact of being ordered to leave a country or region

bank base rate /ˌbæŋk ˈbeɪs ˌreɪt/ *noun* the basic rate of interest which a bank charges

bank charter /ˌbæŋk ˈtʃɑːtə/ *noun* the official government document allowing a banking company to be set up

bank holiday /ˌbæŋk ˈhɒlɪdeɪ/ *noun* in the UK, a day which is a public holiday when the banks are closed (NOTE: The American term is **national holiday**.)

Bank of England /ˌbæŋk əv ˈɪŋlənd/ *noun* the central British bank, owned by the state, which, together with the Treasury, regulates the nation's finances, and which since 1997 has almost complete independence to set interest rates

COMMENT: The Bank of England issues banknotes (which carry the signatures of its officials). It is the lender of last resort to commercial banks and puts into effect the general financial policies of the government. The Governor of the Bank of England is appointed by the government.

bankrupt /ˈbæŋkrʌpt/ *adjective, noun* referring to people that a court has decided are incapable of paying their debts and whose business is taken away from them ○ *a bankrupt property developer* ○ *He was adjudicated* or *declared bankrupt.* ○ *She went bankrupt after two years in business.* ■ *noun* someone who is bankrupt □ **certificated bankrupt** a bankrupt who has been discharged from bankruptcy with a certificate to show he or she was not at fault □ **discharged bankrupt** a person who has been released from being bankrupt □ **undischarged bankrupt** a person who has been declared bankrupt and has not been released from that state ■ *verb* to make someone become bankrupt ○ *The recession bankrupted my father.*

COMMENT: A person who is bankrupt cannot serve as a Member of Parliament, a Justice of the Peace, or a director of a limited company, and cannot sign a contract or borrow money.

bankruptcy /ˈbæŋkrʌptsi/ *noun* the state of being bankrupt ○ *The re-*

*cession has caused thousands of bank-
ruptcies.*

bankruptcy notice /ˌbæŋkrʌptsi
ˈnəʊtɪs/ *noun* a notice warning someone that they will be declared incapable of paying their debts and have their
business taken away from them if they
fail to pay money owed

banner /ˈbænə/ *noun* a piece of material on which a slogan or a political
or other statement is written and dis-
played or carried in a protest ○ *The
demonstrators carried banners with
the words 'Power to the People'.*

bar /bɑː/ *noun* **1.** the profession of a
barrister, or lawyer qualified to speak
in a higher court □ **to be called to the
bar** to pass examinations and fulfil
certain requirements to become a barrister **2.** all barristers or lawyers qualified to speak in the higher courts ◇
the Bar 1. the profession of barrister
2. all barristers ◇ **the Bar of the
House 1.** a line across the floor of the
House of Commons, behind which
people who are not members can
stand to present petitions or to be
questioned ○ *He appeared in person at
the Bar of the House.* **2.** a rail across
the floor of the House of Lords, behind which people who are not peers
can stand

COMMENT: At the State Opening of
Parliament MPs go to the House of
Lords and stand behind the Bar of the
House to hear the Queen's Speech.

baron /ˈbærən/, **Baron** *noun* **1.** a
person of the lowest rank of nobility in
the British House of Lords, or a life
peer **2.** *also* **Baron** a nobleman of various ranks in some European countries

COMMENT: Life peers and peeresses
are barons and baronesses; barons
are directly addressed as 'Lord' followed by their family name. In some
European countries, Baron is used as
a form of address: so, Baron Smith is
addressed as 'Lord Smith', but Baron
Schmidt is addressed as 'Baron
Schmidt'.

baroness /ˈbærənəs/ *noun* **1.** the
wife of a person of the lowest rank of
nobility in the British House of Lords,
a woman of the lowest rank of nobility

in the British House of Lords, or a life
peeress **2.** a noblewoman or the wife
of a nobleman of various ranks in
some European countries

COMMENT: A baroness would usually
be directly addressed as 'Lady' followed by her family name, though she
may be referred to as 'Baroness': *Baroness Thatcher*

baronet /ˈbærənət/ *noun* in the UK
, someone who has the title Sir and
whose right to this title can be passed
from father to son

COMMENT: Baronets are addressed as
'Sir', followed by the Christian name
and family name; their wives are addressed as 'Lady' followed by the family name (so Sir John Smith's wife is
directly addressed as 'Lady Smith');
the title passes to the heir, but does
not qualify the holder for a seat in the
House of Lords. Baronets can be
Members of Parliament.

baronetcy /ˌbærəˈnetsi/ *noun* a title
which can be passed from father to
son but does not qualify the holder for
a seat in the House of Lords

barony /ˈbærəni/ *noun* the title of a
person of the lowest rank of nobility in
the British House of Lords

barricade /ˌbærɪˈkeɪd/ *noun* an informal barrier set up to block a street
or passageway, especially by protestors ■ *verb* to block a street or passageway

Barroso /bəˈrəʊsəʊ/, **Jose Manuel
Durao** (*b.* 1956) the president of the
European Commission (2004–)

basic industry /ˌbeɪsɪk ˈɪndəstri/
noun an industry on which a country's
economy depends

basic rate tax /ˈbeɪsɪk reɪt ˌtæks/
noun the lowest rate of income tax

basics /ˈbeɪsɪks/ *plural noun* **1.** the
most important facts about something
2. the most essential things such as
food and heating ○ *Their weekly income barely covers the basics.* ◇ **to
get back to basics 1.** to start discussing the basic facts again **2.** to return to traditional values

basis /ˈbeɪsɪs/ *noun* **1.** the point or
number from which calculations are
made ○ *We have calculated the costs*

on the basis of a 6% price increase. **2.** the general terms of agreement or general principles on which something is decided ○ *We have three people working on a freelance basis.* □ **on a short-term** or **long-term basis** for a short or long period ○ *He has been appointed on a short-term basis.*

battlebus /'bæt(ə)lbʌs/ *noun* a bus used by a candidate in an election campaign to tour the constituency or country (*informal*)

beat /biːt/ *verb* to defeat someone in an election ○ *The main Opposition party was beaten into third place in the election.*

belli ♦ **casus belli**

belligerency /bə'lɪdʒərənsi/ *noun* the state of being at war or of threatening to start a war

belligerent /bə'lɪdʒərənt/ *adjective* aggressive or at war with another country ○ *two belligerent states* ○ *The UN will try to achieve a ceasefire between the belligerent parties.* ■ *noun* a country at war with another country ○ *The UN tried to set up a meeting where the belligerents could discuss an exchange of prisoners.*

bench /bentʃ/ *noun* a long seat for several people, as found in the Houses of Parliament. ◊ **back benches, front benches, Opposition front bench**

benefit /'benɪfɪt/ *noun* **1.** money or advantage gained from something **2.** a regular payment made to someone under a national or private insurance scheme ○ *She receives £50 a week as unemployment benefit.* ○ *The sickness benefit is paid monthly.* ○ *The insurance office sends out benefit cheques each week.*

benefit claim /'benɪfɪt kleɪm/ *noun* a request for a benefit to be paid

benefit tourism /'benɪfɪt ˌtʊərɪz(ə)m/ *noun* the practice of moving from a poor country to a richer country to receive its health and social benefits

Benelux /'benɪlʌks/ *noun* Belgium, the Netherlands and Luxembourg

Bentham /'benθəm/, **Jeremy** (1748–1832) English philosopher most famous as the founder of Utilitarianism (NOTE: [all senses] Bentham's Utilitarian principle that laws should be made so as to achieve the greatest happiness of the greatest number of people has been interpreted in many ways and is often misunderstood.)

betray /bɪ'treɪ/ *verb* ○ *He betrayed the secret to the enemy.* □ **to betray your country** to give away your country's secrets to an enemy

betting duty /ˌbetɪŋ 'djuːti/, **betting tax** /'betɪŋ tæks/ *noun* a tax raised from gambling on horses and dogs

Bharatiya Janata Party *noun* an Indian political party that advocates Hindu nationalism. Abbr **BJP**

bicameral /ˌbaɪ'kæmərəl/ *adjective* of a legislature or law-making body, having two chambers or houses ○ *The United Kingdom has a bicameral system composed of the House of Commons and House of Lords.* ○ *The United States has a bicameral legislative assembly, composed of the House of Representatives and the Senate.*

bicameralism /ˌbaɪ'kæmərəlˌɪz(ə)m/ *noun* a system of government where there are two houses in the legislature or law-making body (NOTE: The two chambers are usually referred to as the **Upper and Lower Houses**; systems with only one chamber are called **unicameral**.)

Big Ben /ˌbɪg 'ben/ *noun* a large bell which strikes the hours in the Clock Tower of the British Houses of Parliament

big government /ˌbɪg 'gʌv(ə)nmənt/ *noun* government regarded disapprovingly as spending too much and attempting to control too many aspects of people's lives

bilateral /baɪ'læt(ə)rəl/ *adjective* (*of an activity or agreement*) involving two parties or countries ○ *The minister signed a bilateral trade agree-*

ment. ◊ **multilateral, trilateral, unilateral**

'...the Federal Government will try to negotiate with the US to find a bilateral solution for the dispute' [*Toronto Globe & Mail*]

bilaterally /ˌbaɪˈlætər(ə)li/ *adverb* by the action of two parties or countries ○ *The agreement was reached bilaterally.*

bill /bɪl/ *noun* **1.** the draft or first version of a new law which will be discussed in Parliament ○ *The house is discussing the Noise Prevention Bill.* ○ *The Finance Bill had its second reading yesterday.* ◊ **Private Member's Bill, Private Bill, Public Bill 2.** a written paper which is a promise to pay money □ **bill of exchange** a document which orders one person to pay another person a sum of money **3.** a charge to be paid for work done ○ *The bill for cleaning up the beaches will be very large.* ■ *verb* to present a bill to someone so that it can be paid

COMMENT: A Bill passes through the following stages in Parliament: **First Reading, Second Reading, Committee Stage, Report Stage** and **Third Reading**. The Bill goes through these stages first in the House of Commons and then in the House of Lords. When all the stages have been passed the Bill is given the Royal Assent and becomes law as an Act of Parliament. In the USA, a Bill is introduced either in the House or in the Senate. Any number of Senators may jointly sponsor a single bill in the Senate; in the House of Representatives, a maximum of 25 members may jointly sponsor a bill. After its introduction, a bill is referred to a committee which examines it in public hearings, then passes it back for general debate in the full House. The Bill is debated section by section in **Second Reading** and after being passed by both House and Senate is engrossed and sent to the President for signature (or veto).

bill of attainder /ˌbɪl əv əˈteɪndə/ *noun* formerly, a way of punishing people legally without holding a trial, especially in cases of treason, by passing a law in parliament to convict and sentence them

bill of indictment /ˌbɪl əv ɪnˈdaɪtmənt/ *noun US* **1.** a draft of an indictment which is examined by the court, and when signed becomes an indictment **2.** a list of charges given to a grand jury, asking them to indict the accused

bill of rights /ˌbɪl əv ˈraɪts/ *noun* a list of basic human rights guaranteed in the law of a specific country

Bill of Rights /ˌbɪl əv ˈraɪts/ *noun* **1.** an Act passed in 1689, restating the rights of Parliament and people after the Revolution of 1688 **2.** the first ten amendments of the constitution of the United States which refer to the rights and privileges of the individual

binational /baɪˈnæʃ(ə)nəl/ *adjective* between two countries

binding precedent /ˌbaɪndɪŋ ˈpresɪd(ə)nt/ *noun* the decision of a higher court which has to be followed by a judge in a lower court

biological warfare /ˌbaɪə lɒdʒɪk(ə)l ˈwɔːfeə/ *noun* the use of biological material to cause disease during war

bioterrorism /ˈbaɪəʊˌterərɪz(ə)m/ *noun* terrorist attacks involving the use of biological or chemical weapons

bipartisan /ˌbaɪpɑːtɪˈzæn/ *adjective* accepted by the opposition as well as by the government ○ *a bipartisan approach to the problem of municipal finance* □ **a bipartisan foreign policy** a foreign policy agreed between the Government and Opposition

bipartite /baɪˈpɑːtaɪt/ *adjective* with two sides taking part ○ *bipartite talks*

Bircher /ˈbɜːtʃə/ *noun* a member of the John Birch Society, a right-wing political organisation in the United States whose main purpose is fighting Communism

Bishops' Bench /ˌbɪʃəps ˈbentʃ/ *noun* the seats in the House of Lords where the archbishops and bishops who are members of the House of Lords sit. The seats have arms unlike the other seats. ◊ **Lords Spiritual**

bisque /biːsk/ *noun* the absence of an MP from the British House of Commons which is allowed by a whip

BJP *abbreviation* Bharatiya Janata Party

black economy /ˌblæk ɪˈkɒnəmi/ *noun* work which is paid for in cash or goods but not declared to the tax authorities

black list /ˈblæk lɪst/ *noun* a list of persons, organisations or things which are not approved of ○ *the council is drawing up a black list of suppliers*

Black Panther /ˌblæk ˈpænθə/ *noun* a member of a militant African American political organisation opposed to white domination that was active in the United States especially in the late 1960s and early 1970s

Black Power /ˌblæk ˈpaʊə/ *noun* a movement formed by Black people in the United States to encourage social equality and pride in their racial identity

Black Rod /ˌblæk ˈrɒd/ *noun* a member of the Queen's staff in the British Houses of Parliament, who performs ceremonial functions, particularly at the State Opening of Parliament. Also called **Gentleman Usher of the Black Rod**

COMMENT: Like the Sergeant at Arms in the Commons, Black Rod is responsible for keeping order in the House of Lords. His best-known duty is to go from the Lords to summon the Commons to attend the opening of Parliament and hear the Queen's Speech.

Black Sash /ˌblæk ˈsæʃ/ *noun* originally an organisation of white women campaigners against apartheid in South Africa, now a multiracial organisation which promotes civil rights

Blair /bleə/, **Tony** (*b.* 1953) He was elected Labour Party leader in 1994, became prime minister in 1997 and was the first Labour leader to be re-elected, in 2001

Blairism /ˈbleərɪz(ə)m/ *noun* the political policies and style of government of Tony Blair, especially moderate and gradual social reform, prudent

financial management, and tight control over the presentation of policy

blame /bleɪm/ *verb* to say that someone has done something wrong or is responsible for a mistake ○ *The council chairman blamed the opposition for not supporting the amendment.* ○ *The lack of fire equipment was blamed by the coroner for the deaths.* ○ *The spokesman blamed the closure of the hospital on the lack of government funds.*

bloc /blɒk/ *noun* a group of countries who co-operate as a result of having the same political views ○ *a power bloc* ○ *the former Eastern bloc*

block /blɒk/ *verb* to stop something taking place ○ *He used his casting vote to block the motion.* ○ *The planning committee blocked the plan to build a motorway through the middle of the town.* □ **to block a Bill** to prevent a Bill being discussed at a sitting of the House of Commons, by objecting to it formally

blockade /blɒˈkeɪd/ *noun* an act of preventing goods or people going into or out of a place ○ *the government brought in goods by air to beat the blockade* ○ *the enemy lifted the blockade of the port for two months to let in emergency supplies* ■ *verb* to prevent goods or food or people going into or coming out of a place ○ *The town was blockaded by the enemy navy.*

blocked currency /ˌblɒkt ˈkʌrənsi/ *noun* money which cannot be taken out of a country because of exchange controls

block grant /ˌblɒk ˈɡrɑːnt/ *noun* money granted by the central government to a local authority to add to money received from rates or local taxes. Also called **Rate Support Grant**

blocking minority /ˈblɒkɪŋ maɪˌnɒrɪti/ *noun* a group who can veto a proposal even though they are in a minority, as operates in some cases in the EU Council of Ministers

block vote /ˌblɒk ˈvəʊt/ *noun* a vote by someone who is representing the wishes of a large number of people in a particular organisation such as a trade union

Bloquiste /ˌblɒkˈiːst/ *noun* a member or supporter of the Bloc Québécois

blue /bluː/ *noun* the colour traditionally used by the British Conservative Party and other parties of the Right □ **a true-blue Tory** a person who has strongly Conservative views

Blue Book /ˌbluː ˈbʊk/ *noun* a government publication with a blue cover, e.g. the report of a Royal Commission

blue laws /ˈbluː lɔːz/ *plural noun* US laws relating to what can or cannot be done on a Sunday

blue pencil /ˌbluː ˈpensəl/ *verb* formerly, to cross out items from a newspaper or report which it was forbidden to publish

Bn *abbreviation* baron

board /bɔːd/ *noun* a group of people who run an organisation, e.g. a company, trust or society □ **board of directors** a group of directors elected by the shareholders to run a company ○ *the government has two representatives on the board of the nationalized industry* ○ *he sits on the board as a representative of the bank* ○ *two directors were removed from the board at the AGM* □ **board of management** a group of people who manage an organisation

Board of Deputies /ˌbɔːd əv ˈdepjʊtiz/ *noun* a body that represents the legal and political interests of British Jews

Board of Trade /ˌbɔːd əv ˈtreɪd/ *noun* a British government department that regulates commerce and promotes exports, part of the Department for Trade and Industry since 1970. ◊ **President of the Board of Trade**

body /ˈbɒdi/ *noun* **1.** an organisation or group of people who work together ○ *Parliament is an elected body.* ○ *The governing body of the university has to approve the plan to give the President a honorary degree.* ◊ **non-de-** partmental public body **2.** a large amount of something ○ *a growing body of evidence* □ **body of opinion** a group of people who have the same view about something ○ *There is a considerable body of opinion which believes that capital punishment should be reintroduced.*

body politic /ˌbɒdi ˈpɒlɪtɪk/ *noun* all the people of a state considered as a group

bollweevil /ˈbɒlwiːvəl/ *noun* US a senator or congressman from one of the states of the Deep South (*informal*)

Bolshevik /ˈbɒlʃəvɪk/ *adjective* **1.** referring to the main Communist party in Russia at the time of the Revolution of 1917 ○ *Lenin was the leader of the Bolshevik Party.* **2.** Communist, usually referring to the Soviet Union (*dated informal*) ■ *noun* a member of a Communist Party, especially in the Soviet Union, or someone with left-wing views (*dated informal*)

COMMENT: The word comes from the Russian 'bolshinstvo', meaning majority, because this section of the Communist Party was in the majority at the time of the Russian Revolution.

bolshevism /ˈbɒlʃəvɪz(ə)m/ *noun* the form of Communism supported by Lenin

Bolshevism /ˈbɒlʃəvɪz(ə)m/ *noun* **1.** the beliefs of the Bolsheviks, especially the need for the overthrow of capitalism **2.** Communism or revolutionary socialism

bona fide /ˌbəʊnə ˈfaɪdi/ *Latin phrase meaning* 'in good faith' □ **a bona fide offer** an offer which is made honestly or which can be trusted

bona fides /ˌbəʊnə ˈfaɪdiːz/ *Latin phrase meaning* 'good faith': evidence of honesty and good standing ○ *Her bona fides was* or *were accepted by the company.*

bonded /ˈbɒndɪd/ *adjective* held under restrictions

bondholder /ˈbɒndhəʊldə/ *noun* a person who invests in government stocks

boomerang effect /ˈbuːməræŋ ɪˌfekt/ *noun* a decline in votes in an election for a political party or candidate who has been ahead in the opinion polls. Compare **bandwagon effect**

booth /buːð/ *noun* ♦ **polling booth**

border /ˈbɔːdə/ *noun* the frontier between two countries ○ *a border town* ○ *He was stopped by the border guards.*

borough /ˈbʌrə/ *noun* a town which has been given the right to have its own council. ◊ **rotten borough** □ **borough architect, borough engineer, borough treasurer** the officials in charge of the new buildings or machinery or finances of a borough

COMMENT: A borough is an officially incorporated town, which has a charter granted by Parliament. A borough is run by an elected council, with a mayor as its official head. Most boroughs are represented in Parliament by at least one MP.

borough council /ˌbʌrə ˈkaʊnsəl/ *noun* the representatives elected to run a borough

borough valuer /ˌbʌrə ˈvæljuə/ *noun* an official who estimates the value of property, especially where the owner is applying for a grant or where the council is considering buying the property

borrowing /ˈbɒrəʊɪŋ/ *noun* the practice of taking money from someone with their agreement and with the intention of repaying it later ○ *Government borrowing is set to increase.* □ **public sector borrowing requirement (PSBR)** the amount of money which a government has to borrow to pay for its own spending

Boston Tea Party /ˌbɒstən ˈtiː ˌpɑːti/ *noun* a protest against taxes imposed by Britain made by thè citizens of Boston in 1773 that led to the War of American Independence. The protesters boarded three British ships and threw their cargoes of tea overboard.

boundary /ˈbaʊnd(ə)ri/, **boundary line** /ˈbaʊnd(ə)ri laɪn/ *noun* a line marking the edge of an area of land, a border or frontier ○ *The boundary dispute dragged through the courts for years.* ○ *The borough boundary is marked by road signs.*

Boundary Commission /ˌbaʊnd(ə)ri kəˈmɪʃ(ə)n/ *noun* the committee which examines the area and population of constituencies for the House of Commons and recommends changes to make all Members of Parliament represent roughly similar numbers of people

bounty /ˈbaʊnti/ *noun* **1.** a government payment or subsidy made to help an industry **2.** a payment made by government to someone who has saved lives or found treasure

bourgeois /ˈbʊəʒwɑː/ *adjective* **1.** middle class or referring to the class of businessmen and professional people **2.** used by Communists to criticise an outlook which is traditional and conservative and opposed to communism ○ *The Party is trying to reduce its bourgeois image by promoting young activists to the Central Committee.* ■ *noun* a middle-class person

bourgeoisie /bʊəʒwɑˈziː/ *noun* the middle class, usually the richer upper levels of the middle class, formed of businessmen and professional people

boycott /ˈbɔɪkɒt/ *noun* a refusal to buy or to deal in goods from a country or company, used as a punishment ○ *The union organised a boycott against* or *of imported cars.* ■ *verb* to refuse to buy or to deal in goods from a country or company, as a punishment ○ *The company's products have been boycotted by the main department stores.* ○ *We are boycotting all imports from that country.* □ **to boycott a meeting** to refuse to attend a meeting

bracket /ˈbrækɪt/ *noun* a group □ **income bracket, tax bracket** a level of income where a percentage tax applies ■ *verb* to group together

branch /brɑːntʃ/ *noun* **1.** a local office of a bank or large business; a local shop of a large chain of shops ○ *The bank* or *the store has branches in most towns in the south of the country.* ○ *The insurance company has closed its branches in South America.* ○ *He is* the manager of our local branch of Lloyds bank. ○ We have decided to open a branch office in Chicago. ○ The manager of our branch in Lagos or of our Lagos branch. **2.** a section of government ○ The three branches of government are the executive, the legislature and the judiciary. **3.** a part or separate section ○ The school welfare service is a branch of the county education service. ○ The Law of Contract and the Law of Tort are branches of civil law.

branch stacking /'brɑːntʃ ˌstækɪŋ/ noun the practice of recruiting new members to a political party with the aim of influencing the selection of new candidates for office

breach of confidence /ˌbriːtʃ əv 'kɒnfɪd(ə)ns/ noun the act of revealing a secret which someone has told you

breach of privilege /ˌbriːtʃ əv 'prɪvɪlɪdʒ/ noun the act of doing something that may harm the reputation or power of Parliament, e.g. by speaking or writing in a defamatory way about an MP or about Parliament itself

COMMENT: Breaches of parliamentary privilege can take the form of many types of action; the commonest are threats to MPs, or insulting language about MPs; speaking in a rude way about Parliament in public; wild behaviour in the public galleries; trying to influence witnesses appearing before parliamentary committees.

breach of the peace /ˌbriːtʃ əv ðə 'piːs/ noun a disturbance which is likely to annoy or frighten people

breach of trust /ˌbriːtʃ əv 'trʌst/ noun the failure of someone who has undertaken to do a job on behalf of someone else to perform that job honestly or effectively

break down /ˌbreɪk 'daʊn/ verb **1.** to stop or fail ○ the negotiations between Iraq and USA broke down **2.** to show the details section by section ○ The trade figures are broken down into visible and invisible exports.

break off /ˌbreɪk 'ɒf/ verb to stop ○ We broke off the discussion at mid-

night. ○ The government has broken off negotiations with the insurgents. □ **to break off diplomatic relations with a country** to recall the ambassador and close down the embassy in a country

break out /ˌbreɪk 'aʊt/ verb to start suddenly ○ War broke out between the ethnic groups in the region.

break up /ˌbreɪk 'ʌp/ verb **1.** to divide something large into small sections ○ The company was broken up and separate divisions sold off. **2.** to come to an end or to make something come to an end ○ The meeting broke up at 12.30. ○ The police broke up the protest meeting.

bribe /braɪb/ noun money offered to someone to get them to do something to help you, especially something dishonest ○ The minister was accused of taking bribes. ■ verb to give someone money to get them to help you, especially by doing something dishonest ○ He bribed a senior official to get the import licence.

bribery /'braɪb(ə)ri/ noun the crime of paying someone money to get them to do something to help you, especially by doing something dishonest ○ Bribery in the security warehouse is impossible to stamp out.

brief /briːf/ verb to explain something to someone in detail ○ The superintendent briefed the press on the progress of the investigation. □ **to brief a minister, officer** to give a minister or officer all the details of the case which he will argue in Parliament or on TV or in committee

briefing /'briːfɪŋ/ noun an occasion when someone is given information about something ○ All the Whitehall journalists attended a briefing given by the minister.

briefing papers /'briːfɪŋ ˌpeɪpəz/ plural noun documents prepared by officials for a Minister to study

bring down /ˌbrɪŋ 'daʊn/ verb to make a government lose power ○ The government was brought down by the scandal.

bring forward /ˌbrɪŋ ˈfɔːwəd/ *verb* to move something to an earlier date ○ *The date of the hearing has been brought forward to March.*

bring up /ˌbrɪŋ ˈʌp/ *verb* to refer to something for the first time ○ *The chairman brought up the question of corruption in the police force.*

brinkmanship /ˈbrɪŋksmənʃɪp/ *noun* especially in international relations, the practice of allowing a dispute to come close to war in the hope of forcing the opposition to agree to a proposal

Brit /brɪt/ *noun* a British person (*informal*)

Britain /ˈbrɪt(ə)n/, **Great Britain** *noun* the country formed of the islands off the north coast of Europe (NOTE: Britain is formed of England, Wales and Scotland; together with Northern Ireland it forms the United Kingdom of Great Britain and Northern Ireland.)

British /ˈbrɪtɪʃ/ *adjective* referring to Britain or Great Britain ■ *noun* the people who live in Britain or are citizens of Britain living abroad □ **the British** the inhabitants or citizens of Britain

British Isles /ˌbrɪtɪʃ ˈaɪlz/ *noun* the group of islands off the north coast of Europe, consisting of the United Kingdom (England, Wales, Scotland and Northern Ireland) the Republic of Ireland, the Channel Islands and the Isle of Man

British Standards Institute /ˌbrɪtɪʃ ˈstændədz ˌɪnstɪtjuːt/ *noun* an official body which makes rules about standards of quality and safety

Briton /ˈbrɪt(ə)n/ *noun* a British person

budget /ˈbʌdʒɪt/ *noun* a plan of expected spending and income, usually for a period of one year, e.g. the plan made by a government's finance minister □ **the Budget** the annual plan of taxes and government spending proposed by a finance minister □ **the Budget statement** a speech by a Chancellor of the Exchequer presenting his budget to Parliament ○ *the minister put forward a budget aimed at slowing down the economy* ○ *the Chancellor began his budget statement at 3.30* ○ *the budget debate* or *the debate on the budget lasted for two days* □ **to balance the budget** to plan income and expenditure so that they balance ○ *the president is planning for a balanced budget* ■ *verb* to make plans of expected spending and income ○ *The council is budgeting for a 25% increase in expenditure on roads.*

'…the council could refuse to set a legal budget which would result in its being unable to borrow money and pay its employees' [*Local Government News*]

budgetary /ˈbʌdʒɪt(ə)ri/ *adjective* referring to a budget

budgetary control /ˌbʌdʒɪt(ə)ri kənˈtrəʊl/ *noun* the process of keeping a check on spending

budgetary policy /ˌbʌdʒɪt(ə)ri ˈpɒlɪsi/ *noun* the policy of planning income and spending

budgetary requirements /ˌbʌdʒɪt(ə)ri rɪˈkwaɪəməntz/ *plural noun* the spending or income needed by the government's plans

Budget box /ˈbʌdʒɪt bɒks/ *noun* an old red case in which the Chancellor of the Exchequer traditionally carried the Budget papers to Parliament on the day he announced the budget for the next year. ◊ **despatch box**

budget deficit /ˈbʌdʒɪt ˌdefɪsɪt/ *noun* the amount by which what a government spends is more than what it receives in tax and other income

budgeting /ˈbʌdʒɪtɪŋ/ *noun* the activity of preparing plans about spending and income

budget variance /ˌbʌdʒɪt ˈveəriəns/ *noun* the difference between the plans made in a budget and what the actual spending and income is

buffer /ˈbʌfə/ *noun* a country or area of land between two countries which prevents them attacking one another ○ *The UN tried to establish a buffer zone between the two warring factions.* ○

The small country found it had become a buffer state between the two belligerents.

buffer state /ˈbʌfə steɪt/ *noun* a small neutral state that is between two potentially hostile countries and therefore reduces the risk of conflict between them

building permit /ˈbɪldɪŋ ˌpɜːmɪt/ *noun* an official document which allows someone to build on a piece of land

bully pulpit /ˈbʊli ˌpʊlpɪt/ *noun* a position of authority that gives the holder the opportunity of a wide audience for his or her views, e.g. a political office

Bundesbank /ˈbʊndəzbæŋk/ *noun* the German Central Bank

Bundesrat /ˈbʊndəzrɑːt/ *noun* **1.** the upper house of the legislature in Austria and Germany **2.** the federal council in Switzerland, similar to a cabinet

Bundestag /ˈbʊndəztɑːg/ *noun* the lower house of legislature in Germany

bureau /ˈbjʊərəʊ/ *noun* **1.** an office that provides a particular service ○ *a legal advice bureau* ○ *an employment bureau* **2.** a government office or agency **3.** *mainly US* a government department ○ *the European Affairs Bureau* ◊ **Politburo** (NOTE: The plural is **bureaux**.) □ **the Bureau** Same as **FBI 4.** an organisation that collects news

bureaucracy /bjʊəˈrɒkrəsi/ *noun* **1.** the group of civil servants or officials who run central or local government ○ *The investigation of complaints is in the hands of the local bureaucracy.* ○ *The new president found it difficult to change the way the bureaucracy worked.* **2.** an annoying and puzzling system of rules (*informal*) ○ *too much bureaucracy and red tape*

bureaucrat /ˈbjʊərəkræt/ *noun* someone who works in a government or official office (*often disapproving*) ○ *The bureaucrats in the state capital are well-known for the slowness of their decision-making.*

bureaucratic /ˌbjʊərəˈkrætɪk/ *adjective* referring to a bureaucracy or to bureaucrats (*often disapproving*) ○ *You have to follow the correct bureaucratic procedures.* ○ *The investigation has been held up by bureaucratic muddle.*

burgermeister /ˈbɜːgəmaɪstə/ *noun* the mayor of a German town

burgh /ˈbʌrə/ *noun* a Scottish borough or town

burgher /ˈbɜːgə/ *noun* a person who lives in a borough or town

burgomaster /ˈbɜːgəmɑːstə/ *noun* the mayor of a Dutch or Flemish town

Burke, Edmund /bɜːk/ *noun* the Irish politician and writer (1729–97), whose ideas are often said to sum up traditional conservatism best (NOTE: Burke's theory of representation is still quoted in the modern world. He believed that an MP should work for all his constituents, not just those who voted for him, and that the MP should decide for himself how to vote without referring back to seek the views of his constituents.)

Bush /bʊʃ/, **George W.** (*b.* 1946) the 43rd president of the United States (2001–)

business /ˈbɪznɪs/ *noun* **1.** the work of making, buying or selling **2.** a company, shop or factory which makes, buys or sells things ○ *He owns a small car repair business.* ○ *She runs a business from her home.* ○ *He set up in business as an insurance broker.* **3.** things that are discussed in a meeting ○ *The main business of the meeting was finished by 3 p.m.* □ **any other business** item at the end of an agenda, where any matter can be raised. Abbr **AOB** □ **the business of the House, the business of the day** matters for discussion in the House of Commons on a particular day

business committee /ˌbɪznɪs kəˈmɪti/ *noun* a committee set up by the House of Commons to discuss the details of how the work of the House of Commons is to be organised

business rate /ˈbɪznɪs reɪt/ *noun* a local tax paid by businesses in the UK

business ratepayer /ˌbɪznəs ˈreɪtpeɪə/ *noun* a business which pays local taxes on a shop or factory

Butskellism /ˈbʌtskəlɪz(ə)m/ *noun* the relatively similar policies of the Conservative and Labour parties in the United Kingdom in the 1950s, when R. A. Butler and Hugh Gaitskell were the chancellors of the two parties when in power.

by-election /ˈbaɪ ɪˌlekʃən/ *noun* an election for Parliament or for a council in one constituency or ward held because of the death or retirement of the person first elected

bylaw /ˈbaɪ lɔː/, **byelaw, by-law, bye-law** *noun* a rule or law made by a local authority or public body and not by central government ○ *The bylaws forbid playing ball games in the public gardens.* ○ *According to the local bylaws, noise must be limited in the town centre.*

COMMENT: Bylaws must be made by bodies which have been authorized by Parliament, before they can become legally effective.

Byzantine /baɪˈzænatɪn/ *adjective* too complicated to be easily understood ○ *It is difficult to follow the Byzantine discussions between the two countries about the boundary dispute.*

C

CA *abbreviation* consular agent

CAB /ˌsiː eɪ ˈbiː, kæb/, **CABX** *abbreviation* Citizens' Advice Bureau or Bureaux

cabal /kəˈbɑːl/ *noun* a small group of politicians who plan action in secret to get power or advantage

cabinet /ˈkæbɪnət/ *noun* **Cabinet 1.** a committee formed of the most important members of the government, chosen by the Prime Minister or President to be in charge of the main government departments ○ *Cabinet meetings are held in the Cabinet room.* ○ *The Cabinet meets on Thursday mornings.* ○ *The Prime Minister held a meeting of the Cabinet yesterday.* ◊ **inner cabinet, kitchen cabinet 2.** a meeting of the Cabinet ○ *The Prime Minister held a Cabinet yesterday.* ○ *The decision was taken at Thursday's Cabinet.*

Cabinet Committee /ˈkæbɪnət kəˌmɪti/ *noun* one of a number of committees which are formed from Cabinet ministers, junior ministers or civil servants, who advise the Cabinet and Prime Minister on certain matters

Cabinet government /ˌkæbɪnət ˈgʌv(ə)nmənt/ *noun* a form of government where a Prime Minister or President works closely with a group of ministers

COMMENT: In most forms of Cabinet government (as in the UK), the Prime Minister or President chooses the members of his Cabinet and can dismiss them if necessary. In some countries, MPs of the ruling party elect the members of the Cabinet, with the result that the Prime Minister has less overall power over the decisions of the Cabinet, and cannot dismiss ministers easily.

Cabinet Minister /ˌkæbɪnət ˈmɪnɪstə/ *noun* a minister who is a member of the Cabinet

Cabinet Office /ˌkæbɪnət ˈɒfɪs/ *noun* the section of the British Civil Service which works for the Prime Minister and the Cabinet

Cabinet Secretary /ˌkæbɪnət ˈsekrətri/ *noun* the head of the Cabinet Office and of the British Civil Service, who attends Cabinet meetings. Also called **Secretary to the Cabinet**

cadre /ˈkɑːdə/ *noun* an active member or group of key members of a party, especially a Marxist party

calendar /ˈkælɪndə/ *noun* **1.** a book or set of sheets of paper showing the days and months in a year, often attached to pictures **2.** a list of events with the dates on which they will take place **3.** *US* a list of Bills for consideration by committees of the House of Representatives or the Senate

COMMENT: The Senate has only one calendar, but the House of Representatives has several: the Consent Calendar for uncontroversial bills; the Discharge Calendar for motions to discharge a committee of its responsibility for a bill; the House Calendar for bills which do not involve raising revenue or spending money; and the Union Calendar for bills which raise revenue or appropriate money for expenditure.

calendar Wednesday /ˌkælɪndə ˈwenzdeɪ/ *noun* the day of the week when the House of Representatives can consider bills from committees during a short debate

call for /ˈkɔːl fɔː/ *verb* to ask publicly for something, or say that something is necessary ○ *The Opposition called for the Minister's resignation.*

call in /ˌkɔːl ˈɪn/ *verb* **1.** to visit for a short time ○ *The MPs called in to a shopping centre on their campaign trail.* **2.** to ask someone to come to help ○ *The Department of Trade decided to call in the Fraud Squad to help in the investigation.* **3.** to ask for plans to be sent for examination ○ *The minister has called in the plans for the new supermarket.* **4.** to ask for money to be paid ○ *The Central banks have called in the country's debts.*

call off /ˌkɔːl ˈɒf/ *verb* to ask for something not to take place or not to continue ○ *The search for the missing children has been called off.* ○ *The visit was called off because the Foreign Minister was ill.*

call on /ˈkɔːl ɒn/ *verb* **1.** to visit someone ○ *The visiting Swedish Foreign Minister called on the President yesterday for talks.* **2.** to ask someone to do something ○ *The minister called on community leaders to help prevent street crime.*

camarilla /ˌkæməˈrɪlə/ *noun* a small group of advisers, especially a group privately advising an important person

camera /ˈkæm(ə)rə/ ♦ **in camera**

campaign /kæmˈpeɪn/ *noun* **1.** a planned method of working to achieve something ○ *The government has launched a campaign against drunken drivers.* **2.** the work of candidates before an election when they try to win votes ■ *verb* **1.** to try to change something by writing about it or by holding protest meetings or by lobbying Members of Parliament ○ *They are campaigning for the abolition of the death penalty.* or *They are campaigning against the death penalty.* ○ *She is campaigning for the reintroduction of the death penalty.* ○ *He is campaigning for a revision of the Official Secrets Act.* **2.** to try to get people to vote for you in an election ○ *She is campaigning on the issue of more money for the school system.* ○ *He had been campaigning all day from the top of a bus.*

campaigner /kæmˈpeɪnə/ *noun* a person who is campaigning for a party or for a candidate or for a cause ○ *He is an experienced political campaigner.* ○ *She is a campaigner for women's rights.*

campaign trail /kæmˈpeɪn treɪl/ *noun* a series of meetings or visits which are held by a candidate before an election in order to win votes ○ *She is out on the campaign trail again this week.*

Camp David /ˌkæmp ˈdeɪvɪd/ *noun* the official country home of the Presidents of the United States

camp follower /ˌkæmp ˈfɒləʊə/ *noun* a person who supports a party or leader for selfish reasons (*disapproving*)

Canadian Charter of Rights and Freedoms *noun* a statement of the fundamental rights and freedoms of Canadian citizens that forms part of the Constitution Act, 1982

cancel /ˈkænsəl/ *verb* to stop or call off something

cancellation clause /ˌkænsə ˈleɪʃ(ə)n klɔːz/ *noun* a clause in a contract which states when the contract may be brought to an end

candidacy /ˈkændɪdəsi/, **candidature** /ˈkændɪdətʃə/ *noun* the fact of taking part in an election ○ *The Senator has announced his candidacy for the Presidential election.*

candidate /ˈkændɪdeɪt/ *noun* **1.** someone who takes part in an election ○ *the Conservative* or *Labour* or *Liberal candidate* (NOTE: Candidates for election to Parliament must be British citizens over 21 years of age.) **2.** someone or something that is assessed for their suitability for something ○ *We interviewed ten candidates for the post of communications officer.* ○ *The hotel is one of the main candidates for the conference location.*

canton /ˈkæntɒn/ *noun* one of the 22 official regions into which Switzerland and some other countries are divided

canvass /'kænvəs/ *verb* to visit people to ask them to vote for a certain candidate or to say what they think ○ *Party workers are out canvassing voters.* □ **to canvass support** to ask people to support you ○ *She is canvassing support for his Bill among members of the Opposition*

canvasser /'kænvəsə/ *noun* a person who visits people to ask them to vote for a certain candidate or to say what they think

canvassing /'kænvəsɪŋ/ *noun* the action of asking people to vote for some party or candidate, or to say what they think

CAP *abbreviation* Common Agricultural Policy

capita /'kæpɪtə/ ♦ **per capita**

capital /'kæpɪt(ə)l/ *noun* **1.** money and property used in a business **2.** ♦ **capital city**

capital city /,kæpɪt(ə)l 'sɪti/ *noun* the main town in a country, where the government and parliament are usually found

capital crime /,kæpɪt(ə)l 'kraɪm/ *noun* a crime for which the punishment is death. Also called **capital offence**

capital gains /,kæpɪt(ə)l 'geɪnz/ *noun* money made by selling property or shares at a profit

capital gains tax /,kæpɪt(ə)l 'geɪnz ,tæks/ *noun* a tax paid on capital gains

capitalism /'kæpɪt(ə)lɪz(ə)m/ *noun* **1.** the belief in the economic system based on the private ownership of money and property used to create profits **2.** the economic system, where money and property are owned privately and businesses are run for profit by their owners rather than by the state

capitalist /'kæpɪt(ə)lɪst/ *noun* a person who owns money and property and uses them to make profits (*sometimes disapproving*) ■ *adjective* based on capitalism as an economic system □ **capitalist countries** countries, mainly in the West, whose economies are run on capitalist principles □

the capitalist system all capitalist countries working together

capitalistic /,kæpɪtə'lɪstɪk/ *adjective* similar to capitalism (*disapproving*)

capital levy /,kæpɪt(ə)l 'levi/ *noun* a tax on the value of a person's property and possessions

capital transfer tax /,kæpɪt(ə)l 'trænsfɜː ,tæks/ *noun* a tax paid when property or large sums of money are given by one person to another

Capitol /'kæpɪt(ə)l/ *noun* the building in Washington, D.C., where the US Senate and House of Representatives meet

Capitol Hill /,kæpɪt(ə)l 'hɪl/ *noun* a hill in Washington D.C., on which the Capitol building stands, together with other important government buildings □ **on Capitol Hill**, **on the Hill** in the US Senate or House of Representatives ○ *The feeling on Capitol Hill is that the President will veto the proposal.*

Captain of the Honourable Corps of Gentleman-at-Arms /,kæptɪn əv ðɪ ,ɒn(ə)rəb(ə)l kɔː ,dʒent(ə)lmən ət 'ɑːmz/ *noun* in the House of Lords, the Government Chief Whip. ◊ **Parliamentary Secretary to the Treasury**

capture /'kæptʃə/ *verb* to take or get control of something ○ *The Opposition captured six seats in the general election.*

card vote /'kɑːd vəʊt/ *noun* a vote taken at meetings of the Trades Union Congress, where union representatives vote on behalf of the members of their union by holding up a card showing the number of members they are representing

care order /'keə ,ɔːdə/ *noun* an order from a juvenile court, putting a child into the care of a local authority

care proceedings /'keə prə ,siːdɪŋz/ *plural noun* legal action to put a child into the care of someone

caretaker /'keəteɪkə/ *adjective* temporarily responsible for a job or activity

caretaker government /ˌkeəteɪkə ˈɡʌv(ə)nmənt/ *noun* a government that is in power temporarily until an election is held

CARICOM /ˈkærɪkɒm/ *abbreviation* Caribbean Community and Common Market

carousel retaliation /ˌkærəˈsel rɪ ˌtælieɪʃ(ə)n/ *noun* in a trade dispute, especially between the United States and the European Union, the imposition of high import tariffs on a list of imports that is changed regularly to widen the effect

carpetbagger /ˈkɑːpɪtˌbæɡə/ *noun* US a person from one part of a country who goes to another part of that country where he or she is unknown to try to get elected (*informal*)

carpetbagging /ˈkɑːpətˌbæɡɪŋ/ *noun* US the activity of a person going from one part of a country to another part where he or she is unknown to try to get elected (*informal*)

carry /ˈkæri/ *verb* **1.** to take something from one place to another □ **carrying offensive weapons** the offence of holding a weapon or something such as a bottle which could be used as a weapon **2.** to vote to approve a proposal □ **the motion was carried** a formal suggestion to do something was agreed when the majority of people voting supported it **3.** to keep the support of someone □ **the government carried the day** the government won the vote □ **he was not able to carry his supporters with him** his supporters voted against him **4.** (*of a crime*) to be punished with a particular form of punishment ○ *The offence carries a maximum sentence of two years' imprisonment.* **5.** to publish or broadcast news ○ *The newspapers and television bulletins carried the story for a week.* **6.** to display information ○ *All cigarette packets and adverts carry a government health warning,* **7.** to have something as a quality ○ *The policy carries the risk that older people will feel it doesn't meet their needs.* **8.** to accept responsibility for something ○ *The school must carry part of the* blame for the accident. **9.** *US* to win an election in a particular place ○ *The Democrats are expected to carry the state again.* ◇ **to carry conviction** to be considered certain or true ○ *His assurances do not carry conviction.*

carry forward /ˌkæri ˈfɔːwəd/ *verb* to continue to make progress with something ○ *carrying forward policies to support families*

carry out /ˌkæri ˈaʊt/ *verb* to do a job, or obey an order ○ *The police carried out the raid with great speed.* ○ *The agent was only carrying out orders.*

carry through /ˈkæri θruː/ *verb* to do something that it was planned to do ○ *The government carried through reforms to the House of Lords.*

carte blanche /ˌkɑːt ˈblɑːntʃ/ *French phrase meaning* 'white card': permission given by someone to another person, allowing him or her to act in any way necessary to achieve something ○ *He has carte blanche to act on behalf of the government* or *The government has given him carte blanche to act on its behalf.*

cartel /kɑːˈtel/ *noun* an alliance among parties or groups having common aims ○ *the oil cartel*

cartelise /kɑːˈtelaɪz/ *verb* to form a cartel of business companies or political groups

case /keɪs/ *noun* **1.** a question to be investigated by the police or to be decided in a law court **2.** the arguments or facts put forward by one side in a debate or law court ○ *The proposer of the motion put forward a very strong case for repealing the statute.* ○ *The government's case is particularly weak.* ○ *There is a strong case against the accused.*

case law /ˈkeɪs lɔː/ *noun* law as established by the decisions of courts in earlier cases

cast /kɑːst/ *verb* □ **to cast a vote** to vote ○ *Fewer than 50% of the population bothered to cast their votes.*

caste /kɑːst/ *noun* one of the hereditary divisions in a Hindu society where social classes were formerly strictly divided

casting vote /ˌkɑːstɪŋ ˈvəʊt/ *noun* a vote used by the chairman in a case where the votes for and against a proposal are equal ○ *The chairman has a casting vote.* ○ *He used his casting vote to block the motion.*

casual vacancy /ˌkæʒuəl ˈveɪkənsi/ *noun* a position on a committee which is empty and needs to be filled temporarily until the next full committee elections take place

casus belli /ˌkɑːzəs ˈbeliː/ *Latin phrase meaning* 'case for war': a reason which is used to explain why a country has gone to war

catch /kætʃ/ *verb* □ **to catch the Speaker's eye** (*of an MP*) to stand up to show the Speaker a wish to speak in a debate

caucus /ˈkɔːkəs/ *noun* **1.** a group of people in a political party, or a political assembly who meet to influence policy or choose a candidate **2.** *US* a meeting of powerful members of a political party particularly in the US Congress (NOTE: The plural is **caucuses.**)

caudillo *noun* (*in Spanish-speaking countries*) a military or political leader

cause list /ˈkɔːz lɪst/ *noun* a list of cases which are to be heard by a court

CBI /n/ *abbreviation* Confederation of British Industry

Cd *abbreviation* command (paper)

CD /ˌsiːˈdiː/ *abbreviation* Corps Diplomatique

ceasefire /ˈsiːsfaɪə/ *noun* an agreement by two sides in a war to stop fighting for a time ○ *A ceasefire is due to come into effect.* ○ *Both sides have observed the ceasefire.*

cede /siːd/ *verb* to pass possession of territory from one country to another ○ *The Philippines were ceded to the USA by Spain in 1898.* ◊ **cession**

CEHR *abbreviation* Commission for Equality and Human Rights

cell /sel/ *noun* a small group of people who work closely or secretly together within a larger organisation, especially a political organisation

censor /ˈsensə/ *noun* **1.** in some countries, an official whose job is to say whether books, films or television programmes are acceptable and can be published or shown to the public ○ *The film was cut* or *was banned* or *was passed by the censor.* **2.** in some countries, an official whose duty is to prevent the publishing of secret information or of information which may be harmful to the government ○ *All press reports have to be passed by the censor.* ■ *verb* to perform the work of censors ○ *All press reports are censored by the government.* ○ *The news of the riots was censored.* ○ *The TV report has been censored and only parts of it can be shown.*

censorship /ˈsensəʃɪp/ *noun* the act of censoring published or broadcast material ○ *TV reporters complained of government censorship.* ○ *The government has imposed strict press censorship* or *censorship of the press.* (NOTE: no plural)

censure /ˈsenʃə/ *noun* strong criticism □ **motion of censure, censure motion** a proposal from the Opposition to pass a vote to criticise the government ■ *verb* to criticise someone strongly ○ *The Opposition put forward a motion to censure the Government.* ○ *The Borough Architect was censured for failing to consult the engineers.*

central bank /ˌsentrəl ˈbæŋk/ *noun* the main government-controlled bank in a country, which sets interest rates and issues currency and tries to control the foreign exchange rate

Central Committee /ˌsentrəl kə ˈmɪti/ *noun* in a Communist party, the group responsible for party policy

central government /ˌsentrəl ˈgʌv(ə)nmənt/ *noun* the system of administration which operates nationally and deals with matters affecting the whole country, as opposed to local or regional government, which deal with matters which concern only some parts of the country

Central Intelligence Agency /ˌsentrəl ɪnˈtelɪdʒ(ə)ns ˌeɪdʒ(ə)nsi/ *noun US* the main government intelligence office in the USA. Abbr **CIA** (NOTE: The equivalent UK organisations are **MI5** and **MI6**.)

centralisation /ˌsentrəlaɪˈzeɪʃ(ə)n/, **centralization** *noun* a political movement which aims to move towards a situation by which as many government activities as possible take place in one place rather than in many places

centralise /ˈsentrəlaɪz/, **centralize** *verb* to try to achieve control of something from one point rather than many points ○ *The gathering of all personal records has been centralised in the headquarters of the Department of Health.*

centralism /ˈsentrəlɪz(ə)m/ *noun* a political system where decisions are taken by a central group of people

centre /ˈsentə/ *noun* **1.** the position occupied by parties or people in the middle of the range of political ideas ○ *The Liberal Democrats in the UK are often thought to be in the centre.* (NOTE: The US spelling is **center**.) □ **left of centre** tending towards socialism □ **right of centre** tending towards conservatism ○ *a left-of-centre political group* ○ *The Cabinet was formed mainly of right-of-centre supporters of the Prime Minister.* **2.** an important town ○ *an industrial centre* ○ *the centre for the shoe industry* (NOTE: The US spelling is **center**.) **3.** an office (NOTE: The US spelling is **center**.) ■ **1.** a place where people can go for information or advice **2.** a building used for a particular activity ○ *a sports centre* ○ *an out-of-town shopping centre* ○ *a conference centre*

COMMENT: The division of political parties and political ideas into left, right and centre dates from the French Revolution when deputies in the National Assembly sat on the left or right of the chamber according to their views. It was easiest to apply these labels when socialist (left) parties faced

conservative (right) parties in the middle years of the twentieth century. Some commentators say the old divisions of left and right are less and less relevant in the modern world, but they continue to be used.

Centrelink /ˈsentəlɪŋk/ *noun* an Australian government agency that offers to the public services such as advice on finding employment and eligibility for social security payments

centrism /ˈsentrɪz(ə)m/ *noun* support for moderate political or other views

centrist /ˈsentrɪst/ *adjective* referring to the centre in politics ○ *The group advocates a return to centrist politics.* ■ *noun* a person who is in favour of the centre in politics

ceremonial /ˌserɪˈməʊniəl/ *adjective* referring to a ceremony ○ *ceremonial robes* ○ *a ceremonial procession.* ■ *noun* official ceremonies ○ *The book lays out the rules for court ceremonial.* ○ *There is a lot of historic ceremonial attached to the job of Lord Mayor.*

ceremony /ˈserɪməni/ *noun* an official occasion, e.g. the State Opening of Parliament ○ *The mayor presided at the ceremony to open the new council offices.* ○ *Special police were present at ceremonies to mark the National Day.*

certificated /səˈtɪfɪkeɪtɪd/ *adjective* given official permission or approval

certificated bankrupt /sə ˌtɪfɪkeɪtɪd ˈbæŋkrʌpt/ *noun* someone who owed money and who has been given an official document to show that he or she is no longer bankrupt

cession /ˈseʃ(ə)n/ *noun* the act of giving possession of a piece of land by one country to another ○ *the cession of the Philippines to the USA in 1898*

CG /ˌsiː ˈdʒiː/ *abbreviation* Consul General

CGBR *abbreviation* Central Government Borrowing Requirement

CGS *abbreviation* Chief of General Staff

CGT *abbreviation* capital gains tax

chad /tʃæd/ *noun* a piece removed from a ballot paper in order to register a vote for a candidate

chair /tʃeə/ *noun* the position of the person who is in charge of a meeting ○ *to be in the chair* ○ *He was voted into the chair.* ○ *She is Chair of the Finance Committee.* ○ *This can be done by the Chair's action and confirmed later.* (NOTE: The word **chair** is now often used instead of chairman or chairwoman, as it avoids making an unnecessary distinction between men and women.) ■ *verb* to be in charge of a meeting ○ *The meeting was chaired by Mrs Smith.*

chairman /'tʃeəmən/ *noun* **1.** a person who is in charge of a meeting ○ *Mr Howard was chairman* or *acted as chairman.* **2.** a person who is in charge of the board meetings of a company ○ *the chairman of the board* or *the company chairman*

Chairman of Ways and Means /ˌtʃeəmən əv ˌweɪz ən 'miːnz/ *noun* the person elected at the beginning of Parliament to be in charge of the Committee of the Whole House, who also acts as Deputy Speaker (NOTE: The title comes from a former committee of the House of Commons that used to consider the 'ways and means' that Government would use to raise revenue.)

chairmanship /'tʃeəmənʃɪp/ *noun* the position of being in charge of a meeting □ **the committee met under the chairmanship of Mr Jones** Mr Jones chaired the meeting of the committee

chairperson /'tʃeəpɜːs(ə)n/ *noun* the person who is in charge of a meeting

chairwoman /'tʃeəwʊmən/ *noun* a woman who is in charge of a meeting

challenge /'tʃælɪndʒ/ *noun* a statement or action questioning a decision or criticising a person ■ *verb* **1.** to question the truth of something or refuse to accept that something is true ○ *The Leader of the Opposition chal-* lenged the government's unemployment statistics. **2.** to object to or refuse to accept something such as evidence ○ *to challenge a sentence passed by magistrates by appeal to the Crown Court* **3.** to ask someone to do something difficult, which he or she may not be able to do ○ *She challenged the Prime Minister to a debate on television.*

chamber /'tʃeɪmbə/ *noun* **1.** a room where a committee or legislature meets ○ *The meeting will be held in the council chamber.* **2.** a part of a parliament where a group of representatives meet, or the representatives meeting there. In many parliaments there is a lower chamber and an upper chamber. ○ *The British Parliament is formed of two chambers – the House of Commons and the House of Lords.*

Chamber of Commerce /ˌtʃeɪmbər əv 'kɒmɜːs/ *noun* **1.** a group of local businessmen who meet to discuss problems which they have in common, and to support business in the town **2.** an official organisation representing a country's business interests in another country ○ *the Spanish Chamber of Commerce in Britain* ○ *the British Chamber of Commerce in Spain*

Chamber of Deputies /ˌtʃeɪmbə əv 'depjʊtiz/ *noun* the lower section of the legislature in many countries, including Argentina, Bolivia, Belgium, Brazil, Chile, Croatia, Czech Republic, Djibouti, Dominican Republic, Greece, Italy, Luxembourg, Mexico, Paraguay, Spain

Chamber of Representatives /ˌtʃeɪmbə əv ˌreprɪ'zentətɪvz/ *noun* the legislature in Morocco

champagne socialist /ˌʃæmpeɪn 'səʊʃəlɪst/ *noun* someone who is rich but holds socialist principles

Chanc. *abbreviation* **1.** chancellor **2.** chancery

chancellery /'tʃɑːns(ə)ləri/ *noun* **1.** the position of chancellor **2.** an office attached to an embassy

Chancellor /'tʃɑːns(ə)lə/ *noun* same as **Chancellor of the Exchequer** ▪ same as **Lord Chancellor** ▪ *noun* **1.** the head of the government in Austria or Germany **2.** the main secretary of an embassy

Chancellor of the Duchy of Lancaster /ˌtʃɑːnsələ əv ðiː ˈdʌtʃi/ *noun* a title given to a member of the British government with no specific responsibilities attached to it

Chancellor of the Exchequer /ˌtʃɑːnsələr əv ðiː ɪksˈtʃekə/ *noun* the leading finance minister in the British government

chancery /'tʃɑːnsəri/ *noun* an office attached to an embassy or consulate, especially the political section (NOTE: The US term is **chancellery**.)

change of use /ˌtʃeɪndʒ əv ˈjuːs/ *noun* an order allowing a property to be used in a different way, e.g. allowing a shop to be used as a factory

channel /'tʃæn(ə)l/ *noun* a way in which information or goods are passed from one place to another. ◊ **usual channels** □ **to go through the official channels** to deal with government officials, especially when making a request □ **to open up new channels of communication** to find new ways of communicating with someone

chaplain /'tʃæplɪn/ *noun* a priest employed by someone or attached to a group (NOTE: The Speaker's Chaplain says prayers at the beginning of each day's business in the House of Commons.)

charge /tʃɑːdʒ/ *noun* **1.** the cost which must be paid for something ◊ *a policy of opening museums to the public free of charge* ◊ **congestion charge 2.** an accusation made by the police in a criminal case **3.** a serious claim that someone has done something wrong ◊ *The statement led to charges of racism.* ◊ *The MP reacted angrily to the charge that she had not pursued the complaints vigorously enough.*

chargeable /'tʃɑːdʒəb(ə)l/ *adjective* something for which payment may be asked

charge-cap /tʃɑːdʒ kæp/ *verb* to limit the amount of local tax that local authorities in the United Kingdom are allowed to ask people to pay

chargé d'affaires /ˌʃɑːʒeɪ dæˈfeə/ *noun* **1.** a diplomat ranking immediately below an ambassador **2.** a diplomat who is in charge of a minor diplomatic mission

charisma /kəˈrɪzmə/ *noun* the special quality of some public persons, showing charm or strength of character or attraction, that wins them public support

charismatic /ˌkærɪzˈmætɪk/ *adjective* showing the special quality which makes a leader popular ◊ *The old leader has been replaced by a charismatic young politician from the north of the country.*

charter /'tʃɑːtə/ *noun* **1.** a document from the head of state establishing a borough or a corporation or a university or a company, and giving it special rights **2.** an official document containing a list of rights (NOTE: The European Union has issued a Charter of Workers Rights) **3.** a law that appears to allow or encourage something bad (*informal*) ◊ *New restrictions on waste disposal have been labelled as a fly-tipper's charter and bureaucracy gone mad.* ▪ *verb* to hire for a special purpose ◊ *to charter a plane* or *a boat* or *a bus*

Charter of Rights /ˌtʃɑːtər əv ˈraɪts/ *noun* the section of the Canadian Constitution which states the rights of people who have Canadian citizenship

Chartism /'tʃɑːtɪz(ə)m/ *noun* the beliefs of a movement advocating political and social reform in England between 1838 and 1848. Among its aims were: improvements in the education and living conditions of the working classes, payment for Members of Parliament, the right to vote for adult males, electoral districts of equal size and influence, and voting by ballot.

chauvinism /'ʃəʊvɪnɪz(ə)m/ *noun* an excessive feeling of pride in one's country or gender (*used as criticism*) ○ *The President was accused of male chauvinism*

chauvinist /'ʃəʊvɪnɪst/ *noun* a person who is excessively proud of his or her country or gender. Compare **patriot**

check /tʃek/ *noun* to examine carefully

checking /'tʃekɪŋ/ *noun* a careful examination ○ *The inspectors found some defects during their checking of the building.*

Cheney /'tʃeɪni/, **Dick** (*b.* 1941) vice president of the United States (2001–)

Chequers /'tʃekəz/ *noun* the official country house of the British Prime Minister

chief /tʃiːf/ *noun* a traditional tribal leader

Chief Constable /ˌtʃiːf 'kʌnstəb(ə)l/ *noun* the person in charge of a regional police force

chief executive /ˌtʃiːf ɪgˈzekjʊtɪv/ *noun* the president of the United States

Chief Executive /ˌtʃiːf ɪgˈzekjʊtɪv/ *noun* the highest-ranking permanent official of an executive body, e.g. the head of a government, the governor of a US state, or the head of a local authority

Chief Justice /ˌtʃiːf 'dʒʌstɪs/ *noun US* the senior judge in a court

Chief Minister /ˌtʃiːf 'mɪnɪstə/ *noun* the head of government in a federal region such as an Indian state

Chief Officer /ˌtʃiːf 'ɒfɪsə/ *noun* a person who is head of a department in a local authority, responsible to the Chief Executive

COMMENT: A local authority will have several Chief Officers: Chief Education Officer, Chief Housing Officer, Chief Planning Officer, and so on, all of whom are responsible to the Chief Executive. In some authorities they are called Director: Director of Education, Director of Finance, etc.

Chief Secretary to the Treasury /ˌtʃiːf ˌsekrətri tə θə 'treʒ(ə)ri/ *noun* a British government minister, working under the Chancellor of the Exchequer, dealing especially with financial planning

Chief Whip /ˌtʃiːf 'wɪp/ *noun* the main whip of a party, whose job it is to make sure that MPs of that party vote according to the party's policy ○ *The Government Chief Whip made sure the MPs were all present for the vote.* ◊ **Government Chief Whip** (NOTE: Traditionally, Chief Whips do not speak in debates.)

Chiltern Hundreds /ˌtʃɪltən 'hʌndrədz/ *noun* a former administrative division of the country west of London, in Buckinghamshire □ **to apply for the Chiltern Hundreds** to apply to resign from Parliament (*informal*)

COMMENT: As MPs are not allowed to resign from Parliament, the only way in which they can do so is to apply for a paid office or office of profit under the crown, such as this one or the Stewardship of the Manor of Northstead.

Chirac /ʃiˈræk/, **Jacques** (*b.* 1932) prime minister (1974–76, 1986–88) and then president of France (1995–2002, 2002–)

Christian Democrat /'krɪstʃən 'deməkræt/ *noun* in several European countries, a member of a moderate conservative political party

Churchill /'tʃɜːtʃɪl/, **Sir Winston** (1874–1965) prime minister (1940–45, 1951–55) of Britain during World War II. He wrote *The Second World War* (1948–53) and won the Nobel Prize in literature (1953).

churchillian /tʃɜːˈtʃɪliən/ *adjective* a form of strong political leadership or a style of inspiring public speaking similar to that of Winston Churchill who was UK Prime Minister during the Second World War

CIA /ˌsiː ˌaɪ 'eɪ/ *abbreviation* Central Intelligence Agency

circular /'sɜːkjʊlə/ *noun* a leaflet or letter sent to many people

circularise /'sɜːkjʊləraɪz/, **circularize** *verb* to send a circular to many people at the same time ○ *The committee has agreed to circularise the information in advance.*

circulate /'sɜːkjʊleɪt/ *verb* to send something to a number of people ○ *They circulated the proposals in a letter signed by the chairwoman*

circulation /ˌsɜːkjʊ'leɪʃ(ə)n/ *noun* **1.** movement around something ○ *The company is trying to improve the circulation of information between departments.* **2.** the passing of money from one person to another **3.** (*of newspapers*) the number of copies sold

circumstances /'sɜːkəmstənsɪz/ *plural noun* the situation as it is when something happens ○ *The Home Secretary described the circumstances leading to the riot in the prison.*

CIS /ˌsiː aɪ 'es/ *abbreviation* Commonwealth of Independent States

citation /saɪ'teɪʃ(ə)n/ *noun* **1.** a quotation from a text **2.** an official request asking someone to appear in court (NOTE: used mainly in the Scottish and US courts) **3.** a reference to a legal case or authority or precedent **4.** the words used in giving someone an honour, explaining why it is being given

citation clause /saɪ'teɪʃ(ə)n klɔːz/ *noun* the section in a Bill which gives the short title by which it should be known when it becomes an Act

cite /saɪt/ *verb* to refer to something as an example ○ *The letter cited several previous cases of failure to act.*

citizen /'sɪtɪz(ə)n/ *noun* **1.** a person who lives in a city or a particular place ○ *the citizens of Manchester* **2.** a person who has the legal right to live in a particular country ○ *He is a French citizen by birth.*

Citizens' Advice Bureau /ˌsɪtɪzənz əd'vaɪs ˌbjʊərəʊ/ *noun* an office where people can go to get free advice on legal problems. Abbr **CAB**

(NOTE: The plural is **Citizen's' Advice Bureaux**.)

citizen's arrest /ˌsɪtɪz(ə)nz ə'rest/ *noun* the arrest of a suspected criminal by an ordinary citizen, not a policeman

Citizens' Charter /ˌsɪtɪzənz 'tʃɑːtə/ *noun* a document which states what rights a citizen has

citizenship /'sɪtɪz(ə)nʃɪp/ *noun* **1.** the legal status of being a citizen of a country, entitled to its protection and to political rights ○ *She has applied for British citizenship.* **2.** the way people take part in the life of their community as they discuss their rights and carry out their responsibilities (NOTE: In the UK, citizenship is now a part of the curriculum in schools.)

city /'sɪti/ *noun* a large town

civic /'sɪvɪk/ *adjective* referring to a city or the official business of running a city □ **civic dignitaries** the mayor and other senior officials of a city or town □ **civic reception** an official reception for someone, organised by the mayor and council of a city

civic centre /ˌsɪvɪk 'sentə/ *noun* the building in a town or city where its local government is based

civil /'sɪv(ə)l/ *adjective* referring to the rights and duties of citizens

Civil and Public Services Association /'sɪv(ə)l ən 'pʌblɪk 'sɜːvɪsɪz əˌsəʊsi'eɪʃ(ə)n/ *noun* a trade union representing civil servants. It was merged with the Public Services, Tax and Commerce Union in 1996 to become (**PCS**). Abbr **CPSA**

civil defence /ˌsɪv(ə)l dɪ'fens/ *noun* the procedure for protecting the population during a war or emergency

civil disobedience /ˌsɪv(ə)l dɪsə'biːdiəns/ *noun* the activity of breaking the law as an act of protest ○ *The group planned a campaign of civil disobedience as a protest against restrictions on immigrants.*

Civil Guard /'sɪv(ə)l gɑːd/ *noun* one of the police forces in Spain

civilian /sə'vɪliən/ *adjective* referring to an ordinary citizen, who is not a member of the armed forces ○ *Civilian rule was restored after several years of military dictatorship.* ○ *The military leaders called general elections and gave way to a democratically elected civilian government.* ■ *noun* an ordinary citizen who is not a member of the armed forces ○ *The head of the military junta has appointed several civilians to the Cabinet.*

civilisation /ˌsɪvɪlaɪˈzeɪʃ(ə)n/, **civilization** *noun* a social system with a developed culture and organisation

civil law /ˌsɪv(ə)l ˈlɔː/ *noun* the laws relating to people's rights and the agreements made between individuals. Compare **criminal law**

civil liberties /ˌsɪv(ə)l ˈlɪbətiz/ *plural noun* the freedom for people to work or write or speak as they want, providing they keep within the law

Civil List /ˌsɪv(ə)l ˈlɪst/ *noun* the annual sum of money for carrying out official duties, given by Parliament to the Queen and some senior members of the Royal Family

civil marriage /ˈsɪv(ə)l ˈmærɪdʒ/ *noun* a legal marriage without a religious ceremony

civil rights /ˌsɪv(ə)l ˈraɪts/ *plural noun* the rights of each individual according to the law

civil servant /ˌsɪv(ə)l ˈsɜːvənt/ *noun* a person who works in the government departments which administer a country (NOTE: In Britain civil servants have generally been said to be politically neutral, anonymous, and permanently employed. In USA a large part of the civil service changes with a change in the administration.)

civil service /ˌsɪv(ə)l ˈsɜːvɪs/ *noun* the government departments which administer a country ○ *He has a job in the civil service.* ○ *You have to pass an examination to get a job in the civil service* or *to get a civil service job.* (NOTE: Members of the armed forces, magistrates and judges are not part of the British civil service.)

COMMENT: In a liberal democracy, the politicians are elected but the professional administrators or civil servants are not. The civil servants are responsible to the politicians, who in turn are responsible to the people.

civil strife /ˌsɪv(ə)l ˈstraɪf/ *noun* trouble when groups of civilians fight each other

civil war /ˌsɪv(ə)l ˈwɔː/ *noun* a situation inside a country where groups of armed people fight against each other or fight against the government

claim /kleɪm/ *noun* **1.** a legal right which someone believes they have to own something ○ *an historic claim to the territory* **2.** a right to something because of something you have done ○ *a valid claim to be the oldest parliament in the world* **3.** a statement that something has happened or is true ○ *The police deny the claim of assault.*

claimant /ˈkleɪmənt/ *noun* a person who claims money, especially state benefits ○ *Benefit claimants will be paid late because of the bank holiday.* ○ *The government will consider the position of claimants of backdated pensions.*

clarification /ˌklærɪfɪˈkeɪʃ(ə)n/ *noun* making something clear or easy to understand ○ *The wording of the clause is ambiguous and needs clarification.*

Clark /klɑːk/, **Helen Elizabeth** (*b.* 1950) the prime minister of New Zealand (1999–)

class /klɑːs/ *noun* **1.** a group of things or animals which are similar in some way **2.** a social group ○ *Society is traditionally said to be divided into upper class, middle class, and working class.* ■ *verb* to put into groups of similar things ○ *The inspectors classed the food as unfit for sale.* ○ *The magazine was classed as an obscene publication.*

COMMENT: In the UK the population is classified into social classes for statistical purposes. These are: **Class A:** higher managers, administrators and professionals; **Class B:** intermediate managers, administrators and professionals; **Class C1:** supervisors, clerical workers and junior managers; **Class C2:** skilled manual workers; **Class D:** semi-skilled or unskilled manual workers; **Class E:** pensioners, casual workers, long-term unemployed.

class action /ˌklɑːs ˈækʃən/, **class suit** /ˌklɑːs ˈsuːt/ *noun US* a legal action brought on behalf of a group of people

class alignment /ˌklɑːs əˈlaɪnmənt/ *noun* the connection between a class of people and a particular political party (NOTE: In Great Britain, the class alignment between the Labour Party and the working class is in decline as is the class alignment between the Conservative Party and the middle class.)

class-conscious /ˌklɑːs ˈkɒnʃəs/ *adjective* aware of differences of social class

class dealignment /ˌklɑːs ˌdiːəˈlaɪnmənt/ *noun* the way in which in recent years social class has indicated less clearly how people will vote

classification /ˌklæsɪfɪˈkeɪʃ(ə)n/ *noun* **1.** a way of putting things into classes **2.** the process of making information secret

classified information /ˌklæsɪfaɪd ˌɪnfəˈmeɪʃ(ə)n/ *noun* information which is secret and can be told only to specific people

classify /ˈklæsɪfaɪ/ *verb* **1.** to put into groups of similar things **2.** to make information secret

classless /ˈklɑːsləs/ *adjective* a society which has no class divisions o *Over the last twenty years the country has moved towards a classless society.*

class struggle /ˌklɑːs ˈstrʌɡ(ə)l/ *noun* the Marxist concept of the ruling and working classes competing to achieve political and economic power

class war /ˌklɑːs ˈwɔː/, **class strife** *noun* confrontation between different social classes

clause /klɔːz/ *noun* **1.** a section of a contract or of the constitution of a country or political party o *There are ten clauses in the contract.* **2.** a part of a Bill being considered by Parliament, which becomes a section of an Act o *According to clause six, some categories of business will be exempted from tax.*

Clause IV /ˌklɔːz ˈfɔː/ *noun* a part in the constitution of the British Labour Party which before 1995 committed the party to support nationalisation, and which after 1995 committed the party to a broader series of aims, but which included no support for nationalisation (NOTE: Tony Blair's first major step as leader of the Labour Party was to change Clause IV, which had first been adopted by the party in 1918. The reform of Clause IV marked an important stage in the development of what is called 'New Labour'.)

claw back /ˌklɔː ˈbæk/ *verb* to take back money which has been allocated o *Income tax claws back 25% of pensions paid out by the government.*

clawback /ˈklɔːbæk/ *noun* money taken back

clean bill /ˈkliːn bɪl/ *noun US* a bill made up of the original text, with amendments made during Committee, which is presented to the House of Representatives or Senate again as one whole new bill, so as to avoid having to discuss each amendment separately

clerk /klɑːk/ *noun* an official who keeps records of a legislative or administrative body o *accounts clerk* o *sales clerk* o *wages clerk*

clerk assistant /ˌklɑːk əˈsɪst(ə)nt/ *noun* the assistant to the Clerk of the House in the House of Commons

Clerk of the House /ˌklɑːk əv ðə ˈhaʊz/ *noun* **1.** *US* the head of the administrative staff which runs the House of Representatives **2.** the head of the administrative staff which runs the House of Commons and advises the Speaker on points of procedure

Clerk of the Parliaments /ˌklɑːk əv ðə ˈpɑːləmənts/ *noun* the head of the administrative staff in the House of Lords

client country /ˈklaɪənt ˈkʌntri/, **client state** /ˈklaɪənt steɪt/ *noun* a country which depends on another country for such things as defence and trade

client state /'klaɪənt steɪt/ *noun* a country that depends on another for economic, political or military support

Clinton /'klɪntən/, **Bill** (*b.* 1946) 42nd president of the United States (1993–2001). Before his election to the White House he was Democratic governor of Arkansas (1978–80, 1982–92). In 1999 he was impeached and acquitted by the US Senate for perjury and obstruction of justice.

Cllr *abbreviation* Councillor

close /kləʊz/ *noun* the end ○ *At the close of the debate, the government's majority was only six.*

closed /kləʊzd/ *adjective* **1.** shut or not open or not doing business ○ *The office is closed on Mondays.* ○ *All the banks are closed on the National Day.* **2.** restricted to a few people

closed rule /ˌkləʊzd 'ruːl/ *noun* the rule which limits the time available for the discussion of a bill. Also called **gag rule**

closed session /ˌkləʊzd 'seʃ(ə)n/ *noun* a meeting which is not open to the public or to journalists ○ *The town council met in closed session to discuss staff problems in the Education Department.* ○ *The public gallery was cleared when the meeting went into closed session.*

close-run /ˌkləʊs 'rʌn/ *adjective* winning by only a few points more than an opponent ○ *A close-run election is expected.*

closing speeches /ˌkləʊsɪŋ 'spiːtʃəz/ *plural noun* the final speeches for and against a motion in a debate

closure /'kləʊʒə/ *noun* **1.** the act of closing **2.** (*in the House of Commons*) the ending of the debate

closure motion /ˌkləʊʒə 'məʊʃ(ə)n/ *noun* a proposal to end a debate

COMMENT: When wishing to end the debate on a motion, an MP says 'I move that the question be now put' and the Speaker immediately puts the motion to the vote.

cloture /kləʊ'tjʊə/ *noun US* a motion to end a filibuster in the Senate, and thus prevent a measure being defeated, requiring a three-fifths majority to pass

CMEA *abbreviation* Council for Mutual Economic Assistance

Cmnd *abbreviation* Command Papers

CND *abbreviation* Campaign for Nuclear Disarmament

CO *abbreviation* Commonwealth Office

coalition /ˌkəʊə'lɪʃ(ə)n/ *noun* a group of two or more political parties who come together to form a government, when no single party has an absolute majority ○ *The coalition government fell when one of the parties withdrew support.*

'…the question of a coalition has arisen because all three parties are within seven points of each other in the polls and the chances are high that the next election will not give any party a majority' [*Toronto Globe & Mail*]

'England does not love coalitions' [*Benjamin Disraeli*]

Coalition /ˌkəʊə'lɪʃ(ə)n/ *noun* in Australia, a long-standing political coalition between the Liberal Party and the National Party

coalition government /ˌkəʊə'lɪʃ(ə)n 'gʌv(ə)nmənt/ a government in which no party has complete control and two or more parties agree to govern together (NOTE: During World War II, all three major parties in the United Kingdom, Conservative, Labour and Liberal, formed a government together.)

code /kəʊd/ *noun* **1.** an official set of laws or regulations **2.** a set of laws of a country **3.** a set of semi-official rules **4.** a system of signs, numbers or letters which mean something ○ *a message in code* ■ *verb* to write something using secret symbols or signs ○ *coded instructions*

Code Napoleon /ˌkəʊd nə ˈpəʊliən/ *noun* the civil laws of France introduced by Napoleon

code of conduct /ˌkəʊd əv ˈkɒndʌkt/ *noun* the unwritten rules by which a particular group of people are expected to behave

Code of Conduct for Ministers /ˌkəʊd əv ˌkɒndʌkt fə ˈmɪnɪstəz/ *noun* a document authorised by the Prime Minister and first made public in 1992 in which the powers and responsibilities of government ministers are defined

code of practice /ˌkəʊd əv ˈpræktɪs/ *noun* the set of rules by which the members of a profession agree to work

codification /ˌkəʊdɪfɪˈkeɪʃ(ə)n/ *noun* 1. the act of putting all laws together into a single document 2. the act of bringing together of all statutes and case law relating to an issue, to make a single Act of Parliament. ◊ **consolidation**

codify /ˈkəʊdɪfaɪ/ *verb* to write and set out things such as laws or rules in an organised way

coding /ˈkəʊdɪŋ/ *noun* the act of putting a system of signs, numbers or letters on something ○ *the coding of invoices*

cohabitation /ˌkəʊˌhæbɪˈteɪʃ(ə)n/ *noun* the situation where different political parties are in power in different branches of government. In France, the President and Parliament are elected for different periods of time and so may represent different parties.

cold war /ˌkəʊld ˈwɔː/ *noun* the hostile relations between the former Soviet Union and the United States, and their respective allies, from around 1946 to 1989

collaborate /kəˈlæbəreɪt/ *verb* 1. to work together ○ *We are collaborating with a French firm on building a bridge.* ○ *They collaborated on the new aircraft.* 2. to work together with an enemy who is occupying your country

collaboration /kəˌlæbəˈreɪʃ(ə)n/ *noun* 1. working together ○ *Their collaboration on the development of the computer system was very profitable.* 2. the act of helping an enemy

collaborator /kəˈlæbəreɪtə/ *noun* 1. a person who works with another ○ *The head of the research department thanked all her collaborators for their help.* 2. a person who works with an enemy who is occupying his or her country ○ *After the war, several people were executed as collaborators.*

collective /kəˈlektɪv/ *noun* a business such as a farm or factory under state control which is run by the people who work in it

collective leadership /kəˌlektɪv ˈliːdəʃɪp/ *noun* a system of government where several leaders rule the country together, making decisions as a group, without one being in total charge

collective responsibility /kəˌlektɪv rɪˌspɒnsɪˈbɪlɪti/ *noun* the principle that all members of a group are responsible together for the actions of the group (NOTE: In the UK the Cabinet and all ministers are said to be governed by the principle of collective responsibility)

collective security /kəˌlektɪv sɪ ˈkjʊərɪti/ *noun* a system by which a number of states agree to protect each other from attack ○ *The United Nations was set up after the Second World War to create the conditions of collective security which the League of Nations had failed in the period before the war to establish.*

collectivism /kəˈlektɪvɪz(ə)m/ *noun* a political and economic theory based on the desire to protect individuals from exploitation by creating a belief in the value of community action

collectivity /ˌkɒlekˈtɪvɪti/ a community ■ *noun* a group of people

collegial /kəˈliːdʒiəl/ *adjective* relating to control or government based on a number of people working together as a team, rather than by a single person ○ *John Major's style of government was far more collegial than that of his predecessor.*

collegiate /kə'liːdʒiət/ *adjective* sharing responsibilities as a group □ **collegiate decisions** decisions taken by a group of people collectively

colloquium /kə'ləʊkwiəm/ *noun* a meeting for discussion

collusive action /kə,luːsɪv 'ækʃən/ *noun* action taken in secret agreement with another person, which is often dishonest or open to criticism

colonial /kə'ləʊniəl/ *adjective* referring to countries ruled over or settled by other countries ○ *Granting of independence ended a period of a hundred years of colonial rule.* ○ *The colonial government was overthrown by a coup led by the local police force.* □ **colonial powers** countries which rule colonies ■ *noun* a person living in a colony or a person who was born in a colony

colonial dependency /kə,ləʊniəl dɪ'pendənsi/ *noun* a country ruled by another country

colonialism /kə'ləʊniəlɪz(ə)m/ *noun* the theory or practice of establishing colonies in other lands ○ *The meeting denounced colonialism and demanded independence.*

colonialist /kə'ləʊniəlɪst/ *adjective* believing in colonialism ■ *noun* a person who believes in colonialism

colonial status /kə'ləʊniəl 'steɪtəs/ *noun* the legal position of being a colony

colonisation /,kɒlənaɪ'zeɪʃ(ə)n/, **colonization** *noun* the act of making a country into a colony

colonise /'kɒlənaɪz/, **colonize** *verb* to take possession of an area or country and rule it as a colony ○ *The government was accused of trying to colonise the Antarctic Region.*

colonist /'kɒlənɪst/ *noun* a person who goes or is sent to another country or region to settle in a colony

colony /'kɒləni/ *noun* **1.** a country or area ruled and/or settled by another country ○ *Australia was originally a*

group of British colonies. ○ *The Romans established colonies in North Africa.* **2.** a group of people from the same foreign country, settled in a town, who form a separate social group ○ *the Japanese colony in Vancouver* ○ *There is a large German colony in London.*

comity /'kɒmɪti/, **comity of nations** /,kɒmɪti əv 'neɪʃ(ə)nz/ *noun* the respect shown in one country for the laws and customs of another

command /kə'mɑːnd/ *noun* **1.** an order **2.** leadership ○ *He has* or *is in command of the armed forces.* ■ *verb* to order someone to do something ○ *The chairman commanded that the public gallery should be cleared.* ○ *The President commanded the Chief of Police to arrest the Members of Parliament.* □ **to command support** to be good enough to have the support of voters ○ *The measure commands widespread support in the House.* ○ *Can the Minister command enough support to win the vote?*

commander /kə'mɑːndə/ *noun* the officer in charge of a police district in London. Abbr **Cmd., Cmdr, com., Com., Comdr**

Command Papers /kə'mɑːnd ,peɪpəz/ *plural noun* papers such as White Papers or reports of Royal Commissions which are presented to Parliament by the responsible government minister, so called because they are printed 'by Command of Her Majesty' (NOTE: Command Papers are numbered **Cmnd 4546**, etc.)

commence /kə'mens/ *verb* to begin ○ *In the House of Commons, the business of the day commences with prayers.* ○ *The proceedings commenced with the swearing-in of witnesses.* ○ *The committee has commenced the examination of the Bill, clause by clause.*

commencement order /kə'mensmənt ,ɔːdə/ *noun* an order that brings an Act or part of an act into effect after the Royal Assent has been given

comment /'kɒment/ *noun* a remark or spoken or written opinion ○ *The Secretary of State made a comment on the progress of negotiations.* ○ *The newspaper has some short comments about the Bill.* ■ *verb* to remark or to express an opinion ○ *The Speaker commented on the lack of respect shown by MPs.* ○ *The newspapers commented on the result of the vote.*

commentary /'kɒmənt(ə)ri/ *noun* **1.** a set of notes which comment on the main points of a document **2.** a book which comments on the law

commentator /'kɒmənteɪtə/ *noun* a journalist who comments on current events ○ *a report by the political commentator in 'The Times' on unrest on the Government back benches*

commerce /'kɒmɜːs/ *noun* business activities or the buying and selling of goods and services. ◊ **Chamber of Commerce**

commercial /kə'mɜːʃ(ə)l/ *adjective* **1.** referring to business **2.** intended to make money

commercial attaché /kə'mɜːʃ(ə)l ə,tæʃeɪ/ *noun* a diplomat whose job is to encourage business between his country and the country where he works

commercial law /kə,mɜːʃ(ə)l 'lɔː/ *noun* law relating to businesses

commission /kə'mɪʃ(ə)n/ *noun* **1.** a group of people officially appointed to examine a problem ○ *The government has appointed a commission of inquiry to look into the problems of prison overcrowding.* ○ *He is the chairman of the government commission on football violence.* **2.** an official order to someone, giving him or her authority and explaining the duties □ **he has a commission in the armed forces** he is an officer in the armed forces **3.** a payment made by someone to another person who is acting as their agent ○ *She has an agent's commission of 15% of sales.*

commissioner /kə'mɪʃ(ə)nə/ *noun* **1.** a member of an official group which has been appointed to examine

a problem **2.** a person who has a particular official job. ◊ **Parliamentary Commissioner, Local Commissioner 3.** a member of the European Commission

commissioner for oaths /kə ,mɪʃ(ə)nə fər 'əʊðs/ *noun* a lawyer who has the job of administering oaths

Commissioners of Inland Revenue /kə,mɪʃ(ə)nəz əv ,ɪnlənd 'revənjuː/ *noun* the Board of Inland Revenue

Commission for Equality and Human Rights /kə,mɪʃ(ə)n fə ɪ ,kwɒləti ən ,hjuːmən 'raɪts/ the organisation to be set up in 2006 to support human rights especially for minority groups and women. Abbr **CEHR**

Commission for Racial Equality /kə,mɪʃ(ə)n fə ,reɪʃ(ə)l ɪ'kwɒləti/ the organisation which works to improve race relations in the UK and to remove racial discrimination. Abbr **CRE** (NOTE: In 2006 the Commission for Racial Equality will be merged with other bodies to form the Commission for Equality and Human Rights.)

commit /kə'mɪt/ *verb* to send a bill to a parliamentary committee to be reviewed ○ *He was committed for trial at the Crown Court.*

commitment /kə'mɪtmənt/ *noun* a promise or agreement to do something ○ *We have honoured the commitments made in our manifesto.*

commitology /kə,mɪ'ɒlədʒi/ *noun* in the European Union, the system of appointing committees to deal with various areas of action

committed /kə'mɪtɪd/ *adjective* **1.** holding strong political views ○ *She is a committed socialist.* **2.** already promised to be used in a specific way ○ *Half next year's budget is already committed.* ○ *The government's subsidy has been committed to repairs to the Town Hall.* **3.** obliged to act in a particular way ○ *The council is committed to a policy of increasing services and reducing property taxes.*

committee /kə'mɪti/ *noun* **1.** an official group of people who organise or plan for a larger group ○ *to be a member of a committee* or *to sit on a committee* ○ *He was elected to the Finance Committee.* ○ *The new plans have to be approved by the committee members.* ○ *She is attending a committee meeting.* ○ *He is the chairman of the Planning Committee.* ○ *She is the secretary of the Housing Committee.* ◊ **Select Committee** □ **to chair a committee** to be the chairman of a committee **2. Committee** a section of a legislature which considers bills passed to it by the main chamber □ **the House went into Committee** the House of Commons became a Committee of the Whole House

committee meeting /kə'mɪti 'miːtɪŋ/ *noun* a meeting of the members of a committee

Committee of Permanent Representatives /kə,mɪti əv ,pɜːmənənt ,reprɪ'zentətɪvz/ *noun* in the European Union, the institution which prepares for meetings of the Council of Ministers and passes information between member governments and the Council of Ministers. Abbr **COREPER**

Committee of Selection /kə,mɪti əv sɪ'lekʃ(ə)n/ *noun* the committee which chooses the members of the other committees in the House of Commons

Committee of the Parliamentary Commission /kə,mɪti əv ðə ,pɑːlə'ment(ə)ri kə,mɪʃ(ə)n/ *noun* the committee which examines reports by the Ombudsman

Committee of the Regions /kə,mɪti əv ðə 'riːdʒənz/ *noun* in the European Union, the body which brings together representatives of regional and local authorities from all over the Union

Committee of the Whole /kə,mɪti əv ðə 'həʊl/ *noun* the committee formed of at least one hundred members of the House of Representatives in the USA, which discusses a bill which has already been debated in a Standing Committee

Committee of the Whole House /kə,mɪti əv ðə ,həʊl 'haʊz/ *noun* the House of Commons acting as a committee to examine the clauses of a Bill

Committee on Standards and Privileges *noun* the committee of the House of Commons that makes sure that MPs follow the rules of conduct that are designed to stop them making wrong use of the power of their position

Committee on Standards in Public Life *noun* a committee of the House of Commons set up to review the activities of holders of public office, including paid activities outside parliament, and to recommend any changes in practice that are necessary to make sure of high standards. Also called **Nolan Committee**

Committee Stage /kə'mɪti steɪdʒ/ *noun* one of the stages in the discussion of a Bill, where each clause is examined in detail ○ *The Bill is at Committee Stage and will not become law for several months.*

common /'kɒmən/ *adjective* referring to or belonging to several different people or to everyone □ **the common good** the interest of all members of society ○ *the government is working for the common good of the people* □ **common ownership** ownership of a company or a property by a group of people who each own a part

commonalty /,kɒmə'nælɪti/ *noun* ordinary people considered as a political class, as compared with the upper classes

commoner /'kɒmənə/ *noun* an ordinary citizen, who is not a member of a noble family

common law /,kɒmən 'lɔː/ *noun* **1.** law made by decisions of the courts, rather than by act of parliament **2.** the general system of laws which in the past were the only laws existing in England, and which in some cases have been replaced by acts of parliament

common-law /ˈkɒmən lɔː/ *adjective* according to an old system of laws □ **common-law marriage** a situation where two people live together as husband and wife without being married □ **common-law wife** a woman who is living with a man as his wife, although they have not been legally married

common market /ˈkɒmən ˈmɑːkɪt/ *noun* an economic association of countries with the aim of removing or reducing trade barriers

Common Market /ˌkɒmən ˈmɑːkɪt/ *noun* formerly, the European Economic Community, now the European Union

commons /ˈkɒmənz/ *noun* ordinary people as compared with the upper classes

Commons /ˈkɒmənz/ *plural noun* same as **House of Commons** ○ *The Commons voted against the Bill.* ○ *The majority of the Commons are in favour of law reform.* ○ *He was first elected to the Commons in 1979.* ○ *The Bill was passed after an all-night Commons sitting.*

Commonwealth /ˈkɒmənwelθ/ *noun* **1.** the association of independent states which were once ruled by Britain **2.** a self-governing state, usually with a republican system of government (*used in titles*) ○ *the Commonwealth of Australia* ○ *the Commonwealth of Massachusetts* **3.** the period between 1649 and 1660 when there was a republican government in England and Cromwell ruled as Lord Protector

Commonwealth of Independent States /ˈkɒmənwelθ əv ˌɪndɪ ˈpendənt steɪts/ *noun* an organisation formed of the majority of the republics which were in the past part of the USSR. Abbr **CIS**

Commonwealth Secretariat /ˌkɒmənwelθ ˌsekrəˈteəriət/ *noun* an office and officials in London, organising the links between the member states of the Commonwealth. The office is headed by the Commonwealth Secretary-General.

communal /ˈkɒmjʊn(ə)l, kə ˈmjuːn(ə)l/ *adjective* shared by all the members of a group or community ○ *The offices share a communal kitchen.* ○ *Tenants have the right to use the communal gardens.*

commune /ˈkɒmjuːn/ *noun* **1.** a group of people who live and work together, and share their possessions **2.** a small administrative area in some countries such as Switzerland or France, usually with its own mayor and council

communicate /kəˈmjuːnɪkeɪt/ *verb* to pass information to someone ○ *The news was communicated to the press by the Prime Minister's Press Secretary.* ○ *The members of the jury must not communicate with the witnesses.*

communication /kəˌmjuːnɪ ˈkeɪʃ(ə)n/ *noun* **1.** the passing of information □ **to enter into communication with someone** to start discussing something with someone, usually in writing ○ *We have entered into communication with the relevant government department.* **2.** an official message ○ *We have had a communication from the local tax inspector.* ■ *plural noun* **communications** the methods of passing information and of transport ○ *good road and rail communications* ○ *electronic communications systems*

communiqué /kəˈmjuːnɪkeɪ/ *noun* an official announcement ○ *In a communiqué from the Presidential Palace, the government announced that the President would be going on a world tour.*

Communism /ˈkɒmjʊˌnɪz(ə)m/ *noun* **1.** a social system in which all property is owned and shared by society as a whole, with none belonging to individual citizens **2.** the political and economic system in countries governed by Communist parties

Communist /ˈkɒmjʊˌnɪst/ *adjective* practising Communism; referring

to or belonging to a Communist party ○ *Communist ideals were put into practice in Russia after the revolution.*
■ *noun* a member or supporter of a Communist Party ○ *Communists have three seats on the city council.*

communitarianism /kə,mjuːnɪ'teəriənɪz(ə)m/ *noun* the political theory that emphasises the need for strong neighbourhoods and social institutions to provide support to families and individuals

community /kə'mjuːnɪti/ *noun* 1. a group of people living or working in the same place 2. the European Community, now replaced by the European Union □ **the Community ministers** the ministers of Member States of the European Union

community association /kə,mjuːnɪti ə,səʊsi'eɪʃ(ə)n/ *noun* an organisation in which people from a local area meet socially and to discuss local matters

community charge /kə'mjuːnɪti tʃɑːdʒ/ *noun* a local tax paid by each adult person. ◊ **poll tax** (NOTE: This unpopular tax introduced by the government in 1989 was replaced in 1993 by the council tax. The introduction of the tax contributed to the fall of Mrs Thatcher as Prime Minister.)

community council /kə,mjuːnɪti 'kaʊnsəl/ *noun* a body set up to represent people in a small area

community home /kə'mjuːnɪti həʊm/ *noun* a house which belongs to a local authority, where children in care can be kept

Community legislation /kə,mjuːnɪti ledʒɪ'sleɪʃ(ə)n/ *noun* the laws made by the European Union (NOTE: There are two main types of European laws: directives and regulations)

community policing /kə,mjuːnɪti pə'liːsɪŋ/ *noun* a way in which the police can work by consulting the people who live in an area and trying to be sensitive to their particular needs and concerns

community politics /kə,mjuːnɪti 'pɒlɪtɪks/ *noun* the work of politicians in a community who deal with individual problems at local government level and try to encourage as much local participation as possible ○ *The party is strong in community politics.*

community service order /kə,mjuːnɪti 'sɜːvɪs ,ɔːdə/ *noun* a punishment which involves doing unpaid work in the local community

Companies Act /'kʌmp(ə)niz ækt/ *noun* an Act of the British parliament which states the legal limits within which a company may do business

company /'kʌmp(ə)ni/ *noun* 1. the organisation which runs a business 2. **in the company of** being with ○ *He was often seen in the company of the Prime Minister.*

company law /,kʌmp(ə)ni 'lɔː/ *noun* the laws relating to the way business organisations may work

compatriot /kəm'pætriət/ *noun* a person from the same country

compensatory /,kɒmpən'seɪt(ə)ri/ *adjective* providing somebody or a group with payment to help remove the pain or offence cause by some wrong action done to them

competence /'kɒmpɪt(ə)ns/ *noun* being able to do a job ○ *Candidates will be asked to show competence in handling computers.*

competent /'kɒmpɪt(ə)nt/ *adjective* 1. able to do a job ○ *She is a competent manager.* 2. legally able to do something

complainant /kəm'pleɪnənt/ *noun* a person who makes a complaint or who starts a legal action against someone

compliant /kəm'plaɪənt/ *adjective* agreeing with something □ **not compliant with** not in agreement with ○ *The settlement is not compliant with the earlier order of the court.*

comply /kəm'plaɪ/ *verb* □ **to comply with** to obey a rule or law or do what someone asks ○ *The government has* decided it will comply with the requirements of the European Commission ○ She refused to comply with the social worker's instructions.

composite /'kɒmpəzɪt/ *verb* to group together similar proposals from different local branches of an organisation such as a political party or a trade union so that they can be considered in a single discussion at a conference ■ *noun* a group of similar proposals discussed together at a conference of an organisation such as a political party or a trade union

compromise /'kɒmprəmaɪz/ *noun* an agreement between two sides, where each side gives way a little in order to agree ○ After some discussion a compromise solution was reached. ■ *verb* **1.** to reach an agreement by giving way a little **2.** to involve someone in something which damages his or her reputation ○ The minister was compromised in the bribery case.

'…these activists are used to making compromises with their political opponents' [*New Statesman*]

comptroller /kən'trəʊlə/ *noun* a person in charge of accounts

Comptroller and Auditor-General /kən,trəʊlə ən ,ɔːdɪtə 'dʒen(ə)rəl/ *noun* the official in charge of the National Audit Office, whose duty is to examine the accounts of government departments, and to advise the Public Accounts Committee

compulsory /kəm'pʌlsəri/ *adjective* forced or ordered, obligatory for everyone ○ National Service is compulsory in some countries. ○ In Australia, voting in general elections is compulsory.

compulsory purchase /kəm,pʌlsəri 'pɜːtʃɪs/ *noun* the buying of a property by the local council or the government even if the owner does not want to sell

compulsory purchase order /kəm,pʌlsəri 'pɜːtʃɪs ,ɔːdə/ *noun* an official order from a local authority or from the government ordering an owner to sell his or her property to them. Abbr **CPO**

comrade /'kɒmreɪd/ *noun* **1.** a friend or companion **2.** a fellow member of a socialist or communist party **3.** the form of address to a fellow member of a socialist or communist party

Con. *abbreviation* **1.** Conservative **2.** Consul

concede /kən'siːd/ *verb* to admit that someone is right ○ The Minister conceded under questioning that he had not studied the papers. □ **to concede defeat** to admit that you have lost ○ After two recounts the sitting MP had to concede defeat. ◊ **concession**

concession /kən'seʃ(ə)n/ *noun* **1.** an agreement that someone is right, or an agreement to give something which someone wants ○ The government will make no concessions to terrorists. ○ As a concession to the Opposition, the council leader agreed to hold an emergency meeting. ○ The employers have made several concessions in the new wages deal. **2.** an admission of defeat. ◊ **concede**

concession speech /kən'seʃ(ə)n spiːtʃ/ *noun* a speech made by the person who has lost an election, admitting that he or she has lost

conciliate /kən'sɪlieɪt/ *verb* to work with opposing groups to bring them to an agreement, e.g. in an industrial dispute

conciliation /kən,sɪli'eɪʃ(ə)n/ *noun* the process of bringing together the parties in a dispute so that the dispute can be settled

concord /'kɒŋkɔːd/ *noun* a peace treaty

concordat /kən'kɔːdæt/ *noun* an agreement between the Roman Catholic Church and a government, which allows the Roman Catholic Church special rights

concurrent /kən'kʌrənt/ *noun* taking place at the same time

concurrent resolution /kən'kʌrənt ,rezə'luːʃ(ə)n/ *noun* a motion which shows how the House of Representatives feels about a problem

condominium /ˌkɒndə'mɪnɪəm/
noun **1.** the rule of a colony or protected territory by two or more countries
together **2.** *US* a system of ownership,
where a person owns a flat in a building, together with a share of the land
and common parts such as the stairs or
roof

Confederacy /kən'fed(ə)rəsi/,
Confederate States *noun* the group
of eleven Southern states which seceded from the Union and fought the
North in the American Civil War
(1861–65)

confederal /kən'fedərəl/ *adjective*
relating to a confederation

confederate /kən'fed(ə)rət/ *adjective* joined in common purpose

Confederate /kən'fedərət/ *adjective* referring to the Southern states in
the American Civil War ○ *the Confederate Army* ○ *the Confederate headquarters* ○ *the Confederate States* ▪
noun a supporter of the Confederacy
in the American Civil War

confederation /kənˌfedə
'reɪʃ(ə)n/, **confederacy** /kən
'fed(ə)rəsi/ *noun* a group of independent states or organisations working together for common aims ○ *a
loose confederation of states in the
area* (NOTE: A confederation (as in
Switzerland) is a less centralised
form of government than a federation
(as in Canada).)

Confédération Helvétique *noun*
the official French name for Switzerland

**Confederation of British In-
dustry** /kənˌfedəˌreɪʃ(ə)n əv ˌbrɪtɪʃ
'ɪndəstri/ *noun* the organisation representing employers in the UK. Abbr
CBI

confer /kən'fɜː/ *verb* **1.** to give power or responsibility to someone ○ *the
discretionary powers conferred on the
tribunal by statute* **2.** to discuss ○ *The
Leader of the Council conferred with
the Town Clerk.*

conference /'kɒnf(ə)rəns/ *noun* **1.**
a meeting of a group of people to discuss something ○ *The Police Federa-

tion is holding its annual conference
this week.* ○ *The Labour Party Annual
Conference was held in Brighton this
year.* ○ *She presented a motion to the
conference.* ○ *The conference passed a
motion in favour of extending nursery
education.* **2.** *US* a meeting between
representatives of the Senate and
House of Representatives to discuss
differences of opinion over a bill

confidence vote /'kɒnfɪd(ə)ns
vəʊt/ *noun* a vote to show that a person or group is or is not trusted ○ *He
proposed a vote of confidence in the
government.* ○ *The chairman resigned
after the motion of no confidence was
passed at the AGM.*

confidential /ˌkɒnfɪ'denʃəl/ *adjective* secret or not to be told or shown to
other people ○ *She was dismissed for
sending a confidential report to the
newspaper.* ○ *The letter was marked
'Private and Confidential'.*

confidential report /ˌkɒnfɪdenʃəl
rɪ'pɔːt/ *noun* a secret document
which must not be shown to other than
a few named persons

conflict *noun* /'kɒnflɪkt/ a disagreement ○ *Negotiations are taking place
to try to end the conflict in the area.* ▪
verb /kən'flɪkt/ not to agree ○ *The report of the consultant conflicts with
that of the council officers.* ○ *The UK
legislation appears to conflict with the
directives of the EU.*

conflict of interest /ˌkɒnflɪkt əv
'ɪntrəst/ *noun* a situation where a person may profit personally from decisions which are taken by them in an
official position or may not be able to
act properly because of some other
person or matter with which they are
connected

Conflict of Laws /ˌkɒnflɪkt əv
'lɔːz/ *noun* the situation when a legal
case involves the laws of two or more
countries and it is not clear under
whose laws it should be tried

conformity /kən'fɔːmɪti/ *noun* behaviour which is expected by usual
standards

confrontation /ˌkɒnfrʌn'teɪʃ(ə)n/ *noun* a meeting between two people or groups, usually in a situation where there is likely to be conflict

confrontation politics /ˌkɒnfrʌn 'teɪʃ(ə)n 'pɒlɪtɪks/ *noun* the form of political activity, where opposing sides always attack each other and try to reduce each other's popular support, possibly creating an atmosphere of violence. Compare **consensus politics**

congestion charge /kən 'dʒestʃən tʃɑːdʒ/ *noun* a charge made for driving a vehicle into a city during the main part of the day, as an attempt to reduce traffic

Congress /'kɒŋgres/ *noun* 1. the elected federal legislative body in many countries, especially in the USA (formed of a lower and upper house, usually called the House of Representatives and the Senate) ○ *The President is counting on a Democrat majority in Congress.* ○ *He was first elected to Congress in 1975.* ○ *At a joint session of Congress, the President called for support for his plan.* 2. the unicameral legislature in Guatemala and Honduras 3. a large meeting ○ *The Trade Union Congress* 4. used in the name of political parties, e.g. the African National Congress in South Africa

Congressional /kən'greʃ(ə)n(ə)l/ *adjective* referring to Congress ○ *a Congressional subcommittee*

congressional district /kən 'greʃ(ə)n(ə)l 'dɪstrɪkt/ *noun* a district in a US state that can elect one representative to the House of Representatives

Congressional Record /kən 'greʃ(ə)n(ə)l 'rekɔːd/ *noun* the printed record of the work of the House of Representatives and Senate including the speeches made there

Congressman, Congresswoman *noun* a member of the US Congress (NOTE: When used with a name, **Congressman Smith**, it refers to a member of the House of Representatives.)

Congress of Deputies /ˌkɒŋgres əv 'depjutiz/ *noun* the lower house of the legislature in Spain

Congress Party /ˌkɒŋgres 'pɑːti/ *noun* a political party in India

conquer /'kɒŋkə/ *verb* to defeat by force ○ *The victorious army is engaged in establishing the rule of law in the areas which it has conquered.*

conqueror /'kɒŋkərə/ *noun* the person who defeats an enemy or leads the invasion of a country and takes possession of it

conquest /'kɒŋkwest/ *noun* 1. the act of defeating or taking by force 2. the country which has been taken by force

Cons. *abbreviation* Conservative

conscientious objector /ˌkɒnʃienʃəs əb'dʒektə/ *noun* a person who refuses to join the army, because he feels that it is morally wrong

conscript /'kɒnskrɪpt/ *noun* a person who has to join the armed forces as part of legal military service □ **a conscript army** an army formed of conscripts ■ *verb* to order someone to join the armed forces

conscription /kən'skrɪpʃən/ *noun* the legal obligation to join the armed services

consensual /kən'sensjʊəl/ *adjective* happening by agreement

consensus /kən'sensəs/ *noun* general agreement ○ *There was a consensus between all parties as to the next steps to be taken.* ○ *In the absence of a consensus, no decisions could be reached.*

consensus politics /kən,sensəs 'pɒlətɪks/ *noun* a form of political activity, where the main political parties agree in general on policy. Compare **confrontation politics**

consent /kən'sent/ *noun* agreement. ◊ **age of consent**

Consent Calendar /kən'sent 'kælɪndə/ *noun US* a list of bills which are not controversial

conservatism /kən'sɜːvətɪz(ə)m/ *noun* 1. the ideas and beliefs of people who support established ideas and are against sudden change **2. Conservatism** the principles and practice of Conservative politicians or supporters of a Conservative party

conservative /kən'sɜːvətɪv/ *adjective* **1.** supporting established ideas and institutions, and against sudden change ○ *He became more conservative as he grew older.* **2.** careful and cautious ○ *The figures in the document are a conservative estimate.* □ **conservative with a small 'c'** used to show the difference between people who have such ideas and beliefs and those who support the Conservative Party **3. Conservative** referring to the Conservative Party ○ *the Conservative government of 1979* ○ *The manifesto attacks Conservative policies.* Also called **Tory** ■ *noun* **1.** a person who believes that society should not change or should change only very slowly **2. Conservative** a supporter of the Conservative Party

Conservative Party /kən'sɜːvətɪv 'pɑːti/ *noun* the political party which is in favour of only gradual change in society, and against state involvement in industry and welfare

COMMENT: In most countries, the Conservative Party is one of the two main political parties, though it is not always called 'Conservative'. For instance, in many European countries the Christian Democrat Party is the conservative party.

Conservative Party of Canada /kən'sɜːvətɪv 'pɑːti əv 'kænədə/ *noun* a Canadian political party formed from the Progressive Conservative Party and the Canadian Alliance in 2003

consist of /kən'sɪst ɒv/ *verb* to be formed of ○ *The education department consists of advisory and administrative sections, together with the inspectorate.* ○ *A delegation consisting of all the heads of department concerned asked to meet the principal.*

consociation /kən,səʊsi'eɪʃ(ə)n/ *noun* a group of political parties or pressure groups that work together to share power

consolidate /kən'sɒlɪdeɪt/ *verb* to bring several Acts of Parliament together into one act

Consolidated Fund /kən,sɒlɪdeɪtɪd 'fʌnd/ *noun* the total government money formed of all taxes and other government income

Consolidated Fund Bill /kən,sɒlɪdeɪtɪd 'fʌnd ,bɪl/ *noun* a bill in the House of Commons to allow money to be raised for government spending

Consolidating Act /kən'sɒlɪdeɪtɪŋ ,ækt/ *noun* an Act of Parliament which brings together several previous Acts on the same subject

consolidation /kən,sɒlɪ'deɪʃ(ə)n/ *noun* the act of bringing together various Acts of Parliament which deal with one subject into one single Act

consort /'kɒnsɔːt/ *noun* the husband or wife of a King or Queen

conspiracy /kən'spɪrəsi/ *noun* secret agreement or plan to do something wrong or illegal ○ *a conspiracy to oust the leader* □ **conspiracy of silence** an agreement between a group of people to say nothing to anyone else about something that has happened

conspirator /kən'spɪrətə/ *noun* a person who is part of a group who make a secret agreement to do something wrong ○ *After the Gunpowder Plot, the conspirators were rapidly arrested.*

conspiratorial /kən,spɪrə'tɔːriəl/ *adjective* as in a secret agreement made by a group to do something wrong ○ *He spoke in a conspiratorial whisper.*

conspiriologist /kən,spɪri'ɒlədʒɪst/ *noun* someone who believes in conspiracy theories

constable /'kʌnstəb(ə)l/ *noun* **1.** ♦ **police constable 2.** in some towns or townships in the United States and, historically, in British towns and boroughs, a low-ranking law officer

constabulary /kən'stæbjʊləri/ *noun* the police force of a city or a district ■ *adjective* relating to a police force, or involved in being a police officer

constituency /kən'stɪtjʊənsi/ *noun* **1.** an area of a country which is represented by a Member of Parliament ○ *She represents one of the northern constituencies.* ○ *The UK is divided into 650 single-member constituencies.* □ **a good constituency MP** an MP who looks after the interests of his or her constituents well **2.** an area of support ○ *The leader's natural constituency is the working class.*

constituency party /kən,stɪtjʊənsi 'pɑːti/ *noun* a branch of a national political party in a constituency

constituent /kən'stɪtjʊənt/ *noun* a person who lives in a constituency ○ *The MP had a mass of letters from his constituents complaining about aircraft noise.*

constitution /,kɒnstɪ'tjuːʃ(ə)n/ *noun* **1.** the laws under which a country is ruled, which give the people rights and responsibilities, and which give the government powers and duties ○ *The freedom of the individual is guaranteed by the country's constitution.* ○ *The new president asked the assembly to draft a new constitution.* ◊ **European Constitution 2.** the written rules of a society or club ○ *Under the society's constitution, the chairman is elected for a two-year period.* ○ *Payments to officers of the association are not allowed by the constitution.*

'...the Constitution guarantees a very limited number of rights, including free trade among the states, no discrimination against interstate residents, etc.' [*The Age (Melbourne)*]

COMMENT: Most countries have written constitutions, usually drafted by lawyers, which can be amended by an Act of the country's legislative body. The United States constitution was drawn up by Thomas Jefferson after the country became independent, and has numerous amendments (the first ten amendments being the Bill of Rights). Great Britain is unusual in that it has no written constitution and relies on precedent and the body of laws passed over the years to act as a safeguard of the rights of the citizens and the legality of government.

Constitution /,kɒnstɪ'tjuːʃ(ə)n/ *noun* the Constitution of the United States, containing seven articles and 26 amendments, that has been in effect since its adoption in 1789

constitutional /,kɒnstɪ'tjuːʃ(ə)n(ə)l/ *adjective* **1.** referring to a country's constitution ○ *Censorship of the press is not constitutional.* **2.** according to a constitution ○ *The re-election of the chairman for a second term is not constitutional.*

constitutionalise /,kɒnstɪ'tjuːʃənəlaɪz/ *verb* **1.** to make a piece of legislation part of a constitution, or permit a practice through a constitution **2.** to bring a form of government, a country or an organisation under the control of a constitution

constitutionalism /,kɒnstɪ'tjuːʃənəlɪz(ə)m/ *noun* **1.** the system of government based on a constitution **2.** belief in government based on a constitution

constitutionality /,kɒnstɪtjuːʃə'ælɪtin/ *noun* the degree to which something obeys the rules of a constitution

constitutional law /,kɒnstɪ'tjuːʃ(ə)n(ə)l lɔː/ *noun* laws under which a country is ruled or laws relating to the government and its work

constitutional lawyer /,kɒnstɪtjuːʃ(ə)n(ə)l 'lɔːjə/ *noun* a lawyer who specialises in constitutional law

constitutional monarchy /,kɒnstɪtjuːʃ(ə)n(ə)l 'mɒnəki/ *noun* the system of government where the king or queen has limited powers and most power is in the hands of an elected legislature and executive

constitutional right /,kɒnstɪ'tjuːʃ(ə)n(ə)l raɪt/ *noun* a right which is guaranteed by the constitution of a country

constitutive /kən'stɪtjʊtɪv/ *adjective* having the power to create an official body or appoint the members of an official body

constructive engagement /kən'strʌktɪv ɪn'geɪdʒmənt/ *noun* the policy of continuing to have restricted political and business links with a country while still encouraging it to improve political or social conditions

consul /'kɒnsəl/ *noun* **1.** a person who represents a country in a foreign city, and helps his country's citizens and business interests there ○ *the British Consul in Seville* ○ *the French Consul in Manchester* **2.** (*in ancient Roman government*) one of two leaders of the government, elected every year

consular /'kɒnsjʊlə/ *adjective* referring to a consul ○ *The consular offices are open every weekday.* ○ *He spends most of his time on consular duties.*

consular agent /'kɒnsjʊlə ˌeɪdʒ(ə)nt/ *noun* a person with the duties of a representative of a different country in a small foreign town who helps his country's citizens and business interests there. Abbr **CA**

consulate /'kɒnsjʊlət/ *noun* a house or office of someone who represents a different country in a foreign city ○ *There will be a party at the consulate on National Day.*

consul-general /ˌkɒnsəl 'dʒen(ə)rəl/ *noun* the representative of a country in a large foreign city who is responsible for other consuls in the area (NOTE: The plural is **consuls-general** or **consul-generals**.)

consultancy /kən'sʌltənsi/ *noun* the act of giving advice in a specialist area ○ *a consultancy firm* ○ *He offers a consultancy service.*

consultant /kən'sʌltənt/ *noun* someone who gives specialist advice

consultation document /ˌkɒnsəl 'teɪʃ(ə)n ˌdɒkjʊmənt/, **consultative document** /kən'sʌltətɪv 'dɒkjʊmənt/ *noun* a paper with proposals which is given to people who are asked to comment and make suggestions for improvement

consultative /kən'sʌltətɪv/ *adjective* being asked to give advice ○ *the report of a consultative body* ○ *She is acting in a consultative capacity.*

consulting /kən'sʌltɪŋ/ *adjective* referring to a person who gives specialist advice ○ *a consulting engineer*

consumer council /kənˌsjuːmə 'kaʊns(ə)l/ *noun* a group representing the interests of people who buy goods and services

consumer credit /kənˌsjuːmə 'kredɪt/ *noun* the provision of loans by banks to help people buy goods

consumerism /kən'sjuːmərɪz(ə)m/ *noun* the movement for the protection of the rights of people who buy goods and services

consumer legislation /kənˌsjuːmə ˌledʒɪ'sleɪʃ(ə)n/ *noun* the set of laws which give rights to people who buy goods or who pay for services

consumer protection /kənˌsjuːmə prə'tekʃən/ *noun* the legal protection of people who buy goods and services from unfair or illegal business practices

consumption /kən'sʌmpʃən/ *noun* **1.** the use or purchase of goods or services ○ *a car with low petrol consumption* ○ *The factory has a heavy consumption of coal.* **2.** the process of eating or drinking things ○ *increased consumption of fatty sugary foods*

contact group /'kɒntækt gruːp/ *noun* a group of people who meet both sides separately in a dispute to try to achieve agreement through discussion

contempt /kən'tempt/ *noun* behaviour that is rude or shows a lack of respect □ **contempt of Parliament**, **contempt of the House** behaviour which may bring the authority of Parliament into disrepute or which obstructs the work of Parliament □ **to bring Parliament into contempt** to do something which obstructs the work of Parliament or which shows lack of respect for Parliament

content /'kɒntent/ *noun* in the House of Lords, a vote for a motion.

Compare **aye** (NOTE: Disagreement is shown by the phrase 'not content'.)

contents /'kɒntents/ *plural noun* the things contained inside something ○ *The customs officials inspected the contents of the box.*

contest /kən'test/ *noun* a competition, especially in an election ○ *She won the leadership contest easily.* ■ *verb* **1.** to argue that a decision or a ruling is wrong ○ *I wish to contest the claim made by the Leader of the Opposition.* **2.** to fight an election ○ *The seat is being contested by five candidates.*

context /'kɒntekst/ *noun* **1.** a general situation in which something happens ○ *The action of the police has to be seen in the context of the riots against the government.* **2.** the other words which surround a word or phrase ○ *The words can only be understood in the context of the phrase in which they occur.*

Continental Europe /ˌkɒntɪ 'nent(ə)l 'jʊərəp/ *noun* Europe excluding the British Isles

contingent /kən'tɪndʒənt/ *adjective* dependent on something else

contractarianism /ˌkɒntrækt 'eəriənɪz(ə)m/ *noun* the political theory which says that government is based on an agreement between the people and the government

contract law /'kɒntrækt lɔː/ *noun* laws relating to agreements

contradict /ˌkɒntrə'dɪkt/ *verb* not to agree with or to say exactly the opposite ○ *The statement contradicts the report in the newspapers.* ○ *The witness before the committee contradicted himself several times.*

contradiction /ˌkɒntrə'dɪkʃən/ *noun* a statement which disagrees with another statement ○ *The witness' evidence was a mass of contradictions.* ○ *There is a contradiction between the Minister's statement in the House of Commons and the reports published in the newspapers.*

contradictory /ˌkɒntrə'dɪkt(ə)ri/ *adjective* not agreeing ○ *a mass of contradictory evidence*

contrary /'kɒntrəri/ *noun* opposite □ **contrary to** used to emphasise that something is true, even though the opposite may be expected ○ *Contrary to (all) expectations, the party won the election easily.* ○ *Contrary to popular belief* or *opinion, common-law marriage offers little protection to women.*

contravene /ˌkɒntrə'viːn/ *verb* to break or to go against rules or laws ○ *The workshop has contravened the employment regulations.* ○ *The fire department can close a restaurant if it contravenes the safety regulations.*

contravention /ˌkɒntrə'venʃən/ *noun* the act of breaking a rule or law

control /kən'trəʊl/ *noun* **1.** the power of being able to direct something ○ *The company is under the control of three shareholders.* ○ *The Democrats gained control of the Senate.* ○ *The rebels lost control of the radio station.* **2.** the activity of checking something or making sure that something is kept in check ■ *verb* to have power over something □ **to control a council** to have a majority on a council and so direct its business ○ *Senate is controlled by the Conservatives, while the Socialists have a majority in the national Assembly*

controlled economy /kən,trəʊld ɪ'kɒnəmi/ *noun* an economy where most business activity is directed by orders from the government

controversial /ˌkɒntrə'vɜːʃ(ə)l/ *adjective* causing a lot of argument ○ *The council has decided to withdraw its controversial proposal to close the sports club.* ○ *The bill was not controversial and was supported by members of both sides of the house.*

controversy /'kɒntrəvɜːsi, kən 'trɒvəsi/ *noun* a strong argument about an issue ○ *There has been a lot of controversy about the government's tax proposals.*

convener /kən'viːnə/**, convenor** *noun* a person who calls a meeting

convention /kən'venʃən/ *noun* **1.** the general way in which something is usually done, though not enforced by law ○ *It is the convention for American lawyers to designate themselves 'Esquire'.* **2.** a meeting, or series of meetings held to discuss and decide important matters ○ *The Democratic Party Convention to select the presidential candidate was held in Washington.* **3.** an international treaty ○ *the Geneva Convention on Human Rights* ○ *The three countries are all signatories of the convention.*

convention bounce /kən'venʃən baʊns/ *noun* an increase in the support shown for a presidential candidate after nomination at a party convention

convergence criteria /kən ˌvɜːdʒ(ə)ns kraɪ'tɪəriə/ *noun* the economic rules set out in the Maastricht treaty (1993), which members of the European Union have to satisfy in order to move to the single European currency or euro

conviction /kən'vɪkʃən/ *noun* **1.** a feeling of being sure that something is true ○ *It is her conviction that the proposed legislation will result in the sale of council houses being delayed.* **2.** a decision that someone accused of a crime is guilty ○ *She had three convictions for drunken driving.*

conviction politics /kən,vɪkʃən 'pɒlɪtɪks/ *noun* political policies based on firmly held beliefs

convince /kən'vɪns/ *verb* to make someone believe something is true ○ *The government minister tried to convince the strikers that their claims would be heard.* ○ *The Finance Minister had difficulty in convincing Parliament that the budget deficit would be reduced.*

convulsion /kən'vʌlʃən/ *noun* a sudden extreme change (*informal*) ○ *This compromise allowed the court to avoid the political convulsion that would have come with a decision to remove the leader from office.*

cooperate /kəʊ'ɒpəreɪt/ *verb* to work together ○ *The governments are cooperating in the fight against piracy.* ○ *The two firms have cooperated on planning the computer system.*

cooperation /kəʊ,ɒpə'reɪʃ(ə)n/ *noun* working together ○ *The work was completed ahead of schedule with the cooperation of the whole staff.*

cooperative society /kəʊ 'ɒp(ə)rətɪv sə,saɪəti/ *noun* a society where the customers and workers are partners and share the profits

co-opt /ˌkəʊ 'ɒpt/ *verb* □ **to co-opt someone onto a committee** to ask someone to join a committee without having been elected ■ *adjective* **co-opted** made a member of a committee without being elected ○ *She is a co-opted member of the education committee.*

cope /kəʊp/ *verb* to deal with ○ *The House is having difficulty in coping with the mass of legislation before it this session.* ○ *The Chairman of the Finance Committee said that she doubted if the Borough Treasurer's office could cope with the extra workload.*

co-principality /ˌkəʊ ,prɪnsɪ 'pælɪti/ *noun* a state ruled by two princes

COMMENT: The state of Andorra is a co-principality, its two princes being the Bishop of Urgel, in Spain, and the President of the French Republic.

copyright /'kɒpiraɪt/ *adjective* covered by the laws which limit the right to copy books or other written materials ○ *It is illegal to take copies of a copyright work.*

Copyright Act /'kɒpi,raɪt ækt/ *noun* the Act of Parliament controlling the copying of written material without the permission of the author and publisher

copyrighted /'kɒpiraɪtɪd/ *adjective* relating to materials covered by the Copyright Act

copyright law /'kɒpiraɪt lɔː/ *noun* laws concerning the copying of written materials

core executive /ˌkɔː ɪgˈzekjʊtɪv/ *noun* the central figures in the government: Prime Minister, Cabinet, ministers and senior Civil Servants ○ *Rather than thinking of the Prime Minister and Cabinet as struggling for power we should think of the core executive as working most of the time to achieve the same goals.*

COREPER *abbreviation* Committee of Permanent Representatives

coronation /ˌkɒrəˈneɪʃ(ə)n/ *noun* the official ceremony at which a king or queen is crowned

corporate /ˈkɔːp(ə)rət/ *adjective* referring to a group or organisation, especially to a company or business

corporation /ˌkɔːpəˈreɪʃ(ə)n/ *noun* a legal body such as a town council □ **the mayor and corporation** the mayor and other councillors

corporatism /ˈkɔːp(ə)rətɪz(ə)m/ *noun* a system of government where large powerful pressure groups influence the policies of the government

corporatist /ˈkɔːp(ə)rətɪst/ *adjective* referring to corporatism ○ *He holds corporatist views.*

corps diplomatique /ˌkɔː ˌdɪpləməˈtiːk/ *noun* same as **diplomatic corps**

corpus /ˈkɔːpəs/ *noun* a body of laws (NOTE: The plural is **corpora**.)

corpus legis /ˌkɔːpəs ˈledʒɪs/ *Latin phrase meaning* 'body of laws': books containing Roman civil law

correct /kəˈrekt/ *verb* ○ *The assistant will have to correct all these typing errors before you send the contract.* ○ *The minister had to make a statement correcting the information given at the press conference the previous day.* □ **correct the record** *US* to record a change of vote by a Senator after the vote has been counted

correspond /ˌkɒrɪˈspɒnd/ *verb* **1.** to write letters **2.** to be similar or equivalent to something

correspondent /ˌkɒrɪˈspɒndənt/ *noun* **1.** a person who writes letters to someone ○ *As an MP, I have a number* of constituents who are regular correspondents on local issues. **2.** a journalist who writes articles for a newspaper, or reports for radio or TV, on specialist subjects ○ *a financial correspondent* ○ *'The Times' legal correspondent* ○ *She is the Paris correspondent of the 'Telegraph'.* ◊ **court correspondent, lobby correspondent**

corridors of power /ˌkɒrɪdɔːz əv ˈpaʊə/ *plural noun* the places where major political issues are discussed by powerful or influential people and important decisions are taken

corrigendum /ˌkɒrɪˈgendəm/ *noun* a word which is to be corrected (NOTE: The plural is **corrigenda**.)

corrupt /kəˈrʌpt/ *adjective* not honest ■ *verb* to bribe someone to make them act dishonestly

corruption /kəˈrʌpʃən/ *noun* accepting bribes on the part of officials ○ *Magistrates are investigating corruption in the police force.*

Cortes /kɔːˈtez/ *noun* the legislature in Spain

cosignatory /kəʊˈsɪgnət(ə)ri/ *noun* a country which signs a treaty with another ○ *The three countries are all cosignatories to the international convention.*

cosponsor /ˈkəʊˌspɒnsə/ *noun* a person who introduces something such as a bill with someone else ○ *the three cosponsors of the bill*

cost-effective /ˌkɒstɪ ˈfektɪv/ *adjective* giving good value or a good result at little cost ○ *The new scheme will be cost-effective as it improves energy efficiency.*

cost of living /ˌkɒst əv ˈlɪvɪŋ/ *noun* the money which has to be paid for basic needs such as food, heating, and rent ○ *to allow for the rise in the cost of living in salaries* □ **cost-of-living allowance** a special regular addition to normal salary to cover increases in the cost of living □ **cost-of-living increase** an increase in salary to allow it to keep up with the increased cost of living □ **cost-of-living index** a way of measuring the cost of living which is shown as a percentage increase on the figure for the previous year

COTW *noun* the countries that opposed Saddam Hussein in the Iraq War of 2003. Full form **Coalition of the Willing**

council /'kaʊnsəl/ *noun* **1.** an official group chosen to run something or to advise on a problem. ◇ **Security Council 2.** a group of representatives elected to run an area of a country. Also called **local council.** ◇ **borough council, town council, county council 3.** same as **Privy Council 4.** a body of the legislature in several states **5.** a meeting of a council ■ *adjective* relating to or belonging to a local council ○ *a new council policy* ○ *council property*

'…the council could try and cut spending to make a balanced budget' [*Local Government News*]

council chamber /'kaʊnsəl ˌtʃeɪmbə/ *noun* a room in the Town Hall where a local council meets

council estate /'kaʊnsəl ɪˌsteɪt/ *noun* an area of houses and flats belonging to a local council

council house /'kaʊns(ə)l haʊs/, **council flat** /'kaʊns(ə)l flæt/ *noun* a home belonging to a local council, for which rent is paid

council leader /ˌkaʊnsəl 'liːdə/ *noun* a person elected by the main party running a local council as their leader. Compare **mayor**

councillor /'kaʊns(ə)lə/ *noun* an elected member of a council, especially a council that runs a city, county etc.

councilman /'kaʊnsəlmən/ *noun* US a man who is an elected member of a city council in the USA

Council of Europe /'kaʊns(ə)l əv 'jʊərəp/ *noun* the oldest of the European political organisations, with its headquarters in Strasbourg. Abbr **COE**

COMMENT: The Council of Europe was founded in 1949, and currently has 45 members. Its aim is to foster unity of action between European countries in educational, legal and other areas. It established the Convention for the Protection of Human Rights and Fundamental Freedoms (the 'European Convention on Human Rights') in 1950 and the European Court of Human Rights, in Strasbourg, in 1959. The Convention was the first international legal agreement to protect human rights. More recently it has established conventions on the protection of minorities, the prevention of human cloning and cybercrime.

council officer /'kaʊnsəl 'ɒfɪsə/ *noun* a civil servant employed by a town or county council

Council of Ministers /ˌkaʊns(ə)l əv 'mɪnɪstəz/, **Council of the European Union** /ˌkaʊns(ə)l əv ðə ˌjʊərəpiːən 'juːnjən/ *noun* the body made up of ministers of the Member States of the European Union which plays a major part in developing the laws of the Union

COMMENT: The central Council is formed of the Foreign Ministers of the Member States, but the membership of the Council of Ministers varies with the subject being discussed; if it is a question of agricultural policy, then the Ministers of Agriculture of each country form the Council under the chairmanship of the minister whose country then holds the presidency of the EU.

council of war /'kaʊnsəl əv wɔː/ *noun* **1.** a meeting of military leaders in wartime to discuss what action should be taken **2.** a meeting to decide on a plan of action in any emergency

council tax /'kaʊnsəl tæks/ *noun* a local tax raised on each property, paid by the occupier of the property, and calculated according to the value of the property

council tenant /'kaʊnsəl 'tenənt/ *noun* a person who lives in council property and pays rent to the council

councilwoman /'kaʊnsəlwʊmən/ *noun* US a woman who is an elected member of a city council in the USA

counsellor /'kaʊnsələ/ *noun* **1.** a trained person who gives advice or help ○ *They went to see a marriage guidance counsellor.* **2.** a person employed in an embassy **3.** *US* a lawyer who advises a person in a legal case

(NOTE: The US spelling is **coun-selor**.)

count /kaʊnt/ *noun* **1.** the act of counting ○ *the count of votes after an election* ○ *The count started at ten o'clock and finished just after midnight.* ◊ **recount 2.** (*in the House of Commons*) the act of counting how many MPs are present. If there are fewer than 40, the sitting is adjourned. **3.** a separate charge against an accused person read out in court ○ *He was found guilty on all four counts.* **4.** a noble title, used in Europe apart from the United Kingdom (NOTE: The title is used in France **(comte)**, Spain **(Conde)**, Italy **(Conte)**, Germany **(Graf)**, and other countries.)

counter /'kaʊntə/ *noun* something which opposes ○ *The legislation is seen as a counter to the increasing power of local government.* ■ *adverb* in opposition to something

counter- /kaʊntə/ *prefix* against

countercoup /'kaʊntə,kuː/ *noun* a coup against a group that took political power in an earlier coup

counter-demonstration /'kaʊntə,demən'streɪʃ(ə)n/ *noun* a protest held in opposition to another protest

counter-espionage /,kaʊntər'espɪɑːʒ/, **counter-intelligence** /,kaʊntər ɪn'telɪdʒəns/ *noun* the activities involved in working against the spies of another country ○ *The offices were bugged by counter-intelligence agents.*

counterinsurgency /,kaʊnt(ə)rɪn'sɜːdʒ(ə)nsi/ *noun* military action against people who are fighting their own government

countermand /,kaʊntə'mɑːnd/ *verb* to overturn a command made earlier

counterpart /'kaʊntəpɑːt/ *noun* a person who has a similar job or is in a similar situation ○ *The British Minister of Defence wrote to his Spanish counterpart.*

counter-revolution /'kaʊntə,revə'luːʃ(ə)n/ *noun* a violent reaction against a rebellion

counter-revolutionary /,kaʊntə,revə'luːʃ(ə)n(ə)ri/ *adjective* opposing a rebellion or uprising ■ *noun* a person opposed to a rebellion or revolt

countersign /'kaʊntəsaɪn/ *verb* to sign a document which has already been signed by someone else ○ *The payment has to be countersigned by the head of department.*

counterterrorism /,kaʊntə'terərɪz(ə)m/ *noun* military or political activities to prevent terrorist acts

countess /'kaʊntɪs/ *noun* **1.** (*in European aristocracy*) the wife of a count **2.** (*in the British aristocracy*) the wife of an earl

count on /'kaʊnt ɒn/ *verb* **1.** to expect something to happen ○ *The government seems to be counting on winning the votes of the floating voters.* **2.** to rely on someone or something ○ *You can count on Mr Jones, he is an excellent committee chairman.*

country /'kʌntri/ *noun* **1.** a land which is independent and governs itself ○ *The contract covers sales in the countries of the European Union.* ○ *Some African countries export oil.* □ **to go to the country** to call a general election ○ *The Prime Minister has decided to go to the country.* **2.** the area outside a town

Country Party /'kʌntri 'pɑːti/ *noun* now called **National Party of Australia**

county /'kaʊnti/ *noun* one of the administrative divisions of a country ○ *It is illegal to transport cattle across the county boundary.* ○ *The police forces of several counties are cooperating in the search for the missing girl.*

COMMENT: Rural areas in many countries such as Britain and New Zealand and sections of federal states such as the Provinces of Canada and the States in the USA are divided into counties. Most counties in Britain are shires (Berkshire, Staffordshire, etc.). In other cases, the word is used as a title, before the name in Britain (the County of Durham) and after the name in the USA (Marlboro County).

county council /ˌkaʊnti ˈkaʊnsəl/ *noun* a group of people elected to run a county

county town /ˈkaʊnti taʊn/ *noun* the main administrative centre in a county, where the county council offices are situated

coup /kuː/, **coup d'état** /ˌkuː deɪ ˈtæ/ *noun* a rapid change of government which removes one government by force and replaces it by another ○ *After the coup, groups of students attacked the police stations.*

COMMENT: A coup is usually carried out by a small number of people, who already have some power such as army officers, while a revolution is a general uprising of a large number of ordinary people. A coup changes the members of a government, but a revolution changes the whole social system.

court /kɔːt/ *noun* **1.** the place where legal trials are held □ **a settlement was reached out of court, the two parties reached an out-of-court settlement** the dispute was settled between the two parties privately without continuing the court case □ **Criminal Court, Civil Court** a court where criminal or civil cases are heard **2.** the judges or magistrates in a court ○ *The court will retire for thirty minutes.* **3.** a place where a king or queen lives and rules from ○ *The head of the army has a lot of influence at court.* **4.** a king, queen and their officials and servants ○ *When war broke out, the court was moved to the north of the country.* ○ *Members of the court plotted to remove the king and replace him with his brother.*

court correspondent /kɔːt ˌkɒrɪ ˈspɒndənt/ *noun* a journalist who reports on the activities of a king or queen and the royal family

Court of Appeal /ˌkɔːt əv əˈpiːl/, **Court of Appeals** /ˌkɔːt əv əˈpiːlz/ *noun* same as **Appeal Court**

Court of Auditors /ˌkɔːt əv ˈɔːdɪtəz/ *noun* the institution which checks the financial accounts of the European Union

Court of St. James /ˌkɔːt əv sənt ˈdʒeɪmz/ *noun* the official home of the British royal court ○ *He presented his credentials as Ambassador to the Court of St. James.* (NOTE: Foreign ambassadors in Britain are said to be sent to the Court of St. James.)

Court of Session /ˌkɔːt əv ˈseʃ(ə)n/ *noun* the highest civil court in Scotland, consisting of the Inner House and Outer House

covert /ˈkəʊvət, ˈkʌvət/ *adjective* hidden or secret □ **covert action** an action which is secret, e.g. spying

CP *abbreviation* Communist Party (NOTE: In some other languages, it is often written **PC: PCF** (Parti Communiste Français); **PCI** (Partito Comunista Italiano).)

CPO *abbreviation* compulsory purchase order

CPS *abbreviation* Crown Prosecution Service

CPSA *abbreviation* Civil and Public Services Association

CPSU *abbreviation* Community and Public Service Union

crack down on /ˌkræk ˈdaʊn ɒn/ *verb* to use severe measures against something (*informal*) ○ *The government is cracking down on crime.*

CRB *abbreviation* Criminal Records Bureau

CRE *abbreviation* Commission for Racial Equality

credentials /krɪˈdenʃəlz/ *noun* the official documents, proving that an ambassador has been appointed legally by the country he or she represents. Also called **letters of credence** □ **to present his** *or* **her credentials, to present his** *or* **her letters of credence** (*of an ambassador*) to visit for the first time the head of the state of the country where he or she is ambassador, and hand over the documents that show that he or she has been legally appointed

criminal action /ˌkrɪmɪn(ə)l ˈækʃən/ *noun* a case brought usually by the state against someone who is charged with a crime

criminal law /ˌkrɪmɪn(ə)l ˈlɔː/ *noun* the laws relating to acts committed against the laws of the land and which are punished by the state

crisis /ˈkraɪsɪs/ *noun* a time of danger or of great problems requiring action to solve them ○ *The President tried to solve the political crisis after the government was defeated in the Assembly.* ○ *The leader of the council tried to say that the city was not facing a financial crisis.*

crisis management /ˈkraɪsɪs ˌmænɪdʒmənt/ *noun* the process of working through a critical situation, dealing with the problems that arise and trying to control responses to events

crisis measures /ˈkraɪsɪs ˌmeʒəz/ *plural noun* actions taken to try to overcome great dangers or difficulties ○ *We shall have to take crisis measures to deal with the unemployment situation.* (NOTE: The plural is **crises** /ˈkraɪsiːz/ .)

criticise /ˈkrɪtɪsaɪz/, **criticize** *verb* to say that something or someone is wrong or is working badly ○ *The Opposition criticised the government for the way in which it had handled the financial crisis.*

cronyism /ˈkrəʊniɪz(ə)m/ *noun* special treatment given to friends or colleagues, especially in politics

cross /krɒs/ *verb* □ **to cross the floor (of the House)** (*of a sitting MP*) to change from one political party to another

crossbencher /krɒsˈbentʃə/ *noun* a member of the House of Lords who is not a member of one the main political parties. Also called **crossbench Peer**

cross benches /ˌkrɒs ˈbentʃəz/ *plural noun* the seats in the House of Lords where members sit if they are not members of a political party

cross-party /ˌkrɒs ˈpɑːti/ *adjective* involving two or more political parties

crown /kraʊn/ *noun* **1.** a way of describing the state in a country where a king or queen is head of state □ **the Crown** the King or Queen as representing the State ○ *Mr Smith is appearing for the Crown* ○ *the Crown submitted that the maximum sentence should be applied in this case* ○ *the Crown case* or *the case for the Crown was that the defendants were guilty of espionage* **2.** the circular ornament made of gold worn on the head by a king or queen on formal occasions **3.** the monarchy ■ *verb* to put a crown on the head of a king or queen to show that they have become the head of state ○ *British kings and queens are crowned in Westminster Abbey.* ◊ **coronation**

Crown Agent /ˌkraʊn ˈeɪdʒ(ə)nt/ *noun* a member of a government board which provides financial, commercial and other services to some foreign governments and international organisations

Crown Colony /ˌkraʊn ˈkɒləni/ *noun* an overseas territory under the formal control of the UK government

Crown copyright /ˌkraʊn ˈkɒpɪraɪt/ *noun* the right to restrict copying of documents published by the government

Crown Court /ˌkraʊn ˈkɔːt/ *noun* the court, above the level of the magistrates' courts, which has centres all over England and Wales and which hears criminal cases (NOTE: A Crown Court is formed of a circuit judge and jury, and hears major criminal cases.)

crowned head /ˌkraʊnd ˈhed/ *noun* a king or queen ○ *All the crowned heads of Europe attended the state funeral.*

Crown Lands /ˌkraʊn ˈlɑːndz/, **Crown property** *noun* land or property belonging to the King or Queen

Crown Prince /ˌkraʊn ˈprɪns/ *noun* in some countries, the title given to the eldest son of a king, who will become king himself on the death of his father

Crown privilege /ˌkraʊn ˈprɪvɪlɪdʒ/ *noun* the right of the government not to have to produce documents to a court by reason of the interests of the state

Crown Prosecution Service /ˌkraʊn ˌprɒsɪˈkjuːʃ(ə)n ˌsɜːvɪs/ *noun* the office of the Director of Public Prosecutions, whose job is to bring criminals to court. Abbr **CPS**

Crown prosecutor /ˌkraʊn ˈprɒsɪkjuːtə/ *noun* an official of the Director of Public Prosecution's department who is responsible for bringing criminals to court in a local area

crusade /kruːˈseɪd/ *noun* strong action to stop or change something ○ *The government has launched a crusade against drugs.* ■ *verb* to take part in a crusade ○ *She has been crusading for more government action to reduce unemployment.*

crusader /kruːˈseɪdə/ *noun* a person who takes part in a campaign to change something ○ *She was a famous crusader for women's right to vote.*

crypto- /krɪptəʊ/ *prefix* hidden □ **cryptocommunist** a secret communist

CS /ˌsiː ˈes/ *abbreviation* civil service

CSC *abbreviation* Civil Service Commission

CSU *abbreviation* Civil Service Union

cultural /ˈkʌltʃ(ə)rəl/ *adjective* **1.** referring to a society's culture ○ *respect for cultural differences* **2.** referring to the arts ○ *asking for increased public support for cultural activities such as opera and ballet*

cultural attaché /ˈkʌltʃ(ə)rəl ə ˈtæʃeɪ/ *noun* a member of an embassy representing his or her country's interests in the fields of art, music, literature

culture /ˈkʌltʃə/ *noun* **1.** a society's way of thinking and behaving ○ *Euro-*pean history and culture* **2.** activities involving art, music or literature

curfew /ˈkɜːfjuː/ *noun* an order forbidding movement out of doors at specific times ○ *The government has imposed a dusk-to-dawn curfew in the city.*

currency /ˈkʌrənsi/ *noun* the money in coins and notes which is used in a particular country

currency reserves /ˈkʌrənsi rɪ ˌzɜːvz/ *plural noun* the foreign money held by a government to support its own currency and to pay its debts

customs /ˈkʌstəmz/ *plural noun* the government department which organises the collection of taxes on goods brought into a country, or one of its offices at an airport or port

Customs and Excise /ˌkʌstəmz ən ˈeksaɪz/ *noun* the government department which deals with VAT, with taxes on goods brought into the country, and taxes on products such as alcohol produced in the country. Also called **Excise Department**

customs barrier /ˈkʌstəmz ˌbæriə/ *noun* a tax intended to prevent imports

customs duty /ˈkʌstəmz ˌdjuːti/ *noun* same as **import duty**

customs union /ˈkʌstəmz ˌjuːnjən/ *noun* an agreement between several countries that goods can travel between them without paying tax, while goods from other countries are taxed

cutback /ˈkʌtbæk/ *noun* a reduction in the amount of money spent on something, leading to a reduction in something provided ○ *cutbacks on social security spending* ○ *cutbacks in healthcare services*

D

Dáil, Dáil Éireann *noun* the lower house of parliament in the Republic of Ireland ○ *The Foreign Minister reported on the meeting to the Dáil.* (NOTE: The upper house is the Seanad Éireann; the members of the Dáil are called **Teachta Dala (TD)**.)

dark horse /ˌdɑːk ˈhɔːs/ *noun US* a candidate who receives unexpected support in an electoral campaign

data /ˈdeɪtə/ *noun* **1.** information which is available on computer **2.** facts used to come to a decision

data protection /ˈdeɪtə prəˌtekʃən/ *noun* the protection of information such as records about private people in a computer from being copied or used wrongly

date of commencement /ˌdeɪt əv kəˈmensmənt/ *noun* the day of the year when an Act of Parliament or other legal document takes effect

Daughters of the American Revolution /ˌdɔːtəz əv θi əˈmerɪkən ˌrevəˈluːʃ(ə)n/ *plural noun* in the United States, a women's patriotic society founded in 1890 by descendants of those who fought in the War of American Independence. Abbr **DAR**

day-to-day /ˌdeɪ tə ˈdeɪ/ *adjective* taking place as a regular part of normal life ○ *The clerk organises the day-to-day running of the House of Commons.*

Dayton Accords /ˈdeɪtən əˌkɔːdz/ *plural noun* an agreement signed by the presidents of Bosnia, Croatia, and Serbia in 1995, to end hostilities in the former Yugoslavia

DC *abbreviation* **1.** District Council **2.** District of Columbia

dead letter /ˌded ˈletə/ *noun* something which is no longer in use ○ *This law has become a dead letter.*

deadlock /ˈdedlɒk/ *noun* the point when two sides in a dispute cannot agree

deadlocked /ˈdedlɒkd/ *adjective* unable to agree to continue discussing □ **talks have been deadlocked for ten days** after ten days the talks have not produced any agreement

deal /diːl/ *noun* a business agreement or contract ○ *to arrange a deal* or *to set up a deal* or *to do a deal* ○ *to sign a deal*

death duty /ˈdeθ ˌdjuːti/ *noun* same as **estate duty**

death grant /ˈdeθ grɑːnt/ *noun* a state payment to the family of a person who has died to help with the cost of the funeral

death penalty /ˈdeθ ˌpen(ə)lti/ *noun* legal punishment by execution ○ *The president has introduced the death penalty for the worst crimes against the state.*

death squad /ˈdeθ skwɒd/ *noun* an unofficial group of people who murder political opponents or other people considered as enemies

debate /dɪˈbeɪt/ *noun* a formal discussion usually leading to a vote ○ *Several MPs criticised the government in* or *during the debate on the Finance Bill.* ○ *The Bill passed its Second Reading after a short debate.* ○ *The debate continued until 3 a.m.* ■ *verb* **1.** to discuss a proposal before making a decision, usually by a vote ○ *The MPs are still debating the Data Protection Bill.* **2.** to consider something carefully before acting ○ *she de-*

bated whether to approach her MP on the issue

debate on the address /dɪˌbeɪt ɒn ðə əˈdres/ *noun* the debate after the Queen's Speech at the Opening of Parliament, where the motion is to present an address of thanks to the Queen, but the debate is in fact about the government's policies as described in the Queen's Speech

decency /ˈdiːs(ə)nsi/ *noun* polite behaviour that is acceptable to society in general ○ *The film shocked public decency.*

decent /ˈdiːs(ə)nt/ *adjective* following polite behaviour acceptable to society in general ○ *This book will shock any decent citizen.*

decentralisation /diːˌsentrəlaɪˈzeɪʃ(ə)n/, **decentralization** *noun* moving power from the centre to local areas

decentralise /diːˈsentrəlaɪz/, **decentralize** *verb* to move power, authority or action from a central point to local areas ○ *The decision-making processes have been decentralised to semi-autonomous bodies.*

decision /dɪˈsɪʒ(ə)n/ *noun* **1.** a choice made about what to do in a situation ○ *to come to a decision* or *to reach a decision* **2.** the process of thinking clearly and quickly about what to do ○ *acted with decision* **3.** a judgment in a civil court □ **the decision of the House of Lords is final** a decision of the House of Lords, against which there is no appeal **4.** in the European Union, binding legislation. ◊ **directive, recommendation, regulations**

COMMENT: In the EU a decision is binding in its entirety on those to whom it is addressed; a decision may be addressed to a Member State, to an organisation or to an individual person (see Article 189 EC).

decision-maker /dɪˈsɪʒ(ə)n ˌmeɪkə/ *noun* a person who has to decide what is the best thing to do in a situation, especially someone who has important decisions to make

decision-making /dɪˈsɪʒ(ə)n ˌmeɪkɪŋ/ *noun* the process of deciding what is the best thing to do in a situation □ **the decision-making processes** the ways in which decisions are reached

declaration /ˌdekləˈreɪʃ(ə)n/ *noun* **1.** an official or important statement **2.** the official statement that someone has been elected ○ *The count has been going on since 10 o'clock and we are still waiting for the declaration.*

Declaration of Human Rights /ˌdeklərˈeɪʃ(ə)n əv ˌhjuːmən ˈraɪts/ *noun* a United Nations document approved on 10 December 1948, by the General Assembly, setting out the basic rights of all human beings

declaration of independence /ˌdeklərˈeɪʃ(ə)n əv ˌɪndɪˈpendəns/ *noun* a statement from a country making itself independent of another country which was ruling it

Declaration of Independence /ˌdeklərˈeɪʃ(ə)n əv ˌɪndɪˈpendəns/ *noun* the document written by Thomas Jefferson in 1776 by which the American colonies announced their independence from Britain

declaration of war /ˌdeklərˈeɪʃ(ə)n əv ˈwɔː/ *noun* a statement by a country that it considers itself at war with another country

declare /dɪˈkleə/ *verb* to make an official statement, or announce something to the public ○ *to declare someone bankrupt* ○ *to declare that E. Jones has been elected Member of Parliament for the constituency* □ **to declare independence** (*of a country*) to state that it is now independent, and no longer ruled by another country

declared /dɪˈkleəd/ *adjective* **1.** made public ○ *a declared supporter of proportional representation* **2.** officially stated ○ *Taxes are paid on declared income.* □ **declared value** the value of goods entered on a customs declaration

declassification /diːˌklæsɪfɪˈkeɪʃ(ə)n/ *noun* the act of making something no longer secret

declassify /diːˈklæsɪfaɪ/ *verb* to make a secret document or piece of information available to the public ○ *The government papers relating to the war have recently been declassified.*

decolonisation /diːˌkɒlənaɪˈzeɪʃ(ə)n/, **decolonization** *noun* the process by which a state gives its foreign territories their independence

decolonise /diːˈkɒlənaɪz/ *verb* to give a colony its independence

decommission /ˌdiːkəˈmɪʃ(ə)n/ *verb* to officially stop using something such as a weapon

decontrol /diːkənˈtrəʊl/ *verb* to remove controls from something □ **to decontrol the price of something** to stop controlling the price of something so that the price can match demand

decree /dɪˈkriː/ *noun* an order made by a head of state □ **to govern by decree** to rule a country by issuing orders without having them debated and voted in a parliament ■ *verb* to make an order ○ *The President decreed that June 1st should be a National Holiday.*

deductible /dɪˈdʌktɪb(ə)l/ *adjective* taken away from an amount of money ○ *deductible allowance* □ **tax-deductible** deducted from an income before tax is paid

deduction /dɪˈdʌkʃən/ *noun* **1.** business expenses which can be claimed against tax **2.** *US* ♦ **tax deductions**

de facto /ˌdeɪ ˈfæktəʊ/ *Latin phrase* meaning 'in fact': as a matter of fact, even though the legal title may not be certain ○ *He is the de facto owner of the property.* ○ *The de facto government has been recognised.* □ **de facto authority**, **de facto rule** authority or rule of a country by a group because it is in power, whether ruling legally or not □ **de facto recognition** recognition of a new government because it is in power, whether it is ruling legally or not. ◊ **de jure**

defamation /ˌdefəˈmeɪʃ(ə)n/ *noun* the offence of causing harm to somebody by speaking or writing in a dishonest way about them (NOTE: Defamation may be **libel** if it is in a permanent form, such as printed matter, or **slander** if it is spoken.) □ **defamation of character** harm done to someone's reputation by maliciously saying or writing things about him or her

defamatory /dɪˈfæmət(ə)ri/ *adjective* intended to harm someone by saying or writing bad or false things about them

defame /dɪˈfeɪm/ *verb* to say or write bad or false things about the character of someone so as to damage his or her reputation

defeat /dɪˈfiːt/ *noun* the failure to get a majority in a vote ○ *The minister offered to resign after the defeat of the motion in the House of Commons.* ■ *verb* to beat someone or something in a vote ○ *The bill was defeated in the Lords by 52 to 64.* ○ *The government was defeated in a vote on law and order.*

defect /dɪˈfekt/ *verb* **1.** (*of a spy, agent or government employee*) to leave one country or group to work for another country or group **2.** (*of a Member of Parliament*) to leave your party and join another

defection /dɪˈfekʃən/ *noun* the act of leaving one country or group to work for another country or group

defector /dɪˈfektə/ *noun* a person who leaves one country or group to work for another country or group

defence /dɪˈfens/ *noun* **1.** actions taken to protect someone or something against attack (NOTE: The US spelling is **defense.**) **2.** the system of armed forces and weapons that a country uses to protect itself from attack by other countries (NOTE: The US spelling is **defense.**) **3.** something said or done in response to criticism ○ *In his speech he made a strong defence of the decision to raise taxes.* (NOTE: The US spelling is **defense.**) **4.** the case made in a law court in support of the person who is on trial (NOTE: The US spelling is **defense.**) **5.** the lawyer or lawyers who speak in court on behalf of the person who is on trial (NOTE: The US spelling is **defense.**) **6.** measures and structures used to provide protection for something (*often plural*) ○ *a defence against invaders* ○ *flood defences* ■ *adjective* relating to a country's system of defence ○ *defence strategy* ○ *defence budget* (NOTE: The US spelling is **defense.**)

defend /dɪˈfend/ *verb* **1.** to act to protect someone or something **2.** to fight an election to keep an elected position ○ *She is defending a majority of only 2,400.* ○ *He is defending a safe Labour seat.* **3.** to speak to show that your actions were right ○ *The Minister defended his decision.*

defer /dɪˈfɜː/ *verb* to arrange a meeting or activity for a later date than originally planned ○ *to defer judgment* ○ *The decision has been deferred until the next meeting.*

deferment /dɪˈfɜːmənt/ *noun* the act of arranging a meeting or activity for a later date than originally planned ○ *deferment of payment* ○ *deferment of a decision*

deferred /dɪˈfɜːd/ *adjective* delayed until a later date

defiance /dɪˈfaɪəns/ *noun* an open refusal to obey a person, order or rule

defiant /dɪˈfaɪənt/ *adjective* openly refusing to obey ○ *defiant on the issue of ID cards* ○ *The Prime Minister was defiant, insisting there would be no change of direction.*

defiantly /dɪˈfaɪəntli/ *adverb* showing an open refusal to obey a person, order or rule

deficit /ˈdefɪsɪt/ *noun* the amount by which spending is higher than income ○ *The council is trying to agree on how to reduce its current deficit.* ○ *The President has promised to reduce the budget deficit.* ◊ **trade deficit**

'…the Deputy Premier rejected the claim that the budget deficit had developed over a number of years' [*Canberra Times*]

deflation /diːˈfleɪʃ(ə)n/ *noun* the economic situation when prices fall

deflationary /diːˈfleɪʃ(ə)n(ə)ri/ *adjective* leading to a fall in prices ○ *The government has introduced some deflationary measures in the budget.*

Defra /ˈdefrə/ *abbreviation* Department of Environment, Food and Rural Affairs

defy /dɪˈfaɪ/ *verb* **1.** to refuse to obey a person or order ○ *The protesters have defied the court order.* **2.** to be impossible to believe or explain ○ *to defy belief* or *to defy explanation*

de jure /ˌdeɪ ˈdʒʊəri/ *Latin phrase meaning* 'by law': as a matter of law, where the legal title is clear ○ *He is the de jure owner of the property.* □ **de jure recognition** recognition of a new government because it is the legal government of the country. ◊ **de facto**

delegate *noun* /ˈdelɪgət/ a person who is chosen or elected by other people to put their case at a meeting or in an assembly ○ *The company president personally greeted the Japanese delegates.* ■ *verb* /ˈdeləˌgeɪt/ to pass limited authority or responsibility to someone else ○ *The committee delegated the appointment of staff to the chairman.* □ **delegated legislation** orders, which have the power of Acts of Parliament, but which are passed by a minister to whom Parliament has delegated its authority □ **delegated powers** powers which may be legally passed by a council to a committee or by a committee to a sub-committee

delegation /delɪˈgeɪʃ(ə)n/ *noun* **1.** a group of people chosen by other people to put their case at a meeting or in an assembly ○ *a Chinese trade delegation* **2.** the act of passing limited authority or responsibility for making decisions to someone else

delegatus non potest delegare /ˌdelɪgɑːtəs nɒn pɒˌtest ˌdelɪˈgɑːreɪ/ *Latin phrase meaning* 'the delegate cannot delegate to someone else'

deliberations /dɪˌlɪbəˈreɪʃ(ə)nz/ *plural noun* discussions ○ *The result of the committee's deliberations was passed to the newspapers.*

deliberative /dɪˈlɪb(ə)rətɪv/ *adjective* relating to careful discussion

delimit /diːˈlɪmɪt/ *verb* to state clearly what the boundaries of something are ○ *The terms of reference of the commission are strictly delimited.*

deliver /dɪˈlɪvə/ *verb* **1.** to obtain the support of a place or people for a candidate or political party **2.** to do something that was promised ○ *There are increasing signs that people believe the government has delivered on healthcare.*

Dem. *abbreviation* **1.** Democrat **2.** Democratic

demagogic /ˌdeməˈgɒdʒɪk/ *adjective* appealing to people's emotions and prejudices in order to influence them

demagogue /ˈdeməgɒg/ *noun* a leader who is able to get the support of the people by exciting their feelings (*disapproving*)

demagogy, demagoguery *noun* the activity of appealing to feelings such as fear, greed or hatred of the mass of the people

demand /dɪˈmɑːnd/ *noun* the fact that people want goods and services or, the amount of goods or services that people want ○ *Because many people now live alone, the demand for housing is increasing.* ○ *Organic food is being imported to meet the rising demand.*

demarcate /ˈdiːmɑːkeɪt/ *verb* to decide on and set the boundaries of a piece of land

demarcation /ˌdiːmɑːˈkeɪʃ(ə)n/ *noun* the process of deciding on and setting the boundaries of a piece of land

démarche /ˈdeɪmɑːʃ/ *noun* a measure taken by diplomats, especially a spoken protest

demission /diːˈmɪʃən/ *noun* resignation from an important official post

demit /diːˈmɪt/ *verb* to resign from an important official post

demo /ˈdeməʊ/ *noun* same as **demonstration** (*informal*)

democracy /dɪˈmɒkrəsi/ *noun* **1.** a theory or system of government by the people or by the elected representatives of the people ○ *After the coup, democracy was replaced by a military dictatorship.* ◊ **social democracy 2.** a country ruled by its people or their representatives ○ *The pact was welcomed by western democracies.*

democrat /ˈdeməkræt/ *noun* a person who believes in democracy

Democrat /ˈdeməkræt/ *noun* **1.** a member of the Democratic Party, one of the two major political parties in the United States **2.** a member of the Australian Democrats, a centre-left minority political party

democratic /ˌdeməˈkrætɪk/ *adjective* **1.** referring to a democracy ○ *After the coup the democratic processes of government were replaced by government by decree.* **2.** free and fair or reflecting the views of the majority ○ *The resolution was passed by a democratic vote of the council.* ○ *The action of the leader is against the wishes of the party as expressed in a democratic vote at the party conference.*

Democratic /ˌdeməˈkrætɪk/ *adjective* relating to or associated with the Democratic Party of the United States or the Australian Democrats

democratically /ˌdeməˈkrætɪkli/ *adverb* in a democratic way ○ *He is the first democratically elected president following the end of military rule.*

democratic deficit /ˌdeməˈkrætɪk ˈdefɪsɪt/ *noun* the failure of a fully democratic system to behave in a democratic way (NOTE: The European Union has often been accused of having a democratic deficit since the power lies in the Commission and Council of Ministers rather than the European Parliament.)

Democratic Party /ˌdeməˈkrætɪk ˌpɑːti/ *noun* one of the two main political parties in the USA, which is in favour of some social change and state help for poor people, together with restrictions on the power of the federal government. Compare **Republican Party**

Democratic Unionist Party /ˌdeməˈkrætɪk ˈjuːnjənɪst ˈpɑːti/ *noun* a Northern Ireland political party, established by the Reverend Ian Paisley in 1971, and strongly committed to the maintenance of the union between Great Britain and Northern Ireland

democratise /dɪˈmɒkrətaɪz/ *verb* to make a country into a democracy

demonstrate /ˈdemənstreɪt/ *verb* **1.** to show something or make something clear ○ *The police demonstrated how the bomb was planted.* ○ *The MP's comments demonstrated an apparent lack of sympathy for the unemployed.* **2.** to make a public protest about something ○ *Crowds of students were demonstrating against the government.*

demonstration /ˌdemənˈstreɪʃ(ə)n/ *noun* **1.** an act of showing something ○ *The manager gave a demonstration of the new computer system for recording details of tenants and their rents.* **2.** an act of protesting about something ○ *Police broke up the student demonstration.* ○ *Ratepayers are organising a demonstration in front of the Town Hall.*

demonstrator /ˈdemənstreɪtə/ *noun* a person who protests about something publicly ○ *Demonstrators have occupied the municipal building.*

demos /ˈdiːmɒs/ *noun* the ordinary people of a community or nation

demotic /diːˈmɒtɪk/ *adjective* relating to or involving ordinary people

demur /dɪˈmɜː/ *verb* not to agree ○ *The MP stated that there was a question of privilege, but the Speaker demurred.*

denationalise /diːˈnæʃ(ə)nəlaɪz/ *verb* to sell something owned by the state to private investors

denaturalise /diːˈnætʃ(ə)rəlaɪz/ *verb* to take away a naturalised citizen's citizenship, e.g. if it is discovered that they have entered the country illegally

denazify /diːˈnɑːtsifaɪ/ *verb* to remove connections with Nazism

denounce /dɪˈnaʊns/ *verb* **1.** to criticise something or someone publicly and harshly ○ *He denounced the bill as a cheat's charter.* **2.** to accuse someone publicly of an undesirable or illegal act **3.** to announce the formal end of a treaty or other agreement

denuclearise /diːˈnjuːklɪəraɪz/ *verb* to remove or ban nuclear weapons or nuclear power sources from a place

DEP *abbreviation US* Department of Environmental Protection

department /dɪˈpɑːtmənt/ *noun* **1.** a section of a large organisation like a government, company or college ○ *complaints department* ○ *legal department* □ **head of department**, **department head**, **department manager** the person in charge of a department **2.** one of the large local administrative divisions of a country such as France

departmentalism /ˌdiːpɑːtˈmentəlɪz(ə)m/ *noun* **1.** the policy of dividing organisations into departments **2.** the tendency of government departments to follow their own interests

departmental Select Committee /ˌdiːpɑːtˈment(ə)l sɪˈlekt kəˈmɪti/ *noun* a parliamentary committee set up to examine the work of a government department

Department for Constitutional Affairs /dɪˌpɑːtmənt fə ˌkɒnstɪtjuːʃ(ə)nəl əˈfeəz/ *noun* a UK government department whose role is to ensure effective justice for all and protect and extend democratic rights. Abbr **DCA**

Department for Culture, Media and Sport *noun* a UK government department responsible for the arts, cultural activities and heritage, sport, tourism, and press freedom and regulation. Abbr **DCMS**

Department for Education and Skills /dɪˌpɑːtmənt fər edjʊˌkeɪʃ(ə)n ən ˈskɪlz/ *noun* a UK government department responsible for education at all levels and ages, and training people for work. Abbr **DfES**

Department for Environment, Food and Rural Affairs *noun* a UK government department responsible for the natural and developed environment, safe food supplies, rural communities, and the sustainable use of natural resources. Abbr **DEFRA**

Department for International Development /dɪˈpɑːtmənt fə ˌɪntəˈnæʃ(ə)nəl dɪˈveləpmənt/ *noun* a UK government department responsible for policies aimed at reducing global poverty and promoting sustainable development. Abbr **DfID**

Department for Transport /dɪ ˈpɑːtmənt fə ˈtrænspɔːt/ *noun* a UK government department responsible for overseeing the transport system. Abbr **DfT**

Department for Work and Pensions /dɪˌpɑːtmənt fə ˌwɜːk ən ˈpenʃənz/ *noun* a UK government department responsible for Jobcentres, the Child Support Agency, pensions, services for people with disabilities, and other matters relating to individual people's needs. Abbr **DWP**

Department of Defense /dɪ ˌpɑːtmənt əv dɪˈfens/ *noun* the executive department of the US federal government that is mainly responsible for maintaining national security and overseeing the armed forces. Abbr **DOD**

Department of Energy /dɪ ˈpɑːtmənt əv ˈenədʒi/ *noun* the executive department of the US federal government that is mainly responsible for developing energy technology and regulating energy production and use. Abbr **DOE**

Department of Environmental Protection /dɪˈpɑːtmənt əv ɪn ˌvaɪrənˈment(ə)l prəˈtekʃ(ə)n/ *noun* a US state agency responsible for protecting human health by ensuring clean air and water and safe management of hazardous waste materials. Abbr **DEP**

Department of Finance Canada /dɪˌpɑːtmənt əv ˌfaɪnæns ˈkænədə/ *noun* the Canadian government department that is responsible for preparing the federal budget, overseeing tax policies and legislation, and regulating the country's banks and financial institutions

Department of Health /dɪ ˌpɑːtmənt əv ˈhelθ/ *noun* GOV a UK government department with the responsibility of improving the health and well-being of the population. Abbr **DH**

Department of Homeland Security /dɪˈpɑːtmənt əv ˈhəʊmˌlænd sɪˈkjʊərəti/ *noun* the executive department of the US federal government that was established in the aftermath of 11 September 2001, to protect the country against future terrorist attacks. Abbr **DHS** (NOTE: It became an official cabinet department on 24 January 2003, bringing together 22 previously existing agencies to better coordinate defence planning and strategy.)

Department of Housing and Urban Development /dɪ ˈpɑːtmənt əv ˈhaʊzɪŋ ən ˈɜːbən dɪ ˈveləpmənt/ *noun* the executive department of the US federal government that is mainly responsible for promoting community development and enforcing fair housing laws. Abbr **HUD**

Department of Human Resources and Skills Development *noun* the Canadian government department that is responsible for developing and administering policies relating to labour and homelessness. Abbr **HRSD**

Department of Justice /dɪ ˌpɑːtmənt əv ˈdʒʌstɪs/ *noun US* the department of the US government responsible for federal legal cases, headed by the Attorney-General. Also called **Justice Department**

Department of Justice Canada /dɪˌpɑːtmənt əv ˌdʒʌstɪs ˈkænədə/ *noun* the Canadian government department that is mainly responsible for developing policies affecting the justice system and providing legal services to the federal government

Department of National Defense and the Canadian Forces /dɪˈpɑːtmənt əv ˈnæʃ(ə)nəl dɪˈfens ən ðɪ kəˈneɪdiən/ *noun* the Canadian government department that is mainly responsible for national security and overseeing the armed forces. Abbr **DND/CF**

Department of Social Services /dɪˈpɑːtmənt əv ˈsəʊʃ(ə)l ˈsɜːvɪsɪz/ *noun* a US state agency responsible for providing services and protection to people living in poverty or situations of abuse or neglect. Abbr **DSS**

Department of the Interior /dɪ ˌpɑːtmənt əv ðiː ˈɪntɪəriə/ *noun* the executive department of the US federal government that is mainly responsible for developing the nation's natural resources, managing national parks, and overseeing Native American reservations and outlying territories. Abbr **DOI** (NOTE: The UK does not have a government department called the 'Department of the Interior': the Home Office is responsible for supervising the police and policy on law and order.)

Department of Trade and Industry /dɪˌpɑːtmənt əv ˌtreɪd ənd ˈɪndəstri/ *noun* the British government department dealing with business and commerce

dependant /dɪˈpendənt/, **dependent** /dɪˈpendənt/ *noun* a person, especially a relative, who is supported financially by someone else

dependency /dɪˈpendənsi/ *noun* a country or state that belongs to another country with which it does not share a border

dependency theory /dɪˈpendənsi ˌθɪəri/ *noun* a theory of international relations that important countries influence other countries as a result of their economic power

depoliticise, depoliticize *verb* to prevent a discussion about something

being carried out according to fixed political views ○ *The government wants to depoliticise the debate on crime.*

depopulated /diːˈpɒpjʊleɪtɪd/ *adjective* of an area where there are now far fewer people living than there were in the past

deport /dɪˈpɔːt/ *verb* to send someone away from a country ○ *The illegal immigrants were deported.*

deportation /ˌdiːpɔːˈteɪʃ(ə)n/ *noun* the act of sending someone away from a country

deportation order /ˌdiːpɔːˈteɪʃ(ə)n ˌɔːdə/ *noun* an official order to send someone away from a country ○ *The minister signed the deportation order.*

deportee /ˌdiːpɔːˈtiː/ *noun* someone who is being or has been deported

depose /dɪˈpəʊz/ *verb* to remove a political leader or a king or queen from their job

deposit /dɪˈpɒzɪt/ *noun* money paid by a candidate in an election, which is not returned if the candidate does not win enough votes ○ *He polled only 25 votes and lost his deposit.* (NOTE: The deposit is currently £500 and is not returned if a candidate receives less than 5% of the vote.) ■ *verb* to put documents somewhere for safe keeping or for information ○ *We have deposited the deeds of the house with the bank.* ○ *She deposited her will with her solicitor.*

COMMENT: Information which has not been presented to MPs in any other way may be placed in either the House of Commons or the House of Lords library by a Minister or the Speaker as a 'deposited paper'. Most deposited papers are replies to written parliamentary questions.

deprived /dɪˈpraɪvd/ *adjective* not having the basic things regarded as necessary for a pleasant life ○ *a deprived childhood* ○ *a deprived area*

dept *abbreviation* department

deputation /ˌdepjʊˈteɪʃ(ə)n/ *noun* a group of people who have been chosen to represent and act on behalf of a larger group of people

depute /dɪ'pjuːt/ *verb* to give someone the job of doing something ○ *He was deputed to act as chairman.* ■ *adjective* same as **deputy** (*used after nouns*)

deputise /'depjʊtaɪz/, **deputize** *verb* to take the place of a higher official

deputy /'depjʊti/ *noun* **1.** a person who takes the place of a higher official or who helps a higher official ○ *She acted as deputy for the chairman* or *She acted as the chairman's deputy.* **2.** *US* a person who acts for or helps a sheriff **3.** (*in some countries*) a member of a legislative body ○ *After the Prime Minister resigned, the deputies of his party started to discuss the election of a successor.* ◊ **Chamber of Deputies**

Deputy Mayor /'depjʊti meə/ *noun* a member of a town council who acts for a mayor if he or she is absent

Deputy Minister /ˌdepjʊti 'mɪnɪstə/ *noun in Canada* the chief civil servant in charge of a ministry (NOTE: In the UK, the post is called the **Permanent Secretary**.)

Deputy Prime Minister /ˌdepjʊti praɪm 'mɪnɪstə/ *noun* the title given to a senior Cabinet minister who acts for the Prime Minister if he or she is absent

Deputy Speaker /ˌdepjʊti 'spiːkə/ *noun* a MP, elected by other MPs, who acts as chair of the House of Commons when the Speaker is absent (NOTE: There are three Deputy Speakers: one has the additional title of the Chairman of Ways and Means, the others are Deputy Chairmen of Ways and Means.)

derecognition /ˌdiːrekəg'nɪʃ(ə)n/ *noun* the situation when one country decides not to accept the government of another country as the rightful government

deregulate /diː'regjʊleɪt/ *verb* to remove government controls from an industry

deregulation /diːˌregjʊ'leɪʃ(ə)n/ *noun* reducing government control over an industry

dereliction /ˌderə'lɪkʃ(ə)n/ *noun* □ **dereliction of duty** failure to do what you ought to do ○ *he was found guilty of gross dereliction of duty*

derogation /ˌderə'geɪʃ(ə)n/ *noun* in the European Union, the temporary suspension of a regulation or directive

desegregate /diː'segrɪgeɪt/ *verb* to end the separation of people based on their ethnic background

desegregation /ˌdiːsegrɪ'geɪʃ(ə)n/ *noun* the ending of the separation of people based on ethnic background

deselect /ˌdiːsɪ'lekt/ *verb* to decide that a person who had been chosen by a political party as a candidate for a constituency is no longer the candidate

deselection /ˌdiːsɪ'lekʃ(ə)n/ *noun* the act of deselecting a candidate ○ *Some factions in the local party have proposed the deselection of the candidate.*

desert /dɪ'zɜːt/ *verb* to leave the armed forces without permission

designate /'dezɪgneɪt/ *adjective* a person who has been given a job but who has not yet started work ○ *the chairman designate* ■ *verb* to name or to appoint officially ○ *The area was designated a National Park.*

despatch /dɪ'spætʃ/ *verb* to send ○ *The letters about the rates were despatched yesterday.* ○ *The Defence Minister was despatched to take charge of the operation.*

despatch box /dɪ'spætʃ bɒks/ *noun* **1.** the red leather case in which government papers are sent to ministers. Also called **red box 2.** one of two boxes facing each other on the centre table in the House of Commons at which a Minister or member of the Opposition Front Bench stands to speak □ **to be at the despatch box** (*of a minister*) to be speaking in parliament

despot /'despɒt/ *noun* a ruler with great power

despotic /dɪ'spɒtɪk/ *adjective* like a ruler with great power

despotism /'despɒtɪz(ə)m/ *noun* the system of government where the ruler has great power

destabilise /diː'steɪbɪlaɪz/ *verb* to make a government or economy unable to function successfully

détente /'deɪˌtɒnt/ *noun* an improvement in the relations between two or more countries who have been unfriendly

detention centre /dɪ'tenʃ(ə)n ˌsentə/ *noun* a place where people can be kept while their request to enter and remain in a country is considered

deterrent /dɪ'terənt/ *noun* **1.** something which discourages someone from doing something ○ *Means testing is a deterrent to the take-up of benefits.* **2.** weapons, particularly nuclear weapons, seen as threat that will prevent another country from attacking

dethrone /dɪ'θrəʊn/ *verb* to remove a king or queen from their official position

developer /dɪ'veləpə/ *noun* a business person who buys up land in order to build houses on it

developing country /dɪˌveləpɪŋ 'kʌntri/, **developing nation** /dɪˌveləpɪŋ 'neɪʃ(ə)n/ *noun* a country which is not yet fully industrialised

development /dɪ'veləpmənt/ *noun* **1.** the process of encouraging business activities in a region or country and helping its economy grow **2.** the process of planning the production of a new product or new town **3.** a change which takes place ○ *a new development in healthcare*

development area /dɪ'veləpmənt ˌeəriə/ *noun* an area which has been given special help from a government to encourage businesses and factories to be set up there. Also called **development zone**

development plan /dɪ'veləpmənt plæn/ *noun* a plan drawn up by a government or council to show how an area should develop over a period of time

deviate /'diːvieɪt/ *verb* to move away from a planned course of action

deviationism /ˌdiːvi'eɪʃ(ə)nɪz(ə)m/ *noun* departure from accepted political views, especially from orthodox communism

devolution /ˌdiːvə'luːʃ(ə)n/ *noun* the passing of power from a central government to a local or regional authority (NOTE: In the UK, devolution is the process by which since 1997 a parliament has been set up in Scotland, and assemblies have been created in Northern Ireland, Wales and Greater London.)

COMMENT: Devolution involves the transfer of more power than decentralisation. In a devolved state, the regional authorities are almost autonomous.

devolutionist /ˌdiːvə'luːʃ(ə)nɪst/ *noun* someone who favours transferring power from a central government to smaller political units

devolve /dɪ'vɒlv/ *verb* to transfer power from a central to a regional or local authority ○ *Power is devolved to regional assemblies.*

Devolved Assembly /dɪˌvɒlvd ə'sembli/ *noun* one of the representative bodies set up in the UK in 1998, which are the Scottish Parliament, Welsh Assembly, Northern Ireland Assembly and, in 2000, the Greater London Assembly

devolved government /dɪˌvɒlvd 'gʌv(ə)nmənt/ *noun* government with the power to make laws on the internal affairs of a region of a country (NOTE: Devolved governments were established in Scotland, Wales and Northern Ireland in 1998, but in 2004 the one in Northern Ireland is in abeyance.)

DFES *abbreviation* Department for Education and Skills

DFID /'dɪfɪd/ *abbreviation* Department for International Development

DfT *abbreviation* Department for Transport

DH *abbreviation* Department of Health

DHS *abbreviation US* Department of Homeland Security

dialogue /'daɪəlɒg/ *noun* **1.** formal discussion between two people or groups in order to reach a decision ○ *engage in constructive dialogue* ○ *enter into dialogue* **2.** official diplomatic contact between two countries

diarchy /'daɪɑːki/ *noun* **1.** a form of government in which power is held by two rulers or governing bodies **2.** a country controlled by two rulers or governing bodies

diary /'daɪəri/ *noun* a book in which you can write notes or appointments for each day of the week and record events which have taken place

dictator /dɪk'teɪtə/ *noun* a ruler who has complete power ○ *The country has been ruled by a military dictator for six years.* ○ *The MPs accused the party leader of behaving like a dictator.*

dictatorial /ˌdɪktə'tɔːriəl/ *adjective* **1.** referring to a ruler who has complete power ○ *a dictatorial form of government* **2.** behaving like a ruler with complete power ○ *Officials disliked the Minister's dictatorial way of working.*

dictatorship /dɪk'teɪtəʃɪp/ *noun* **1.** rule by someone with complete power ○ *Under the dictatorship of Mussolini, personal freedom was restricted.* □ **the dictatorship of the proletariat** in Marxist theory, the period after a revolution when the Communist Party takes control until a true classless society develops **2.** a country ruled by someone with complete power □ **a military dictatorship** a country ruled by an army officer as a dictator

diehard *noun, adjective* a person who strongly opposes any form of change ○ *He's a diehard Conservative.* ○ *Diehard Labour supporters criticised the new style of leadership.*

Diet /'daɪət/ *noun* the legislative body in Japan and some other countries

dilatory motion /ˌdɪlət(ə)ri 'məʊʃ(ə)n/ *noun* a motion in the House of Commons to put off the debate on a proposal until a later date

diplomacy /dɪ'pləʊməsi/ *noun* **1.** the management of a country's interest in another country ○ *The art of diplomacy is to anticipate the next move by the other party.* □ **quiet diplomacy** discussing problems with officials of another country in a calm way, without telling the press about it □ **secret diplomacy** discussing problems with another country in secret **2.** a quiet way of persuading people to do what you want or of settling problems without force ○ *solved the dispute with tact and diplomacy*

diplomat /'dɪpləmæt/ *noun* a person such as an ambassador who is an official representative of his or her country in another country

diplomatic /ˌdɪplə'mætɪk/ *adjective* **1.** referring to diplomats ○ *His car had a diplomatic number plate.* ○ *She was using a diplomatic passport.* □ **to grant someone diplomatic status** to give someone the rights of a diplomat **2.** quietly persuasive in dealing with other people

diplomatic bag /ˌdɪplə'mætɪk bæg/ *noun* a bag containing official government documents which is carried from one country to another by diplomats and cannot be opened by customs ○ *He was accused of shipping arms into the country in the diplomatic bag.*

diplomatic channels /ˌdɪpləmætɪk 'tʃæn(ə)lz/ *plural noun* the ways in which diplomats communicate between countries ○ *The message was delivered by diplomatic channels.* ○ *They are working to restore diplomatic channels between the two countries.*

diplomatic corps /ˌdɪplə'mætɪk kɔː/ *noun* all the foreign ambassadors and their staff in a city or country

diplomatic etiquette /ˌdɪplə 'mætɪk 'etɪket/ *noun* formal conventions of behaviour between diplomats

diplomatic immunity /ˌdɪpləmætɪk ɪˈmjuːnɪti/ *noun* the right of not being subject to the laws of the country in which you are living, because you are a diplomat ○ *She claimed diplomatic immunity to avoid being arrested.*

diplomatic relations /ˌdɪplə ˈmætɪk rɪˈleɪʃ(ə)nz/ *plural noun* the arrangements by which two countries have representatives in each other's country and deal with each other formally ○ *The countries have broken off diplomatic relations.*

diplomatic service /ˌdɪpləˈmætɪk ˈsɜːvɪs/ *noun* the government department concerned with relations with other countries, including those who work in embassies, consulates, and other representatives abroad ○ *He has decided on a career in the diplomatic service.*

diplomatist /dɪˈpləʊmətɪst/ *noun* same as **diplomat** (*formal*)

direct action /daɪˌrekt ˈækʃən/ *noun* political or industrial action intended to have immediate and noticeable effect that will influence opinion, e.g. a strike, boycott or civil disobedience

direct democracy /daɪˈrekt dɪ ˈmɒkrəsi/ *noun* rule of the people by the people without the intervention of representatives ○ *The only really viable form of direct democracy for the modern world is the use of referendums.*

direct election /daɪˈrekt ɪˈlekʃən/ *noun* an election where the voters vote for the person who will represent them, as opposed to elections where the voters vote for people who then choose the representative

direction /daɪˈrekʃən/ *noun* **1.** control or leadership **2.** the general progress of something ○ *unhappy about the direction the party has taken in recent years* ■ **directions** instructions which explain how something should be done ○ *The court is not able to give directions to the local authority.*

directive /daɪˈrektɪv/ *noun* **1.** an order to someone to do something **2.** a piece of legislation made by the European Commission ○ *The Commission issued a directive on food prices.* (NOTE: A directive of the European Commission is binding as to the result to be achieved, but leaves to the national authorities the choice of form and method (Article 189 EC).)

direct labour organisation /daɪ ˈrekt ˈleɪbə ˌɔːɡənaɪˈzeɪʃ(ə)n/ *noun* a group of workers employed by a council or other government department, as opposed to a group who are privately employed by a company which has a contract to do the work from the council or government department. Abbr **DLO**

director /daɪˈrektə/ *noun* **1.** a person whose job involves managing all or part of an organisation or company ○ *He is the director of a government institute.* ○ *She was appointed director of the charity.* **2.** the person appointed by the shareholders to manage a company **3.** the chief officer of a department in a council **4. Director of Education** or **Housing** or **Social Services** the chief officer in a local government administration, in charge of the education or housing or social services in his or her area

directorate-general /daɪ ˈrekt(ə)rət ˈdʒen(ə)rəl/ *noun* an administrative section of the European Commission

director-general /daɪˌrektə ˈdʒen(ə)rəl/ *noun* **1.** a person in charge of a large organisation, with several directors responsible to him or her **2.** in the European Union, a civil servant in charge of one of the directorates-general in the European Union

Director-General of Fair Trading /daɪˌrektə ˌdʒen(ə)rəl əv ˌfeə ˈtreɪdɪŋ/ *noun* the official in charge of the Office of Fair Trading, a body which regulates businesses and protects consumers

Director of Education /daɪˈrektə əv ˌedjʊˈkeɪʃ(ə)n/ *noun* an officer of a local authority who is responsible for schools and colleges in the area

Director of Public Prosecutions /daɪˌrektə əv ˌpʌblɪk ˌprɒsɪ'kjuːʃ(ə)nz/ *noun* the government official in charge of the Crown Prosecution Service, reporting to the Attorney-General, who advises on criminal cases brought by the police, prosecutes in important cases and advises other government departments if prosecutions should be started ○ *The papers in the case have been sent to the Director of Public Prosecutions.* Abbr **DPP**

directory /daɪ'rekt(ə)ri/ *noun* a list of people or businesses with their addresses and telephone numbers, and sometimes further information about them

direct primary /daɪ'rekt 'praɪməri/ *noun* in the United States, a primary election in which the candidates for an office are each chosen by popular vote

direct tax /daɪˌrekt 'tæks/ *noun* tax which is paid on money that has been earned or profits, e.g. income tax

direct taxation /daɪˌrekt tæk'seɪʃ(ə)n/ *noun* the system of taxing a person or organisation on money that has been earned or on profits

dirigisme *noun* tight government control of a country's economy and social institutions

dirty trick /ˌdɜːti 'trɪk/ *plural noun* tactics used in a political campaign against an opponent that are not completely fair or honest

Disability Rights Commission /ˌdɪsəbɪlɪti 'raɪts kəˌmɪʃ(ə)n/ an organisation which works to improve the conditions of people with disabilities and to remove any discrimination against them. Abbr **DRC** (NOTE: In 2006 the Disability Rights Commission will be merged with other bodies to form the Commission for Equality and Human Rights.)

disadvantage /ˌdɪsəd'vɑːntɪdʒ/ *noun* something which makes someone or something less successful than others ○ *It is a disadvantage for a tax lawyer not to have studied to be an accountant.* □ **at a disadvantage** less likely to be successful ○ *not having studied law puts him at a disadvantage* ■ *verb* to put someone or something in a more difficult position than someone else, making success less likely ○ *She is disadvantaged by not having the right qualifications for the job.*

disadvantaged /ˌdɪsəd'vɑːntɪdʒd/ *adjective* referring to people who have less money, education or opportunities than others, or to places where conditions are more

disappear /dɪsə'pɪə/ *verb* to arrest or kill a political opponent without the process of law

disarmament /dɪs'ɑːməmənt/ *noun* the process of reducing the number of arms held by a country

disburse /dɪs'bɜːs/ *verb* to pay money to somebody out of a large amount which has been collected for a purpose

disbursement /dɪs'bɜːsmənt/ *noun* the payment of money from a large amount which has been collected for a purpose

discharge /dɪs'tʃɑːdʒ/ *verb* ○ *The judge discharged the jury.* □ **to discharge a committee** *US* to remove control of a bill from a committee, especially if a committee has not reported on a bill within 30 days

COMMENT: Committees of both House of Representatives and the Senate can be discharged; the action to discharge a committee in the House of the Representatives is called a 'discharge petition' and in the Senate a 'discharge resolution'.

Discharge Calendar /ˌdɪstʃɑːdʒ 'kælɪndə/ *noun* a list of motions for discharging committees

disciplinary /ˌdɪsɪ'plɪnəri/ *adjective* relating to punishment for breaking rules □ **disciplinary procedure** a way of warning someone officially that he or she is not doing things in the expected way □ **to take disciplinary action against someone** to punish someone for not doing things in the expected way

disclaimer /dɪs'kleɪmə/ *noun* a legal refusal to accept responsibility or to accept a right

disclosure /dɪs'kləʊʒə/ *noun* the act of telling details or of publishing a secret ○ *The disclosure of the takeover bid raised the price of the shares.* ○ *The defendant's case was made stronger by the disclosure that the plaintiff was an undischarged bankrupt.* □ **disclosure of confidential information** an act of telling someone information which should not be made public

discretionary /dɪ'skreʃ(ə)n(ə)ri/ *adjective* available to use if necessary □ **the minister's discretionary powers** powers which the minister could use if he thought he should do so

discriminate /dɪ'skrɪmɪneɪt/ *verb* to note real or imagined differences between things and act on these judgments, sometimes unfairly ○ *The planning committee finds it difficult to discriminate between applications which improve the community, and those which are purely commercial.*

discrimination /dɪˌskrɪmɪ'neɪʃ(ə)n/ *noun* action which treats different groups of people in different ways, sometimes unfairly ○ *Racial discrimination is against the law.* ○ *She accused the council of sexual discrimination in their recruitment policy.*

disenfranchise /ˌdɪsɪn'fræntʃaɪz/, **disfranchise** *verb* to deprive a person or organisation of a privilege or legal right, especially the right to vote

disestablish /ˌdɪsɪ'stæblɪʃ/ *verb* to end a legal relationship between a state and a church or religion

disloyal /dɪs'lɔɪəl/ *adjective* not supporting your country, friends or political party

disloyalty /dɪs'lɔɪəlti/ *noun* behaviour that does not support your country, friends or political party

dispensation /ˌdɪspen'seɪʃ(ə)n/ *noun* special permission to do something which is usually not allowed or is against the law

displaced person /dɪsˌpleɪsd 'pɜːs(ə)n/ *noun* a man or woman who has been forced to leave their home and move to another country because of war

disqualification /dɪsˌkwɒlɪfɪ'keɪʃ(ə)n/ *noun* the situation of being prevented from continuing to do something because you have broken the rules in some way □ **disqualification from office** a rule which forces a director to be removed from a directorship if he does not fulfil its conditions

disqualify /dɪs'kwɒlɪfaɪ/ *verb* to prevent someone from continuing to do something because they have done something wrong, or because it is not allowed by a set of rules ○ *After the accident he was fined £1,000 and disqualified from driving for two years.* ○ *Being a judge disqualifies her from being a Member of Parliament.* ○ *Applicants will be disqualified for canvassing.*

Disraeli /dɪz'reɪli/, **Benjamin, 1st Earl of Beaconsfield** (1804–81) British politician and novelist. British Conservative prime minister (1868, 1874–80).

dissent /dɪ'sent/ *noun* strong lack of agreement ○ *The opposition showed its dissent by voting against the Bill.* ■ *verb* not to agree with someone ○ *The motion was carried, three councillors dissented.* □ **dissenting opinion** the opinion of a member of a committee, showing that he or she disagrees with the other members

dissident /'dɪsɪdənt/ *adjective* not in agreement with a political group or government ○ *a dissident writer* ■ *noun* a person who is not in agreement with a political group or government

dissolution /ˌdɪsə'luːʃ(ə)n/ *noun* the formal process of ending a business or legal relationship ■ *also* **dissolution of Parliament** the formal process of ending a parliament, which is followed by a general election ○ *The government lost the vote of no confidence, and so the Prime Minister asked for a dissolution of Parliament.*

dissolve /dɪ'zɒlv/ *verb* to bring a business or legal relationship to an end □ **to dissolve Parliament** to end a session of Parliament, and so force a general election

district /'dɪstrɪkt/ *noun* a section of a town or of a country

District Auditor /'dɪstrɪkt 'ɔːdɪtə/ *noun* a local official of the Audit Commission

district council /ˌdɪstrɪkt 'kaʊnsəl/ *noun* an elected body which runs a local area

COMMENT: There are two kinds of district council: metropolitan districts, covering large urban areas, are responsible for all local matters; non-metropolitan districts deal with some local matters, but leave other matters to be dealt with by the county council.

district court /'dɪstrɪkt kɔːt/ *noun* US a court in a federal district

District of Columbia /ˌdɪstrɪkt əv kə'lʌmbiə/ *noun* the district of which the US capital Washington is the centre, which is not part of any state of the USA and is administered directly by Congress. Abbr **DC**

district registry /ˌdɪstrɪkt 'redʒɪstri/ *noun* the office where records of births, marriages and deaths are kept for an area

divide /dɪ'vaɪd/ *verb* **1.** to make into separate sections ○ *The country is divided into six administrative regions.* ○ *The two departments agreed to divide the work between them.* **2.** (*in the House of Commons*) to vote ○ *The House divided at 10.30.* **3.** to disagree, or make people disagree ○ *They were divided on the issue of the benefits of membership of the European Union.*

division /dɪ'vɪʒ(ə)n/ *noun* **1.** a section of something which is divided into several sections ○ *Smith's is now a division of the Brown group of companies.* **2.** one of the separate sections of the High Court (the Queen's Bench

Division, the Family Division and the Chancery Division) or the sections of the Appeal Court (Civil Division and Criminal Division) **3.** (*in the House of Commons*) a vote ○ *In the division on the Law and Order Bill, the government had a comfortable majority.* ◊ **divide 2 4.** the act of dividing or of being divided □ **division of responsibility** the act of sharing the responsibility for something between several people

COMMENT: When a division is called in the House of Commons, the Speaker names four MPs as tellers, bells are rung and the doors out of the division lobbies are closed. MPs file through the lobbies and are counted as they pass through the doors and go back into the chamber. At the end of the division, the tellers report the numbers of Ayes and Noes, and the Speaker declares the result by saying 'the Ayes have it' or 'the Noes have it'.

divisional /dɪ'vɪʒ(ə)n(ə)l/ *adjective* referring to a division ○ *a divisional education officer*

division bell /dɪ'vɪʒ(ə)n bel/ *noun* the bell which is rung to warn MPs that a vote is going to be taken

division bell area /dɪˌvɪʒ(ə)n bel 'eəriə/ *noun* the area round the House of Commons which is near enough for MPs to come to vote after the division bell has rung. Eight minutes is allowed between the bell and the vote. ○ *She has a flat in the division bell area.*

division list /dɪ'vɪʒ(ə)n lɪst/ *noun* a list of MPs who voted for and against a motion, usually included in Hansard on the day after the vote

division lobby /dɪ'vɪʒ(ə)n ˌlɒbi/ *noun* one of two rooms in the House of Commons through which MPs pass to vote. Also called **voting lobby** (NOTE: The Aye lobby is to the right of the Speaker's chair, behind the seats where the MPs who form the government sit, and the No lobby is to the left.)

division vote /dɪ'vɪʒ(ə)n vəʊt/ *noun* US a vote in the House of Representatives, where members stand up to be counted and the vote is not recorded in the record. Also called **standing vote**

DLO *abbreviation* Direct Labour Organization

'...a good DLO will subcontract work to the private sector, if only to give itself a benchmark for performance measurement' [*Local Government News*]

DMK *noun* in Tamil Nadu, India, a political party advocating the promotion of Tamil society and culture. Full form **Dravida Munnetra Kazgham**

DND/CF *abbreviation* Department of National Defense and the Canadian Forces

D-notice /ˈdiː ˌnəʊtɪs/ *noun* a government statement, without legal force, containing official guidance to news editors that the publication of a specific piece of information is not advisable ○ *should be DA-notice* Full form **Defence Advisory notice**

doctrine /ˈdɒktrɪn/ *noun* a statement of policy

document /ˈdɒkjʊmənt/ *noun* **1.** a paper with information in it ○ *Deeds, contracts and wills are all legal documents.* **2.** an official paper from a government department ■ *verb* to put something in a published document ○ *The cases of unparliamentary language are well documented in Hansard.*

documentary /ˌdɒkjʊˈment(ə)ri/ *adjective* in the form of documents ○ *documentary evidence* ○ *documentary proof*

documentation /ˌdɒkjʊmen ˈteɪʃ(ə)n/ *noun* all the documents referring to something ○ *Please send me the complete documentation concerning the sale.*

DOD *abbreviation US* Department of Defense

Dod's Parliamentary Companion /ˌdɒdz ˌpɑːləment(ə)ri kəm ˈpænjən/ *noun* a small book containing details of all MPs, their constituencies and government posts

DOE *abbreviation US* Department of Energy

dogma /ˈdɒgmə/ *noun* a belief or set of beliefs of a political, religious or other group of people

dogmatic /dɒgˈmætɪk/ *adjective* relating to a religious, political, philosophical or moral dogma

DOI *abbreviation US* Department of the Interior

dollar diplomacy /ˈdɒlə dɪ ˈpləʊməsi/ *noun* **1.** the use of money to establish good relations with other countries **2.** in the United States, a policy aimed at encouraging and protecting US interests abroad

domain /dəʊˈmeɪn/ *noun* the territory ruled by a specific government or leader

Domesday Book /ˈduːmzdeɪ bʊk/ *noun* a record made for King William I in 1086, which recorded lands in England and their owners for tax purposes

domestic /dəˈmestɪk/ *adjective* **1.** referring to a family or home **2.** referring to the home country or to the country where a business has its head offices ○ *The remarks by the ambassador were regarded as interference in the country's domestic affairs.*

domestic consumption /də ˌmestɪk kənˈsʌmpʃən/ *noun* the use of goods in a country, or the amount used

domestic production /dəˌmestɪk prəˈdʌkʃən/ *noun* production of goods in a country

domestic rate /dəˈmestɪk reɪt/ *noun* a local tax which is levied on houses and flats

domicile /ˈdɒmɪsaɪl/ *noun* the country where someone is said to live permanently or where a company's office is registered, especially for tax purposes □ **domicile of origin** the domicile which a person has from birth, usually the domicile of the father □ **domicile of choice** country where someone has chosen to live, which is not the domicile of origin ■ *verb* to live in a particular place □ **he is domiciled in Denmark** he lives in Denmark officially

dominant party /'dɒmɪnənt 'pɑːti/ *noun* In a democracy, the way in which one political party tends to be stronger and more successful in winning elections than the others for a period of time ○ *The dominant party in US politics after 1932 was the Democrat Party, but its dominance was probably at an end by the end of the century.*

dominion /də'mɪnjən/ *noun* **1.** *also* **Dominion** an independent state which is part of the British Commonwealth **2.** the power of control over something ○ *to exercise dominion over a country*

domino effect /'dɒmɪnəʊ ɪ,fekt/ *noun* the situation that happens when one event causes another which then causes another to happen (NOTE: In the 1960s some Americans argued that if Vietnam became a communist country the rest of Southeast Asia would also become communist according to the domino effect.)

domino theory /'dɒmɪnəʊ ,θɪəri/ *noun* a theory that political events are connected and that one event can start a chain of others (NOTE: The theory was developed by US President Dwight D. Eisenhower to warn of the spread of Communism in Southeast Asia.)

donate /dəʊ'neɪt/ *verb* to give money to an organisation, especially a political party or charity

donation /dəʊ'neɪʃ(ə)n/ *noun* the money given to an organisation such as a political party or charity

donkey vote /'dɒŋki vəʊt/ *noun* in the preferential voting system, a vote in which the preferences are just marked in the order that they appear on the ballot sheet (NOTE: In Australia, where voting is compulsory, this is often a way of registering a protest vote or abstention.)

doorstep /'dɔːstep/ *verb* to talk to people at their doors in order to persuade them to buy something, to vote for a candidate in an election, or to find out their opinions

doorstep poll /'dɔːstep pəʊl/ *noun* an opinion survey carried out by asking people questions at their front doors ○ *A doorstep poll suggested that the sitting MP might lose her seat.*

door-to-door /,dɔː tə 'dɔː/ *adjective* going from one house to the next ○ *Before the election, the party had carried out a lot of door-to-door canvassing, talking to voters and handing out leaflets.*

Dorothy Dixer /,dɒrəθi 'dɪksə/ *noun* a question asked in parliament which allows a politician, especially a minister, to give a prepared answer

double agent /'dʌb(ə)l 'eɪdʒənt/ *noun* someone who spies for one government and also gives secret information about that government to the other

double dissolution /'dʌb(ə)l ,dɪsə'luːʃ(ə)n/ *noun* in Australia, the dissolution of both houses of the federal parliament by the governor general when the upper house has repeatedly refused to pass legislation already passed by the lower house

double taxation /,dʌb(ə)l tæk'seɪʃ(ə)n/ *noun* a system of taxing the same income twice, e.g. by a direct tax and an indirect tax, or by paying tax in two countries

double tax treaty /,dʌb(ə)l tæks 'triːti/ *noun* an agreement between two countries so that citizens or businesses pay tax in one country only

dove /dʌv/ *noun* a person who tries to achieve peace through discussion. Compare **hawk**

doveish /'dʌvɪʃ/, **dovish** *adjective* favouring diplomatic solutions to foreign policy issues and preferring to avoid confrontation or war ○ *He was accused of having doveish tendencies.* Compare **hawkish**

Downing Street /'daʊnɪŋ striːt/ *noun* the street in London where the Prime Minister and Chancellor of the Exchequer have their official houses. Also called **No. 10 Downing Street** (NOTE: The words 'Downing Street' are often used to mean 'the Prime

Minister' or even 'the British government': *a Downing Street spokesman revealed that the plan had still to be approved by the Treasury; Downing Street sources indicate that the Prime Minister has given the go-ahead for the change; Downing Street is angry at suggestions that the treaty will not be ratified.*)

doyen of the diplomatic corps /ˌdɔɪən əv ðɪ ˌdɪplə'mætɪk kɔː/ *noun* the foreign ambassador who has been in that country for the longest time

DPP *abbreviation* Director of Public Prosecutions

draconian /drə'kəʊniən/ *adjective* extremely severe ○ *The government took draconian measures against the student protesters.*

draft /drɑːft/ *noun* a first rough plan or document which has not been finished ○ *a draft of a contract* or *a draft contract* ○ *He drew up a draft agreement* ○ *The draft minutes were sent to the chairman for approval.* ○ *The draft Bill is with the House of Commons lawyers.* ○ *The draft of the press release was passed by the Minister.* ■ *verb* to make a first rough plan of a document ○ *to draft a contract* or *a document* or *a bill* ○ *The contract is still being drafted*

draft bill /ˌdrɑːft 'bɪl/ *noun* a Bill that is examined by a departmental Select Committee before it is introduced in Parliament, allowing MPs who have special knowledge of the subject to make comments at an early stage

drafter /'drɑːftə/ *noun* a person who makes a first rough plan of a document

drafting /'drɑːftɪŋ/ *noun* the act of preparing the first rough plan of a document ○ *the drafting stage of a parliamentary Bill* ○ *The drafting of the contract took six weeks.*

draftsman /'drɑːftsmən/, **draughtsman** /'drɑːftsmən/, **draftswoman**, **draughtswoman** *noun* same as **drafter**

draw up /ˌdrɔː 'ʌp/ *verb* to write a legal document ○ *to draw up a con-*tract or *an agreement* ○ *to draw up a company's articles of association*

DRC *abbreviation* Disability Rights Commission

dream ticket /ˌdriːm 'tɪkɪt/ *noun* a pair or team of candidates standing for associated political offices who seem to share between them all the qualities that will make them successful in an election

DSS *abbreviation US* Department of Social Services

DTI *abbreviation* Department of Trade and Industry

dual nationality /'djuːəl ˌnæʃə 'nælɪti/ *noun* the right to be a citizen of two countries

ducal /'djuːkəl/ *adjective* referring to a person who holds the title of duke or duchess

duchess /'dʌtʃɪs/ *noun* the wife of a man who holds the title of duke

duchy /'dʌtʃi/ *noun* the area once ruled by a person with the title of duke. ◊ **Chancellor of the Duchy of Lancaster**

duke /djuːk/ *noun* a person with the highest noble title

Duma /'duːmə/ *noun* the Russian parliament

dummy /'dʌmi/ *noun* a paper with the titles of a Bill, presented in the House of Commons for the First Reading when the short title is read out by the clerk

dutiable /'djuːtjəb(ə)l/ *adjective* carrying a tax □ **dutiable goods**, **dutiable items** goods on which a customs or excise duty has to be paid

duty /'djuːti/ *noun* **1.** the responsibility for something that someone has ○ *It is the duty of every citizen to serve on a jury if called.* ○ *The government has a duty to protect its citizens from criminals.* **2.** the official work which someone has to do in their job **3.** the tax which is paid on goods ○ *to take the duty off alcohol* ○ *to put a duty on cigarettes* □ **goods which are liable to duty** goods on which customs or excise tax has to be paid

duty bound /ˈdjuːti baʊnd/ *adjective* having to do something because it is your duty ○ *Witnesses under oath are duty bound to tell the truth.*

duty of care /ˌdjuːti əv ˈkeə/ *noun* the responsibility to be careful at work not to harm other people

duumvir /ˈduːəmvɪə/ *noun* either of two people who share a position of authority equally between them

DWP *abbreviation* Department for Work and Pensions

dyarchy *noun* another spelling of **diarchy**

dynast /ˈdaɪnəst/ *noun* a ruler who is member of a powerful ruling family, especially a hereditary monarch

dynastic /dɪˈnæstɪk/ *adjective* referring to a family of rulers ○ *the rules of dynastic succession*

dynasty /ˈdɪnəsti/ *noun* **1.** a family of rulers, following one after the other ○ *The Ming dynasty ruled China from 1368 to 1644.* **2.** a period of rule by members of the same family

dystopia /dɪsˈtəʊpiə/ *noun* an imaginary place where everything is as bad as it possibly can be. Compare **utopia**

E

earl /ɜːl/ *noun* a lord of middle rank, below a marquess and above a viscount (NOTE: The wife of an **earl** is a **countess**.)

earldom /'ɜːldəm/ *noun* the title of earl

early day motion /ˌɜːli deɪ 'məʊʃ(ə)n/ *noun* a motion proposed in the House of Commons for discussion 'at an early date'. Usually used to introduce the particular point of view of the MP proposing the motion, and seldom actually followed by a full debate.

earning power /'ɜːnɪŋ ˌpaʊə/ *noun* the amount of money someone should be able to earn

East Asia /ˌiːst 'eɪʒə/ the area of China, Hong Kong, Japan, North Korea, South Korea, Macau, Mongolia, parts of Russia, and Taiwan. Also called **Far East**

EC *abbreviation* European Community. Now called **European Union**

ECHR *abbreviation* European Court of Human Rights

ECJ *abbreviation* European Court of Justice

economic /ˌiːkə'nɒmɪk/ *adjective* **1.** referring to a country's economy ○ *The government's economic policy was shown to be working.* **2.** not needing much money to be spent ○ *It would not be economic to open the advice office on Sundays.*

economic migrant /ˌiːkənɒmɪk 'maɪɡrənt/ *noun* a worker who travels to an area or country where work or an easier life is available

economic planning /ˌiːkənɒmɪk 'plænɪŋ/ *noun* the activity of planning the future financial state of a country for the government

economic sanctions /ˌiːkənɒmɪk 'sæŋkʃ(ə)ns/ *plural noun* restrictions place by one country on trade with another country in order to influence its political situation or in order to make its government change its policy ○ *to impose sanctions on a country* or *to lift sanctions* ○ *The imposition of sanctions has had a marked effect on the country's economy.*

economic trend /ˌiːkənɒmɪk 'trend/ *noun* the way in which a country's economy is growing or shrinking

economic union /ˌiːkənɒmɪk 'juːnjən/ *noun* the economies of two or more countries merged to function as a unit that shares a common financial policy and currency

economism /ɪ'kɒnəmɪz(ə)m/ *noun* **1.** the belief that economics is the most important element to consider in a society **2.** the belief that improvement of the living standards of its members is the chief goal of a political or trade union organisation

economy /ɪ'kɒnəmi/ *noun* **1.** the financial state of a country or the way in which a country makes and uses its money **2.** the careful use of waste money or materials

ecoterrorism /'iːkəʊˌterərɪz(ə)m/ *noun* disruption of the activities of people or companies who are regarded as polluting or destroying the natural environment

ECU *abbreviation* European Currency Unit

e-democracy /'iː dɪˌmɒkrəsi/ *noun* the use of electronic systems for people to use in order to vote or for the government to consult people's opinion

edict /ˈiːdɪkt/ *noun* an official order or announcement

Eduskunta *noun* the legislature in Finland

EEA *abbreviation* European Economic Area

EEC *abbreviation* European Economic Community. Now called **European Community (EC)**

Eerste Kamer *noun* the upper house of the legislature in the Netherlands. ◊ **States-General**

EFTA *abbreviation* European Free Trade Area

egalitarian /ɪˌgælɪ'teəriən/ *adjective* referring to egalitarianism ○ *She holds egalitarian views.* ▪ *noun* a person who supports egalitarianism

egalitarianism /ɪˌgælɪ'teəriənɪz(ə)m/ *noun* the political theory that all members of society have equal rights and should have equal treatment

EGM *abbreviation* Extraordinary General Meeting

e-government /ˈiː ˌgʌv(ə)nmənt/ *noun* government services made available to the public by electronic means such as the Internet

Eire *noun* now called **Republic of Ireland**

Éireann ♦ Seanad Éireann

Eisenhower /ˈeɪzənhaʊə/**, Dwight D.** (1890–1969) supreme commander of Allied forces in Europe during World War II and 34th president of the United States

elect /ɪ'lekt/ *verb* **1.** to choose someone by a vote ○ *a vote to elect the officers of an association* ○ *She was elected chair of the committee.* ○ *He was first elected for this constituency in 1979.* **2.** to choose to do something ○ *He elected to stand trial by jury.*

-elect /ɪlekt/ *suffix* the person who has been elected but has not yet started the term of office ○ *She is the president-elect.* (NOTE: The plural is **presidents-elect**.)

election /ɪ'lekʃən/ *noun* **1.** the act of electing a representative or representatives. ◊ **general election, local election 2.** the act of choosing ○ *his recent election as president of the society* ○ *The accused made his election for jury trial.*

election agent /ɪˌlekʃən 'eɪdʒənt/ *noun* a person appointed by a party to organise its campaign in a constituency during an election ○ *The ruling party lost votes in the general election* or *in the elections for local councils.* ○ *The election results are shown on television.*

election campaign /ɪˌlekʃən kæm 'peɪn/ *noun* the period immediately before an election, when candidates try to gain support

Election Day /ɪ'lekʃ(ə)n deɪ/ *noun* in the United States, a day designated by law for the election of people to public office (NOTE: In the United States, Election Day for national elections is designated by law as the Tuesday after the first Monday in November in even-numbered years.)

electioneer /ɪˌlekʃə'nɪə/ *verb* (*often as criticism*) to get votes in an election, e.g. by visiting people and giving interviews to the media ○ *Cutting taxes just before the election is pure electioneering.*

election expenses /ɪˌlekʃən ɪk 'spensɪz/ *plural noun* the money spent by a candidate or political party during an election campaign, which has to be publicly declared

elective /ɪ'lektɪv/ *adjective* **1.** relating to voting **2.** chosen by a vote, or held by someone who is chosen by a vote ○ *elective office*

elector /ɪ'lektə/ *noun* a person who is qualified to vote in an election (NOTE: There is an important distinction to be made between electors, who are qualified to vote but may not choose to do so, and voters, who do actually vote)

electoral /ɪ'lekt(ə)rəl/ *adjective* relating to elections ○ *the electoral process*

electoral college /ɪˌlekt(ə)rəl ˈkɒlɪdʒ/ *noun* a small group of people elected by the whole population to vote on their behalf in an election with two stages

COMMENT: The President of the USA is elected by an electoral college made up of people elected by voters in each of the states of the USA. Each state elects the same number of electors to the electoral college as it has Congressmen, plus two. This guarantees that the college is broadly representative of voters across the country. The presidential candidate with an overall majority in the college is elected president.

Electoral Commission /ɪˈlekt(ə)rəl kəˌmɪʃ(ə)n/ *noun* an independent body that reviews donations to political parties and the amount of money spent on election campaigns and examines electoral law and practice. It also tries to make people more aware of the process of electing people. (NOTE: It was established by the Political Parties, Elections and Referendums Act 2000.)

electoral platform /ɪˌlekt(ə)rəl ˈplætfɔːm/ *noun* the set of proposals for future policy set out by a candidate or party before an election which the candidate claims he or she will carry out if elected ○ *The party is campaigning on a platform of lower taxes and less government interference in municipal affairs.*

electoral quota /ɪˌlekt(ə)rəl ˈkwəʊtə/ *noun* in Australia, the number of representatives of a state or territory that can be elected to the House of Representatives, in proportion to the population of the state or territory, i.e. approximately 1:70,000 inhabitants

electoral reform /ɪˌlekt(ə)rəl rɪˈfɔːm/ *noun* the process of changing the system of voting

electoral register /ɪˌlekt(ə)rəl ˈredʒɪstə/, **electoral roll** /ɪˌlekt(ə)rəl ˈrəʊl/ *noun* a list of the names of all the people who are eligible to vote who have registered to do so. Also called **electoral roll**

electoral ward /ɪˌlekt(ə)rəl ˈwɔːd/ *noun* an area, city or country represented by a councillor on a local council ○ *Councillor Smith represents Central Ward on the council.* (NOTE: The US term is **precinct**.)

electorate /ɪˈlekt(ə)rət/ *noun* all the people in an area or country qualified to vote ○ *The electorate is tired of party political broadcasts.* ○ *The British electorate want a change of government.*

electronic voting /ˌelekˈtrɒnɪk ˈvəʊtɪŋ/ *noun* the use of electronic means to vote. Also called **e-voting** (NOTE: In the UK, trials of different methods such as text message, Internet, electronic kiosk and, for the first time ever, digital TV were carried out in 2004.)

eligible /ˈelɪdʒɪb(ə)l/ *adjective* able to do or have something according to a rule ○ *Once you are over 18, you are eligible to vote.* ○ *The family is eligible for financial help.*

elite /ɪˈliːt/ *noun* **1.** a small group of people in a group or society who have high status, power and special advantages ○ *a political elite* ○ *a social elite* **2.** the best people at a particular activity ■ *adjective* **1.** having high status, power and special advantages **2.** very good, usually the best of its kind ○ *an elite army unit*

elitism /ɪˈliːtɪz(ə)m/ *noun* the belief that only people with the best education or other social advantages should be allowed to do something ○ *accused the legal profession of elitism*

elitist /ɪˈliːtɪst/ *noun* someone who supports elitism ■ *adjective* supporting elitism ○ *elitist opinions*

emancipation /ɪˌmænsɪˈpeɪʃ(ə)n/ *noun* the process of making a group free from former legal and political restrictions

embargo /ɪmˈbɑːɡəʊ/ *noun* a government order which stops something, e.g. a type of trade □ **to lay** or **put an embargo on trade with a country** to say that trade with a country must not take place □ **to put an embargo on a**

press release to say that information given to the media must not be made public before a specific date □ **to lift an embargo** to allow trade to start again ■ *verb* to stop something, or not to allow something to take place ○ *The government has embargoed trade with the Eastern countries.* □ **the press release was embargoed until 1st January** the information in the release could not be published until 1st January

embassy /'embəsi/ *noun* **1.** a building where an ambassador and other diplomats work in a foreign country ○ *the American embassy* ○ *Each embassy is guarded by special police.* **2.** an ambassador and his staff, sent by a government to represent it in another country ○ *Queen Elizabeth I sent an embassy to the Tsar Ivan the Terrible.*

COMMENT: An embassy is the territory of the country which it represents. The police and armed forces of the country where the embassy is situated are not allowed to enter the embassy without official permission. People seeking asylum in a specific country can take refuge in its embassy, but it is not easy for them to leave, as to do so they have to step back into the country against which they are seeking protection.

emblem /'embləm/ *noun* an object used as the symbol of a country, state or town ○ *The leek and the red dragon are emblems of Wales.*

emergency /ɪ'mɜːdʒənsi/ *noun* a dangerous situation where decisions have to be taken quickly

emergency debate /ɪˌmɜːdʒənsi dɪ'beɪt/ *noun* a special debate on a subject of great national importance, which takes place within 24 hours of being requested (NOTE: Only one or two emergency debates are accepted each year.)

emergency planning department /ɪˌmɜːdʒənsi 'plænɪŋ dɪ ˌpɑːtmənt/ *noun* a department in a local council which plans for action to be taken in case of major accidents

emergency planning officer /ɪ ˌmɜːdʒənsi 'plænɪŋ ˌɒfɪsə/ *noun* a

council official who prepares the actions needed to deal with dangerous situations such as major accidents

emergency powers /ɪˌmɜːdʒənsi 'paʊəz/ *plural noun* the special powers granted to a government or to a minister to deal with a dangerous situation

emergency services /ɪ 'mɜːdʒənsi ˌsɜːvɪsɪz/ *plural noun* the police, fire and ambulance services, which are ready for action if a dangerous situation happens

emergent /ɪ'mɜːdʒənt/ *adjective* still in the process of developing ○ *emergent countries*

emigrant /'emɪgrənt/ *noun* a person who leaves one country to live permanently in another

emigrate /'emɪgreɪt/ *verb* to go to another country to live permanently

emigration /ˌemɪ'greɪʃ(ə)n/ *noun* the act of leaving a country to go to live permanently in another country

emissary /'emɪsəri/ *noun* a person who carries a special message from one government to another

emoluments /ɪ'mɒljʊmənts/ *plural noun* the pay earned by someone for the work they have done (NOTE: The US term is **emolument**.)

emperor /'emp(ə)rə/ *noun* a man who rules a country or a group of countries ○ *the Emperor of Japan* or *the Japanese Emperor* ◊ **empress**

empire /'empaɪə/ *noun* a large group of countries ruled by one country ○ *The British Empire came to an end after the Second World War, and was replaced by the Commonwealth.*

employ /ɪm'plɔɪ/ *verb* to give someone regular paid work ○ *The council employs people with disabilities in its offices.* ○ *She runs a department employing two hundred people.*

employed /ɪm'plɔɪd/ *adjective* in regular paid work ■ *plural noun* the people who are working ○ *the employers and the employed*

employee /ɪm'plɔɪiː/ *noun* a person paid to work for someone or for a company ○ *Employees of the firm are eligible to join a profit-sharing scheme.* ○ *Relations between management and employees have improved.* ○ *The council has decided to stop taking on new employees.*

employer /ɪmˈplɔɪə/ *noun* a person or company which has paid workers

employer's contribution /ɪm ˌplɔɪəz ˌkɒntrɪˈbjuːʃ(ə)n/ *noun* the money paid by an employer towards an employee's pension

employment /ɪmˈplɔɪmənt/ *noun* the state of being employed or paid to work for someone or for a company

employment programme /ɪm ˈplɔɪmənt ˈprəʊɡræm/ *noun* a government plan to create more jobs

employment statistics /ɪm ˈplɔɪmənt stəˈtɪstɪks/ *plural noun* government figures on the numbers of people who are working

empress /ˈemprɪs/ *noun* **1.** a woman who rules an empire ○ *Queen Victoria was the Empress of India.* **2.** the wife of an emperor

enabling legislation /ɪnˌeɪblɪŋ ˌledʒɪˈsleɪʃ(ə)n/ *noun* an Act of Parliament which gives a minister the power to put other legislation into effect

enact /ɪnˈækt/ *verb* to make a proposal for legislation into a law

enacting clause /ɪnˈæktɪŋ klɔːz/, **enacting words** *noun* the first section of a bill, starting with the words 'be it enacted that' which gives the bill its official legal status when parliament has voted to accept it

enactment /ɪˈnæktmənt/ *noun* **1.** the act of making a proposal for legislation into a law **2.** an Act of Parliament

enclave /ˈeŋkleɪv/ *noun* a region which belongs to one country or is independent but is completely surrounded by another country

endorse /ɪnˈdɔːs/ *verb* **1.** to agree with or support something ○ *The council endorsed the action taken by the Chief Executive.* ○ *Many MPs endorsed the efforts made by the soldiers to*

gain compensation. **2.** to formally approve or permit something ○ *These practices have not been endorsed by any official.* **3.** to make a note on a driving licence that the holder has been convicted of a traffic offence **4.** to sign a receipt or cheque

endorsement /ɪnˈdɔːsmənt/ *noun* **1.** an act of approving or permitting something **2.** a signature on a document which approves or permits something **3.** a note on a driving licence to show that the holder has been convicted of a traffic offence

enemy /ˈenəmi/ *noun* a person or country which is hostile to another ○ *His political enemies took the opportunity to oust him from the post.*

enforce /ɪnˈfɔːs/ *verb* to make sure something is done or is obeyed ○ *to enforce the terms of a contract*

enforceable /ɪnˈfɔːsəb(ə)l/ *adjective* something which can be enforced ○ *In practice the bylaw was not easily enforceable.*

enfranchise /ɪnˈfræntʃaɪz/ *verb* to give someone the right to vote. ◊ **franchise**

enfranchisement /ɪn ˈfræntʃaɪzmənt/ *noun* the action of giving someone the right to vote

engagé /ɒnˈɡæʒeɪ/ *adjective* (*of artists, writers, etc.*) showing political involvement

engross /ɪnˈɡrəʊs/ *verb* to draw up a legal document in its final form

engrossed Bill /ɪnˈɡrəʊst bɪl/ *noun US* a Bill which has been passed by either the House of Representatives or Senate which is written out in its final form with all amendments to be sent to the other chamber for discussion

engrossment /ɪnˈɡrəʊsmənt/ *noun* **1.** the drawing up of a legal document in its final form **2.** a legal document in its final form

enquire /ɪŋˈkwaɪə/ same as **inquire**

enquiry /ɪŋˈkwaɪri/ same as **inquiry**

enrolled bill /ɪnˈrəʊld bɪl/ *noun US* the final copy of a bill which has been passed by both House and Senate, and is written out with all its amendments for signature by the Speaker of the House of Representatives, the President of the Senate and the President of the USA

entente /ɒnˈtɒnt/ *noun* an agreement between two or more countries, used especially of the 'Entente Cordiale' between Britain and France in 1904

enterprise /ˈentəpraɪz/ *noun* **1.** a system where businesses are developed privately rather than by the state **2.** a business ○ *She runs a mail order enterprise.*

Enterprise, Transport and Lifelong Learning Department *noun* a department of the Scottish Executive, responsible for industrial development, transport and communications, and further education. Abbr **ETLLD**

enterprise zone /ˈentəpraɪz zəʊn/ *noun* an area of a country, where the government offers special payments to companies to encourage them to set up businesses

entitlement /ɪnˈtaɪt(ə)lmənt/ *noun* something to which someone has a right

entitlement card /ɪnˈtaɪt(ə)lmənt kɑːd/ *noun* a national identity card proposed by the UK government that could include personal information such as health and tax records as well as enable the bearer to claim state benefits

entitlement program /ɪnˈtaɪt(ə)lmənt ˌprəʊɡræm/ *noun* in the United States, a government programme that targets a particular section of the population to receive specific social benefits

entrenched /ɪnˈtrentʃt/ *adjective* fixed and difficult to change ○ *the government's entrenched position on employees' rights*

entrenched clause /ɪnˈtrentʃt klɔːz/ *noun* a section in a constitution which cannot be amended except by an unusual and difficult process

entryism /ˈentriˌɪz(ə)m/ *noun* a way of taking control of a political party or elected body, where extremists join or are elected in the usual way, and are able to take over because of their numbers or because they are more active than other members

entryist /ˈentriɪst/ *adjective* referring to entryism ○ *The party leader condemned entryist techniques.*

environment /ɪnˈvaɪrənmənt/ *noun* **1.** the surroundings in which somebody or something exists and which affect the development of that person or thing ○ *the working environment* **2. the environment** the earth, its natural features and resources

environmental /ɪnˌvaɪrən ˈment(ə)l/ *adjective* referring to the environment ○ *the Opposition spokesman on environmental issues*

environmental health /ɪn ˌvaɪrənmənt(ə)l ˈhelθ/ *noun* the health of the public and how their surroundings and living conditions affect it

Environmental Health Officer /ɪnˌvaɪrənmənt(ə)l ˈhelθ ˌɒfɪsə/ *noun* an official of a local authority who examines the environment and tests for air pollution or bad sanitation or noise levels. Also called **Public Health Inspector**

environmentalism /ɪnˌvaɪrən ˈmentəlɪz(ə)m/ *noun* the belief that political policy should have the protection of the natural world and its resources as its first consideration

environmentalist /ɪnˌvaɪrən ˈment(ə)lɪst/ *noun* a supporter of environmentalism ■ *adjective* referring to environmentalism

envoy /ˈenvɔɪ/ *noun* **1.** a person who is sent with a message from one government or organisation to another ○ *the President's special envoy to the Middle East* **2.** a senior diplomat with a rank below that of ambassador

EOC *abbreviation* Equal Opportunities Commission

equalisation /ˌiːkwəlaɪˈzeɪʃən/, **equalization** *noun* the process of making something the same in size, amount or importance for all the members of a group

equalitarian, equalitarianism ♦ **egalitarian**

equality /ɪ'kwɒlɪti/ *noun* the condition where all citizens are equal, have equal rights and are treated equally by the state

equality of opportunity /ɪ ˌkwɒlɪti əv ˌɒpə'tjuːnɪti/ *noun* a situation where each citizen has the same chance to get a job, be elected or have other opportunities

equal opportunities /ˌiːkwəl ɒpə 'tjuːnɪtiz/ *noun* a policy of avoiding discrimination against groups in society like women, disabled people and ethnic and religious groups (NOTE: The US term is **affirmative action program**.)

Equal Opportunities Commission /ˌiːkwəl ɒpə'tjuːnɪtiz kə ˌmɪʃ(ə)n/ *noun* the official organisation set up in 1975 to make sure that men and women have equal chances of employment and to remove discrimination between the sexes (NOTE: From 2006 the Equal Opportunities Commission is to be merged with other similar bodies into the Commission for Equality and Human Rights)

equivalence /ɪ'kwɪvələns/ *noun* the same value as something else

equivalent /ɪ'kwɪvələnt/ *adjective* being of the same value as something else

Erskine May /ˌɜːskɪn 'meɪ/ *noun* the book which gives detailed information on how Parliament conducts its business

COMMENT: Erskine May's 'Treatise on the Law, Privileges, Proceedings and Usage of Parliament' was originally published in 1844. The author, Sir Thomas Erskine May, was Clerk of the House of Commons. The book is updated frequently, and is the authority on questions of parliamentary procedure.

escalation /ˌeskə'leɪʃ(ə)n/ *noun* an increase in something

espionage /'espiənɑːʒ/ *noun* the use of spies to get important secret information about another country or company. ◊ **counter-espionage**

established post /ɪ'stæblɪʃt pəʊst/ *noun* a permanent post in the civil service or similar organisation

establishment /ɪ'stæblɪʃmənt/ *noun* **1.** an organisation or institution **2.** □ **the Establishment** powerful and important people who run the country and its government ○ *the judiciary and the old universities form the basis of the Establishment* ◊ **great 3.** the permanent staff of a government department or military force

establishment officer /ɪ ˌstæblɪʃmənt 'ɒfɪsə/ *noun* a civil servant in charge of personnel in a government department

estate /ɪ'steɪt/ *noun* any of three divisions of parliament or constitutional government, either the Lords Temporal, Lords Spiritual, and the Commons, or the Crown, the House of Lords, and the House of Commons. The Scottish parliament before the Union was composed of the three estates of the high-ranking clergy, the barons, and the representatives of the royal burghs.

estate duty /ɪ'steɪt ˌdjuːti/ *noun* the tax paid on the property left by a dead person. Also called **death duty**

estimate *noun* /'estɪmət/ an attempt to say what future costs or income will be □ **estimates of expenditure** calculation of future expenditure prepared for each government department by the minister ■ *verb* /'estɪmeɪt/ to attempt to say what future costs or income will be ◊ **estimates 1.** detailed statements of future expenditure for each government department (divided into Civil Estimates and Defence Estimates) presented to the House of Commons for approval **2.** detailed statements of future expenditure for each department of a local authority

ethical /'eθɪk(ə)l/ *adjective* morally correct

ethnic /ˈeθnɪk/ *adjective* referring to some nation or race

ethnic cleansing /ˌeθnɪk ˈklenzɪŋ/ *noun* violent action to remove people of a different culture from an area

ethnic group /ˈeθnɪk gruːp/ *noun* a group of people who have the same culture and traditions, especially when they are living in a country with a different culture

ethnicity /eθˈnɪsɪti/ *noun* the fact of belonging to a specific ethnic group ○ *The form asks you to state your ethnicity.*

ethnic minority /ˌeθnɪk maɪ ˈnɒrɪti/ ♦ **ethnic group**

ETLLD *abbreviation Scotland* Enterprise, Transport and Lifelong Learning Department

EU *abbreviation* European Union

euro /ˈjʊərəʊ/ *noun* the currency of the European Union

Euro- /jʊərəʊ/ *prefix* referring to Europe or the European Union

Eurocentric /ˌjʊərəʊˈsentrɪk/ *adjective* focusing on Europe, sometimes in a way that is dismissive of other parts of the world

Euro-constituency /ˌjʊərəʊ kən ˈstɪtjʊənsi/ *noun* an electoral district which elects an MEP to the European Parliament. Also called **Euro-seat**

Eurocrat /ˈjʊərəʊkræt/ *noun* a civil servant working in any of the European Union institutions (*informal*)

Euro-MP /ˌjʊərəʊ ˌem ˈpiː/ *noun* a Member of the European Parliament

European /ˌjʊərəˈpiːən/ *adjective* referring to Europe

European Commission /ˌjʊərəpiːən kəˈmɪʃ(ə)n/ *noun* the main executive body of the European Union made up of commissioners nominated by the Member States. Also called **Commission of the European Community**

COMMENT: The European Commission is the executive body of the European Union. The commissioners are nominated by the Member States for a five-year term and their appointments are ratified by the European Parliament.

Each commissioner has responsibility for a Directorate-General or department with specific policy interests like transport or agriculture.

European Community /ˌjʊərəpiːən kəˈmjuːnɪti/, **European Economic Community** /ˌjʊərəpiːən ˌiːkənɒmɪk kəˈmjuːnɪti/ *noun* now called **European Union**

European Constitution /ˌjʊərə ˈpiːən ˌkɒnstɪˈtjuːʃ(ə)n/ *noun* a constitution that brings together the many treaties and agreements on which the European Union is based. It defines the powers of the EU, stating where it can and cannot act and in what cases the Member States have a right of veto, and also defines the role of the EU institutions. (NOTE: It was ratified in Brussels on 18 June 2004.)

European Council /ˌjʊərəpiːən ˈkaʊns(ə)l/ *noun* a group formed of the heads of state or of government of the member states of the European Union, which meets at least twice a year under the chairmanship of the member state which holds the presidency, to discuss EU matters. The presidency of the council passes from country to country every six months.

European Court of Human Rights /ˌjʊərəpiːən kɔːt əv ˌhjuːmən ˈraɪts/ *noun* the court which sits in Strasbourg considering the rights of citizens of states which have signed the European Convention of Human Rights

European Court of Justice /ˌjʊərəpiːən ˌkɔːt əv ˈdʒʌstɪs/ *noun* the court which sits in Luxembourg and is responsible for judging cases under the law of the European Union and hearing appeals under European law from Member States of the EU

European Economic Area /ˌjʊərəpiːən ˌiːkənɒmɪk ˈeərɪə/ *noun* the area covered by the treaty signed between the European Union and some other European countries outside the EU which allows free trade with these countries. Abbr **EEA**

European External Action Service /ˌjʊərəˈpiːən ɪkˈstɜːn(ə)l 'ækʃ(ə)n 'sɜːvɪs/ *noun* a provision of the European Constitution for a European diplomatic service

European Free Trade Association /ˌjʊərə'piːən friː treɪd əˌsəʊsi 'eɪʃ(ə)n/ *noun* a union of Western European countries established to eliminate trade tariffs among member states The original members in 1960 were Austria, Denmark, the United Kingdom, Norway, Portugal, Sweden and Switzerland. Current members are Iceland, Liechtenstein, Norway and Switzerland. Abbr **EFTA**

Europeanism /ˌjʊərə'piːənɪz(ə)m/ *noun* support for the European Union and its further development

European Parliament /ˌjʊərəpiːən 'pɑːləmənt/ *noun* the parliament made up of people (MEPs or Euro-MPs) elected by the voters of each member state of the European Union

European Social Charter /ˌjʊərəpiːən ˌsəʊʃ(ə)l 'tʃɑːtə/ *noun* a charter for workers drawn up by the European Union in 1989, setting out the rights for workers to fair treatment and pay

European Union /ˌjʊərəpiːən 'juːniən/ *noun* the 25 European countries which have joined together to work for peace in Europe, economic growth and improvements in the living and working conditions of their citizens. Abbr **EU**

Europol /'jʊərəʊpɒl/ *abbreviation* European Police

Eurosceptic /'jʊərəʊ'skeptɪk/ *adjective* opposed to further growth of the powers of the European Union over its Member States

Euro-seat /'jʊərəʊ siːt/ *noun* same as **Euro-constituency**

evacuate /ɪ'vækjueɪt/ *verb* to make the people who live in a place move away from it because of the threat of disaster or invasion

evidence /'evɪd(ə)ns/ *noun* **1.** a written or spoken statement of facts which helps to prove something at a trial ○ *The National Association of Teachers of English gave evidence to the committee.* **2.** a spoken statement made to a committee of the House of Commons or House of Lords, which is then printed in the official record ○ *The Home Secretary gave evidence before the Select Committee.* **3.** a spoken or written statement made to a government or other inquiry ○ *In evidence presented to the tribunal, the employees showed that their wages had not risen in line with the cost of living.* ■ *verb* to show something ○ *the lack of good faith, as evidenced by the minister's refusal to make a statement to the Commons*

e-voting /'iː ˌvəʊtɪŋ/ *noun* same as **electronic voting**

excellency /'eksələnsi/ *noun* □ **His Excellency, Her Excellency** the way of referring to an ambassador

exceptional needs payment /ɪk ˌsepʃən(ə)l niːdz 'peɪmənt/ *noun* a payment made by the social services to a person who has a particular urgent need, such as for clothes

excess vote /'ekses vəʊt/ *noun* a vote to approve the spending of more money than was originally approved

exchangeable /ɪks'tʃeɪndʒəb(ə)l/ *adjective* possible to exchange

exchange controls /ɪks'tʃeɪndʒ kənˌtrəʊlz/ *plural noun* government restrictions on changing local money into foreign money ○ *The government imposed exchange controls to stop the rush to buy dollars.*

Exchange Equalisation Account /ɪksˌtʃeɪndʒ ˌiːkwəlaɪ'zeɪʃən əˌkaʊnt/ *noun* an account with the Bank of England used by the government when buying or selling foreign money to influence the exchange rate for the pound

Exchequer /ɪks'tʃekə/ *noun* the government department which deals with taxes and government spending. Also called **Treasury**. ◊ **Chancellor of the Exchequer**

excise /'eksaɪz/ *noun* a government tax on some goods used, made or sold

Excise Department /'eksaɪz dɪ
ˌpɑːtmənt/ *noun* same as **Customs
and Excise**

excise duty /'eksaɪz ˌdjuːti/ *noun*
a tax on the sale of goods such as alcohol and petrol which are produced in
the country or on some goods brought
into the country

exclusion zone /ɪk'skluːʒ(ə)n
ˌzəʊn/ *noun* an area, usually of sea,
near a country, which the military
forces of other countries are ordered
not to use

execute /'eksɪkjuːt/ *verb* to carry
out a decision, plan or order

executive /ɪg'zekjʊtɪv/ *adjective*
1. putting decisions into action □ **executive session** *US* a meeting of a congressional committee where only
committee members, witnesses and
other members of Congress may attend, and the public is excluded **2.** referring to the branch of government
which puts laws into effect ■ *noun* **1.**
a person in an organisation who takes
decisions **2.** □ **the Executive** the section of a government which puts into
effect the laws passed by Parliament
(NOTE: In the USA, this is the president.)

'...the principles of a free constitution
are lost when the legislative power is
nominated by the executive'
[*Edward Gibbon*]

executive agency /ɪgˌzekjʊtɪv
'eɪdʒənsi/ *noun* a semi-independent
organisation set up to carry out some
of the responsibilities of government
department

executive agreement /ɪg
ˌzekjʊtɪv ə'griːmənt/ *noun* an agreement between a US president and a
foreign head of state that has not been
given approval by the Senate

Executive Branch /ɪg'zekjʊtɪv
brɑːntʃ/ *noun* the part of government
which puts legislation into action
(NOTE: The other two branches are
the judicial and the legislative.)

Executive Council /ɪgˌzekjʊtɪv
'kaʊns(ə)l/ *noun* **1.** in Australia and
New Zealand, a body made up of the

Governor-General or Governor and
government ministers which meets to
brief the Governor-General or Governor on policies and formally approve
government appointments and legislation **2.** in Canada, the cabinet of a provincial government

executive document /ɪg
ˌzekjʊtɪv ˌdɒkjʊ'ment/ *noun* a document such as a treaty, sent by the President of the USA to the Senate for ratification

executive order /ɪgˌzekjʊtɪv
'ɔːdə/ *noun* an order made by the
President of the USA or by a state
governor

executive power /ɪgˌzekjʊtɪv
'paʊə/ *noun* the right to put decisions
into action

executive privilege /ɪgˌzekjʊtɪv
'prɪvɪlɪdʒ/ *noun* the right of the President of the USA not to reveal matters
which are considered secret

executive session /ɪgˌzekjʊtɪv
'seʃ(ə)n/ *noun US* a meeting of a
committee of Congress which only
committee members, witnesses and
other members of Congress may attend, and the public is not allowed to
attend

exempt /ɪg'zempt/ *adjective* not
covered by a law, or not forced to obey
a law □ **exempt from tax** not required
to pay tax, or not subject to tax ○ *Food
is exempt from sales tax.* ■ *verb* to free
something from having tax paid on it
or from having to pay tax ○ *Non profit-
making organisations are exempted
from tax.* ○ *The government exempted
trusts from tax.*

exempt information /ɪgˌzempt
ˌɪnfə'meɪʃ(ə)n/ *noun* information
which may be kept secret from the
public, because if it were not it might
be unfair to an individual or harmful to
the council ○ *The council resolved that
the press and public be excluded for
item 10 as it involved the likely disclosure of exempt information.*

exemption /ɪg'zempʃ(ə)n/ *noun*
the act of freeing something from a
contract or from a tax

exemption clause /ɪgˈzempʃ(ə)n klɔːz/ *noun* a section in a contract freeing a party from specific liabilities

exempt supplies /ɪgˌzempt sə ˈplaɪz/ *plural noun* sales of goods or services on which tax does not have to be paid

exercise /ˈeksəsaɪz/ *noun* **1.** the use of a power ○ *A court can give directions to a local authority as to the exercise of its powers in relation to children in care.* **2.** a test or trial to get experience or information ○ *Getting the residents' views on the new road will be a useful exercise.* ○ *The leaflets prepared by the department are just a public relations exercise.* ■ *verb* to use or to put into practice

exile /ˈeksaɪl/ *noun* **1.** the punishment of being sent to live in another country ○ *The ten members of the opposition party were sent into exile.* □ **government in exile** a government formed outside a country to oppose the government inside it **2.** a person who has been sent to live in another country as a punishment ○ *The new leadership hopes that after the amnesty several well-known exiles will return home.* ■ *verb* to send someone to live in another country as a punishment ○ *He was exiled for life.*

exit poll /ˈegzɪt pəʊl/ *noun* a survey taken outside a place where people have voted, asking those who have just voted how they voted, to get an idea of the likely result of an election

ex officio /ˌeks əˈfɪʃiəʊ/ *Latin phrase meaning* 'because of an office held' ○ *The mayor is ex officio a member* or *an ex officio member of the finance committee.*

expansionism /ɪkˈspænʃ(ə)nɪz(ə)m/ *noun* a policy of expanding a country's economy or territory

expansionist /ɪkˈspænʃ(ə)nɪst/ *adjective* (*of a country or government*) wanting to increase the lands it controls

expatriate *noun* /eksˈpætriət/ a person who lives in a country which is not his or her own ○ *There is a large expatriate community* or *a large community of expatriates in Geneva.* ■ *verb* /eksˈpætrieɪt/ to force someone to leave the country where he or she is living

expatriation /eksˌpætriˈeɪʃ(ə)n/ *noun* the act of forcing someone to leave the country where he or she is living. Compare **repatriation**

expenditure /ɪkˈspendɪtʃə/ *noun* the amount of money spent on something ■ the major costs of a council or central government (such as schools, roads, hospitals, etc.)

expire /ɪkˈspaɪə/ *verb* (*(of an official document)*) to stop being valid on a particular date □ **his passport** or **visa has expired** his passport or visa is no longer valid

explanatory note /ɪkˌsplænət(ə)ri ˈnəʊt/ *noun* a short piece of text that explains something in more detail or helps you to understand it better ■ *plural noun* **explanatory notes** general information about a Bill, explaining its legal and political implications, written by the relevant Government Department

export *verb* /ɪkˈspɔːt/ to send goods to foreign countries for sale ○ *We have exported more goods this month than ever before.* ■ *noun* /ˈekspɔːt/ **1.** the sending of goods out of a country to be sold ○ *The export of firearms is forbidden.* **2.** something sent out of the country for sale

export restitution /ˌekspɔːt ˌrestɪˈtjuːʃ(ə)n/ *noun* money paid by the European Union to subsidise European food exporters

exports /ˈekspɔːts/ *plural noun* goods sent abroad for sale ○ *Exports have fallen because the exchange rate is too high.*

expropriate /eksˈprəʊprieɪt/ *verb* to take private property for public use

expropriation /ɪksˌprəʊpriˈeɪʃ(ə)n/ *noun US* the action of the state in taking private property for public use, and paying compensation to the former owner (NOTE: The UK term is **compulsory purchase**.)

expunge /ɪk'spʌndʒ/ *verb* to remove something from an official record ○ *The Chairman ordered the remarks to be expunged from the record.*

extension /ɪk'stenʃən/ *noun* the act of increasing something

extension of remarks /ɪk ˌstenʃən əv rɪ'mɑːks/ *noun US* additional material which a member of Congress adds to the Congressional Record after a sitting

external /ɪk'stɜːn(ə)l/ *adjective* involving relations with foreign countries

exterritorial /ˌeksterɪ'tɔːriəl/ *adjective* same as **extraterritorial**

extra-authority payments /ˌekstrə ɔːˌθɒrɪti 'peɪmənts/, **extra-borough, extra-district** *plural noun* payments made to another authority for services provided by that authority

extradite /'ekstrədaɪt/ *verb* to bring an arrested person from one country to another country because she or he is wanted for trial for a crime which she or he committed in that country ○ *She was arrested in France and extradited to stand trial in Germany.*

extradition /ˌekstrə'dɪʃ(ə)n/ *noun* the action of bringing an arrested person from one country to be tried for a crime he or she committed in another country ○ *The USA requested the extradition of the leader of the drug gang.*

extradition treaty /ˌekstrə'dɪʃ(ə)n ˌtriːti/ *noun* an agreement between two countries that a person arrested in one country can be sent to the other to stand trial for a crime committed there

Extraordinary General Meeting /ɪkˌstrɔːd(ə)n(ə)ri ˌdʒen(ə)rəl 'miːtɪŋ/ *noun* a special meeting of members to discuss an important matter which cannot wait until the next Annual General Meeting

extraterritorial /ˌekstrəˌterɪ'tɔːriəl/ *adjective* **1.** situated or coming from outside a country's borders **2.** relating to exemption from the legal control of a country of residence

extra-territoriality /ˌekstrə ˌterɪtɔːri'ælɪti/ *noun* (*of diplomats*) the fact of being outside the territory of a country and so not subject to its laws

extra-territorial waters /ˌekstrə ˌterɪtɔːriəl 'wɔːtəz/ *plural noun* international waters, outside the jurisdiction of a country

extremism /ɪk'striːmɪz(ə)m/ *noun* ideas and practices that support very strong action such as the use of violence to achieve change

extremist /ɪk'striːmɪst/ *noun* (*as criticism*) a person who supports very strong or sometimes violent methods to achieve change ○ *The party has been taken over by left-wing extremists.* ○ *The meeting was broken up by extremists from the right of the party.* ■ *adjective* in support of strong methods ○ *The electorate decisively rejected the extremist parties.*

F

Fabian /'feɪbiən/ *adjective* relating to the Fabian Society ■ *noun* a member or supporter of the Fabian Society

Fabianism /'feɪbiənɪz(ə)m/ *noun* the beliefs of the Fabian Society

Fabian Society /'feɪbiən sə,saɪəti/ *noun* a political organisation founded in Britain in 1884 with the aim of developing socialism by gradual and lawful means rather than by revolution

facedown /'feɪsdaʊn/ *noun* a determined confrontation between two opposing people or groups

facie ♦ **prima facie**

facsimile /fæk'sɪmɪli/, **facsimile copy** /fæk,sɪmɪli 'kɒpi/ *noun* an exact copy of a document

fact-finding /'fækt ,faɪndɪŋ/ *adjective* looking for information □ **a fact-finding delegation** a group of people who visit somewhere to get information about an issue

faction /'fækʃən/ *noun* a group of people within a larger organisation such as a political party, who have different views or special aims ○ *Arguments broke out between different factions at the party conference.*

factional /'fækʃən(ə)l/ *adjective* referring to factions ○ *Factional infighting has weakened the party structure.*

factionalise /'fækʃənəlaɪz/ *verb* to split into factions, or cause a group to split into factions

factionalism /'fækʃənəɪz(ə)m/ *noun* the existence of or conflict between groups within a larger group

factor /'fæktə/ *noun* a thing which is important or which influences something ○ *The need to encourage tourism is a major factor in increased council spending on amenities.* ○ *The rise in unemployment is an important factor in the job market.*

Factortame case *noun* a legal case in 1991 which showed clearly that British law, made by Parliament, had to give way to European Law (NOTE: The Spanish fishing company, Factortame, had been stopped from fishing according to the Merchant Shipping Act of 1988, but the law lords struck down this Act because, according to European law, Factortame had done nothing illegal. This seemed to some commentators to show that Parliament had given away its legal sovereignty to the European Union.)

Faculty of Advocates /,fæk(ə)lti əv 'ædvəʊkəts/ *noun* the legal body to which Scottish barristers belong

fair trade /,feə 'treɪd/ *noun* an international business system where countries agree not to charge duties on goods imported from their trading partners

fall /fɔːl/ *verb* to lose political power or be defeated (NOTE: **falling – fell – fallen**) □ **to fall outside** not to be part of a list or not to be covered by a rule ○ *the case falls outside the jurisdiction of the local planning authority* □ **to fall within** to become part of a list or to be covered by a rule ○ *the newspaper report falls within the category of defamation* ○ *the case falls within the competence of the local authority* ■ *noun* a loss of political power or control

FAO *abbreviation* Food and Agriculture Organization (of the UN)

fascism /ˈfæʃɪz(ə)m/ *noun* extreme right-wing nationalist ideas, in favour of the power of the state, the army and the leader of the nation, violently opposed to Communism

fascist /ˈfæʃɪst/ *adjective* referring to fascism ○ *a fascist dictatorship* ○ *The leader of the party has made speeches advocating fascist principles.* ■ *noun* a supporter of fascism

Fatah, Al *noun* ♦ **Al Fatah**

Father of the House /ˈfɑːðə əv ði haʊz/ *noun* the MP who has been an MP for the longest time without a break (NOTE: It is also sometimes used to refer to the oldest member of the House of Lords.)

fatwa /ˈfætwə/ *noun* an official order made by a Muslim religious leader

FBI /ˌef biː ˈaɪ/ *abbreviation* Federal Bureau of Investigation

FCO *abbreviation* Foreign and Commonwealth Office

FCSD *abbreviation Scotland* Financial and Central Services Department

FDA *abbreviation* First Division Association

feasibility study /ˌfiːzəˈbɪlɪti ˌstʌdi/, **feasibility report** /ˌfiːzə ˈbɪlɪti rɪˌpɔːt/ *noun* work done to see if something which has been planned is a good idea ○ *The council asked the planning department to comment on the feasibility of the project.* ○ *The department has produced a feasibility report on the development project.*

feasibility test /ˌfiːzəˈbɪlɪti test/ *noun* a test to see if something proposed is possible

fed. *abbreviation* **1.** federal **2.** federated **3.** federation

Fed. *abbreviation* **1.** Federal **2.** Federated **3.** Federation

federal /ˈfed(ə)rəl/ *adjective* **1.** referring to a system of government in which a group of states are linked together in a federation □ **a federal constitution** a constitution such as that in Germany which provides for a series of semi-autonomous states joined together in a national federation **2.** refer-

ring especially to the central government of the United States □ **federal court, federal laws** court or laws of the USA, as opposed to state courts or state laws

Federal Assembly /ˈfed(ə)rəl əˈsembli/ *noun* the legislature in Russia

Federal Bureau of Investigation /ˌfed(ə)rəl ˌbjʊərəʊ əv ɪnˌvestɪˈɡeɪʃ(ə)n/ *noun* a section of the US Department of Justice, which looks into crimes against federal law and subversive acts in the USA. Abbr **FBI**

Federal Chancellor /ˈfed(ə)rəl ˈtʃɑːns(ə)lə/ *noun* the head of the executive in Germany

federal district /ˈfed(ə)rəl ˈdɪstrɪkt/ *noun* an area in which the seat of the national government of a federation such as the United States is located

federal government /ˈfed(ə)rəl ˈɡʌv(ə)nmənt/ *noun* the central government of a federal state

federalise /ˈfed(ə)rəlaɪz/ *verb* **1.** to bring various states together in a federal union **2.** to place something under the control of a federal government

federalism /ˈfed(ə)rəlɪz(ə)m/ *noun* the system of government which operates in a country which is a federation of semi-autonomous provinces or states, with a central federal government linking them together

federalist /ˈfed(ə)rəlɪst/ *noun* a supporter of a federal system of government

Federal Reserve /ˈfedrəl rɪzɜːv ˈbæŋk/ *noun US* the national system of banks in the United States

COMMENT: The Federal Reserve system is the central bank of the USA. The system is run by the Federal Reserve Board, under a chairman and seven committee members (or 'governors') who are all appointed by the President. The twelve Federal Reserve Banks act as lenders of last resort to local commercial banks. Although the board is appointed by the president, the whole system is relatively independent of the US government.

Federal Reserve Board /ˈfedrəl rɪˈzɜːv ˈbɔːd/ *noun* in the USA , the government organisation which runs the central banks and sets US interest rates

federate /ˈfedəreɪt/ *verb* to join together in a federation, or cause various bodies to join together in a federation

federation /ˌfedəˈreɪʃ(ə)n/ *noun* **1.** a group of organisations which are linked together and have a central body which represents their interests ○ *the American Federation of Labor* **2.** a group of semi-autonomous states which have a central government which represents them and looks after their common interests, in areas such as foreign policy and the armed forces

COMMENT: Many federations exist, though they are not often called such: the USA, Russia, Canada, Australia and Germany are all federations. Federations differ in how much independence the component regions or states have. A very loose form of federation is known as a confederation.

Federation Council /ˌfedə ˈreɪʃ(ə)n ˈkaʊns(ə)l/ *noun* the upper house of the legislature in Russia. ◊ **Duma**

federative /ˈfed(ə)rətɪv/ *adjective* relating to a federation

fellow traveller /ˈfeləʊ ˈtræv(ə)lə/ *noun* someone who sympathises with the cause of a group, especially the Communist Party, without becoming an official member

feminism /ˈfemɪnɪz(ə)m/ *noun* a movement supporting equality of women with men

feminist /ˈfemɪnɪst/ *adjective, noun* referring to feminism ○ *the feminist movement*

feudalise /ˈfjuːdəlaɪz/ *verb* to make a system similar to the feudal system

feudalism /ˈfjuːd(ə)lɪz(ə)m/ *noun* the medieval system where land was granted by a king to his nobility, and by the nobility to the peasants, on condition that each performed a service for their superior

feudal society /ˌfjuːd(ə)l sə ˈsaɪəti/ *noun* a society where each class or level has a duty to serve the class above it

feudal system /ˈfjuːdəl ˌsɪstəm/ *noun* ♦ **feudalism**

Fianna Fáil *noun* the republican party, one of the two main political parties in the Republic of Ireland

fide ♦ **bona fide**

fief /fiːf/ *noun* same as **fiefdom**

fiefdom /ˈfiːfdəm/ *noun* **1.** the lands controlled by a feudal lord **2.** something such as territory or a sphere of activity that is controlled or dominated by a specific person or group ○ *The company has an ethical responsibility to the existing residents of the area since this is their community and not the personal fiefdom of the developer.*

Fifth /fɪfθ/ *noun* same as **Fifth Amendment**

Fifth Amendment /ˌfɪfθ ə ˈmendmənt/ *noun* an amendment to the constitution of the USA, which says that no person can be forced to give evidence which might incriminate himself or herself

fifth column /ˌfɪfθ ˈkɒləm/ *noun* a secret group that works to promote its own ends and undermines the efforts of others

figure /ˈfɪɡə/ *noun* **1.** a particular number ○ *By 1982 unemployment had reached a very high figure* **2.** a person ○ *He was one of the more colourful figures to lead the party.*

file /faɪl/ *noun* a collection of papers stored away ○ *The official files are usually opened after 50 years and the contents made public.* ■ *verb* **1.** to store away a collection of papers **2.** to make an official request **3.** to present something officially so it can be recorded ○ *to file an application for a patent* ○ *to file a return to the tax office*

filibuster /ˈfɪlɪbʌstə/ *noun* in a debate, a speech which carries on for a long time so that the debate cannot be closed and a vote taken ○ *The Democrats organised a filibuster in the Senate.* ◊ **talk out**

COMMENT: Filibusters are possible in the US Senate, because the rules of the Senate allow unlimited debate. A filibuster may be ended by a closure motion which requires a three-fifths majority to pass. The filibuster is also used in the UK but in practice only for Private Members Bills, since government bills can be pushed through using the closure or guillotine.

filibustering /ˈfɪlɪbʌstərɪŋ/ *noun* the organising or carrying out of a filibuster

finance /ˈfaɪnæns/ *noun* public money used by a government or local authority ○ *Where will the authority find the finance to pay the higher salaries?* ○ *He is the secretary of the local authority finance committee.* ■ *verb* to pay for something ○ *a government-financed programme of prison construction* ○ *The new building must be financed by the local authority.*

Finance Act /ˈfaɪnæns ækt/ *noun* the annual Act of the British Parliament which gives the government power to raise taxes as proposed in the budget

Finance Minister /ˌfaɪnæns ˈmɪnɪstə/ *noun* the government minister responsible for finance, both taxation and spending. Also called **Minister of Finance**

financial /faɪˈnænʃəl/ *adjective* referring to finance ○ *She has a financial interest in the company.*

Financial and Central Services Department /faɪˌnænʃ(ə)l ən ˌsentrəl ˈsɜːvɪsɪz dɪˌpɑːtmənt/ *noun* a department of the Scottish Executive, responsible for collecting taxes and managing public revenue. Abbr **FCSD**

financial assistance /faɪˌnænʃəl əˈsɪstəns/ *noun* help in the form of money

financial commitments /faɪˌnænʃəl kəˈmɪtmənts/ *plural noun* money which is owed

financial institution /faɪˌnænʃəl ˌɪnstɪˈtjuːʃ(ə)n/ *noun* a bank or investment company or insurance company whose work involves lending or investing money

Financial Secretary to the Treasury /faɪˌnænʃəl ˌsekrət(ə)ri tə ðə ˈtreʒəri/ *noun* the minister of state in the Treasury, responsible to the Chancellor of the Exchequer

findings /ˈfaɪndɪŋz/ *noun* the decisions reached by an official group □ **the findings of a commission of inquiry** the conclusions of the commission

Fine Gael *noun* one of the two main political parties in the Republic of Ireland, considered more moderate than Fianna Fail

finlandisation, **finlandization** *noun* a policy of neutrality, similar to that formerly adopted by Finland because of its geographical position between the West and the USSR

fire regulations /ˈfaɪə ˌregjʊleɪʃ(ə)nz/ *plural noun* the local or national laws which owners of buildings used by the public have to obey in order to be given a fire certificate

First Amendment /ˌfɜːst ə ˈmen(d)mənt/ *noun* the first amendment to the Constitution of the USA, which protects freedom of speech and religion

First Division Association /ˌfɜːst dɪˌvɪʒ(ə)n əˌsəʊsiˈeɪʃ(ə)n/ *noun* same as **Association of First Division Civil Servants**

first estate /ˌfɜːst ɪˈsteɪt/ *noun* the social and political class that consists of senior members of the clergy

first lady /ˌfɜːst ˈleɪdi/ *noun* the wife or woman partner of a high government official, especially of a country's leader

First Lord of the Treasury /ˌfɜːst lɔːd əv ðə ˈtreʒəri/ *noun* a former British government post, now combined with that of Prime Minister

First Minister /ˌfɜːst ˈmɪnɪstə/ *noun* the leader of the National Assembly of Northern Ireland, Scotland or Wales

first-past-the-post /ˌfɜːst pɑːst ðə ˈpəʊst/ *noun* an electoral system such as that used in the UK, where the candidate with most votes wins the election even if he or she does not have more than half of all votes. Also called **Single Member Plurality System**

First Reading /ˌfɜːst ˈriːdɪŋ/ *noun* the formal introduction of a Bill into the House of Commons, after which it is printed

First World /ˌfɜːst wɜːld/ *noun* the principal industrialised countries of the world, including the United States, the United Kingdom, the nations of western Europe, Japan, Canada, Australia and New Zealand

fiscal /ˈfɪskəl/ *adjective* referring to tax or to government money ○ *the government's fiscal policies*

fiscal measures /ˌfɪskəl ˈmeʒəz/ *plural noun* tax changes made by a government

fiscal year /ˌfɪskəl ˈjɪə/ *noun* the twelve-month period on which taxes are calculated (NOTE: In the UK it is April 6th to April 5th; in the USA it is from July 1st to June 30th.)

Five-Year Plan /ˌfaɪv jɪə ˈplæn/ *noun* a set of proposals for running a country's economy over a five-year period

fixture /ˈfɪkstʃə/ *noun* a permanently arranged meeting ○ *The council meeting is a fixture on the third Wednesday of every month.*

flag /flæg/ ◇ **to fly a flag 1.** to attach a flag in an obvious position to show that your ship belongs to a certain country ○ *a ship flying the British flag* **2.** to act in a way that shows that you are proud of belonging to a certain country or working for a certain company ○ *The Trade Minister has gone to the World Fair to fly the flag.*

flag conservative /ˌflæg kən ˈsɜːvətɪv/ *noun* a neoconservative who believes that the United States' role is to engage in global policing in order to secure the national interest, national security, and the security of US allies

flag of convenience /ˌflæg əv kən ˈviːniəns/ *noun* the flag of a country

which may have no ships of its own but allows ships of other countries to be registered in its ports and fly its flag

flag of truce /ˌflæg əv ˈtruːs/ *noun* a white flag used to end a conflict temporarily, to allow negotiations to take place. Also called **white flag**

flag-waving /ˈflæg ˌweɪvɪŋ/ *noun* activities showing obvious and emotional patriotism

floating vote /ˌfləʊtɪŋ ˈvəʊt/ *noun* the votes of floating voters ○ *The Opposition is trying to capture the bulk of the floating vote.*

floating voter /ˌfləʊtɪŋ ˈvəʊtə/ *noun* **1.** a voter who has not decided how to vote **2.** a voter who does not always vote for the same party, but changes from election to election (NOTE: The US term is **swing voter**.)

floor /flɔː/ *noun* □ **the floor of the House** the main part of the House of Commons, House of Lords or Congress where business is conducted ○ *Debates on the floor of the House are often lively.*

floor leader /ˈflɔː ˌliːdə/ *noun* a member of an American legislative body chosen by fellow party members to organise their activities and strategy on the floor of the legislature

floor manager /ˈflɔː ˌmænɪdʒə/ *noun* a member, usually the chairman, of the reporting committee in the House of Commons who is responsible for trying to get agreement on a bill

floor spokesman /ˈflɔː ˌspəʊksmən/ *noun* in the US Senate, the spokesperson for a particular party ○ *The Senate majority leader is the floor spokesman for his party in the Senate.*

FO *abbreviation* Foreign Office

focus group /ˈfəʊkəs gruːp/ *noun* a small group of representative people who are questioned about their opinions as part of political or market research

Foggy Bottom /ˌfɒgi ˈbɒtəm/ *noun US* the State Department (*informal*) (NOTE: Foggy Bottom is an area in Washington DC where the State Department has its offices.)

FOL *abbreviation* Federation of Labour

Folketing *noun* the legislature in Denmark

follower /'fɒləʊə/ *noun* a person who supports a party, without being a member of that party

follow up /ˌfɒləʊ 'ʌp/ *verb* to examine something further ○ *The tax inspectors are following up the information they received.*

Food and Drug Administration /ˌfuːd ən 'drʌg ədˌmɪnɪstreɪʃ(ə)n/ *noun* full form of **FDA**

force /fɔːs/ *noun* **1.** strength or power ○ *took control by force* **2.** effect or influence □ **to come into force** to start to operate or work ○ *The new regulations will come into force on January 1st.* □ **to put into force** to make something apply □ **the new regulations have the force of law** they are the same as if they had been voted into law by parliament **3.** an organised group of people ○ *a military force* ○ *a police force* ■ *verb* to make someone do something ○ *The government has been forced to reconsider its plans.*

force majeure /ˌfɔːs mæˈʒɜː/ *noun* something which happens which is out of the control of the parties who have signed a contract and which prevents one of the parties keeping to the contract, e.g. a war or storm

foreign /'fɒrɪn/ *adjective* not belonging to one's own country ○ *Foreign cars have flooded our market.* ○ *We are increasing our trade with foreign countries.*

foreign affairs /'fɒrɪn əˈfeəz/ *plural noun* matters concerning other countries

Foreign and Commonwealth office /'fɒrɪn ən 'kɒmənwelθ 'ɒfɪs/ *noun* same as **Foreign Office**. abbr **FCO**

foreign currency /ˌfɒrɪn 'kʌrənsi/ *noun* the money of another country

foreigner /'fɒrɪnə/ *noun* a person from another country

foreign exchange /ˌfɒrən ɪks'tʃeɪndʒ/ *noun* the system of changing the money of one country for that of another

foreign exchange dealing /ˌfɒrɪn ɪks'tʃeɪndʒ ˌdiːlɪŋ/ *noun* the activity of buying and selling foreign money

foreign exchange market /ˌfɒrɪn ɪks'tʃeɪndʒ ˌmɑːkɪt/ *noun* the place where foreign money is bought and sold

foreign exchange reserves /ˌfɒrɪn ɪks'tʃeɪndʒ rɪˌzɜːvz/ *noun* the foreign money held by a government to support its own currency

foreign goods /ˌfɒrɪn 'gʊdz/ *plural noun* things produced in other countries

foreign investments /ˌfɒrɪn ɪn'vestmənts/ *plural noun* money invested in other countries

foreign minister /'fɒrɪn 'mɪnɪstə/ *noun* in many countries, a minister in a government who is responsible for relations with other countries

foreign ministry /'fɒrɪn 'mɪnɪstri/ *noun* in many countries, the department of government responsible for relations with other countries

foreign mission /'fɒrɪn 'mɪʃ(ə)n/ *noun* a group of diplomats who represent their country abroad

Foreign Office /'fɒrɪn ˌɒfɪs/ *noun* the British government department dealing with relations with other countries. Abbr **FO**. Also called **Foreign and Commonwealth Office**

COMMENT: In most countries, the government department dealing with other countries is called the Foreign Ministry, with the Foreign Minister in charge. In the UK, they are called the Foreign Office and Foreign Secretary. In the USA, they are called the State Department and the Secretary of State.

foreign policy /ˌfɒrɪn 'pɒlisi/ *noun* the policy followed by a country when dealing with other countries

Foreign Secretary /ˌfɒrɪn 'sekrɪt(ə)ri/ *noun* the British government minister in charge of relations with other countries

Foreign Service /ˌfɒrɪn ˈsɜːvɪs/ *noun* the government department responsible for a country's relations with other countries

foreign trade /ˌfɒrɪn ˈtreɪd/ *noun* trade with other countries

formal /ˈfɔːm(ə)l/ *adjective* according to correct and suitable methods ○ *to make a formal application* ○ *to send a formal order*

formality /fɔːˈmælɪti/ *noun* a thing which has to be done to obey the law or because it is the custom ○ *The chairman dispensed with the formality of reading the minutes.*

formation /fɔːˈmeɪʃ(ə)n/ *noun* the act of organizing ○ *The formation of the new splinter group has altered the voting pattern in the assembly.*

formulate /ˈfɔːmjuleɪt/ *verb* to write down or state clearly ○ *The Government's proposals are formulated in a White Paper.*

forty-ninth parallel /ˈfɔːti naɪnθ ˈpærəlel/ *noun* the border between the United States and Canada, that runs at 49° latitude along most of its length

forum /ˈfɔːrəm/ *noun* a place or opportunity for matters to be discussed ○ *The debate should be carried out in the forum of the council chamber, not on the pages of the local newspaper.*

founder /ˈfaʊndə/ *noun* a person who establishes a party, institution or company

founder member /ˌfaʊndə ˈmembə/ *noun* a member of a party or organisation who has been a member from the beginning

fourth estate /ˌfɔːθ ɪˈsteɪt/ *noun* journalists, the press, or the media in general

Fourth World /ˈfɔːθ ˈwɜːld/ *noun* the poorest countries of the world

franchise /ˈfræntʃaɪz/ *noun* **1.** a right given to someone to do something, especially the right to vote in local or general elections. ◊ **enfranchise, universal franchise 2.** a right

given by a company to someone to trade in the company's name in a particular area ○ *She has bought a printing franchise* or *a hot dog franchise.* ■ *verb* to sell the right to trade in a company's name in a particular area ○ *Her sandwich bar was so successful that she decided to franchise it.*

frank /fræŋk/ *noun* the right of sending official post free of charge, used by members of Congress

free circulation of goods /ˌfriː ˌsɜːkjʊˈleɪʃ(ə)n əv ɡʊdz/ *noun* the movement of goods from one country to another without legal restrictions

free collective bargaining /ˌfriː kəˌlektɪv ˈbɑːɡɪnɪŋ/ *noun* negotiations over pay and working conditions between the management and the workers' representatives without government interference

free competition /ˌfriː ˌkɒmpəˈtɪʃ(ə)n/ *noun* being free to compete without government interference

free currency /ˌfriː ˈkʌrənsi/ *noun* a currency which is allowed by the government to be bought and sold without restriction

freedom /ˈfriːdəm/ *noun* **1.** the state of being free or not being held in prison or as a slave ○ *The president gave the accused man his freedom.* **2.** the state of being free to do something without restriction **3.** □ **freedom of the city** the highest honour given to a person by a town or city ○ *In a ceremony at the Town Hall yesterday, Lord Smith was given the Freedom of the City.*

Freedom Charter /ˈfriːdəm ˈtʃɑːtə/ *noun* a document setting out the basic rights of all South Africans, composed in 1955 in opposition to the Nationalist government and constituting the manifesto of the African National Congress

freedom fighter /ˈfriːdəm ˌfaɪtə/ *noun* a guerrilla fighting against an oppressive government or to free the country from foreign control

freedom of assembly /ˌfriːdəm əv əˈsembli/ *noun* the right to hold a meeting or a peaceful demonstration without being afraid of prosecution. Also called **freedom of meeting**

freedom of association /ˌfriːdəm əv əsəʊsiˈeɪʃ(ə)n/ *noun* the right to join together with other people in a group, such as a church or trade union, without being afraid of prosecution

freedom of information /ˌfriːdəm əv ɪnfəˈmeɪʃ(ə)n/ *noun* the right of government information being available to ordinary people, or of official records about private people being available to each person concerned

Freedom of Information Act /ˈfriːdəm əv ˌɪnfəˈmeɪʃ(ə)n ˌeɪ siː ˈtiː/ *noun* the Act of Parliament (2000) which allows people to gain access to government documents (NOTE: The UK Freedom of Information Act is a weaker measure than most people had hoped for, and gives British citizens less access to information than similar measures in the USA and other countries do.)

freedom of meeting /ˈfriːdəm əv ˈmiːtɪŋ/ *noun* same as **freedom of assembly**

freedom of speech /ˌfriːdəm əv ˈspiːtʃ/ *noun* the right to say, write or publish what you want without being afraid of prosecution

freedom of the press /ˌfriːdəm əv ðə ˈpres/ *noun* the right to write and publish in a newspaper what you wish without being afraid of prosecution

free elections /ˌfriː ɪˈlekʃ(ə)nz/ *plural noun* elections which are honest and not rigged by one of the parties or by the government ○ *the right to hold free elections*

free enterprise /ˌfriː ˈentəpraɪz/ *noun* the economic system where business is free from government interference and the economy is largely in private hands rather than under state control

freelance /ˈfriːlɑːns/ *noun* someone, especially a politician, who is not committed to any group and takes action or forms alliances independently

freeman /ˈfriːmæn/ *noun* a person who has received the honour of freedom of the city

free market economy /ˌfriː ˌmɑːkɪt ɪˈkɒnəmi/ *noun* the economic system where the government does not interfere in business activity and where the economy is largely in private hands rather than under state control

free movement of capital /ˌfriː ˌmuːvmənt əv ˈkæpɪt(ə)l/ *noun* the ability to transfer capital from one country to another without any restrictions

free port /ˈfriː pɔːt/, **free trade zone** /ˌfriː ˈtreɪd ˌzəʊn/ *noun* a port or area where there are no customs duties

free speech /ˌfriː ˈspiːtʃ/ *noun* ⟶ **freedom of speech**

free trade /ˌfriː ˈtreɪd/ *noun* the economic system where goods can go from one country to another without any restrictions

free trade area /ˌfriː ˈtreɪd ˌeəriə/ *noun* a group of countries practising free trade

free trader /ˌfriː ˈtreɪdə/ *noun* a person who supports free trade

free vote /ˌfriː ˈvəʊt/ *noun* an occasion in a parliament when members are allowed to decide how to vote according to their consciences and personal opinions rather than as instructed by their party leaders

free world /ˌfriː ˈwɜːld/ *noun* the countries of the world with democratic governments, as opposed to those with totalitarian or communist governments

French Community /ˌfrentʃ kəˈmjuːnəti/ *noun* an association linking France and several former French colonies

French Revolution /ˌfrentʃ ˌrevəˈluːʃ(ə)n/ *noun* the violent overthrow of the French king by the people of France in 1789

fringe /frɪndʒ/ *noun* the members of a group or organisation whose views are not representative of the group as a whole ○ *a fringe meeting* ○ *Some on the conservative fringes argue that the state should not grant any rights at all to gay couples.*

front /frʌnt/ *noun* a political group, usually an alliance of several smaller groups, formed to resist a threat □ **to form a common front** to join into a group against a threat. ◊ **Popular Front**

frontbencher /ˌfrʌnt'bentʃə/ *noun* a Member of Parliament who sits on the front rows of seats in the chamber and who is a government minister or a member of the Opposition shadow cabinet. Also called **frontbench MP**

front benches /ˌfrʌnt 'bentʃɪz/ *plural noun* two rows of seats in the House of Commons, facing each other with a table between them, where Government ministers or members of the Opposition Shadow Cabinet sit □ **the Government front bench** the seats where the members of the Government sit facing the Opposition. Also called **Treasury bench**. ◊ **Opposition front bench**

frontier /frʌn'tɪə/ *noun* the boundary of a country

frontline /'frʌntlaɪn/ *adjective* relating to countries that have a border with another country in which fighting is taking place

frontline state /ˌfrʌntlaɪn 'steɪt/ *noun* a nation situated on the border of an area where fighting is happening or is likely to happen

front organisation /ˌfrʌnt ˌɔːɡənaɪ'zeɪʃ(ə)n/ *noun* an organisation which pretends to be neutral, but in fact supports a political party or other interest group

full title /ˌfʊl 'taɪt(ə)l/ *noun* the summary of an Act of Parliament, printed at the beginning of the Act. Also called **long title**

function /'fʌŋkʃən/ *noun* **1.** an official ceremony ○ *At a function held in the council offices, the mayor gave testimonials to two of the library staff.* ○ *The council offices are closed for an official function.* **2.** a job or duty ○ *It is not the function of the clerk to give an opinion on the candidates.* ○ *The job description lists the various functions of a Chief Education Officer.* ■ *verb* to work ○ *Lack of qualified engineers is hindering the functioning of the council's maintenance department.*

functionary /'fʌŋkʃənəri/ *noun* an official, especially someone who is regarded as having unimportant duties

fund /fʌnd/ *verb* to pay for something ○ *The scheme is funded by the local education committee.* ○ *Redevelopment of the centre of the town has been funded partly by government and partly by local industry.* ■ *noun* a collection of money for a special purpose ○ *The mayor has opened a fund to help poor families.*

fundamentalism /ˌfʌndə'ment(ə)lɪz(ə)m/ *noun* **1.** the practice of following extremely traditional religious beliefs **2.** a government based on extremely traditional religious beliefs

fundamentalist /ˌfʌndə'ment(ə)lɪst/ *adjective* referring to fundamentalism ○ *a fundamentalist regime* ■ *noun* a person who holds fundamentalist views

fund-raising /'fʌnd ˌreɪzɪŋ/ *noun* the activity of asking people or organisations to give money ○ *The mayor launched a fund-raising scheme to get more money for the children's club.*

further education /ˌfɜːðər edjʊ'keɪʃ(ə)n/ *noun* the teaching of students after they have left school at 16 ○ *The borough's College of Further Education offers a wide range of courses.*

fusionism /'fjuːʒ(ə)nɪz(ə)m/ *noun* the formation of political coalitions, support for their formation or belief in their effectiveness

G

G8 *noun* the group of the eight most industrialised nations in the world, i.e. Canada, France, Germany, Italy, Japan, Russia, the United Kingdom, and the United States. Representatives from these countries meet regularly for discussions, especially on global economic policies. Full form **Group of Eight**

Gaeltacht *noun* the parts of Ireland or Scotland where Gaelic is spoken by a large part of the population

gag /gæg/ *verb* to try to stop someone talking or writing ○ *The government was accused of using the Official Secrets Act as a means of gagging the press.*

gag rule /ˈgæg ruːl/ *noun* a rule in the House of Representatives which limits the time for debate. Also called **closed rule**

gain /geɪn/ *noun* **1.** an increase **2.** an increase in a share of the vote ○ *The latest poll shows a socialist gain of 2%.* **3.** a seat won in an election ○ *The Conservatives had 20 gains and 10 losses in the local elections.* ■ *verb* **1.** to get or to obtain something **2.** to win a seat in an election ○ *The Socialists gained six seats on the council at the expense of the Tories.*

gainful /ˈgeɪnf(ə)l/ *adjective* □ **gainful employment** employment which pays money

gainfully employed /ˈgeɪnf(ə)li ɪmˈplɔɪd/ *adverb* paid for the work carried out

gallery /ˈgæləri/ *noun* the seats above the House of Commons and House of Lords, where the public and journalists sit □ **the Speaker ordered the galleries to be cleared** the Speaker asked for all visitors to leave

Gallup poll /ˈgæləp pəʊl/ *noun* a survey in which a group of people taken as a representative sample of a larger group are asked their opinions on a specific subject

gaming licence /ˈgeɪmɪŋ ˌlaɪs(ə)ns/ *noun* a document which allows someone to run a gambling club

gangway /ˈgæŋweɪ/ *noun* the space between the benches running down the middle of the House of Commons □ **below the gangway** further away from the Speaker

garda /ˈgɑːdə/ *noun* a police officer in the Republic of Ireland

Garda /ˈgɑːdə/ *noun* the police force of the Republic of Ireland

gardaí plural of **garda**

GATT *abbreviation* General Agreement on Tariffs and Trade

Gaullism /ˈgɔːlɪz(ə)m/ *noun* the nationalist and conservative policies of General Charles de Gaulle, leader of France after World War II, and his followers

gavel /ˈgæv(ə)l/ *noun* a small wooden hammer used by the chairman of a meeting to call the meeting to order ○ *The chairman banged his gavel on the table and shouted to the councillors to be quiet.*

COMMENT: In the American Senate, a ceremonial gavel is placed on the Vice-President's desk when the Senate is in session.

GCHQ *abbreviation* Government Communications Headquarters

GDP *abbreviation* gross domestic product

General Agreement on Tariffs and Trade /ˌdʒen(ə)rəl əˌgriːmənt ɒn ˌθærɪfs ən 'treɪd/ *noun* the international treaty which aimed to try to reduce restrictions in trade between countries. Abbr **GATT** (NOTE: Replaced on 1st January 1995 by the World Trade Organization (WTO).)

general amnesty /ˌdʒen(ə)rəl 'æmnəsti/ *noun* a pardon granted to all prisoners or unconvicted criminals

General Assembly /ˌdʒen(ə)rəl ə'sembli/ *noun* the meeting of all the members of the United Nations, where each country is represented and each has a vote

General Assembly of the United Nations /ˌdʒen(ə)rəl əˌsembli əv θi juːˌnaɪtɪd 'neɪʃ(ə)nz/ *noun* the meeting of all the members of the United Nations to discuss international problems, where each member state has one vote

general election /ˌdʒen(ə)rəl ɪ 'lekʃən/ *noun* choosing a legislature or executive by all the voters in a country

COMMENT: In Britain, a Parliament can only last for a maximum of five years, and a dissolution is usually called by the Prime Minister before the end of that period. The Lord Chancellor then issues a writ for the election of MPs. All British subjects (including Commonwealth and Irish citizens), are eligible to vote in British elections provided they are on the electoral register, are over 18 years of age, are sane, are not members of the House of Lords and are not serving prison sentences for serious crime. In the USA, members of the House of Representatives are elected for a two-year period. Senators are elected for six-year terms, one third of the Senate being elected every two years. The President of the USA is elected by an electoral college made up of people elected by voters in each of the states of the USA. Each state elects the same number of electors to the electoral college as it has Congressmen, plus two. This guarantees that the college is broadly representative of voters across the country. The presidential candidate with an overall majority in the college is elected president. A presidential term of office is four years, and a president can stand for re-election once.

general instrument /'dʒen(ə)rəl 'ɪnstrʊmənt/ *noun* a form of Statutory Instrument which does not need approval by both Houses of Parliament

Generalitat *noun* the parliament in Catalonia

General Purposes Committee /'dʒen(ə)rəl 'pɜːpəsɪz kəˌmɪti/ *noun* a local council committee which deals with matters which do not come under any other committee

general strike /ˌdʒen(ə)rəl 'straɪk/ *noun* a strike involving all or most workers in a country

Geneva Convention /dʒɪˌniːvə kən'venʃ(ə)n/ *noun* the international treaty governing the behaviour of countries relating to behaviour in time of war

Geneva Protocol /dʒɪ'niːvə ˌprəʊtəkɒl/ *noun* the international agreement to limit the use of chemical and biological weapons

genocide /'dʒenəʊsaɪd/ *noun* the killing of an entire ethnic group

Gentleman Usher of the Black Rod /ˌdʒent(ə)lmən 'ʌʃə əv ðə blæk rɒd/ *noun* same as **Black Rod**

geopolitical /ˌdʒiːəʊpə'lɪtɪkəl/ *adjective* relating to political relations between different countries and groups of countries

geopolitics /ˌdʒiːəʊ'pɒlətɪks/ *noun* the political relations between different countries and groups of countries

geostrategy /'dʒiːəʊˌstrætədʒɪ/ *noun* the policy of a country based on a combination of geographical and political factors

gerontocracy /ˌgerənt'ɒkrəsi/ *noun* **1.** a system of government in which older people are chosen as rulers **2.** a group of older people who make up a government

gerrymander /'dʒerimændə/ *verb* to change the boundaries of an electoral area in order to gain an unfair political advantage in an election

gerrymandering
/ˈdʒerimændərɪŋ/ *noun* the reorganisation of parliamentary constituencies or electoral districts to get an advantage in the next election

get out /ˌget ˈaʊt/ *verb* to produce something ○ *The Royal Commission got out the report in time for the meeting.* ○ *The party was late in getting out its election manifesto.*

get round /ˌget ˈraʊnd/ *verb* **1.** to find the time to do something ○ *hadn't got round to reading the report* **2.** to avoid ○ *We tried to get round the embargo by shipping from Canada.* ○ *Can you advise me how we can get round the quota system?*

GG *abbreviation* Governor General

ghetto /ˈgetəʊ/ *noun* the area of a town where many people of the same ethnic group or background live, separately from the rest of the population

ginger group /ˈdʒɪndʒə gruːp/ *noun* a group of people within a political party or organisation who try to make the organisation more radical

give away /ˌgɪv əˈweɪ/ *verb* **1.** to give something as a free present **2.** to reveal a secret

give rise to /ˌgɪv ˈraɪz tə/ *verb* to be the cause of something ○ *The decisions of the planning committee have given rise to complaints from applicants.*

give up /ˌgɪv ˈʌp/ *verb* to agree that someone else should have something that was once yours ○ *gave up their claim to the land* ○ *give up sovereignty*

give way /ˌgɪv ˈweɪ/ *verb* to allow someone else to speak (NOTE: used frequently in the House of Commons when a Member wants to say something when someone else is speaking: *Will the hon. Gentleman give way? No, I will not give way* or *I will give way shortly.*)

Gladstone /ˈglædstəʊn/, **W. E.** (1809–98) leader of the Liberal Party after 1867 and four times prime minister (1868–74, 1880–85, 1886, and 1892–94). He introduced national education in Britain (1870).

glasnost /ˈglæznɒst/ *noun* openness in government or freedom of information (NOTE: The term was first used by president Gorbachev to describe the system he developed in Russia after the fall of communism.)

global /ˈgləʊb(ə)l/ *adjective* referring to the whole world □ **global conflict** a world war

globalism /ˈgləʊbəlɪz(ə)m/ *noun* the belief that political policies should consider national concerns in the context of international situations and issues

gloss /glɒs/ *verb* words in a document used to explain it more fully or to explain specific words

GNP *abbreviation* gross national product

go-ahead /ˈgəʊ əˌhed/ *noun* permission to begin to do something

go back on /ˌgəʊ ˈbæk ɒn/ *verb* not to do what has been promised ○ *Two months later they went back on the agreement.*

God Save the Queen /ˌgɒd seɪv ðə ˈkwiːn/ *noun* the title of the British national anthem

go into /ˌgəʊ ˈɪntuː/ *verb* **1.** to enter **2.** to examine carefully ○ *The bank wants to go into the details of the council's loans to the club.* ○ *The fraud squad is going into the facts behind the property deals.*

good cause /ˌgʊd ˈkɔːz/ *noun* **1.** a group or charity which deserves to be helped ○ *The money collected by the Mayor's Christmas Fund will go to good causes in the borough.* **2.** a reason which is accepted in law ○ *The court asked the accused to show good cause why she should not be sent to prison.*

good faith /ˌgʊd ˈfeɪθ/ *noun* general honesty

good neighbour /ˌgʊd ˈneɪbə/ *noun* a country which has good relations with other countries near it

good neighbourliness /ˌgʊd ˈneɪbəlinəs/ *noun* good relations between a country and those that are near it

goods /gʊdz/ *plural noun* things that are produced to be sold

good title /ˌgʊd ˈtaɪt(ə)l/ *noun* the legal right to own a property

go on /ˌgəʊ ˈɒn/ *verb* **1.** to continue ○ *The staff went on working in spite of the fire.* ○ *The chairman went on speaking for two hours.* **2.** to use to help find something or decide something ○ *Two bank statements are all the tax investigators have to go on.* ○ *The Foreign Office has only a report in a Hong Kong newspaper to go on.*

gov. *abbreviation* government

govern /ˈgʌv(ə)n/ *verb* **1.** to rule a country ○ *The country is governed by a group of military leaders.* ○ *The Chief Minister governs in the name of the Federal Government.* **2.** to control something ○ *the rules governing elections to the National Assembly* **3.** to influence something ○ *Their behaviour will govern our response.*

governance /ˈgʌv(ə)nəns/ *noun* the theory or activity of governing ○ *The Bill is a threat to the governance of Britain.*

government /ˈgʌv(ə)nmənt/ *noun* **1.** the way of ruling or controlling a country ○ *People want democratic government.* ○ *The leader of the Opposition is promising to provide effective government.* **2.** an organisation which administers a country or part of a country ○ *The government has decided to introduce new immigration laws.* ○ *The Labour government introduced nationalisation.* ○ *Succeeding governments have been unable to deal with the rising crime rate.* **3.** coming from the government or referring to the government ○ *government intervention* or *intervention by the government* ○ *a government ban on the import of arms* ○ *a government investigation into organised crime* ○ *Government officials prevented him leaving the country.* ○ *Government policy is outlined in the Green Paper.* ○ *Government regulations state that*

import duty has to be paid on expensive items.

governmental /ˌgʌv(ə)nˈment(ə)l/ *adjective* relating to a government

governmentalise /ˌgʌv(ə)nˈmentəlaɪz/ *verb* to put a sphere of activity under the control of a government

Government Chief Whip /ˈgʌv(ə)nmənt tʃiːf wɪp/ *noun* the main whip of the party in power, who reports to the Cabinet and whose job it is to make sure that government bills are passed by Parliament (NOTE: In the House of commons the Government Chief Whip's official title is Parliamentary Secretary to the Treasury and in the House of Lords it is Captain of the Honourable Corps of Gentleman-at-Arms.)

government contractor /ˌgʌv(ə)nmənt kənˈtræktə/ *noun* a company which supplies goods or services to the government on contract (NOTE: **government** can take a singular or plural verb: *the government have decided to repeal the Act*; *the government feels it is not time to make a statement.* Note also that the word **Government** is used, especially by officials, without the article: *Government has decided that the plan will be turned down*; *the plan is funded by central government.*)

government economic indicators /ˌgʌv(ə)nmənt ˌiːkənɒmɪk ˈɪndɪkeɪtəz/ *plural noun* figures which show how the country's economy is expected to perform

government of national unity /ˈgʌv(ə)nmənt əv ˈnæʃ(ə)nəl ˈjuːnɪti/ *noun* a government formed of a coalition of several parties, usually to deal with a specific emergency such as a war

governor /ˈgʌv(ə)nə/ *noun* **1.** a person who governs a state or province ○ *the governor of Uttar Pradesh* ○ *Ronald Reagan was Governor of California before becoming President.* **2.** a person representing the Crown, e.g. the official in charge of a colony **3.** a person in charge of a prison ○ *a prison governor* ○ *The prisoners applied to the governor for parole.* **4.** a member of a group responsible for controlling a public institution such as a hospital or school

Governor-General /ˌgʌv(ə)nə 'dʒen(ə)rəl/ *noun* a person representing the United Kingdom in a Commonwealth country which still has the British Queen as head of state. ◊ **Lieutenant-Governor**

govt *abbreviation* government

graft /grɑːft/ *noun* bribery of officials ○ *He was accused of graft when it was learnt that he had tried to bribe the Planning Officer.*

Grand National Assembly /ˌgrænd ˌnæʃ(ə)nəl əˈsembli/ *noun* the legislature in Turkey

grant /grɑːnt/ *noun* **1.** the act of giving something to someone, permanently or temporarily, by a written document ○ *She made a grant of land to her son.* **2.** money given by the government or local authority or other organisation to help pay for something ○ *The institute has a government grant to cover the cost of the development programme.* ○ *The local authority has allocated grants towards the costs of the scheme.* ○ *Many charities give grants for educational projects.* ■ *verb* to agree to give someone something or to agree to allow someone to do something ○ *to grant someone permission to build a house* or *to leave the country* ○ *The local authority granted the company an interest-free loan to start up the new factory.* ○ *She was granted leave to appeal.* ○ *The government granted an amnesty to all political prisoners.*

grant-aided /ˌgrɑːmnt 'eɪdɪd/ *adjective* supported by funds from the government ○ *a grant-aided scheme*

grantee /grɑːnˈtiː/ *noun* a person who receives money as a grant

grant-in-aid /ˌgrɑːnt ɪn 'eɪd/ *noun* money given by central government to local government to help pay for a project

grantor /grɑːnˈtɔː/ *noun* a person who makes a grant of money

Grant-Related Expenditure Assessment /ˌgrɑːnt rɪˌleɪtɪd ɪk 'spendɪtʃə əˌsesmənt/ *noun* the government calculation of what each local authority needs to spend each year. Abbr **GREA**

grass roots /ˌgrɑːs 'ruːts/ *noun* the ordinary members of a political party or of society in general ○ *What is the grass-roots reaction to the constitutional changes?* ○ *The party has considerable support at grass-roots level.* ○ *The Chairman has no grass-root support.*

grata ♦ **persona**

GREA *abbreviation* Grant-Related Expenditure Assessment

great /greɪt/ *noun* □ **the great and the good** important public figures

Great Hural /ˌgreɪt 'hjʊərəl/ *noun* the legislative body in Mongolia

Great Power /ˌgreɪt 'paʊə/ *noun* a nation that has international political, social, economic and usually military influence

Great Seal /ˌgreɪt 'siːl/ *noun* the ceremonial seal, kept originally by the Lord Chancellor, used for authenticating important public documents on behalf of the Queen (NOTE: The use of a seal to authenticate public documents dates back hundreds of years but is now only used for reasons of tradition and ceremony.)

green /griːn/ *adjective* supporting or promoting the protection of the environment ■ *noun* a supporter or advocate of protecting the environment, especially a member of a political party concerned with environmental issues

green card /ˌgriːn 'kɑːd/ *noun* a work permit needed by a foreigner in the USA

greenie /'griːni/ *noun* a conservationist or environmentalist

Green Line /ˌgriːn 'laɪn/ *noun* in the state of Israel, the pre-1967 border along the West Bank and the Gaza Strip

Green Paper /ˌgriːn ˈpeɪpə/ *noun* in the United Kingdom or Canada, a discussion document from the government on possible proposals for a new law. Compare **White Paper** (NOTE: A Green Paper is issued when plans for legislation are at quite an early stage and the government is open to further suggestions. A White Paper is issued generally when plans are more fully developed and it may be very close to the final Bill.)

Green Party /ˈgriːn ˈpɑːti/, **the Greens** /ðə ˈgriːnz/ *noun* the political party existing in several countries, which is concerned mainly with environmental and health issues

greymail /ˈgreɪmeɪl/ *noun* a threat used by the defence in a spy trial to reveal national secrets unless the government drops the case against the defendant

grey vote /ˈgreɪ vəʊt/ *noun* older people considered as a group that can be influenced to vote in a specific way ○ *The healthcare issue will affect the grey vote.*

Grit /grɪt/ *noun, adjective* in Canada, a Liberal (*informal*)

gross domestic product /ˌgrəʊs dəˌmestɪk ˈprɒdʌkt/ *noun* the annual value of goods sold and services paid for inside a country. Abbr **GDP**

gross national product /ˌgrəʊs ˌnæʃ(ə)nəl ˈprɒdʌkt/ *noun* the annual value of goods and services in a country including income from other countries. Abbr **GNP**

grounds /graʊndz/ *noun* the basic reasons for believing something or for doing something ○ *She retired on medical grounds.* ○ *Does he have good grounds for complaint?* ○ *There are no grounds for thinking any misconduct has occurred.*

Group of Eight /ˌgruːp əv ˈeɪt/ *noun* full form of **G8**

groupuscule /ˈgruːpəskjuːl/ *noun* a very small and extreme political group

gubernatorial /ˌguːbənəˈtɔːriəl/ *adjective* relating to a governor, especially a governor of a US state

guerrilla /gəˈrɪlə/, **guerilla** *noun* a person or small group fighting an enemy often in a civil war, but not a member of an official army ○ *After the defeat of the army, guerrilla groups sprang up all over the country.* ○ *Guerrillas have attacked government outposts in many parts of the North.*

guest country /ˌgest ˈkʌntri/ *noun* a country invited to an international meeting, without the right to vote

guidelines /ˈgaɪdlaɪnz/ *plural noun* instructions or suggestions as to how something should be done ○ *The government has issued guidelines on increases in wages and prices.* ○ *The National Union of Teachers has issued guidelines to its members on dealing with claims.* ○ *The Secretary of State can issue guidelines for expenditure.* ○ *The minister said he was not laying down guidelines for the spending of money which was not earmarked for special projects.*

guillotine /ˈgɪlətiːn/ *noun* **1.** a motion in the House of Commons to end a debate on a clause of a Bill at an agreed time and generally without allowing a full debate **2.** the machine formerly used in France for executing criminals by cutting off their heads ■ *verb* **1.** in the House of Commons, to end a debate at an agreed time, and generally without allowing a full debate to take place **2.** to execute someone by cutting his or her head off with a guillotine

gulag /ˈguːlæg/ *noun* the network of political prisons and labour camps in the former Soviet Union

Gulf States /ˌgʌlf ˈsteɪts/ *noun* **1.** the countries that border the Persian Gulf and are producers of oil, i.e. Iran, Iraq, Kuwait, Saudi Arabia, Bahrain, Qatar, the United Arab Emirates and Oman **2.** the states of the southern United States that border the Gulf of Mexico, i.e. Florida, Alabama, Mississippi, Louisiana and Texas

gun amnesty /ˈgʌn ˌæmnəsti/ *noun* an arrangement where any person having a gun illegally can hand the gun in to the police without being prosecuted for it

gunboat diplomacy /ˌgʌnbəʊt dɪˈpləʊməsi/ *noun* the attempt to solve international problems by force or by threatening to use force. ◊ **diplomacy**

Gunpowder Plot /ˈgʌnˌpaʊdə plɒt/ *noun* a conspiracy by a group of Roman Catholics, including Guy Fawkes, to blow up Parliament in 1605

gynaecocracy /ˌgaɪnɪˈkɒləkrəsi/ *noun* political control by women, or a political system that gives power to women

gynarchy /ˈgaɪnɑːki/ *noun* same as **gynaecocracy**

gynocracy /gaɪˈnɒkrəsi/ *noun* same as **gynaecocracy**

H

hack /hæk/ *noun* **1.** a journalist or writer, especially one who does routine work or work that is not very good **2.** a political party member who works for the party uncritically in a routine job

Hail to the Chief /ˌheɪl tə ðə ˈtʃiːf/ *noun* the piece of military music played to greet the President of the United States

Hamas /ˈhæmæs/ *noun* a fundamentalist Islamic Palestinian organisation engaged in resistance to Israel in the Israeli-occupied territories

hamlet /ˈhæmlət/ *noun* a small village

hammer and sickle /ˌhæmə ən ˈsɪk(ə)l/ *noun* a symbol of Soviet Communism representing industrial and agricultural workers, used on the flag of the former Soviet Union

hand down /ˌhænd ˈdaʊn/ *verb* **1.** to pass something from one generation to another ○ *The house has been handed down from father to son since the nineteenth century.* **2.** to deliver a judgment or decision

hand over /ˌhænd ˈəʊvə/ *verb* to pass something to someone ○ *She handed over the documents to the lawyer.*

Hansard /ˈhænsɑːd/ *noun* the official report of everything that is said and done in the House of Commons and the House of Lords

COMMENT: These reports were first published by Luke Hansard in 1774 and are now published daily by the Stationery Office. Each page is divided into two numbered columns, so a reference to a particular speech in Hansard could read: Vol.120, No.24, 22 July 1987, Col. 370.

Hansard reporter /ˈhænˌsɑːd rɪ ˈpɔːtə/ *noun* one of the people who take notes of the debates in Parliament for printing in Hansard

hard currency /ˌhɑːd ˈkʌrənsi/ *noun* the currency of a country which has a strong economy and which can be changed into other currencies

hardliner /hɑːdˈlaɪnə/ *noun* a person who is inflexible, especially over policy ○ *Hardliners in the Government are pushing the President to refuse to talk to the rebel leader.*

harmonisation /ˌhɑːmənaɪ ˈzeɪʃ(ə)n/, **harmonization** *noun* the process of bringing a number of different rules or systems in different countries into a position where they are parallel or similar to one another ○ *harmonisation of tax policies throughout the EU*

harmonise /ˈhɑːmənaɪz/, **harmonize** *verb* to bring a number of different rules or systems into a position where they are similar or parallel to one another

hawk /hɔːk/ *noun* a person who believes in threatening or using armed force as a means of settling problems between countries. Compare **dove**

hawkish /ˈhɔːkɪʃ/ *adjective* favouring military force rather than diplomatic solutions to foreign policy issues ○ *The agreement will not satisfy the more hawkish members of the Cabinet.* Compare **doveish**

HE /ˌaɪtʃ ˈiː/ *abbreviation* His Excellency *or* Her Excellency

head /hed/ *noun* **1.** the most important person **2.** the most important or main ○ *head clerk* ○ *head porter* ○ *head salesman* ○ *head waiter* **3.** the top part or first part ○ *Write the name of the company at the head of the list.* **4.** a person ○ *Allow £10 per head for expenses.* ○ *Factory inspectors cost on average £25,000 per head per annum.* ■ *verb* to be the manager or to be the most important person ○ *to head a department* ○ *She is heading a government delegation to China.*

headed /ˈhedɪd/ *adjective* having a name and address printed at the top of a piece of paper

headhunt /ˈhedhʌnt/ *verb* to look for suitable people and offer them jobs in other companies

heading /ˈhedɪŋ/ *noun* the title printed at the beginning of a section of a document

head of government /ˌhed əv ˈɡʌv(ə)nmənt/ *noun* the leader of a country's government. ◊ **Prime Minister**

head of protocol /ˌhed əv ˈprəʊtəkɒl/ *noun* an official in an embassy who is concerned with relations with the government of the country where the embassy is and with other embassies

head of state /ˌhed əv ˈsteɪt/ *noun* the official leader of a country, who in some cases is also the head of the government, e.g. a king, queen or president

COMMENT: A head of state may not have much political power and may be restricted to ceremonial duties such as meeting ambassadors, laying wreaths at national memorials, opening parliament, etc. The head of government is usually the effective ruler of the country, except in countries where the President is the executive ruler, and the head of government is in charge of the administration. In the United Kingdom, the Queen is head of state, and the Prime Minister is head of government. In the United States, the President is both head of state and head of government.

headquarters /hedˈkwɔːtəz/ *plural noun* the main office of an organisation. Abbr **HQ**

heads of agreement /ˌhedz əv ə ˈɡriːmənt/ *noun* a draft agreement containing the most important points but not all the details

Health and Safety at Work Act /ˌhelθ ən ˌseɪfti ət ˈwɜːk ˌækt/ *noun* the Act of Parliament which regulates what employers must do to make sure that their workers are kept healthy and safe at work

Health Canada /ˌhelθ ˈkænədə/ *noun* the Canadian government department that is responsible for protecting the health and safety of the people of Canada

Health Service Commissioners /ˌhelθ ˌsɜːvɪs kəˈmɪʃənəz/, **Health Service Ombudsmen** *noun* the officials who investigate complaints from the public about the National Health Service

hear /hɪə/ *verb* □ **hear! hear!** words used in a meeting to show that you agree with the person speaking

hearing /ˈhɪərɪŋ/ *noun* **1.** a case which is being heard by a committee, tribunal or court of law ○ *The hearing about the planning application lasted ten days.* **2.** the opportunity of speaking to an official body about something ○ *He asked to be given a hearing by the full council so that he could state his case.*

heartland /ˈhɑːtlænd/ *noun* **1.** a central area of a country or region that has special economic, political, military or sentimental significance **2.** an area of a country where a particular activity or opinion is common ○ *the industrial heartland* ○ *The new party has made advances into the Conservative heartlands.*

heckle /ˈhek(ə)l/ *verb* to shout remarks, insults or questions in order to upset someone who is making a speech

hegemony /hɪˈɡeməni/ *noun* the leadership by one strong state over a group of other states, usually in the same area

heir apparent /ˌeər əˈpærənt/ *noun* an heir whose inheritance cannot be altered by the birth of another heir

heir presumptive /ˌeə prɪ
ˈzʌmptɪv/ *noun* an heir whose inheritance will pass to another heir if one is born whose entitlement is greater

helotism /ˈhiːlətɪz(ə)m/ *noun* a political or social system in which one group, class or country is systematically oppressed by another

hemicycle /ˈhemiˌsaɪk(ə)l/ *noun* a meeting room with seats in the form of a semicircle ○ *MEPs meet in the hemicycle.*

henceforth /hensˈfɔːθ/ *adverb* from this time on ○ *Henceforth it will be more difficult to avoid customs examinations.*

henchman /ˈhentʃmən/ *noun* someone, especially a man, who is a close supporter or associate of someone in an important position, often using strong methods to carry out their wishes

henchwoman /ˈhentʃwʊmən/ *noun* a woman who is a close supporter or associate of someone in an important position, often using strong methods to carry out their wishes

heptarch /ˈheptɑːk/ *noun* one of the seven rulers in a heptarchy

heptarchy /ˈheptɑːki/ *noun* **1.** government by seven rulers or leaders **2.** a state governed by seven rulers, or a state divided into seven parts, each ruled by a different leader

here- /hɪə/ *prefix* this time or this point

hereafter /hɪərˈɑːftə/ *adverb* from this time or point on

hereby /hɪəˈbaɪ/ *adverb* in this way or by this letter ○ *We hereby revoke the agreement of January 1st 1982.*

hereditament /ˌherɪˈdɪtəmənt/ *noun* property which can be passed from parents to their children

hereditary /həˈredɪt(ə)ri/ *adjective* passed from one member of a family to another

hereditary office /həˌredɪt(ə)ri ˈɒfɪs/ *noun* an official position which is passed from one member of a family to another

herein /ˌhɪərˈɪn/ *adverb* in this document ○ *the conditions stated herein* ○ *See the reference herein above.*

hereinafter /ˌhɪərɪnˈɑːftə/ *adverb* stated later in this document ○ *the conditions hereinafter listed*

hereof /ˌhɪərˈɒv/ *adverb* of this

hereto /ˌhɪəˈtuː/ *adverb* to this ○ *according to the schedule of payments attached hereto* □ **as witness hereto** as a witness of this fact

heretofore /ˈhɪətəˌfɔː/ *adverb* previously or earlier

hereunder /ˌhɪərˈʌndə/ *adverb* below this point in a document ○ *See the documents listed hereunder.*

Her Majesty's government /ˌhɜː
ˌmædʒəstiz ˈgʌv(ə)nmənt/ *noun* the official title of the government of the United Kingdom

Her Majesty's pleasure /ˌhɜː
ˌmædʒəstiz ˈpleʒə/ *noun* □ **detention or during Her Majesty's pleasure** detention for an indefinite period, until the Home Secretary decides that a prisoner can be released

Her Majesty's Stationery Office *noun* the government department which prints documents for all government departments and also publishes and sells books for the government. Abbr **HMSO**. Also called **The Stationery Office**

heteronomous /ˌhetəˈrɒnəməs/ *adjective* subject to laws and rules imposed by other people or institutions. Compare **autonomous**

hierarchy /ˈhaɪərɑːki/ *noun* the arrangement of an organisation in various ranks, with fewer and fewer people in the higher ranks ○ *He started as a local official and rapidly rose through the ranks of the party hierarchy.*

hierocracy /ˌhaɪəˈrɒkrəsi/ *noun* **1.** government by clergy **2.** a body of clergy that rules a place or country

High Commission /ˌhaɪ kə
ˈmɪʃ(ə)n/ *noun* **1.** in a Commonwealth country, an embassy ○ *the British High Commission in Ottawa* or *the*

UK High Commission in Ottawa ○ *The High Commission staff were told not to speak to journalists.* ○ *She is joining the High Commission as an interpreter.* **2.** the office of a High Commissioner

High Commissioner /ˌhaɪ kə'mɪʃ(ə)nə/ *noun* a person who represents a Commonwealth country in another Commonwealth country, having the same rank and the same duties as an ambassador

High Court /ˌhaɪ 'kɔːt/, **High Court of Justice** /ˌhaɪ kɔːt əv 'dʒʌstɪs/ *noun* the main civil court in England and Wales

High Court of Justiciary /ˌhaɪ kɔːt əv dʒʌ'stɪʃiəri/ *noun* the highest criminal court of Scotland

high flyer /ˌhaɪ 'flaɪə/ *noun* **1.** a person who is very successful or who is likely to get a very important job **2.** a share whose market price is rising rapidly

high-level /ˌhaɪ ˌlev(ə)l/ *adjective* involving participation by people who have important positions in their organisation or country ○ *high-level talks*

highlight /'haɪlaɪt/ *verb* to emphasise an important point ○ *The report highlighted weaknesses in the work of the department.* ■ *noun* the best part of something ○ *The speech of the Deputy Prime Minister was the highlight of the Party Conference.*

high-profile /ˌhaɪ 'prəʊfaɪl/ *adjective* in or intended to be noticeable to the public, e.g. to attract attention, support or business ○ *a high-profile politician* ○ *a high-profile public information campaign*

High Sheriff /ˌhaɪ 'ʃerɪf/ *noun* the senior representative appointed by the Crown in a county

high treason /ˌhaɪ 'triːz(ə)n/ *noun* the formal way of referring to treason

highway /'haɪweɪ/ *noun* a main road

Highway Code /ˌhaɪweɪ 'kəʊd/ *noun* the rules which govern the behaviour of people and vehicles using roads

Highways Agency /'haɪweɪz ˌeɪdʒənsi/ *noun* an executive agency of the Department of Transport that operates, maintains and improves the main roads in Britain

highways committee /'haɪweɪz kə,mɪti/ *noun* the committee of a local council with deals with roads and paths

Highways Department /'haɪweɪz dɪ,pɑːtmənt/ *noun* the part of a local council that looks after the main roads

Hilary /'hɪləri/ *noun* one of the four law terms in a year

historic /hɪ'stɒrɪk/ *adjective* **1.** old or having a long history ○ *The council is trying to redevelop the historic centre of the city.* ○ *The building is preserved as a historic monument.* **2.** important and likely to be remembered ○ *The MP, opening the town's first shopping precinct, said that it was a historic occasion.*

HK *abbreviation* House of Keys

HL /ˌeɪtʃ 'el/ *abbreviation* House of Lords

HMG *abbreviation* **1.** Her Majesty's Government **2.** His Majesty's Government

HMS /ˌeɪtʃ ˌem 'es/ *abbreviation* **1.** Her Majesty's Service **2.** His Majesty's Service

HMSO *abbreviation* Her Majesty's Stationery Office

Hobbes, Thomas /hɒbz/ *noun* the English philosopher (1588–1679) whose Leviathan defended the right of a ruler to use absolute power in order to keep peace (NOTE: Hobbes said that without government, life for people in a state of nature or anarchy would be 'nasty, solitary, brutish and short'.)

hoc ♦ ad hoc

hold /həʊld/ *verb* □ **to hold a seat** (*of a party or candidate*) to have a member elected for a constituency of the same party as the previous member ○ *Labour held the seat with an increased majority.*

hold back /ˌhəʊld 'bæk/ *verb* to wait or not to go forward

hold down /ˌhəʊld 'daʊn/ *verb* to control strictly or to keep in check ○ *The Government is trying to hold down food prices.* ○ *The army has been sent to hold down the rebel areas.*

hold out /ˌhəʊld 'aʊt/ *verb* **1.** to offer ○ *The negotiators held out the possibility of increased aid.* ○ *The chairman held out the possibility of rapid promotion.* **2.** to remain in a place or position, while being attacked ○ *The rebels are holding out in the government radio station.*

hold over /ˌhəʊld 'əʊvə/ *verb* to put back to a later date ○ *Discussion of item 4 was held over until the next meeting.*

holdover /'həʊldəʊvə/ *noun* someone who remains in a job or other position that has come under different control ○ *A holdover from the previous administration at the Pentagon agency ordered the destruction of classified documents.*

hold to /'həʊld tuː/ *verb* to keep or limit □ **the government hopes to hold wage increases to 5%** the government hopes that wage increases will not be more than 5%

hold up /ˌhəʊld 'ʌp/ *verb* **1.** to show or display ○ *The agreement was held up as an example of good management-worker relations.* **2.** to stay at a high level ○ *Share prices have held up well.* ○ *Sales held up during the tourist season.* **3.** to delay ○ *The shipment has been held up at the customs.* ○ *Payment will be held up until the contract has been signed.*

holiday /'hɒlɪdeɪ/ *noun* a period away from work. ◊ **bank holiday**

home /həʊm/ *noun* **1.** a place where a person lives **2.** someone's country of origin, or the country where a company is based

homeland /'həʊmlænd/ *noun* **1.** the country where someone was born or where they live and have a sense of belonging to **2.** in South Africa under the apartheid system, a partly self-governing region set aside for the Black population

homeland security /'həʊmlænd sɪ'kjʊərɪti/ *noun US* safety and protection from terrorist attack of a country (NOTE: Following the terrorist attack of 11 September 2001, President Bush created a new executive department, the Department of Homeland Security.)

Home Office /'həʊm ˌɒfɪs/ *noun* the UK government ministry dealing with crime, the police and prisons

COMMENT: In most countries the government department dealing with the internal order of the country is called the Ministry of the Interior, with a Minister of the Interior in charge.

home rule /ˌhəʊm 'ruːl/ *noun* the right of an area of a country to rule itself after being governed by another country

COMMENT: Home Rule was the aim of Irish Nationalists between 1870 and 1920 when they were trying to achieve independence for Ireland.

Home Secretary /ˌhəʊm 'sekrət(ə)ri/ *noun* the minister of the UK government in charge of the Home Office, dealing with law and order, the police and prisons. Also called **Secretary of State for Home Affairs**

hon. *abbreviation* honourable

honest broker /ˌɒnɪst 'brəʊkə/ *noun* a person, group or country that helps two sides to come together in a dispute

honorary /'ɒnərəri/ *adjective* not paid a salary

honorary consul /ˌɒnərəri 'kɒnsəl/ *noun* a person who represents one country in a different country but is not paid a salary, and is not a professional diplomat

honourable /'ɒn(ə)rəb(ə)l/ *noun* the title used when one MP addresses another in the House of Commons ○ *The hon. Member for London East would do well to remember the conditions in her constituency.* ○ *Will my hon. Friend give way?* ○ *The hon.*

Gentleman is perfectly entitled to ask that question.

COMMENT: Various conventions are attached to the use of the word in Parliament. In general, MPs can refer to each other as 'the hon. Member for...'; the Speaker will refer to all MPs as 'hon. Members'. To distinguish MPs of one's own party from those on the other side of the House, an MP will say 'my hon. Friend'. To distinguish between women and men MPs, you can say 'the hon. Lady' or 'the hon. Gentleman'. Lawyers may be addressed as 'hon. and learned'.

Honours List /'ɒnəz lɪst/ *noun* a list of the people who have been or are to be awarded honours such as a peerage or membership of a chivalric order by the British monarch

hopper /'hɒpə/ *noun US* a box where bills are put after being introduced in the House of Representatives

horse-trading /'hɔːs ˌtreɪdɪŋ/ *noun* the negotiations between political parties or politicians or members of a committee to obtain a general agreement for something ○ *After a period of horse-trading, the committee agreed on the election of a member of one of the smaller parties as Chairman.*

hostile /'hɒstaɪl/ *adjective* not friendly, or aggressive ○ *The proposal was given a hostile reception by the main committee.*

hostile act /'hɒstaɪl ækt/ *noun* an unfriendly action which suggests that the country committing it is an enemy ○ *We consider the violation of our air space a hostile act.*

hostilities /hɒ'stɪlɪtiz/ *plural noun* armed fighting ○ *The president is trying to negotiate an end to hostilities in the region.*

hostility /hɒ'stɪlɪti/ *noun* an unfriendly attitude towards someone ○ *Her proposal was greeted by the rest of the committee with hostility.* ○ *Members of the public showed their hostility by throwing eggs.*

hot button /'hɒt ˌbʌt(ə)n/ *noun* something that is known to be likely to provoke a strong response, especially among voters or consumers

hot pursuit /ˌhɒt pə'sjuːt/ *noun* in international law, the right which is sometimes claimed to chase a ship into international waters or to chase suspected criminals across an international border into another country

house /haʊs/ *noun* **1.** one of the two chambers of a legislature, usually the lower chamber **2.** *also* **House** one of the two parts of the UK Parliament, either the House of Commons or the House of Lords ○ *The minister brought a matter to the attention of the House.* **3.** one of the two chambers of the United States Congress ○ *The bill was passed by both houses and sent to the President for signature.*

household /'haʊshəʊld/ *noun* the people living together in a house

householder /'haʊshəʊldə/ *noun* person who occupies a private house

House leader /ˌhaʊz 'liːdə/ *noun* **1.** (*in the UK*) the Leader of the House, a government minister and member of the cabinet, who is responsible for the administration of legislation in the House of Commons or House of Lords, and is the main government spokesman in the House **2.** (*in the USA*) the chief of one of the political parties in the House of Representatives

House of Assembly /ˌhaʊs əv ə 'sembli/ *noun* the legislative body in Barbados, Dominica, Tasmania and Zimbabwe

House of Chiefs /ˌhaʊz əv 'tʃiːfs/ *noun* the upper consultative council in Botswana

House of Commons /ˌhaʊs əv 'kɒmənz/ *noun* **1.** the lower house of the British Parliament, made up of 659 elected members **2.** the lower house of a legislature with two parts such as that in Canada

COMMENT: Members of the House of Commons (called MPs) are elected for five years, which is the maximum length of a Parliament. Bills can be presented in either the House of Commons or House of Lords, and sent to the other chamber for discussion and amendment. All bills relating to revenue must be introduced in the House of Commons, and most other bills are introduced there also.

House of Councillors /ˌhaʊz əv ˈkaʊnsɪləz/ *noun* the upper house of the legislature in Japan

House of Keys /ˌhaʊs əv ˈkiːz/ *noun* the lower house of the legislature of the Isle of Man

House of Lords /ˌhaʊs əv ˈlɔːdz/ *noun* the non-elected upper house of Parliament in the United Kingdom, made up of life peers, some hereditary peers and some bishops

COMMENT: The composition of the House of Lords was changed by the House of Lords act 1999; hereditary peers no longer sit there by right, although 92 remain, elected by their own party or crossbench (non-party) groups, or as Deputy Speakers, Committee Chairs, or to fill two hereditary royal appointments, the Earl Marshal and the Lord Great Chamberlain. The House of Lords was for centuries the highest court of appeal; now the only appeal from the House of Lords is to the European Court of Justice. Proposals for reform introduced in 2003–4 will remove the 'law lords' from the House of Lords and create a new Supreme Court. This is being done to make it quite clear that the judiciary is independent from the other two branches of government.

House of Representatives /ˌhaʊs əv reprɪˈzentətɪvz/ *noun* **1.** the lower house of the Congress of the United States of America, made up of 435 elected members **2.** the legislative body in many countries, including Antigua, Australia, Colombia, Cyprus, the Gambia, Jamaica, Japan, Jordan, Nepal, New Zealand, the Philippines, Trinidad and Tobago, Yemen

COMMENT: The members of the House of Representatives (called Congressmen or Congresswomen) are elected for two years. All bills relating to revenue must originate in the House of Representatives; otherwise bills can be proposed in either the House or the Senate and sent to the other chamber for discussion and amendment.

House of the People /ˌhaʊz əv ðə ˈpiːp(ə)l/ *noun* same as **Lok Sabha**

House Republican Leader /ˌhaʊz rɪˌpʌblɪkən ˈliːdə/ *noun* the head of the Republican Party in the House of Representatives

Houses of Parliament /ˌhaʊzɪz əv ˈpɑːləmənt/ **1.** the building where the British Parliament meets, containing the chambers of the House of Commons and the House of Lords **2.** the British Parliament

housing /ˈhaʊzɪŋ/ *noun* the supply of houses or flats for people to live in ○ *The council provides low-cost housing for families in the borough.* ○ *The family lives in council housing.*

housing association /ˈhaʊzɪŋ əˌsəʊsieɪʃ(ə)n/ *noun* an organisation subsidised by government, which provides cheap housing for people

housing department /ˈhaʊzɪŋ dɪˌpɑːtmənt/ *noun* the department of a local authority which deals with council houses and flats

housing list /ˈhaʊzɪŋ lɪst/ *noun* the list of people waiting to be placed in council housing ○ *They have been on the housing list for three years.*

Howard /ˈhaʊəd/, **John** (*b.* 1939) Australian prime minister (1996–)

Howard /ˈhaʊəd/, **Michael** (*b.* 1941) Elected as a Conservative to Parliament in 1982, he was Home Secretary from 1993 to 1997 and became leader of the Opposition in 2003

HP *abbreviation* Houses of Parliament

HQ *abbreviation* headquarters ○ *The party HQ was surrounded by demonstrators.*

HR *abbreviation* House of Representatives

HSE *abbreviation* Health and Safety Executive

HUD /hʌd/ *abbreviation US* Department of Housing and Urban Development

humanitarian aid /hjuːˌmænɪˈteəriən eɪd/ *noun* help in the form of essential basic food and medicines sent to countries suffering from famine or other disasters

humanitarian space /hjuː‚mænɪ
'teəriən speɪs/ *noun* a neutral zone
occupied by international aid agencies
in a region which is at war

human rights /‚hjuːmən 'raɪts/
plural noun the rights of individual
men and women to basic freedoms
such as freedom of speech and freedom of association

Human Rights Act /‚hjuːmən
'raɪts ‚ækt/ *noun* the Act of Parliament (1998) which incorporated the
European Convention on Human
Rights into British law

humble address /‚hʌmbəl ə'dres/
noun a formal communication from
one or both Houses of Parliament to
the Queen

Hundred Days /‚hʌndrəd 'deɪz/
plural noun the first 100 days of a new
administration in the USA, seen as a
test of that administration's ability

COMMENT: It was originally applied to
the first 100 days of president Roosevelt's administration in 1933, and is
now applied to all new administrations.

hung /hʌŋ/ *adjective* with no majority □ **hung council, hung parliament**
a council or parliament in which no
single party has enough votes to form
a government

hunger march /'hʌŋgə mɑːtʃ/
noun a march organised by unemployed people to draw attention to
their problems

hunger strike /'hʌŋgə straɪk/
noun a refusal to eat over a period of
time as a form of protest, especially by
a prisoner

Hural /'hjʊərəl/ *noun* the legislative
body in Mongolia

hustings /'hʌstɪŋz/ *noun* □ **at the
hustings** at a parliamentary election

COMMENT: The hustings were formerly
the booths where votes were taken, or
the platform on which candidates
stood to speak, but now the phrase is
used simply to mean 'at an election'.

Hutton Enquiry /'hʌtən ɪŋ
‚kwaɪəri/ *noun* a judicial enquiry
headed by Lord Justice Hutton in 2003
into the events surrounding the suicide
of a senior government scientist with
expertise on weapons of mass destruction in connection with the war with
Iraq (NOTE: Lord Hutton found that
the BBC had misreported government actions over the war with Iraq
and, to most people's surprise, made
very few criticisms of the government.)

Hybrid Bill /'haɪbrɪd bɪl/ *noun* a
parliamentary bill with some provisions affecting the public domain and
others affecting private interests

I

ICC *abbreviation* International Criminal Court

ICM /ˌaɪ siː ˈem/ *abbreviation* Intergovernmental Committee for Migrations

ID *abbreviation* identity *or* identification

ID card /ˌaɪ ˈdiː ˌkɑːd/ *noun* same as **identity card**

idem /ˈɪdem/ *pronoun* the same thing or the same person

identic /aɪˈdentɪk/ *adjective* referring to diplomatic notes sent, or diplomatic action taken, by two or more governments in exactly the same form

identity /aɪˈdentɪti/ *noun* who someone is

identity card /aɪˈdentɪti kɑːd/ *noun* a card carried by citizens of a country or members of a group to prove who they are

identity theft /aɪˈdentɪti θeft/ *noun* the stealing of personal information that makes it possible to use someone's bank account, credit card etc.

ideological /ˌaɪdiəˈlɒdʒɪk(ə)l/ *adjective* referring to ideology ○ *The two sections of the party have important ideological differences.*

ideologist, ideologue *noun* a person who follows a particular ideology (*often disapproving*)

ideology /ˌaɪdiˈɒlədʒi/ *noun* a set of basic ideas about life and society, such as religious or political opinions ○ *Most political parties are based on ideologies.* ○ *Marxist ideology states that a classless society will be established.*

IGC *abbreviation* Intergovernmental Conference

ignore /ɪɡˈnɔː/ *verb* to reject a bill of indictment because there is not enough evidence

illegal immigrant /ɪˌliːɡ(ə)l ˈɪmɪɡrənt/ *noun* a person who enters a country to live permanently without having the permission of the government to do so

ILO *abbreviation* International Labour Organisation

immigrant /ˈɪmɪɡrənt/ *noun* a person who moves into a country to live permanently

immigrate /ˈɪmɪɡreɪt/ *verb* to move into a country to live permanently

immigration /ˌɪmɪˈɡreɪʃ(ə)n/ *noun* moving into a country to live permanently

Immigration Laws /ˌɪmɪˈɡreɪʃ(ə)n lɔːz/ *plural noun* the legislation controlling the movement of people into a country to live there

immunity /ɪˈmjuːnɪti/ *noun* protection against arrest or prosecution ■ *US* the protection of members of Congress against being sued for libel or slander for statements made on the floor of the House (NOTE: The UK term is **privilege**.)

COMMENT: Immunity from prosecution is granted to magistrates, counsel and witnesses as regards their statements in judicial proceedings. Families and servants of diplomats may be covered by diplomatic immunity.

impartial /ɪmˈpɑːʃ(ə)l/ *adjective* not biased towards one group or political party or one side in a dispute or competition ○ *to give someone a fair and impartial hearing* ○ *A judgment must be impartial.*

impartiality /ɪmˌpɑːʃiˈælɪti/ *noun* the state of being impartial ○ *The newspapers doubted the impartiality of the Ombudsman.*

impartially /ɪmˈpɑːʃ(ə)li/ *adverb* not showing any bias towards one group or political party or one side in a dispute or competition ○ *ACAS has to act impartially towards the two parties in the dispute.*

impeach /ɪmˈpiːtʃ/ *verb* to charge a head of state, minister or judge with treason, bribery or with serious crimes

impeachment /ɪmˈpiːtʃmənt/ *noun* the charge of treason, bribery or serious crimes brought against a head of state, judge or minister (NOTE: Impeachments ended in Britain in the late 18th century, but have continued to be used occasionally under the Constitution of USA. In 1999 impeachment proceedings against President Clinton failed to gain sufficient support in the Senate.)

impending /ɪmˈpendɪŋ/ *adjective* about to happen soon ○ *The newspapers carried stories about the impending general election.*

imperial /ɪmˈpɪəriəl/ *adjective* referring to an empire ○ *the power of imperial Rome*

imperialism /ɪmˈpɪəriəlɪz(ə)m/ *noun* (*disapproving*) **1.** the idea or practice of having an empire formed of colonies **2.** the practice of controlling other countries as if they were part of an empire

imperialist /ɪmˈpɪəriəlɪst/ *adjective* referring to imperialism ■ *noun* a person who is in favour of empires and imperialism

imperialistic /ɪmpɪəriəˈlɪstɪk/ *adjective* referring to imperialism

COMMENT: Although imperialism is used to refer to states which have or had colonies such as Britain, France, Belgium or the Netherlands, it is now widely used to refer to states which exert strong influence over other states. This influence can be political, military or commercial: *cultural imperialism.*

implicate /ˈɪmplɪkeɪt/ *verb* to suggest or show that someone is involved in something ○ *Several ministers were implicated in the arms-selling scandal.*

import *noun* /ˈɪmpɔːt/ the bringing of foreign goods into a country to be sold ○ *The import of firearms is forbidden.* ■ *verb* /ɪmˈpɔːt/ to bring foreign goods into a country

import duty /ˈɪmpɔːt ˌdjuːti/ *noun* a tax on foreign goods brought into a country. Also called **customs duty**

import levy /ˈɪmpɔːt ˌlevi/ *noun* a tax on foreign goods brought into a country, e.g. in the European Union a tax on imports of farm produce from outside the EU

import quota /ˈɪmpɔːt ˌkwəʊtə/ *noun* a fixed quantity of a particular type of foreign goods which the government allows to be brought into the country ○ *The government has imposed a quota on the import of cars.* ○ *The quota on imported cars has been lifted.*

imports /ˈɪmpɔːts/ *plural noun* foreign goods brought into a country ○ *All imports must be declared to the customs.*

impose /ɪmˈpəʊz/ *verb* to ask someone to pay a fine ○ *to impose a tax on bicycles* ○ *The court imposed a fine of £100.* ○ *They tried to impose a ban on smoking.* ○ *The government imposed a special duty on oil.* ○ *The customs have imposed a 10% tax increase on electrical items.*

imposition /ˌɪmpəˈzɪʃ(ə)n/ *noun* **1.** the act of putting a tax on goods or services ○ *Council officials consider having to attending all-night sittings to be an imposition.* **2.** an unreasonable request

impound /ɪmˈpaʊnd/ *verb* to take something and keep it, usually because something illegal has been done ○ *The lorries were impounded by customs.*

impunity /ɪmˈpjuːnɪti/ *noun* freedom from threat of punishment

in abeyance /ˌɪn əˈbeɪəns/ *noun* being out of operation or use for a period □ **this law is in abeyance** this law in not being enforced at the present time

in absentia /ˌɪn æbˈsenʃə/ *adverb* while someone is not present ○ *The former President was tried and sentenced to death in absentia.*

inalienable /ɪnˈeɪliənəb(ə)l/ *adjective* which cannot be taken away or given away or sold

inaugurate /ɪˈnɔːɡjʊreɪt/ *verb* to mark the start of someone's period of office with a formal ceremony

inauguration /ɪˌnɔːɡjʊˈreɪʃ(ə)n/ *noun* the formal act of confirming someone in an official position, especially the President of the United States, or a ceremony held for this purpose

in camera /ˌɪn ˈkæm(ə)rə/ *adverb* in private or with no members of the public present ○ *The case was heard in camera.*

incitement /ɪnˈsaɪtmənt/ *noun* the crime of encouraging, persuading or advising someone to commit a crime □ **incitement to racial hatred** the offence of encouraging people to attack others because of their race, by words, actions or writing

inclusive /ɪnˈkluːsɪv/ *adjective* not excluding any group or section of society ○ *inclusive of tax* or *not inclusive of VAT* □ **the party conference runs from the 12th to the 16th inclusive** it starts on the morning of the 12th and ends on the evening of the 16th

inclusive language /ɪnˌkluːsɪv ˈlæŋɡwɪdʒ/ *noun* language that avoids careless discrimination against some people because of gender, class, ethnic group, etc. in the words and descriptions used

incomes policy /ˈɪnkʌmz ˌpɒlɪsi/ *noun* an economic policy that plans to control inflation by keeping control of wage levels

income tax /ˈɪnkʌm tæks/ *noun* a tax, mainly on what someone is paid

incoming /ˈɪnkʌmɪŋ/ *adjective* recently elected or appointed □ **the incoming government, the incoming Minister** the new government or the Minister who has just been appointed and is about to start working ○ *The chairman welcomed the incoming committee.* ○ *The incoming cabinet was sworn in at the Presidential palace.*

incompetency /ɪnˈkɒmpɪt(ə)nsi/ *noun* the state of not being legally able to do something

incompetent /ɪnˈkɒmpɪt(ə)nt/ *adjective* **1.** unable to work well or to perform some duty ○ *The Finance Minister is quite incompetent, but he is the President's brother-in-law.* ○ *The company has an incompetent sales director.* **2.** not legally able to do something ○ *She is incompetent to sign the contract.*

incorporate /ɪnˈkɔːpəreɪt/ *verb* **1.** to bring something in to form part of a main group or to make a document part of another document ○ *Income from the 1994 acquisition is incorporated into the accounts.* ○ *The list of markets is incorporated into the main contract.* **2.** to form a registered company ○ *a company incorporated in the USA* ○ *an incorporated company* ○ *J. Doe Incorporated* **3.** to give legal status and the right to have a council to a town

incorporation /ɪnˌkɔːpəˈreɪʃ(ə)n/ *noun* act of incorporating something

incumbency /ɪnˈkʌmbənsi/ *noun* the situation of being the holder of an elected position

incumbency effect /ɪnˈkʌmbənsi ɪˌfekt/ *noun* the way in which people who have already been elected to an office tend to be re-elected for a further term

incumbent /ɪnˈkʌmbənt/ *adjective* holding an official position ○ *the incumbent President* ■ *noun* a person who holds an official position ○ *There will be no changes in the governor's staff while the present incumbent is still in office.*

incursion /ɪnˈkɜːʃ(ə)n/ *noun* **1.** a raid or limited military attack on another country **2.** entry into an area where someone or something should not be

indefeasible right /ˌɪndɪfiːzɪb(ə)l 'raɪt/ *noun* a right which cannot be taken or given away

indemnification /ɪnˌdemnɪfɪ 'keɪʃən/ *noun* a promise of payment for loss or damage

independence /ˌɪndɪˈpendəns/ *noun* **1.** freedom from rule or control or influence of others ○ *The colony struggled to achieve independence.* ○ *Britain granted her colonies independence in the years after the Second World War.* ○ *An independence movement grew in the colony.* **2.** the time when a country became independent from another country ○ *The ten years since independence have seen many changes.*

Independence Day /ˌɪndɪ 'pendəns deɪ/ *noun* the day when a country celebrates its independence, e.g. July 4th in the USA

independent /ˌɪndɪˈpendənt/ *adjective* free or not controlled by anyone ○ *The council has asked an independent consultant to report on the housing department.* ○ *The country has been independent since 1956.*

Indian National Congress /ˈɪndiən ˈnæʃ(ə)nəl ˈkɒŋgres/ *noun* an Indian political party that led the struggle for independence from the British Empire and has dominated the post-independence government

Indian Subcontinent /ˌɪndiən ˌsʌbˈkɒntɪnənt/ *noun* India, Pakistan and Bangladesh

individual /ˌɪndɪˈvɪdʒuəl/ *noun* a single person ○ *He was approached by two individuals on a constituency matter.* ■ *adjective* referring to a single person or thing ○ *The records are kept in individual files.*

individualism /ˌɪndɪ 'vɪdʒuəlɪz(ə)m/ *noun* the political theory which places most importance on the rights of each person and tries

to free each person from too much social control and restriction

industrial /ɪnˈdʌstriəl/ *adjective* relating to work

industrial development /ɪn ˌdʌstriəl dɪˈveləpmənt/ *noun* the planning and building of new industries in special areas

industrial processes /ɪnˌdʌstriəl ˈprəʊsesɪz/ *plural noun* the methods and systems involved in making products in factories

Industrial Revolution /ɪn ˌdʌstriəl revəˈluːʃ(ə)n/ *noun* the period in the late 18th and early 19th centuries when industry began to develop

infiltrate /ˈɪnfɪltreɪt/ *verb* to enter an organisation secretly, without the officials knowing ○ *The club has been infiltrated by right-wing agitators.*

inflation /ɪnˈfleɪʃ(ə)n/ *noun* the situation where prices rise to keep up with increased money available to buy goods

influence /ˈɪnfluəns/ *noun* the effect on someone or something ○ *They said the president was acting under the influence of the Ambassador.* ○ *The decision of the court was not influenced by the speech of the Prime Minister.* ○ *We are suffering from the influence of a high exchange rate.* ■ *verb* to have an effect on someone or something ○ *The House was influenced in its decision by the gravity of the financial crisis.* ○ *The price of oil has influenced the price of industrial goods.* ○ *He was accused of trying to influence the Select Committee.*

influence peddling /ˈɪnfluəns ˌpedlɪŋ/ *noun* offering to use your influence, especially political power, for payment, to help a person or group achieve something

influential /ˌɪnfluˈenʃəl/ *noun* having the power to influence someone or something ○ *He is the chairman of the influential Foreign Affairs Committee.*

informal vote /ɪnˈfɔːm(ə)l vəʊt/ *noun* a ballot paper which is not filled in or is incorrectly filled in and is therefore declared invalid

information /ˌɪnfə'meɪʃ(ə)n/ *noun* details or facts about something or somebody

information office /ˌɪnfə 'meɪʃ(ə)n ˌɒfɪs/ *noun* an office where someone can answer questions from the public

infringe /ɪn'frɪndʒ/ *verb* to break a law or a right

inhabitant /ɪn'hæbɪt(ə)nt/ *noun* a person who lives in a building or town or country ○ *Spain has 39 million inhabitants.*

initiative /ɪ'nɪʃətɪv/ *noun* **1.** a decision to start doing something ○ *The president took the initiative in asking the rebel leader to come for a meeting.* ○ *The minister has proposed several initiatives to try to restart the deadlocked negotiations.* **2.** (*in Switzerland and the USA*) a move by a group of citizens to propose that something should be decided by a referendum

injunction /ɪn'dʒʌŋkʃ(ə)n/ *noun* a court order telling someone to stop doing something or not to do something ○ *He got an injunction preventing the company from selling his car.* ○ *The council applied for an injunction to stop the developer from continuing with the demolition.*

injustice /ɪn'dʒʌstɪs/ *noun* a lack of justice ○ *She complained about the injustice of the system.*

Inkatha *noun* a Zulu political party that was founded in South Africa in 1975

INLA *abbreviation* Irish National Liberation Army

inland /'ɪnlənd/ *adjective* inside a country □ **inland freight charges** charges for carrying goods from one part of the country to another

Inland Revenue /ˌɪnlənd 'revənjuː/ *noun* the department of the British government dealing with tax ○ *to make a declaration to the Inland Revenue*

Inland Revenue Department /ˌɪnlænd 'revəˌnjuː dɪˌpɑːtmənt/

noun in New Zealand, the government department responsible for the collection and administration of taxes. Abbr **IRD**

inner cabinet /ˌɪnə 'kæbɪnət/ *noun* an informal group of the most important members of the Cabinet, who under some Prime Ministers may meet with the Prime Minister and decide policy away from the rest of the Cabinet

inner city /ˌɪnə 'sɪti/ *noun* the central part of a large urban area, often an area of poverty, poor housing and other social problems

input tax /'ɪnpʊt tæks/ *noun* VAT paid on goods or services bought

inquire /ɪn'kwaɪə/, **enquire** /ɪŋ 'kwaɪə/ *verb* to ask questions about something ○ *He inquired if anything was wrong.* ○ *She inquired about the rate of inflation in other European countries.* ○ *The commission is inquiring into corruption in the customs service.*

inquiry /ɪn'kwaɪəri/, **enquiry** /ɪn 'kwaɪri/ *noun* an official investigation ○ *There has been a government inquiry into the loss of the secret documents.*

inquorate /ɪn'kwɔːreɪt/ *adjective* without the required number of people to hold or carry on a meeting ○ *The meeting was declared inquorate and had to be abandoned.*

in-service training /ˌɪn ˌsɜːvɪs 'treɪnɪŋ/ *noun* training offered by an employer to his or her staff ○ *The report suggested increasing in-service training facilities in the department.* Abbr **INSET**

inspector /ɪn'spektə/ *noun* **1.** an official whose job is to check that a particular activity or situation is follows approved standards □ **inspector of taxes, tax inspector** an official of the Inland Revenue who examines tax returns and decides how much tax each person should pay **2.** a British police officer of a rank above sergeant

inspectorate /ɪn'spekt(ə)rət/ *noun* a group of inspectors with the same area of responsibility □ **the school inspectorate** all local or national inspectors of schools

institute /'ɪnstɪtjuːt/ *noun* **1.** an official organisation **2.** the title of a professional organisation ○ *The Royal Institute of British Architects.* ■ *verb* to start something ○ *to institute proceedings against someone*

institution /ˌɪnstɪ'tjuːʃ(ə)n/ *noun* **1.** an organisation or society set up for a particular purpose **2.** a building for a special purpose

institutionalised /ˌɪnstɪ'tjuːʃ(ə)nəlaɪzd/, **institutionalized** *adjective* **1.** unable to live independently after having been in prison, hospital or other institution for a long time **2.** happening so often that it is considered to be normal even though wrong or harmful ○ *The office of US President has become institutionalised.*

instrument /'ɪnstrʊmənt/ *noun* **1.** a tool or piece of equipment **2.** a legal document

instrumentality /ˌɪnstrʊmen'tælɪti/ *noun* in the United States, a subsidiary branch of a department or agency

insular /'ɪnsjʊlə/ *adjective* **1.** referring to islands **2.** not interested in anything outside one's immediate surroundings

insularity /ˌɪnsjʊ'lærɪti/ *noun* indifference to anything outside one's immediate surroundings

insurable /ɪn'ʃʊərəb(ə)l/ *adjective* possible to insure

insurance /ɪn'ʃʊərəns/ *noun* the business of insuring

insurgency /ɪn'sɜːdʒənsi/ *noun* a state where many groups fight to try to bring down a government over a long period of time

insurgent /ɪn'sɜːdʒənt/ *noun* a person who fights to bring down a government by force ○ *The army tried to capture the leaders of the insurgents.*

insurrection /ˌɪnsə'rekʃən/ *noun* an armed attempt to overthrow a gov-

ernment ○ *The insurrection lasted two weeks.*

insurrectionist /ˌɪnsə'rekʃənɪst/ *noun* a person who takes part in an armed attempt to overthrow a government

integrationist /ˌɪntɪ'greɪʃ(ə)nɪst/ *noun* someone who works to promote or maintain integration ■ *adjective* promoting or maintaining integration

intelligence /ɪn'telɪdʒəns/ *noun* secret information

intelligence service /ɪn'telɪdʒəns ˌsɜːvɪs/ *noun* the government department which tries to discover other countries' secrets

inter- /ɪntə/ *prefix* between

inter alia /ˌɪntə 'eɪliə/ *Latin phrase meaning* 'among other things'

intercameral /ˌɪntə'kæmərəl/ *adjective* between the two chambers of a bicameral legislature

intercontinental /ˌɪntəkɒntɪ'nent(ə)l/ *adjective* between continents

interdependent /ˌɪntədɪ'pendənt/ *adjective* dependent on each other ○ *Great Britain and the EU are economically interdependent.*

interest /'ɪntrəst/ *noun* **1.** special attention ○ *The managing director takes no interest in the staff club.* ○ *The government has shown a lot of interest in the scheme.* **2.** the payment made by a borrower for the use of money, calculated as a percentage of the capital borrowed ○ *The bank pays 10% interest on deposits.* **3.** money paid as income on investments or loans ○ *to receive interest at 5%* ○ *the loan pays 5% interest* ○ *deposit which yields* or *gives* or *produces* or *bears 5% interest* ○ *account which earns interest at 10%* or *which earns 10% interest* **4.** the percentage to be paid for borrowing **5.** the right or title to a property or money invested in a company or financial share in, and part control over, a company

interest group /'ɪntrəst gruːp/ *noun* a group of people who work together for a specific reason, often by putting pressure on the government

interfere /ˌɪntəˈfɪə/ *verb* to get involved or to try to change something which is not your concern

intergovernmental /ˌɪntəˌgʌv(ə)n'ment(ə)l/ *adjective* between governments □ **intergovernmental communications** messages passed from one government to another

Intergovernmental Conference /ˌɪntəgʌv(ə)nment(ə)l 'kɒnf(ə)rəns/ *noun* **1.** a meeting for discussion in which many countries take part **2.** a special meeting of all the heads of the governments of the European Union, held every few years to make important decisions on the future development of the EU ► abbr **IGC**

Intergovernmental Panel on Climate Change /ˌɪntəgʌv(ə)n ment(ə)l 'pæn(ə)l ɒn 'klaɪmət tʃeɪndʒ/ *noun* an international body set up in 1988 to assess information relating to climate change caused by human activities. Abbr **IPCC**

interim /'ɪntərɪm/ *adjective* serving temporarily until a permanent replacement can be elected or appointed

interior /ɪn'tɪəriə/ *adjective* relating to the internal affairs of a country, especially as opposed to its foreign relations

internal /ɪn'tɜːn(ə)l/ *adjective* referring to the inside □ **an internal memo** a memo from one department in an organisation to another □ **internal affairs of a country** the way in which a country deals with its own citizens ○ *It is not usual for one country to criticise the internal affairs of another.*

Internal Revenue Service /ɪn ˌtɜːn(ə)l 'revənjuː ˌsɜːvɪs/ *noun* the department of the US government dealing with income tax. Abbr **IRS** (NOTE: The UK equivalent is the **Inland Revenue.**)

international /ˌɪntə'næʃ(ə)nəl/ *adjective* involving two or more countries

International /ˌɪntə'næʃ(ə)nəl/ *noun* any of four international Socialist, Communist, or Anarchist organisations formed in 1864, 1889, 1919, and 1938 respectively

International Court of Justice /ˌɪntənæʃ(ə)nəl ˌkɔːt əv 'dʒʌstɪs/ *noun* the court of the United Nations, which is in The Hague, Netherlands

International Criminal Court /ˌɪntə'næʃ(ə)nəl 'krɪmɪn(ə)l kɔːt/ *noun* the court set up by the United Nations to deal with war crimes and crimes against humanity committed by political leaders and those engaged in warfare. Abbr **ICC**

International Development Association /ˌɪntəˌnæʃ(ə)nəl dɪ 'veləpmənt əˌsəʊsieɪʃ(ə)n/ *noun* a specialised agency of the United Nations that provides credit to nations on less strict terms than the World Bank. Abbr **IDA**

Internationale /ˌɪntəˌnæʃ(ə)'nɑːl/ *noun* the song used as an anthem by Socialists and Communists

International Finance Corporation /ˌɪntənæʃ(ə)nəl 'faɪnæns ˌkɔːpəreɪʃ(ə)n/ *noun* a specialised agency of the United Nations that is affiliated with the World Bank and promotes private enterprise in developing nations by providing risk capital. Abbr **IFC**

internationalise /ˌɪntə 'næʃ(ə)nəlaɪz/ *verb* to place something under the protection or control of several countries instead of one country

internationalism /ˌɪntə 'næʃ(ə)nəlɪz(ə)m/ *noun* the idea that different countries should try to work together more closely

internationalist /ˌɪntə 'næʃ(ə)nəlɪst/ *noun* someone who supports greater cooperation between countries ■ *adjective* favouring greater cooperation between countries

International Labour Organisation /ˌɪntə'næʃ(ə)nəl 'leɪbə/ *noun* the organisation set up by the United Nations which tries to improve working conditions and workers' pay in member countries. Abbr **ILO**

international law /ˌɪntənæʃ(ə)nəl ˈlɔː/ *noun* the laws governing relations between countries

International Monetary Fund /ˌɪntəˈnæʃ(ə)nəl ˈmʌnɪt(ə)ri fʌnd/ *noun* an organisation of the United Nations, which is a type of bank that helps member states in financial difficulties, gives financial advice to members and encourages world trade. Abbr **IMF**

international politics /ˌɪntənæʃ(ə)nəl ˈpɒlɪtɪks/ *noun* the diplomatic and political interaction between the governments of different countries

international relations /ˌɪntə ˈnæʃ(ə)nəl rɪˈleɪʃ(ə)nz/ *plural noun* political activities undertaken between two or more countries ■ *noun* the branch of political science that studies relations between different countries

International Telecommunication Union *noun* a specialised agency of the United Nations that promotes international cooperation in telecommunications and allots radio frequencies for various purposes. Abbr **ITU**

internuncial /ˌɪntəˈnʌnsiəl/ *adjective* relating to an internuncio of the Roman Catholic Church

internuncio /ˌɪntəˈnʌnsiəʊ/ *noun* a diplomatic representative of the pope of a rank below a nuncio

interpellate /ɪnˈtɜːpəleɪt/ *verb* to interrupt a parliamentary debate by asking a question on an aspect of government policy

Interpol /ˈɪntəpɒl/ *noun* an international police organisation through which the member countries co-operate in solving crimes ○ *They warned Interpol that the man was thought to have gone to France or Spain.*

interpret /ɪnˈtɜːprɪt/ *verb* **1.** to say what you think something such as a document, law or decision means ○ *The chairman asked the Chief Executive to interpret the clause in the White Paper.* **2.** to translate what someone has said into another language ○ *My* assistant knows Spanish, so she will interpret for us.

interpretation /ɪnˌtɜːprɪˈteɪʃ(ə)n/ *noun* **1.** what someone thinks is the meaning of something such as a document, law or decision **2.** a translation of what has been said in one language into another

Interpretation Act /ɪnˌtɜːprɪ ˈteɪʃ(ə)n ækt/ *noun* an Act of Parliament which rules how words used in other Acts of Parliament are to be understood

interpreter /ɪnˈtɜːprɪtə/ *noun* a person who translates what someone has said into another language ○ *My assistant will act as interpreter.* ○ *The witness could not speak English and the court had to appoint an interpreter.*

interregnum /ˌɪntəˈregnəm/ *noun* the period between the end of the reign of one king or ruler and the beginning of the next

interrupt /ˌɪntəˈrʌpt/ *verb* to try to speak or to shout when someone else is talking

COMMENT: In the House of Commons, an MP is allowed to interrupt another MP only if he wants to ask the member who is speaking to explain something or to raise a point of order.

interstate controls /ˌɪntəsteɪt kənˈtrəʊlz/ *noun* restrictions on trade or the movement of people between one state and another

intervener /ˌɪntəˈviːnə/ *noun* a person who gets involved in an action to which he or she was not originally a party

intervention /ˌɪntəˈvenʃən/ *noun* **1.** acting to make a change ○ *the government's intervention in the foreign exchange markets* ○ *the central bank's intervention in the banking crisis* ○ *the Association's intervention in the labour dispute* **2.** an act of interfering in another country's affairs ○ *The Minister of Foreign Affairs said the President's remarks were an intervention in the domestic affairs of his country.*

interventionism /ˌɪntə ˈvenʃənɪz(ə)m/ *noun* political interference or military involvement by one country in the affairs of another

intitule *verb* to give a title to an Act of Parliament

intolerant /ɪn'tɒlərənt/ *adjective* refusing to accept that other people can have different opinions or ways of doing things ○ *Extremist political parties tend to be very intolerant.*

intranational /ˌɪntrə'næʃ(ə)nəl/ *adjective* existing or occurring within the boundaries of a single nation

intransigent /ɪn'trænsɪdʒənt/ *adjective* refusing to change or discuss compromise

intra vires /ˌɪntrə 'vaɪriːz/ *Latin phrase meaning* 'within the legal powers' ○ *The minister's action was ruled to be intra vires.* Compare **ultra vires**

introduce /ˌɪntrə'djuːs/ *verb* to present something or to put something forward ○ *He is introducing a Bill in Parliament to prevent the sale of drugs.* ○ *The department has introduced some new evidence to the Committee.* ○ *The education department has decided to introduce vegetarian meals in schools.*

introduction /ˌɪntrə'dʌkʃən/ *noun* an act of presenting something or putting something forward ○ *the introduction of new evidence into the case* □ **introduction of a Bill** putting forward a Bill for discussion in Parliament

invade /ɪn'veɪd/ *verb* **1.** to attack and enter another country **2.** to enter somewhere in large numbers or in a way that causes problems ○ *Corruption had invaded every area of public life.* □ **to invade someone's privacy** to prevent someone from doing what they want to do without being watched or interrupted by someone else ○ *The press even invaded their privacy on family holidays.*

invalidate /ɪn'vælɪdeɪt/ *verb* **1.** to make something legally or officially unacceptable ○ *Because the company has been taken over, the contract has been invalidated.* **2.** to show that

something previously said or done is wrong ○ *The recent findings invalidate the earlier study.*

invalidation /ɪnˌvælɪ'deɪʃən/ *noun* an act of making something legally or officially unacceptable

invalidity /ˌɪnvə'lɪdɪti/ *noun* **1.** the fact of being legally or officially unacceptable ○ *the invalidity of the contract* **2.** the condition of being ill and unable to work

invasion /ɪn'veɪʒ(ə)n/ *noun* an act of attacking and entering the territory of another country

ipso facto /ˌɪpsəʊ 'fæktəʊ/ *Latin phrase meaning* 'by this very fact' or 'the fact itself shows' ○ *The writing of the letter was ipso facto an admission that the Minister knew of the case.* ○ *He was chairman of the committee at the time of the investigation and ipso facto was seen to be under suspicion.*

IRA /'aɪrə/ *noun* an organisation of Irish nationalists who originally fought for an independent Ireland and who still want to achieve the unity of the island of Ireland. Full form **Irish Republican Army**

IRD *abbreviation* Inland Revenue Department

Irish Republican Army /'aɪrɪʃ rɪ'pʌblɪkən 'ɑːmi/ *noun* full form of **IRA**

IRO *abbreviation* **1.** International Refugee Organization **2.** international relief organization

Iron Curtain /'aɪən 'kɜːt(ə)n/ *noun* the imaginary barrier created by the policy of isolation which prevented freedom of travel and communication between Western and Eastern Europe during the Cold War

iron triangle /'aɪən 'traɪæŋɡəl/ *noun US* the close connection between interest groups, executive departments and Congressional committees in making policy

irredenta /ˌɪrɪ'dentə/ *noun* a territory that was formerly part of one country but is now ruled by another and is subject to claims that it should be returned to its former country

irredentism /ˌɪrɪˈdentɪz(ə)m/ *noun* the policy of trying to get back a region which has been lost to another country, or trying to take over a region which is felt to belong to the country because of similar language or culture

irredentist /ˌɪrɪˈdentɪst/ *noun* a supporter of irredentism ○ *The meeting was disrupted by Albanian irredentists.*

irregularity /ɪˌregjʊˈlærɪti/ *noun* something which does not conform to the rules

irresponsibility /ˌɪrɪspɒnsəˈbɪlɪti/ *noun* a failure to act in a responsible way

IRS *abbreviation* Internal Revenue Service

Islamic Jihad /ɪzˌlæmɪk dʒɪˈhæd/ *noun* an Islamic fundamentalist organisation that wants to create an Islamic Palestinian state by armed opposition to Israel and opposes pro-Western Arab governments

isolation /ˌaɪsəˈleɪʃ(ə)n/ *noun* **1.** the situation of a country which is not allied to other countries **2.** the situation of being alone or kept apart from other people

isolationism /ˌaɪsəˈleɪʃ(ə)nɪz(ə)m/ *noun* the political policy of a country refusing to make alliances with other countries

isolationist /ˌaɪsəˈleɪʃ(ə)nɪst/ *noun* a person who believes that his or her country should not make alliances with other countries

issue /ˈɪʃuː/ *noun* **1.** the subject of a dispute or discussion ○ *The speaker was told to deal with the issue being discussed.* ○ *The sale of the site raises a completely new issue.* **2.** an occasion of making new shares available ■ *verb* to announce something or make something available officially ○ *to issue a writ against someone* ○ *The chairman's office issued a statement.* ○ *The council was forced to issue a denial.* ○ *The government issued a report on London's traffic.* ○ *The Secretary of State issued guidelines for expenditure.* ○ *The Minister issued writs for libel in connection with allegations made in a Sunday newspaper.*

item /ˈaɪtəm/ *noun* **1.** something for sale **2.** a piece of information **3.** a matter for discussion □ **we will now take item four on the agenda** we will now discuss the fourth subject listed on the agenda

J

Janata Dal *noun* an Indian political party founded in India

Jefferson, Thomas /ˈdʒefəsən/ *noun* the American politician and writer (1743–1826) who wrote the Declaration of Independence and had a considerable influence on the American Constitution (NOTE: Jefferson was a democrat who wanted an educated population and believed that government ought to be limited by a system of checks and balances.)

Jerga /ˈdʒɜːgə/ ♦ **Loya Jerga**

Jim Crow /ˌdʒɪm ˈkrəʊ/ *noun* discrimination against Black people, especially by public segregation

jingoism /ˈdʒɪŋgəʊɪz(ə)m/ *noun* extreme patriotism

Job Centre /ˈdʒɒb ˌsentə/ *noun* the government office which lists and helps to fill jobs

job creation scheme /ˌdʒɒb kri ˈeɪʃ(ə)n ˌskiːm/ *noun* a government-backed plan to encourage new work for the unemployed

John Birch Society /ˌdʒɒn ˈbɜːtʃ səˌsaɪəti/ *noun* a right-wing political organisation formed in the United States to fight Communism

join /dʒɔɪn/ *verb* **1.** to put things together ○ *The appendix is joined to the report.* **2.** to become part of something ○ *They joined the Labour Party.*

joint /dʒɔɪnt/ *adjective* **1.** with two or more organisations or people linked together **2.** one of two or more people who work together or who are linked ○ *joint managing director* ○ *joint owner* ○ *joint signatory*

joint and several /ˌdʒɔɪnt ən ˈsev(ə)rəl/ *adjective* as a group together and also separately

joint commission of inquiry /ˌdʒɔɪnt kəˌmɪʃ(ə)n əv ɪnˈkwaɪəri/ *noun* a committee set up to look into something with representatives of various organisations on it

joint committee /ˌdʒɔɪnt kəˈmɪti/ *noun* **1.** a committee formed of equal numbers of members of the House of Commons and House of Lords **2.** *US* a committee with members of both House of Representatives and Senate, usually set up to investigate a serious problem

joint resolution /ˌdʒɔɪnt ˌrezə ˈluːʃ(ə)n/ *noun US* a motion passed by both the House of Representatives and the Senate

journal /ˈdʒɜːn(ə)l/ *noun* **1.** a diary or record of something which happens each day ○ *The chairman kept a journal during the negotiations.* **2.** an official record of the proceedings of a legislature such as the House of Commons, House of Lords, House of Representatives or Senate ○ *the Official Journal of the European Union*

journalist /ˈdʒɜːn(ə)lɪst/ *noun* someone who writes articles for a newspaper, or reports for TV or radio ○ *The council chairman asked the journalists to leave the committee room.*

JP *abbreviation* Justice of the Peace (NOTE: The plural is **JPs**.)

judge /dʒʌdʒ/ *noun* an official of the judicial branch who presides over a law court, and in civil cases decides which party is in the right ○ *a County Court judge* ○ *a judge in the Divorce Court* ○ *The judge sent him to prison for embezzlement.*

COMMENT: At present the appointment of judges is the work of the Lord Chancellor and Prime Minister. Under reforms announced in 2003–4, all judges will be appointed by an Independent Judicial Appointments Commission. The minimum requirement is that one should be a barrister or solicitor of ten years' standing. The majority of judges are barristers, but they cannot practise as barristers. The appointment of judges is not a political appointment, and judges remain in office unless they are found guilty of gross misconduct. In the USA, state judges can be appointed by the state governor or can be elected; in the Federal courts and the Supreme Court, judges are appointed by the President, but the appointment has to be approved by Congress.

Judge Advocate-General /ˌdʒʌdʒ ˌædvəkət ˈdʒen(ə)rəl/ *noun* a lawyer employed by the state to advise on all legal matters concerning the Army

Judge Advocate of the Fleet /ˌdʒʌdʒ ˌædvəkət əv ðə ˈfliːt/ *noun* a lawyer employed by the state to advise on all legal matters concerning the Royal Navy

judgement /ˈdʒʌdʒmənt/, **judgment** *noun* **1.** the ability to make a good decision ○ *The officer was criticised for showing lack of judgement.* ○ *The Minister's judgement is at fault.* **2.** a legal decision or an official decision of a court

Judges' Rules /ˌdʒʌdʒɪz ˈruːlz/ *plural noun* an informal set of rules governing how the police may question someone suspected of a crime

judicature /ˈdʒuːdɪkətʃə/ *noun* judges and the justice system as a whole

judice ♦ **sub judice**

judicial /dʒuːˈdɪʃ(ə)l/ *adjective* relating to judges and the justice system

Judicial Branch /dʒuːˈdɪʃ(ə)l brɑːntʃ/ *noun* same as **judiciary**

Judicial Committee of the House of Lords /dʒuː ˌdɪʃ(ə)l kə ˌmɪti əv ðə ˌhaʊs əv ˈlɔːdz/ *noun* the highest appeal court in England and Wales (NOTE: Reforms introduced in

2003–4 are likely replace the law lords with a Supreme Court)

Judicial Committee of the Privy Council /dʒuː ˌdɪʃ(ə)l kə ˌmɪti əv ðə ˌprɪvi ˈkaʊns(ə)l/ *noun* the appeal court for appeals from some Commonwealth countries and colonies

judicial review /dʒuː ˌdɪʃ(ə)l rɪ ˈvjuː/ *noun, noun* an examination of a case a second time by a higher court because a lower court has acted wrongly ■ *noun* an examination by a court of administrative or legislative decisions taken by an authority or government

judiciary /ˈdʒʊˈdɪʃəri/ *noun* the branch of government concerned with the system of justice. Also called **judicial branch** (NOTE: The other two branches are the executive and the legislative)

junior minister /ˈdʒuːniə ˈmɪnɪstə/ *noun* in a government or department, the Under-Secretary of State or Minister of State

junta /ˈdʒʌntə/ *noun* a ruling group which has taken power in a country by force ○ *The junta came to power six years ago and is formed of representatives of each of the armed forces.* (NOTE: The term is used mainly of military governments, and usually in South America; the word is correctly pronounced as /ˈhʊntə/ but this pronunciation is not often used in English.)

jurisdiction /ˌdʒʊərɪsˈdɪkʃən/ *noun* legal power over someone or something

jury /ˈdʒʊəri/ *noun* a group of twelve people who decide whether someone is guilty or not guilty on the basis of the evidence they hear in court

jury service /ˈdʒʊəri ˌsɜːvɪs/ *noun* the duty which each person has of serving on a jury if asked to do so (NOTE: The US term is **jury duty**.)

just /dʒʌst/ *adjective* fair or right □ **just war** war which is considered to be morally right

justice /'dʒʌstɪs/ *noun* **1.** the legal process of dealing with someone accused of a crime in court **2.** a judge or magistrate **3.** the title given to a High Court judge ○ *Mr Justice Adams* (NOTE: It is sometimes written as **J** after the judge's name: *Adams J.*)

Justice Department /'dʒʌstɪs dɪ 'pɑːtmənt/ *noun* **1.** a department of the Scottish Executive, responsible for all aspects of the legal system and the police **2.** *US* same as **Department of Justice**

justice of the peace /ˌdʒʌstɪs əv ðə 'piːs/ *noun* a person without legal training who works as a judge in a local court. Abbr **JP**

justice system /'dʒʌstɪs 'sɪstəm/ *noun* the legal process of judging people and giving punishments in court

justiciary /dʒʌs'tɪʃəri/ *noun* the system of justice or legal system □ **High Court of Justiciary** the highest criminal court in Scotland

K

kakistocracy /ˌkækɪstˈɒkrəsi/ *noun* government by the most unscrupulous or unsuitable people, or a state governed by such people

Kamer ◆ **Eerste Kamer, Tweede Kamer**

kangaroo /ˌkæŋɡəˈruː/ *noun* the system used when discussing a Bill, where some clauses are not discussed at all, but simply voted on, with the discussion then moving on to the next clause

keep down /ˌkiːp ˈdaʊn/ *verb* to control or oppress ○ *The generals have managed to keep down the country districts by stationing troops in the area.*

Keeper of the Great Seal /ˌkiːpər əv ðiː ˌɡreɪt ˈsiːl/ *noun* same as **Lord Chancellor** (NOTE: Reforms introduced in 2003–4 are likely to abolish the office of Lord Chancellor)

Keeper of the Seal /ˈkiːpə əv ðɪ siːl/ *noun* same as **Lord Chancellor** (NOTE: Reforms introduced in 2003–4 are likely to abolish the office of Lord Chancellor)

Kenesh ◆ **Uluk Kenesh**

Kennedy /ˈkenɪdi/, **John F.** (1917–63) 35th president of the United States, assassinated in Dallas, Texas, on 22 November 1963

Keynesianism *noun* the theory that government must compensate for insufficient business investment in times of recession by spending on its own projects

keynote /ˈkiːnəʊt/ *verb* **1.** to deliver the most important speech at a conference or meeting **2.** to outline an important policy in a speech or report

keynote address /ˈkiːnəʊt əˈdres/, **keynote speech** /ˈkiːˌnəʊt spiːtʃ/ *noun* the main speech at a conference by an important speaker who sums up the main areas to be discussed

kill /kɪl/ *verb* to stop discussion of a proposal ○ *The veto in the Security Council killed the resolution.*

king /kɪŋ/ *noun* the man who rules in a monarchy (NOTE: often used with a name as a title: *King Juan Carlos*)

kingdom /ˈkɪŋdəm/ *noun* a country ruled by a king or queen ○ *the United Kingdom of Great Britain and Northern Ireland* ○ *the kingdom of Saudi Arabia*

kingly /ˈkɪŋli/ *adjective* suitable for a king or like a king (NOTE: **kingly** shows approval, as opposed to **royal** which does not imply approval or condemnation)

kingmaker /ˈkɪŋˌmeɪkə/ *noun* someone with sufficient power to have an influence on who is appointed to important positions, usually within a government

kingship /ˈkɪŋʃɪp/ *noun* the rule of a king

King's Messenger /ˌkɪŋz ˈmesɪndʒə/ *noun* ◆ **Queen's Messenger**

kitchen cabinet /ˌkɪtʃɪn ˈkæbɪnət/ *noun* a private, unofficial committee of ministers, advisers and friends who advise some Prime Ministers or Presidents (NOTE: The term was first used to describe the advisors of the President of the USA, Andrew Jackson, who used to meet literally in the kitchen of the White House.)

Knesset *noun* the legislature in Israel

knight /naɪt/ *noun* a man who has received a title of honour from the king or queen ■ *verb* to make someone into a knight ○ *He was knighted in the Birthday honours list.*

knighthood /'naɪthʊd/ *noun* the position of being a knight

knock-on effect /ˌnɒk ɒn ɪ,fekt/ *noun* an indirect effect, following on from something ○ *The political unrest had a knock-on effect on the tourist industry.* ○ *The coup had a knock-on effect on the governments of neighbouring states.*

Kremlin /'kremlɪn/ *noun* a series of buildings surrounded by a high wall in the centre of Moscow, where the offices of the main ministers of the Russian Federation are situated (NOTE: often used to mean 'the Russian Government': *a Kremlin spokesman said the letter was helpful*)

Kremlinologist, Kremlin-watcher *noun* a non-Russian who specialises in studying the actions of the Russian political leadership and tries to guess what is really going on in Russia

L

Lab. *abbreviation* Labour

Labor /'leɪbə/ *noun* the Australian Labor Party ∎ *adjective* relating to the Australian Labor Party

Laborite /'leɪbəraɪt/ *noun* a member or supporter of the Australian Labor Party

labor union /'leɪbə ˌjʊnjən/ *noun* US an organisation which represents workers who are its members in discussions about pay and conditions of work with management (NOTE: The UK term is **trade union**.)

labour /'leɪbə/ *noun* **1.** heavy work (NOTE: The US spelling is **labor**.) **2.** workers in general (NOTE: The US spelling is **labor**.) □ **skilled labour** workers who have special knowledge or qualifications **3.** □ **labour law, labour laws, labour legislation** laws relating to the employment of workers (NOTE: The US spelling is **labor**.)

Labour, the Labour Party *adjective* relating to the Labour Party in the United Kingdom or New Zealand

labour force /'leɪbə fɔːs/ *noun* all the people who are available to work

labour-intensive /ˌleɪbər ɪn'tensɪv/ *adjective* a type of work that needs many people to do it

labourism /'leɪbərɪz(ə)m/ *noun* a political or social movement that works to ensure the rights of workers, or support for such a movement

labourist /'leɪbərɪst/ *noun* a supporter of the rights of workers

Labourite /'leɪbəraɪt/ *noun* a member or supporter of the Labour Party in the United Kingdom or New Zealand

labour mobility /ˌleɪbə məʊ'bɪlɪti/ *noun* the ability of people to move easily from one job to another, or from one place to another to find work

labour movement /'leɪbə 'muːvmənt/ *noun* the organisations working for the improvement of working conditions for workers

Labour Party /'leɪbə 'pɑːti/ *noun* a political party, one of the main parties in Britain which is on the left of the political spectrum. Also called **Labour**

COMMENT: The British Labour Party was founded in 1906 as a fusion of the Independent Labour Party and other workers' groups, including representatives from the Trades Union Congress. The Labour Party has been closely allied to the Trades Union Congress in the past. Members of trade unions pay a political levy to support the Party, and some Labour MPs are sponsored by trade unions.

ladies' gallery /'leɪdiz ˌɡæləri/ *noun* an area of the public gallery of the UK House of Commons that is kept for women only

Lady /'leɪdi/ *noun* a title given to the wife of a knight or baronet or baron or earl

COMMENT: In most case, the title is used before the family name without the Christian name. Where the title is used to indicate the daughter of a nobleman, the Christian name is used. So the wife of Sir Edwin Smith is Lady Smith; the daughter of the Duke of Northumberland is Lady Jane Percy.

Lady Mayoress /'leɪdi ˌmeə'res/ *noun* the wife of a Lord Mayor

laissez-faire, laisser-faire *noun* the political theory that a government should do nothing to control the economy ○ *Laissez-faire resulted in increased economic activity, but contributed to a rise in imports.*

lame duck /ˌleɪm ˈdʌk/ *noun* a company or administration which is in difficulties and which needs support ○ *The government has promised a rescue package for lame duck companies.*

lame duck administration or **presidency** /ˌleɪm dʌk ədˌmɪnɪ ˈstreɪʃ(ə)n/ *noun* a US administration towards the end of a President's second term, when there is very little incentive to do much

lame duck president /ˌleɪm dʌk ˈprezɪd(ə)nt/ *noun* a US president in the last part of the term of office, who cannot stand for re-election, and so lacks political force

LAMSAC *abbreviation* Local Authorities Management Services and Computer Committee

land /lænd/ *noun* **1.** an area of earth **2.** a nation or country ○ *The President welcomed the official delegation from the land of his ancestors.* **3. Land** one of the regions which make up the federal republic of Germany and also Austria (NOTE: The plural is **Länder**.)

COMMENT: Under English law, the ownership of all land is vested in the Crown, although individuals or other legal persons may hold estates in land, the most important of which are freehold estates, which amount to absolute ownership, and leasehold estates, which last for a fixed period of time. Ownership of land usually confers ownership of everything above and below the land. The process of buying and selling land is 'conveyancing'. Any contract transferring land or any interest in land must be in writing. Interests in land can be disposed of by a will.

Landlord and Tenant Act /ˌlændlɔːd ən ˈtenənt ˌækt/ *noun* the Act of Parliament which regulates the letting of property

landmark /ˈlændmɑːk/ *noun* **1.** a famous building or natural feature ○ *The Houses of Parliament and Westminster are well-known London landmarks.* **2.** an important event or decision ○ *The opening of the new bridge is a landmark in the town's history.*

landmark decision /ˌlændmɑːk dɪˈsɪʒ(ə)n/ *noun* an important legal or political decision

land office /ˈlænd ˌɒfɪs/ *noun* a government office that administers and records sales and transfers of public land

land reform /ˈlænd rɪˌfɔːm/ *noun* the policy of changing the ownership of agricultural land by government law, so that those owning no land receive some

Land Registry /ˈlænd ˌredʒɪstri/ *noun* the British government office where land is registered

landslide /ˈlændslaɪd/ *noun* a very large majority obtained in an election ○ *The Socialists won in a landslide.* □ **a landslide victory** or **win** an election success with a very large majority

Lands Tribunal /ˈlɑːndz traɪ ˌbjuːn(ə)l/ *noun* a court which deals with compensation claims relating to land

Landtag /ˈlænttɑːg/ *noun* the legislative assembly of a German or Austrian state

land tax /ˈlænd tæks/ *noun* a tax on the value of land owned

laodicean *adjective* lacking in religious or political commitment ■ *noun* someone who has no strong commitment to religion or politics

lapse /læps/ *noun* the ending of a right, contract or offer ■ *verb* to stop being valid or to stop being active ○ *The insurance policy lapsed because the premiums had not been paid.* □ **lapsed passport** a passport which is out of date

late-night /ˈleɪt naɪt/ *adjective* happening late at night ○ *The House of Commons had a late-night sitting.* ○ *Their late-night negotiations ended in an agreement signed at 3 a.m.*

law /lɔː/ *noun* **1.** a rule by which a country is governed and by which the activities of people and organisations are controlled ○ *A law has to be passed by Parliament.* ○ *The government has proposed a new law to regulate the sale of goods on Sundays.* **2.** all the statutes of a country taken together □ **inside the law**, **within the law** obeying the laws of a country □ **against the law**, **outside the law** not according to the laws of a country ○ *Dismissing an employee without reason is against the law.* ○ *The agents were operating outside the law.* □ **in law** according to the law ○ *What are the duties in law of a guardian?* □ **to break the law** to do something which is not allowed by law ○ *He is breaking the law by selling goods on Sunday.* ○ *You will be breaking the law if you try to take the goods out of the country without an export licence.* **3.** a general rule

law and order /ˌlɔː ənd ˈɔːdə/ *noun* a situation in which the laws of a country are being obeyed by most people ○ *There was a breakdown of law and order following the assassination of the president.*

Law Centre /ˈlɔː ˌsentə/ *noun* a local office with full-time staff who advise and represent people free of charge

Law Commission /ˈlɔː kə ˌmɪʃ(ə)n/ *noun* a permanent committee which reviews English law and recommends changes to it

law court /ˈlɔː kɔːt/ *noun* a place where a trial is held or where a judge listens to cases

law enforcement /ˈlɔː ɪn ˌfɔːsmənt/ *noun* the official activity of making sure that a law is obeyed

Law Lords /ˈlɔː lɔːdz/ *plural noun* the members of the House of Lords who are judges, including the Lord Chancellor and the Lords of Appeal in Ordinary (NOTE: Reforms proposed in 2003–4 are likely to remove these law lords from the House of Lords and set up a separate Supreme Court)

lawmaker /ˈlɔːmeɪkə/ *noun* a person who makes or passes laws, e.g. an MP or a Congressman

law-making /ˈlɔː ˌmeɪkɪŋ/ *noun* the making of laws ○ *Parliament is the law-making body in Great Britain.*

Law Officers /ˈlɔːr ˌɒfɪsːəz/ *plural noun* the posts of Attorney-General and Solicitor-General (in England and Wales) and Lord Advocate and Solicitor-General (in Scotland)

law reform /ˌlɔː rɪˈfɔːm/ *noun* the continuing process of revising laws to make them better suited to the needs of society

Law Reports /ˈlɔː rɪˌpɔːts/ *plural noun* the collection of reports of cases of special interest and importance, which may set legal precedents

lay /leɪ/ *verb* to put or present something ○ *The report of the planning committee was laid before the council.* □ **to lay an embargo on trade with a country** to forbid trade with a country □ **to lay a proposal before the House** to introduce a new Bill before Parliament ■ *adjective* not belonging to a profession or not trained to a professional standard in a subject ○ *The Committee has a chairman and several lay advisers.*

lay down /ˌleɪ ˈdaʊn/ *verb* to state clearly ○ *The conditions are laid down in the document.* ○ *The guidelines lay down rules for dealing with traffic offences.* (NOTE: **laying – laid – has laid**)

LC *abbreviation* Lord Chancellor

lead /liːd/ *verb* **1.** to be the first or to be in front ○ *The company leads the world in waste disposal.* **2.** to be the main person in a group ○ *The Parliamentary delegation is led by J.M. Jones, MP.* **3.** to start to do something, especially to start to present a motion for debate ○ *The Home Secretary will lead for the Government in the emergency debate.*

leader /ˈliːdə/ *noun* **1.** someone who is responsible for organising or controlling a group of people ○ *our political and military leaders* ○ *a meeting of world leaders* ○ *She was appointed leader of the delegation.* **2.** someone such as a person, company, country or something such as a product that is the most successful of its type ○ *a world leader in biomedical research* ○ *indus-*

try leaders in electronic surveillance systems

Leader of the Council /'li:də əv ðə 'kaʊns(ə)l/ *noun* same as **council leader** ○ *Councillor Jenkins, Leader of the Council, stated that the report would be examined at the next meeting.*

Leader of the House /ˌli:də əv ðə 'haʊs/ *noun* the senior government minister and member of the Cabinet, who is responsible for the administration of legislation in the House of Commons or House of Lords, and is the main government spokesman in the House (NOTE: Both people can be referred to as Leader of the House and more specific terms are Leader of the Commons and Leader of the Lords.)

Leader of the Opposition /ˌli:də əv ðɪ ˌɒpəˈzɪʃ(ə)n/ *noun* the head of the largest party opposing the government

leadership /'li:dəʃɪp/ *noun* **1.** the quality of being a good leader ○ *He showed leadership in defending the party against attacks by splinter groups.* **2.** the position of leader ○ *There are six candidates for the leadership of the party.* ○ *The leadership contest is wide open.* **3.** the few people who are the most important members of a party or group ○ *None of the party leadership appeared at the meeting.*

leading /'li:dɪŋ/ *adjective* most important ○ *He was the leading figure in the movement to increase pensions.*

lead to /'li:d tə/, **lead up to** /ˌli:d 'ʌp tuː/ *verb* to be the cause of ○ *The discussions led to a big argument between the management and the union.* ○ *We received a series of approaches leading up to the takeover bid.*

leaflet /'li:flət/ *noun* a sheet of paper advertising something, usually a single sheet perhaps folded in two ○ *Party workers distributed leaflets to all the householders in the constituency.* ■ *verb* to give leaflets to people in an area ○ *They leafleted all the houses in*

the electoral ward early on the morning of the election.

leafleting /'li:flətɪŋ/ *noun* the activity of giving out leaflets

league /li:g/ *noun* a group of people or states with similar aims, who come together to form a group and take action to further their aims

League of Nations /ˌli:g əv 'neɪʃ(ə)nz/ *noun* the group of states which joined between the First and Second World Wars in a group similar to the present United Nations

leak /li:k/ *noun* the unofficial passing of secret information or information which has not yet been published to newspapers or television stations ■ *verb* to pass information unofficially to newspapers or television stations ○ *The details of the plan have been leaked to the press to test public reaction.* ○ *Information about the government plans has been leaked to the Sunday papers.*

leakage /'li:kɪdʒ/ *noun* the unofficial release of secret information, usually to the media

leakproof /'li:kpruːf/ *adjective* not allowing secret information to be made public unofficially ○ *No committee is leakproof.*

leaky /'li:ki/ *adjective* allowing secret information to be made public unofficially

leave /li:v/ *noun* **1.** permission to do something ○ *The representative of the construction company asked leave of the council to show a detailed plan of the proposed development.* □ **'by your leave'** with your permission **2.** □ **leave of absence** permission to be absent from work or, in the case of an MP, to be away from the House of Commons

left /left/, **Left** *noun* **1.** the political parties which hold ideas in favour of change and furthering the interests of the working class and the poor **2.** the political ideas which support change, especially in the interests of the working class and the poor □ **swing to the left** a movement of support towards socialist principles □ **on the left** with views that are more strongly progressive and less conservative ○ *She's always been on the left of the Tory party.*

COMMENT: The division of political parties and political ideas into left, right and centre dates from the French Revolution when deputies in the National Assembly sat on the left or right of the chamber according to their views. It was easiest to apply these labels when socialists (left) parties faced conservative (right) parties in the middle years of the twentieth century. Some commentators say the old divisions of left and right are less and less relevant in the modern world, but they continue to be used.

leftism /ˈleftɪz(ə)m/ *noun* belief in a policy of liberal, socialist or communist political and social change or reform

leftist /ˈleftɪst/ *adjective* (*usually disapproving*) supporting the views of the left ○ *The minister is showing leftist tendencies.* ■ *noun* a person with left-wing ideas

left-of-centre /ˌleft əv ˈsentə/ *adjective* relating to political views that are slightly left-wing

left wing /ˌleft ˈwɪŋ/ *noun* the people who are more strongly socialist than others of their party ○ *the left wing of the Labour Party.*

left-wing /ˌleft ˈwɪŋ/ *adjective* strongly favouring the left ○ *She was criticised for abandoning her left-wing principles.* ○ *The party caucus has been infiltrated by left-wing activists.*

left-winger /left ˈwɪŋə/ *noun* a person with left-wing political ideas

legal /ˈliːg(ə)l/ *adjective* **1.** according to the law or allowed by the law ○ *The company's action was completely legal.* **2.** referring to the law ○ *legal advice*

Legal Aid scheme /ˌliːg(ə)l ˈeɪd skiːm/ *noun* the British government scheme where a person with very little money can have legal advice paid for by the state

legalisation /ˌliːgəlaɪˈzeɪʃ(ə)n/, **legalization** *noun* the process of making something legal that was previously not legal

legalise /ˈliːgəlaɪz/, **legalize** *verb* to make something legal ○ *a proposal to legalise certain drugs*

legality /lɪˈgælɪti/ *noun* the fact of something being legal ○ *They questioned the legality of the police action.*

legally /ˈliːgəli/ *adjective* according to the law ○ *In Australia, you are legally obliged to vote.* □ **legally binding** enforced by law ○ *signed a legally binding agreement*

legal system /ˈliːg(ə)l ˈsɪstəm/ *noun* the way in which the laws of a particular country are used to judge people in court

legate /ˈlegət/ *noun* an official representative of a government, especially a diplomat

legation /lɪˈgeɪʃ(ə)n/ *noun* **1.** a group of diplomats representing their country in another country at a lower level than an embassy **2.** a building in which a group of diplomats below the rank of ambassador works

legis ♦ **corpus legis**

legislate /ˈledʒɪsleɪt/ *verb* to make a law ○ *Parliament has legislated against the sale of drugs* or *to prevent the sale of drugs.*

legislation /ˌledʒɪˈsleɪʃ(ə)n/ *noun* laws or written rules which are passed by a parliament and implemented by the courts

'...the greatest happiness of the greatest number is the foundation of morals and legislation' [*Jeremy Bentham*]

legislative /ˈledʒɪslətɪv/ *adjective* relating to laws and the process or function of making new laws ○ *the legislative processes* ○ *Parliament has a legislative function.*

Legislative Assembly /ˌledʒɪslətɪv əˈsembli/ *noun* the lower house of the legislature in Australian states, Canadian provinces, Costa Rica, Panama and El Salvador

Legislative Branch /ˈledʒɪslətɪv brɑːntʃ/ *noun* same as **legislature**

Legislative Council /ˈledʒɪslətɪv ˈkaʊns(ə)l/ *noun* the upper house of the legislature in some Commonwealth countries, e.g. in most South Asian and Australian states

legislative day /'ledʒɪslətɪv deɪ/ *noun US* the time from the start of a meeting of one of the Houses of Congress to its adjournment. The House of Representatives usually adjourns at the end of each day, but the Senate may not, so that the Senate's legislative day can last several calendar days.

legislative veto /ˌledʒɪslətɪv 'viːtəʊ/ *noun* in the USA, a clause written into legislation which gives powers to government agencies stating that Congress may override a decision taken by the agency using of these powers

legislator /'ledʒɪsleɪtə/ *noun* a person who makes or passes laws, e.g. an MP or a Congressman

legislature /'ledʒɪslətʃə/ *noun* **1.** a body such as a parliament which makes laws ○ *Members of the legislature voted against the proposal.* Also called **Legislative Branch** (NOTE: The other two branches are the executive and the judicial.) **2.** the building where a parliament meets ○ *The protesters marched towards the State Legislature.*

legitimation /lɪˌdʒɪtɪ'meɪʃ(ə)n/ *noun* the way in which a political system or part of a political system is given the respect of the people so that it can do its work with authority (NOTE: One of the functions of parliament is said to be legitimation because laws made by parliament are the work of elected representatives of the people.)

legitimise /lɪ'dʒɪtɪmaɪz/, **legitimize** *verb* to make something legitimate and give it authority ○ *The support of the Prime Minister has legitimised attacks on the party activists.*

legitimist /lɪ'dʒɪtɪmɪst/ *noun* a person who supports the return to the throne of the rightful king or the rightful descendant of the last king

Leninism /'lenɪnɪz(ə)m/ *noun* Communist ideas put forward by the Russian follower of Marx, Vladimir Ilyich Lenin (1870 – 1924) who ruled Russia after the Revolution of 1917 (NOTE: Lenin believed that Marxism could be applied successfully only if the proletariat was led by an intellectual group which formed the main leadership of a governing and authoritarian party.)

Leninist /'lenɪnɪst/ *adjective* referring to Leninism ■ *noun* a person who supports and believes in Leninism

lese majesty /ˌleɪz 'mædʒəsti/ *noun* a criminal offence against a ruler or head of state

letters patent /ˌletəz 'peɪtənt/ *plural noun* an official document from the Crown, which gives someone the exclusive right to do something, especially making and selling an invention

leveller /'lev(ə)lə/ *noun* somebody who wants everyone in society to be equal

levy /'levi/ *noun* a tax or extra payment placed on goods or services ■ *verb* to collect a tax or an extra payment ○ *to levy a duty on the import of computer parts* ○ *The government has decided to levy a tax on imported cars.*

liability /ˌlaɪə'bɪlɪti/ *noun* the state of being legally responsible for paying for damage or loss ○ *The council has admitted liability but the amount of damages has not yet been agreed.*

liable /'laɪəb(ə)l/ *adjective* being legally responsible for paying for damage or loss

Lib. *abbreviation* Liberal

Lib Dem /ˌlɪb 'dem/ *abbreviation* Liberal Democrat

liberal /'lɪb(ə)rəl/ *adjective* **1.** allowing freedom to people or not controlling people ○ *The government has adopted a very liberal attitude towards tax reform.* (NOTE: To show the difference between the different meanings of the adjective, people sometimes say 'liberal with a small l' when not referring to political ideas.) **2.** generous ○ *He has given a liberal donation to party funds.* ■ *noun* a person who believes in individual freedom and the improvement of society

Liberal /'lɪb(ə)rəl/ *adjective* relating to the Liberal Party in the United Kingdom, Canada, or Australia ■ *noun* a member or supporter of the Liberal Party, e.g. in the United Kingdom, Canada, or Australia

liberal democracy /'lɪb(ə)rəl dɪ 'mɒkrəsi/ *noun* a political system that has free elections, many political parties, political decisions made by an independent legislature, independent judges, and law enforcement by the state

Liberal Democrat /'lɪb(ə)rəl 'deməkræt/ *noun* a member of the British Liberal and Social Democratic Party

Liberal Democratic Party /'lɪbrəl demə'krætɪk 'pɑːti/ *noun* a British political party formed in 1988 from the existing Liberal Party and some members of the Social Democratic Party (NOTE: often called **the Lib Dems**)

liberalism /'lɪb(ə)rəlɪz(ə)m/ *noun* the ideals and beliefs of liberals

Liberal Party /'lɪb(ə)rəl ˌpɑːti/ *noun* a political party which supports some social change, some involvement of the state in industry and welfare, but opposes the centralisation of government and has no fixed connections with either workers or employers (NOTE: The British Liberal Party developed from the Whig Party of the 17th and 18th centuries. The name Liberal was applied from the middle of the 19th century onwards.)

Liberal Party of Australia /'lɪb(ə)rəl 'pɑːti əv ɒs'treɪliə/ *noun* a conservative Australian political party which has almost always been in coalition with the National Party

liberation /ˌlɪbə'reɪʃ(ə)n/ *noun* the process of being set free from an oppressive regime

liberation theology /ˌlɪbə 'reɪʃ(ə)n θi'ɒlədʒi/ *noun* the religious theory developed in Latin America,

which involves the church in finding solutions to social problems

libertarian /ˌlɪbə'teəriən/ *noun* someone who believes that people should have complete freedom to think and act as they wish

liberty /'lɪbəti/ *noun* freedom □ **liberty of the individual** the freedom for each person to act within the law □ **liberty of the press** the freedom of newspapers to publish what they want within the law without censorship □ **liberty of the subject** the right of a citizen to be free unless convicted of a crime which is punishable by imprisonment ◇ **at liberty 1.** free or not in prison ○ *They are still at liberty while waiting for charges to be brought.* **2.** free to do something ○ *You are at liberty to complain if you are not satisfied with the service of the department.*

'...liberty is the right to do everything which the laws allow' [*Montesquieu*]

licence /'laɪs(ə)ns/ *noun* **1.** official permission to do something or to use something ○ *He granted his neighbour a licence to use his field.* (NOTE: The US spelling is **license.**) **2.** an official document showing that someone has permission to do something (NOTE: The US spelling is **license.**) □ **import licence, export licence** a document which allows goods to be imported or exported □ **licence to sell liquor, liquor licence** a document given by a Magistrates' Court allowing someone to sell alcohol

license /'laɪs(ə)ns/ *verb* to give someone official permission to do something ○ *licensed to sell beers, wines and spirits* ○ *to license a company to produce spare parts* ○ *She is licensed to drive a bus.* ○ *She is licensed to run an employment agency.* ■ *noun* US spelling of **licence**

lie upon the table /ˌlaɪ ʌˌpɒn ðə 'teɪb(ə)l/ *verb* (*of a petition*) to have been put before the House of Commons (NOTE: After a petition has been presented by an MP it is said to 'lie upon the table'.)

lieutenant /lef'tenənt/ *noun* a US police or fire department officer of a rank above sergeant ○ *The party leader's main lieutenant has decided to quit Parliament.*

lieutenant governor /lef,tenənt 'gʌv(ə)nə/ *noun* **1.** an elected official in a US state government of a rank below governor **2.** an official appointed by the Canadian federal government who acts for the Crown as the representative of the British monarch in a Canadian province

Lieutenant-Governor /lef,tenənt 'gʌv(ə)nə/ *noun* **1.** a representative of the British Crown in states or provinces of countries which are members of the Commonwealth ○ *the Lieutenant-Governor of Nova Scotia* **2.** *US* a deputy to the governor of a state

life peer /'laɪf pɪə/ *noun* a member of the House of Lords who is appointed for life, and whose title is not inherited when he or she dies

life peeress /'laɪf ,pɪəres/ *noun* a woman who is a life peer

limitrophe *adjective* on the border between countries or areas (*French*)

Lincoln /'lɪŋkən/, **Abraham** (1809–65) 16th president of the United States. 16th president of the United States, he led the North to victory in the US Civil War, and announced the emancipation of slaves in the southern states (1863). His Gettysburg Address, delivered on 19 November 1863, became one of the great texts of US history. He was assassinated by John Wilkes Booth while attending a performance at Ford's Theatre in Washington, DC.

Line of Control /,laɪn əv kən'trəʊl/ *noun* the line separating the areas of the disputed territory of Kashmir controlled by India and Pakistan, established in 1972

lingua franca /,lɪŋgwə 'fræŋkə/ *noun* a language which serves as the language of communication between different countries or different regions

linkage /'lɪŋkɪdʒ/ *noun* progress towards an objective which depends on concessions made by the various parties on other related issues

list system /'lɪst ,sɪstəm/ *noun* ♦ party list system

living standards /'lɪvɪŋ ,stændədz/ *plural noun* ♦ standard of living

Lloyd George /,lɔɪd 'dʒɔːdʒ/, **David, 1st Earl of Dwyfor** (1863–1945) the last Liberal prime minister of the United Kingdom (1916–22)

Lloyd's Register /,lɔɪdz 'redʒɪstə/ *noun* a list showing details of all the ships in the world

lobby /'lɒbi/ *noun* **1.** ♦ division lobby **2.** a group of people which tries to influence MPs or the passage of legislation □ **the car lobby** people who try to persuade MPs that cars should be encouraged and not restricted □ **the environmentalist lobby** group who try to persuade MPs that the environment must be protected, pollution stopped, etc. **3.** the group of journalists attached to the House of Commons, who are given information in regular official meetings by senior ministers or their assistants ■ *verb* to ask someone such as an MP or local official to do something on your behalf ○ *A group of local businessmen has gone to London to lobby their MPs on the problems of unemployment in the area.*

lobby correspondent /'lɒbi kɒrɪ,spɒndənt/ *noun* a journalist who is one of those attached to the House of Commons who receive information from ministers in regular official meetings

lobby fodder /,lɒbi 'fɒdə/ *noun* ordinary MPs who vote as their party tells them without thinking

lobbyist /'lɒbiɪst/ *noun* a person who is paid to represent a pressure group

lobby system /'lɒbi 'sɪstəm/ *noun* the system of employing professional lobbyists to attempt to influence political policy

local authority /,ləʊk(ə)l ɔː'θɒrɪti/ *noun* a section of elected government which runs an area, e.g. a district council

Local Commissioner /'ləʊk(ə)l kə'mɪʃ(ə)nə/, **Local Government Ombudsman** /'ləʊk(ə)l 'gʌv(ə)nmənt 'ɒmbʊdzmən/ *noun* an official who investigates complaints against local authorities

local council /'ləʊk(ə)l 'kaʊnsəl/ *noun* same as **council** *noun* 2

local election /'ləʊk(ə)l ɪ'lekʃən/ *noun* the elections to choose representatives for local government or for a town, city or county council. Also called **municipal elections**

local government /,ləʊk(ə)l 'gʌv(ə)nmənt/ *noun* administration and politics at the level below national government, e.g. county and borough councils

COMMENT: Local government in England and Wales is a two-tier system: county councils, with non-metropolitan district councils under them, and metropolitan district councils which are self-governing large urban areas. In Scotland there are nine large Regional Councils instead of county councils.

Local Government Ombudsman /'ləʊk(ə)l 'gʌv(ə)nmənt 'ɒmbʊdzmən/ *noun* same as **Local Commissioner**

Locke, John /lɒk/ *noun* the English philosopher (1632–1704) who justified the overthrow of royal power in England and the creation of a system based on the power of parliament (NOTE: Locke believed that the power of a government was based on a contract between the government and the people, and that if the government broke their side of the contract the people did not have to obey it.)

Lodge /lɒdʒ/ *noun* the official residence of the Australian prime minister in Canberra

logroll /'lɒgrəʊl/ *verb* to agree with political colleagues that each will support the other's piece of legislation

logrolling /'lɒgrəʊlɪŋ/ *noun* an understanding between colleagues in a legislature that each will support the other's piece of legislation

Lok Sabha *noun* the lower house of Parliament in India (NOTE: The upper house is the **Rajya Sabha**.)

London Mayor /'lʌndən meə/ *noun* the directly elected mayor of Greater London, a job first created in 2000 (NOTE: Ken Livingstone was elected first mayor of London in 2000 as an independent candidate, having failed to secure the nomination of the Labour Party. He was re-elected, this time as a Labour candidate, in 2004.)

loophole /'luːphəʊl/ *noun* a mistake in a law or contract which allows people to avoid their obligations ○ *The measure was largely introduced to close a loophole in the law.*

lord /lɔːd/ *noun* **1.** a member of the House of Lords **2. Lord** a title given to barons and to the sons of dukes and marquesses

COMMENT: When used for a baron, the title is given with the family name: *Lord Smith*; but when used for the son of a duke or marquess, the Christian name is used as well: *Lord James Stuart.*

Lord Advocate /,lɔːd 'ædvəkət/ *noun* a member of the government who is one of the two Law Officers in Scotland

Lord Chamberlain /,lɔːd 'tʃeɪmbəlɪn/, **Lord Great Chamberlain** *noun* a hereditary peer with various ceremonial duties especially for the sovereign (NOTE: Under the changes to the House of Lords, the Lord Chamberlain remains a member of the House despite being an hereditary peer.)

Lord Chancellor /,lɔːd 'tʃɑːnsələ/ *noun* a member of the government and cabinet who presides over the debates in the House of Lords, is responsible for the administration of justice, plays an important role in appointing judges, and who is the most important judge in England (NOTE: In 2003 the government announced plans to abolish the office of Lord Chancellor, which was thought to be incompatible with the independence of the judiciary.)

Lord Chief Justice /ˌlɔːd tʃiːf 'dʒʌstɪs/ *noun* the chief judge of the Queen's Bench Division of the High Court, and second most important judge after the Lord Chancellor

Lord Justice /ˌlɔːd 'dʒʌstɪs/ *noun* the title given to a judge who is a member of the House of Lords (NOTE: It is sometimes written as **LJ** after the name: *Smith LJ*)

Lord Justice Clerk /ˌlɔːd ˌdʒʌstɪs 'klɑːk/ *noun* the second most important judge in the Scottish High Court of Justiciary (NOTE: It is sometimes written as **LJ** after the name: *Smith LJ*)

Lord Justice General /ˌlɔːd ˌdʒʌstɪs 'dʒen(ə)rəl/ *noun* the most important judge in the Scottish High Court of Judiciary

Lord Lieutenant /ˌlɔːd lef'tenənt/ *noun* a person who is a representative of the Crown in a county

Lord Mayor /ˌlɔːd 'meə/ *noun* in the United Kingdom except Scotland, the mayor of a large city such as London or Dublin, elected for a year by other councillors. ◊ **Lord Provost**

Lord of Appeal /ˌlɔːd əv ə'piːl/, **Lord of Appeal in Ordinary** /ˌlɔːd əv əˌpiːl ɪn 'ɔːd(ə)n(ə)ri/ *noun* one of the law lords who sit as judges in the House of Lords when the House is acting as a Court of Appeal (NOTE: Reforms proposed in 2003–4 are likely to remove these law lords from the House of Lords and set up a separate Supreme Court.)

Lord of Appeal in Ordinary /ˌlɔːd əv əˌpiːl ɪn 'ɔːd(ə)n(ə)ri/ *noun* same as **Lord of Appeal**

Lord Ordinary /ˌlɔːd 'ɔːd(ə)n(ə)ri/ *noun* a judge of the upper house of the Scottish Court of Session

Lord President /ˌlɔːd 'prezɪdənt/ *noun* a judge of the Scottish Court of Session

Lord President of the Council /ˌlɔːd ˌprezɪdənt əv ðə 'kaʊns(ə)l/ *noun* a senior member of the government and member of the House of Lords who is the head of the Privy Council Office and has other duties given by the Prime Minister

Lord Privy Seal /ˌlɔːd ˌprɪvi 'siːl/ *noun* a senior member of the government, often a member of Cabinet, with duties given by the Prime Minister

Lord Protector /ˌlɔːd prə'tektə/ *noun* the title taken by Oliver Cromwell during the Protectorate

Lord Provost /ˌlɔːd 'prɒvəst/ *noun* in Scotland, the chairperson of the city councils of Glasgow, Edinburgh, Aberdeen and Dundee, elected by the other councillors. ◊ **Lord Mayor**

Lords /lɔːdz/ *plural noun* the House of Lords as a whole, or the members of the House of Lords ○ *The Bill goes before the Lords next week.* ○ *The Lords voted to amend the Bill.*

Lords Spiritual /ˌlɔːdz 'spɪrɪtʃuəl/ *noun* the archbishops and bishops who are members of the House of Lords, not associated with a political party (NOTE: The Archbishop of Canterbury, the Archbishop of York, the Bishops of London, Durham and Winchester and 21 other bishops, in order of seniority, are the Lords Spiritual.)

Lords Temporal /ˌlɔːdz 'temp(ə)rəl/ *noun* the members of the House of Lords who are not bishops

lose /luːz/ *verb* **1.** not to win something such as an election, vote or court case ○ *The government lost the vote of no confidence.* ○ *The government is going to lose the next election.* ○ *He lost his appeal to the House of Lords.* ○ *She lost her case for compensation.* □ **the motion was lost** the motion did not receive enough votes to be approved **2.** not to have something any more ○ *He lost his seat at the last election.* ○ *The Opposition lost several seats in the council election.* **3.** to have less money ○ *He lost £25,000 in his father's computer company.* **4.** to drop to a lower price ○ *The dollar lost two cents against the pound.* ○ *Gold shares lost 5% on the market yesterday.*

loudspeaker van /laʊd'spiːkə væn/ *noun* a vehicle with a loudspeaker so that political or other messages can be delivered to people in the streets and adjacent houses (NOTE: The US term is **sound truck**.)

lower chamber /ˌləʊə 'tʃeɪmbə/, **lower house** *noun* one of the two parts of a parliament that has two chambers, e.g. the British House of Commons or the American House of Representatives. ◊ **upper chamber** (NOTE: In practice the House of Commons is now far more important than the House of Lords, although it is still called the lower house. The Senate and House of Representatives in the USA are considered 'co-equal', but the Senate is still the upper house there.)

Loya Jerga /'lɔɪə 'dʒɜːgə/ *noun* the Grand Council in Afghanistan, which is a type of parliament

loyal /'lɔɪəl/ *adjective* continuing to support somebody or something ○ *He has been loyal to the party, even though the leader criticised him in public.*

loyalist /'lɔɪəlɪst/ *noun* a person who continues to support something, especially a king or political party

Loyalist /'lɔɪəlɪst/ *noun* a Northern Ireland Protestant who supports the continuation of Northern Ireland's political union with Britain

loyally /'lɔɪəli/ *adverb* in a way that supported something even in difficult situations ○ *She has served the council loyally for ten years.*

loyalty /'lɔɪəlti/ *noun* support given out of a sense of duty and respect ○ *All the members of the government have sworn an oath of loyalty to the President.*

Lumpenproletariat *noun* in the philosophy of Marxism, the ordinary workers who are not strongly interested in Marxism

M

Maastricht Treaty /ˈmɑːstrɪkt ˌtriːti/ *noun* the treaty of 1st November 1993 by which the member states of the European Community established the European Union. It significantly extended the scope of the previous treaties, preparing the way for the adoption of the single European currency, adopting a Social Chapter which gave rights to workers, strengthening European institutions and suggesting further scope for development in the fields of education, justice, defence and foreign policy. The British Prime Minister at the time, John Major, signed the treaty with the exclusion of the Single Currency and the Social Chapter. In trying to have the treaty ratified by Parliament, Major's Conservative government almost fell from power. Also called **Treaty of Maastricht** (NOTE: Maastricht is a town in the southeastern part of the Netherlands.)

MacDonald /məkˈdɒnəld/, **Ramsay** (1866–1937) a founder member of the Labour Party and the United Kingdom's first Labour prime minister (1924, 1929–35)

mace /meɪs/ *noun* a large ornamental stick, made of gold or silver, which is ceremonially placed on the table in the House of Commons or House of Lords, or in some local council chambers to show that business can begin

COMMENT: The significance of the mace in the House of Commons is so great that if it is not on the table, no business can be done. The mace is carried by the Serjeant at Arms in official processions. It is kept under the table in the House of Commons and placed on the table at the beginning of each sitting. It is taken off the table when the House goes into Committee. In the House of Lords, the mace is placed on the Woolsack. Local authorities usually also have maces which are carried in front of the mayor on ceremonial occasions by the mace-bearer, and often placed on the table at full council meetings. In the US House of Representatives, the mace is placed beside the Speaker's chair when the House is in session. There is no mace in the Senate, but a ceremonial gavel is placed on the vice-president's desk when the Senate is in session.

mace-bearer /ˈmeɪs ˌbeərə/ *noun* the official who carries a mace in procession

Machiavellian /ˌmækiəˈveliən/ *adjective* using trickery and dishonesty to achieve what you want. Compare **Byzantine**

COMMENT: The Italian writer, Niccolo Machiavelli (1469–1527) published a book *The Prince* in 1516. In it Machiavelli encouraged rulers to ignore all the rules of morality in the pursuit of power, but to try at the same time to appear to be acting morally.

machine /məˈʃiːn/ *noun* **1.** a complicated mechanical tool which can do difficult, heavy and repetitive jobs better than an individual person **2.** the people and system used to achieve or control something ○ *to get the party machine geared up for the next election* ○ *the Allied war machine* ○ *an effective propaganda machine*

machinery /məˈʃiːnəri/ *noun* an established organisation or system for achieving something ○ *the local government machinery* or *the machinery of local government* ○ *the machinery for awarding government contracts* ○ *The council's administrative machin-*

ery seems to have broken down in this case.

Macmillan /məkˈmɪlən/, **Harold, 1st Earl of Stockton** (1894–1986) prime minister of the United Kingdom (1957–63). twice Conservative prime minister (1957–63) during which time many former British colonies became independent.

Madam /ˈmædəm/ *noun* a formal way of addressing a woman, especially one whom you do not know, sometimes used in front of the title of a post □ **Madam Chairman** a formal way of addressing the chair of a committee who is a woman □ **Madam Speaker** the correct way to address a woman Speaker in the Commons

Magna Carta /ˌmægnə ˈkɑːtə/ *noun* the Great Charter, granted by King John in 1215, which gave his subjects political and personal freedoms

COMMENT: The Magna Carta is supposed to be the first step taken towards democratic rule, since it gave political power to the aristocracy and reduced the power of the King to override the law. It did not give power to the ordinary people, but confirmed the rights of the individual to own property and receive impartial justice.

maiden speech /ˌmeɪd(ə)n ˈspiːtʃ/ *noun* the first speech by a new MP in the House of Commons

mailbag /ˈmeɪlbæg/ *noun US* same as **postbag**

mainstream /ˈmeɪnstriːm/ *noun* the opinions held by a majority of people ○ *He is in the mainstream of Conservative politics.* ○ *Environmentally-friendly policies quickly entered the mainstream.*

majesty /ˈmædʒəsti/ *noun* an impressive or royal quality, or appearance ○ *the majesty of the State Opening of Parliament*

Majesty /ˈmædʒəsti/ *noun* a title given to a King or Queen ○ *His Majesty, the King* ○ *Their Majesties, the King and Queen* ○ *'Your Majesty, the Ambassador has arrived'* □ **on Her Majesty's Service** words printed on

official letters from government departments. Abbr **OHMS**. ◊ **Her Majesty's Stationery Office**

majeure /mæˈʒɜː/ ◆ **force majeure**

Majlis *noun* the Consultative Assembly in Iran, Saudi Arabia, Oman and Turkmenistan, which is a type of parliament

Major /ˈmeɪdʒə/, **John** (*b.* 1943) Conservative prime minister of the United Kingdom(1990–97)

majoritarian /məˌdʒɒrɪˈteəriən/ *adjective* relating to control by the majority in any group of people ■ *noun* someone who supports the view that a group should be controlled in the way decided on by the majority of its members

majority /məˈdʒɒrɪti/ *noun* **1.** a larger group than any other □ **a majority of members** more than 50% of MPs or councillors □ **the cabinet accepted the proposal by a majority of ten to seven** ten members of the cabinet voted to accept and seven voted against **2.** the age at which someone becomes responsible for his or her actions and can be given the rights and responsibilities of an adult

COMMENT: The age of majority in the UK and US is eighteen.

majority decision /məˈdʒɒrɪti dɪˌsɪʒ(ə)n/ *noun* a decision made after a vote according to the wishes of the larger group

majority leader /məˌdʒɒrɪti ˈliːdə/ *noun US* the spokesman for the majority party in the House of Representatives or the Senate, elected by other members of the party

majority rule /məˈdʒɒrɪti ruːl/ *noun* control of a group of people according to the decision of the majority of its members

majority system /məˌdʒɒrɪti ˈsɪstəm/ *noun* the system of voting where half the votes plus one more must be cast for a proposal for it to be accepted

majority vote /məˈdʒɒrɪti vəʊt/ *noun* a vote for or against a proposal of more than half of the people voting

majority whip /məˈdʒɒrɪti wɪp/ *noun US* one of the assistants to majority leaders in the House of Representatives or the Senate, whose responsibility is to make sure the members of their party vote

maladministration /ˌmæləd.mɪnɪˈstreɪʃ(ə)n/ *noun* managing a business or a government organisation in a bad or dishonest way ○ *The ombudsman found the council guilty of maladministration.*

malcontent /ˈmælkəntent/ *noun* someone who is unhappy or not satisfied with a particular system

manage /ˈmænɪdʒ/ *verb* **1.** to direct or to be in charge of a business or organisation ○ *to manage a department* ○ *to manage a branch office* **2.** to succeed in doing something **3.** to use money or time successfully

management /ˈmænɪdʒmənt/ *noun* **1.** the activity of directing or running a business ○ *to study management* ○ *good management* or *efficient management* **2.** a group of managers or directors

manager /ˈmænɪdʒə/ *noun* **1.** the head of a department **2.** a person in charge of a branch or shop **3.** a politician who helps in the detailed business of running a political party or a legislative body **4.** *US* a member of the House of Representatives or Senate, elected to represent the chamber in a conference to discuss differences of opinion over a bill

mandarin /ˈmændərɪn/ *noun* □ **Whitehall mandarin** an important British civil servant (*informal*)

mandate /ˈmændeɪt/ *noun* the authority given to a person or group to do something for somebody else ○ *The government has a mandate from the people to carry out the plans put forward in its manifesto.* (NOTE: In the case of a democratic government the mandate is given by the electors.) □ **to seek a new mandate** to try to be re-elected to a position ■ *verb* **1.** to give a government the authority to carry out policies ○ *The government* has been mandated to revise the tax system. **2.** to give a person authority to vote for a group ○ *The delegates were mandated to vote on behalf of their membership.*

mandatory /ˈmændət(ə)ri/ *adjective* required by law ○ *a mandatory pension provision*

mandatory meeting /ˌmændət(ə)ri ˈmiːtɪŋ/ *noun* a meeting which must be held, or a meeting which all members have to attend

manhood suffrage /ˈmænhʊd ˈsʌfrɪdʒ/ *noun* the right to vote given to all adult men

Manifest Destiny /ˈmænɪˌfest ˈdestəni/ *noun* a belief held in the 19th century that the United States had the God-given right to expand into and control the whole North American continent

manifesto /ˌmænɪˈfestəʊ/ *noun* a written public statement of the aims and policies of a group or party ○ *The Labour Party manifesto was published at the beginning of the election campaign.* ○ *Will the government implement all its manifesto promises?*

Mansion House /ˈmænʃən haʊs/ *noun* the official residence of the Lord Mayor of London

manual /ˈmænjuəl/ *noun* **1.** a book which explains how a piece of equipment works **2.** *US* a book which explains the organisation and procedures of the Houses of Congress

Maoism /ˈmaʊɪz(ə)m/ *noun* the communist ideas developed by Mao Zedong

COMMENT: Maoism is different from Marxism, because it is based on the wisdom of the people as a whole. Party officials and technical experts can be criticised if they do not follow the people's wishes. Maoists also believe that Communist principles may be adapted to different circumstances in different countries, though the basic aim of imposing Communism is most important and is to be achieved by force if necessary.

Maoist /ˈmaʊɪst/ *adjective* referring to Maoism ■ *noun* a person who follows the ideas taught by Mao Zedong

Mao Zedong /ˌmaʊ zeɪ ˈdɒŋ/ *noun* a dictator (1893–1976) who was chairman of the People's Republic of China form 1949 until his death and head of the Chinese Communist Party. He developed Marx's ideas of communism into Maoism. Also called **Chairman Mao**

march /mɑːtʃ/ *noun* a political protest in the form of an organised walk through the streets by a group of people in support of a cause

marchioness /ˌmɑːʃəˈnes/ *noun* the wife or widow of a marquess

marginal /ˈmɑːdʒɪn(ə)l/ *adjective* not very large ○ *The rate increases had only a marginal effect on the council's loan repayments.* ■ *noun also* **marginal constituency** *or* **marginal seat** a constituency where the sitting MP has a small majority ○ *The swing in several crucial marginals showed that the government was going to lose the election.* ○ *MPs representing marginal seats are worried about the government's poor showing in the opinion polls.*

market /ˈmɑːkɪt/ *noun* **1.** a place where goods are sold, often in the open air **2.** a place where a product might be sold or a group of people who might buy a product ○ *the home market* ○ *overseas markets* ○ *We want to increase our activity in the European Market.* **3.** the trade or business in a particular type of goods ○ *the property market* ○ *the job market* **4.** the economic system of buying and selling goods ○ *We need to let prices find their market level.*

market forces /ˌmɑːkɪt ˈfɔːsɪz/ *plural noun* economic pressure caused by free trade and not governed by the action of the government ○ *The government decided to stop paying subsidies to the farmers and to leave food supply to market forces*

mark up /ˌmɑːk ˈʌp/ *verb* □ **to mark up a bill** *US* to make changes to a bill as it goes through committee

marquess /ˈmɑːkwɪs/ *noun* a member of the nobility, the rank below a duke (NOTE: The wife of a **marquess** is a **marchioness**.)

marshal /ˈmɑːʃ(ə)l/ *noun* **1.** in some US cities, the head of the fire or police service **2.** in some US cities, a law enforcement officer

martial /ˈmɑːʃ(ə)l/ *adjective* relating to war, fighting or military forces ○ *martial music*

martial law /ˌmɑːʃ(ə)l ˈlɔː/ *noun* the rule of a country or part of a country by the army on the orders of the main government, the ordinary law having been suspended ○ *The president imposed* or *declared martial law in two provinces.* ○ *The government lifted martial law.*

Martin /ˈmɑːtɪn/, **Paul** (*b.* 1938) Canadian prime minister (2003–)

Marx, Karl /mɑːks/ *noun* the German philosopher (1818–83) who lived most of his life in London and whose ideas were the inspiration for communism (NOTE: Marx believed that people all over the world would eventually live in a state of perfect liberation, free from government, social class and misleading ideas. Lenin, Stalin and Mao changed Marx's ideas in order to maintain themselves as dictators.)

Marxism /ˈmɑːksˌɪz(ə)m/ *noun* the communist ideas of Karl Marx

Marxism-Leninism /ˌmɑːksɪz(ə)m ˈlenɪnɪz(ə)m/ *noun* Marxism adapted by the inclusion of Lenin's ideas that imperialism is the final stage of capitalism and that the focus of class struggle should shift from industrialised to nonindustrialised societies

Marxist /ˈmɑːksɪst/ *adjective* referring to Marxism ○ *a Marxist analysis of economic history* ○ *The book is an account of Marxist ideology.* ■ *noun* a person who supports the ideas of Karl Marx

Master of the Rolls /ˌmɑːstə əv ðə ˈrəʊlz/ *noun* the judge who presides over the Court of Appeal

matter /ˈmætə/ *noun* a problem or issue to be discussed ○ *the most im-*

portant matter on the agenda ○ *We shall consider first the matter of last month's fall in prices.* □ **matter of concern** an issue which causes concern ■ *verb* to be important ○ *Does it matter if the staff are paid a day late?*

matters arising /ˌmætəz əˈraɪzɪŋ/ *plural noun* a section in a meeting, where problems or questions which refer to items in the minutes of the previous meeting can be discussed

mayor /meə/ *noun* **1.** a person who is elected by the public as the official in control of a city, as in London or New York (NOTE: 'Mayor' is also used in English to apply to persons holding similar positions in other countries: *the Mayor of Berlin; the Mayor of Paris; the Mayor of New York.*) **2.** an honorary title held for a year by a town councillor who has been elected to the position by the other councillors. The Mayor may act as chair of the council and has a role in civic, social and charitable activities in the town. ▸ ◊ **Lord Mayor**

COMMENT: Previously, a mayor was the head of the elected government of a town and the head of the majority party. The mayor's responsibilities have now been taken over by the Council Leader, and the office of mayor is largely ceremonial. It is an honour often given to a long-serving or distinguished councillor. In Scotland, a mayor is called a Provost. In the USA, mayors are elected by popular vote, and appoint their team to run the various departments in a city. In 1999 Londoners voted in a referendum to have a directly-elected mayor with limited powers over transport and police. Other towns and cities have also been given the power to have such an official, but only one in three have chosen to do so after referendums have been held.

mayoral /ˈmeər(ə)l/ *noun* referring to a mayor ○ *mayoral duties*

mayoralty /ˈmeər(ə)lti/ *noun* the position of a mayor

mayoress /meərˈes/ *noun* the wife of a mayor, or another woman chosen by the mayor as an official partner for the term of office

mayor-making /ˈmeə ˌmeɪkɪŋ/ *noun* a ceremony which takes place at a council's Annual Meeting, when the new mayor is invested with the chain of office

Mbeki /əmˈbeki/, **Thabo** (*b.* 1942) president of South Africa (1999–)

McCarthyism /məˈkɑːθiɪz(ə)m/ *noun* the policy of searching for Communists or Communist sympathisers in the USA in the 1950s (NOTE: Senator Joseph McCarthy was the leading figure on the committee which questioned Americans, among them prominent figures from the world of films and entertainment, about their political beliefs, and ruined their careers if they showed communist sympathies. McCarthyism was strongly opposed in the 1950s by many people in America and thoroughly discredited by the 1960s.)

means of production /ˌmiːnz əv prəˈdʌkʃən/ *plural noun* in Marxism, the raw materials, machinery and other things needed to manufacture goods

means test /ˈmiːnz test/ *noun* a test to see if someone is entitled to government financial assistance because they have a low income

measure /ˈmeʒə/ *noun* **1.** a way of calculating size or quantity **2.** an action taken to deal with a problem, e.g. a law passed by Parliament ○ *a government measure to reduce crime in the inner cities* ○ *This is one of a series of measures to be introduced in the next session of Parliament.* □ **as a precautionary measure** to prevent something taking place ■ *verb* **1.** to find out the size or quantity of something **2.** □ **to measure the government's** or **the company's performance** to judge how well the government or the company is doing

media /ˈmiːdiə/ *noun* the newspapers, radio and television ○ *The main way that people learn about politics today is through the media.*

mediate /ˈmiːdieɪt/ *verb* to try to make the two sides in an argument come to an agreement ○ *to mediate be-*

tween the manager and staff ○ *to mediate in a dispute*

mediation /ˌmiːdɪˈeɪʃ(ə)n/ *noun* an attempt by a third party to make the two sides in an argument agree ○ *The employers refused an offer of government mediation.*

mediatise /ˈmiːdɪətaɪz/ *verb* to take control of another country while allowing its ruler to have some part in governing it

mediator /ˈmiːdɪeɪtə/ *noun* a person who attempts to make the two sides in an argument agree

megalomania /ˌmegələʊˈmeɪniə/ *noun* extreme pleasure in someone's own power or importance

megalomaniac /ˌmegələʊˈmeɪniæk/ *adjective, noun* a person who takes extreme pleasure in their own power and importance

member /ˈmembə/ *noun* **1.** a person who belongs to a group or a society **2.** a Member of Parliament, or a member of Congress ○ *the member for Oxford* ○ *the newly elected member for Windsor* **3.** a person elected to a local council ○ *The members asked for a report from the planning officer.* ○ *Officers must carry out the wishes of members.* **4.** an organisation or country which belongs to a group ○ *the members of the United Nations* ○ *the member countries of the European Free Trade Association* ○ *the member companies of a trade association*

Member of Congress /ˈmembə əv ˈkɒŋgres/ *noun* someone who is elected to the US Congress, especially to the House of Representatives

Member of Parliament /ˌmembər əv ˈpɑːləmənt/ *noun* a person elected to represent the people of an area of the United Kingdom in parliament. Abbr **MP**

COMMENT: Any British subject over 21 is eligible for election as an MP, but the following are disqualified: peers, ministers of the Church of Scotland, persons holding a paid job granted them by the monarch, judges, civil servants, bankrupts, people who are insane, and some categories of prisoners.

Member of the European Parliament /ˌmembə əv ðə ˌjʊərəpiːən ˈpɑːləmənt/ *noun* a person elected to represent the people of an area of Europe in the European Parliament. Abbr **MEP**

Member of the Northern Ireland Assembly /ˈmembə əv ðɪ ˈnɔːð(ə)n ˈaɪələnd/ *noun* a person elected to represent the people of an area of Northern Ireland in the devolved representative body. Abbr **MNIA**

Member of the Scottish Parliament /ˈmembə əv ðɪ ˈskɒtɪʃ ˈpɑːləmənt/ *noun* a person elected to represent the people of an area of Scotland in the devolved assembly. Abbr **MSP**

Member of the Welsh Assembly /ˈmembə əv ðɪ welʃ/ *noun* a person elected to represent the people of an area of Wales in the devolved representative body. Abbr **MWA**

Members' Gallery /ˈmembəz ˌgæləri/ *noun* the seats in the House of Commons for visitors invited by Members of Parliament

membership /ˈmembəʃɪp/ *noun* **1.** the fact of belonging to a group ○ *membership qualifications* ○ *conditions of membership* ○ *to pay your membership* or *your membership fees* ○ *Is Iceland going to apply for membership of the European Union?* **2.** all the members of a group ○ *The membership was asked to vote for the new president.*

Member State /ˈmembə steɪt/ *noun* one of the countries that is part of the European Union

memo /ˈmeməʊ/ *noun* a short note

memorandum /ˌmeməˈrændəm/, **memo** /ˈmeməʊ/ *noun* **1.** a short written statement about a subject from officials to other officials ○ *a memorandum to all the Chief Officers about the new arrangements* **2.** a written communication circulated among diplomats, especially one that summarises a country's position on an issue **3.** a written summary of a legal document **4.** a memo (*formal*)

memorial /mɪ'mɔːriəl/ *noun* **1.** a written statement of facts presented by a group of citizens, asking a legislature such as a parliament or town council to perform some action **2.** a ceremony which is performed in order to remember an important event or person, or a building or statue which is created to remember something or somebody

Memorial Day /mə'mɔːriəl deɪ/ *noun* a public holiday in the USA to remember those who died in wars, celebrated at the end of May

memorialise /mɪ'mɔːriəlaɪz/ *verb* to present a memorial accompanying a petition to a person or group in power

memorialist /mɪ'mɔːriəlɪst/ *noun* someone who writes, supports or presents a memorial accompanying a petition

MEP *abbreviation* Member of the European Parliament (NOTE: The plural is **MEPs.**)

mercenary /'mɜːs(ə)n(ə)ri/ *noun* a soldier who fights for a foreign country for money

meritocracy /ˌmerɪ'tɒkrəsi/ *noun* a society where people of ability have higher status than people of inherited wealth and good birth

merit system /'merɪt 'sɪstəm/ *noun* in the USA, the way in which the majority of civil servants and appointments to the federal bureaucracy are permanent specialists who win their jobs by a competitive selection process (NOTE: Most of the important figures in the federal bureaucracy are appointed by the spoils system, which means they are temporary appointments made by the incoming President.)

mesocracy /mez'ɒkrəsi/ *noun* a society governed by the middle class

Met /met/ *abbreviation* Metropolitan Police

metropolis /mɪ'trɒpəlɪs/ *noun* a very large town, usually the capital of a country

metropolitan /ˌmetrə'pɒlɪt(ə)n/ *adjective* referring to a large city

metropolitan county /ˌmetrə'pɒlɪt(ə)n 'kaʊnti/ *noun* in England, any of the six large urban administrative units that existed in the system of local government in force between 1974 and 1986

metropolitan district /ˌmetrə'pɒlɪt(ə)n 'dɪstrɪkt/ *noun* in England, any of the principal units of local government that used to be metropolitan counties, each with an elected council

Metropolitan District Council /ˌmetrəpɒlɪt(ə)n ˌdɪstrɪkt 'kaʊns(ə)l/ *noun* in England and Wales, a large administrative area covering an urban area

Metropolitan Police /ˌmetrəpɒlɪt(ə)n pə'liːs/ *noun* the police force of Greater London

COMMENT: The higher ranks in the Metropolitan Police are Deputy Assistant Commissioner, Assistant Commissioner, and Commissioner.

Metropolitan Police Commissioner /ˌmetrəpɒlɪt(ə)n pəˌliːs kə'mɪʃ(ə)nə/ *noun* the head of the Metropolitan Police

MFN *abbreviation* most-favoured nation

MHA *abbreviation* Member of the House of Assembly

MI5, MI6 *noun* the British government intelligence agencies (NOTE: The US equivalent is **the Central Intelligence Agency.**)

COMMENT: MI5 (or the Security Service) is concerned with national security, in particular counter-terrorism and counter-espionage. MI6 (or the Secret Intelligence Service) is concerned with obtaining information about other countries which may be of use to the government's defence, security, economic and foreign services.

Middle America /'mɪd(ə)l ə'merɪkə/ *noun* a section of the middle class in the United States regarded as politically conservative with traditional social and moral values

Middle East /ˈmɪd(ə)l ˈiːst/ *noun* countries to the east of Egypt and west of Pakistan

Middle England /ˌmɪd(ə)l ˈɪŋɡlənd/ *noun* a section of the middle class in England regarded as politically conservative with traditional social and moral values

middle-of-the-road /ˌmɪd(ə)l əv ðə ˈrəʊd/ *adjective* not extreme (*informal*) ○ *middle-of-the-road political opinions*

midterm /ˌmɪdˈtɜːm/ *adjective* relating to the middle of a term of office

militant /ˈmɪlɪtənt/ *adjective, noun* very actively supporting and working for a cause ○ *The speaker was shouted down by militant environmental campaigners.*

Militant Tendency /ˈmɪlɪtənt ˈtendənsi/ *noun* a former Trotskyite faction of the Labour Party, active in the 1970s and 1980s

militarise /ˈmɪlɪtəraɪz/ *verb* to greatly strengthen a country's armed forces

militarism /ˈmɪlɪtərɪz(ə)m/ *noun* **1.** strong influence or control by military leaders on the government or policies of a country or state **2.** a government policy of greatly strengthening a country's armed forces

military /ˈmɪlɪt(ə)ri/ *adjective* referring to the armed services □ **a period of military rule** government by the army ○ *The country was ruled by a military government for nine years.* ○ *The military dictatorship has agreed to return to civilian rule next year.* ■ *noun* □ **the Military** the Army

military attaché /ˌmɪlɪt(ə)ri ə ˈtæʃeɪ/ *noun* an army officer who works in an embassy and reports on military affairs to his or her home government

Mill, John Stuart /mɪl/ *noun* the British philosopher (1806–73) whose best known work of political philosophy is *On Liberty* (NOTE: Mill argued that people should be free to do anything they liked as long as it did not harm others.)

Min. *abbreviation* **1.** Minister **2.** Ministry

minibudget /ˌmɪniˈbʌdʒɪt/ *noun* a statement of the government's financial position and plans made at some point before the main annual budget

minimum wage /ˌmɪnɪməm ˈweɪdʒ/ *noun* the lowest hourly wage which a company can legally pay its workers, set at a rate decided by the government

minister /ˈmɪnɪstə/ *noun* a senior diplomat below the rank of ambassador

Minister, Minister of the Crown *noun* a member of a government who is in charge of a department ○ *a government minister* ○ *the Minister of Information* or *the Information Minister* ○ *the Minister of Foreign Affairs* or *the Foreign Minister* ○ *the Minister of Justice* or *the Justice Minister*

COMMENT: In the USA, heads of government departments have the title of **secretary**: *the Secretary for Commerce;* in the UK, ministers in charge of government departments have the title of **Secretary of State**: *the Secretary of State for Defence.*

Minister for the Civil Service /ˈmɪnɪstə fə ðɪ ˈsɪv(ə)l ˈsɜːvɪs/ *noun* a former British government post, now combined with that of Prime Minister

ministerial /ˌmɪnɪˈstɪəriəl/ *adjective* referring to a minister ○ *ministerial responsibilities* ○ *The ministerial car was waiting at the airport.*

ministerial tribunal /ˌmɪnɪstɪəriəl traɪˈbjuːn(ə)l/ *noun* a sort of court set up by a government minister to hear appeals from local courts of a similar sort

Minister of State /ˌmɪnɪstə əv ˈsteɪt/ *noun* a member of a government who is in charge of a section of a government department. Also called **junior minister, Under-Secretary of State**

Minister-President /ˈmɪnɪstə ˈprezɪdənt/ *noun* in Germany, the title of the premier in a Land

Minister without Portfolio
/ˌmɪnɪstə wɪˌðaʊt pɔːtˈfəʊliəʊ/ *noun*
a minister who does not have responsibility for any particular department

ministry /ˈmɪnɪstri/ *noun* **1.** a department of state in the government ○
a ministry official or *an official from
the ministry* ○ *She works in the Ministry of Finance* or *the Finance Ministry.*
○ *He is in charge of the Ministry of Information* or *of the Information Ministry.* (NOTE: In Britain and the USA,
important ministries are called **departments**: *the Department of
Trade*; *the Commerce Department.*)
2. a government □ **during the Wilson
ministry** when the government headed by Prime Minister Wilson was in
office

Ministry of Defence /ˌmɪnɪstri əv
dɪˈfens/ *noun* a government department in charge of the armed forces

Ministry of Foreign Affairs
/ˌmɪnɪstri əv ˌfɒrɪn əˈfeəz/ *noun* a
government department dealing with a
country's relations with other countries (NOTE: The UK equivalent is **the
Foreign Office** and the US equivalent is **the State Department**.)

minor /ˈmaɪnə/ *noun* a person less
than eighteen years old ○ *Minors cannot vote in a general election.*

minoritarianism /maɪˌnɒrɪ
ˈteəriənɪz(ə)m/ *noun* support for or
political action on behalf of a minority

minority /maɪˈnɒrɪti/ *noun* **1.** a
number or quantity which is less than
half of the total ○ *A minority of council
members opposed the chairman.* ○
*Only a small minority of football sup-
porters get involved in violence.* □ **in
the minority** being fewer than half ○
*the small parties are in the minority on
the local council* **2.** a small group of
people who differ in some way from a
large group ○ *It's only a minority of
the supporters who are violent and
causing trouble.* **3.** a part of a society
that differs from the rest of it in some
way, especially in ethnic background,
religion or culture **4.** being less than
eighteen years old, or the time when

someone is less than eighteen years
old ○ *A person is not liable for debts
contracted during minority.*

minority government /maɪˌnɒrɪti
ˈɡʌv(ə)nmənt/ *noun* a government
which does not have majority over all
other groups in the House of Commons

minority leader /maɪˌnɒrɪti ˈliːdə/
noun US the person who speaks for
the minority party in the House or
Senate, elected by other members of
the party

minority report /maɪˌnɒrɪti rɪ
ˈpɔːt/ *noun* a statement of their views
made by a small number of people
who hold an opposing view from the
rest of the group asked to consider
something ○ *Two of the members of
the Royal Commission disagreed with
the others and submitted a minority
report.*

minority whip /maɪˌnɒrɪti ˈwɪp/
noun US one of the assistants to minority leaders in the House or Senate,
whose responsibility is to make sure
the members of their party vote

minute /ˈmɪnɪt/ *noun* a note or document about a subject ○ *Have you read
his minute about the report? I have
asked the Chief Education Officer to
prepare a minute about the discussions.* ■ *verb* to put something into the
record of a meeting ○ *The chairman's
remarks about the auditors were min-
uted.*

minutebook /ˈmɪnɪtbɒk/ *noun* a
book in which the minutes of a meeting are kept

miscellaneous /mɪsəˈleɪniəs/ *adjective* not all of the same sort ○ *miscellaneous items* ○ *a box of miscellaneous pieces of equipment* ○ *miscellaneous expenditure*

miscount *noun* /ˈmɪskaʊnt/ a mistake in counting ■ *verb* /mɪsˈkaʊnt/ to
make a mistake in counting ○ *The
votes were miscounted, so the ballot
had to be taken again.*

misgovern /mɪsˈɡʌv(ə)n/ *verb* to
govern badly

misgovernment /mɪs
'gʌv(ə)nmənt/ *noun* bad government

misinterpret /ˌmɪsɪn'tɜːprɪt/ *verb*
to understand something wrongly ○
The protestors misinterpreted the in-
structions of the police.

misinterpretation /ˌmɪsɪn,tɜːprɪ
'teɪʃ(ə)n/ *noun* a wrong understanding of something □ **clause which is**
open to misinterpretation a clause
which can be wrongly interpreted

mislead /mɪs'liːd/ *verb* to make
someone understand something
wrongly ○ *The instructions in the doc-*
ument are quite misleading. ○ *The*
wording of the Bill is misleading and
needs to be clarified. ○ *The minister*
misled the House in his statement on
the affair.

misrepresent /ˌmɪsreprɪ'zent/
verb to report facts or statements or
opinions wrongly ○ *The Minister com-*
plained that the TV news report had
misrepresented him.

misrepresentation /ˌmɪs
ˌreprɪzen'teɪʃ(ə)n/ *noun* a wrong
statement, especially in order to trick
someone

misrule /mɪs'ruːl/ *noun* bad government ○ *13 years of misrule*

mission /'mɪʃ(ə)n/ *noun* **1.** a special
purpose for which someone is sent
somewhere ○ *Her mission was to try to*
persuade the rebels to accept the gov-
ernment's terms. **2.** an important plan
or goal ○ *a mission to end child pover-*
ty □ **mission in life** a personal goal ○ *It*
was her mission in life to see a Labour
MP elected for her constituency for
the first time. **3.** a group of people who
visit another country for a special purpose, generally on government or official business ○ *a trade mission to Ja-*
pan ○ *The members of the government*
mission are staying in the embassy. **4.**
an embassy or consulate or building
where representatives of a foreign
country work ○ *The crowd gathered*
outside the gates of the British Mis-
sion.

misunderstanding /ˌmɪsʌndə
'stændɪŋ/ *noun* a mistake ○ *There was*
a misunderstanding over the date of
the next meeting.

MLA *abbreviation* Member of the
Legislative Assembly

MMP *abbreviation* Mixed Member
Proportional

MNA *abbreviation* Member of the
National Assembly (of Quebec)

MNIA *abbreviation* Member of the
Northern Ireland Assembly

mob /mɒb/ *noun* **1.** a large violent
crowd ○ *The embassy was burned*
down by a mob of students. ○ *The po-*
lice fired on the mob of demonstrators.
2. (*old*) the lower classes of society

mobilise /'məʊbɪlaɪz/, **mobilize**
verb **1.** to get the armed forces ready
for war **2.** to encourage people to take
decisions or protest about something ○
The opposition is trying to mobilise
public opinion against the draft legis-
lation.

mobocracy /mɒb'ɒkrəsi/ *noun* **1.**
political control exercised by a mob **2.**
a place where a mob has political control

mob rule /ˌmɒb 'ruːl/ *noun* **1.** the
rule of a town or country by an angry
crowd or by the lower classes **2.** (*old*)
rule by the lower classes of society

MoD *abbreviation* Ministry of Defence

moderate /'mɒd(ə)rət/ *adjective*
not extreme or not very large ○ *a mod-*
erate increase in government spend-
ing ○ *She holds very moderate politi-*
cal views. ○ *We had only moderate*
success in our negotiations. ■ *noun* a
person with moderate ideas or opinions ○ *The moderates were defeated*
by the extremists. ■ *verb* to make
something less extreme ○ *The rebels*
were forced to moderate their de-
mands.

moderation /ˌmɒdə'reɪʃ(ə)n/ *noun*
1. the avoidance of extremes or becoming less extreme ○ *The negotiators*
practised moderation in their dealings
with the enemy. **2.** a reduction ○ *a*
moderation in the speed of political
change

Modernisation Committee /ˌmɒdənaɪˈzeɪʃ(ə)n kəˌmɪti/ *noun* a Select Committee of the House of Commons set up 1997 to recommend changes in the practices and procedures of the House to meet modern standards

modus vivendi /ˌməʊdəs vɪ ˈvendiː/ *Latin phrase meaning* 'way of living', an informal agreement between parties to exist peacefully together ○ *After years of confrontation, they finally have achieved a modus vivendi.*

mole /məʊl/ *noun* someone who anonymously reveals sensitive information about the organisation they work for

monarch /ˈmɒnək/ *noun* a royal ruler of a country, e.g. a king, queen or emperor

monarchic /mɒˈnɑːkɪk(ə)l/, **monarchical** *adjective* referring to or in favour of a monarchy

monarchism /ˈmɒnəkɪz(ə)m/ *noun* 1. the belief in monarchy as a system of government 2. the system of government in which a monarch has power

monarchist /ˈmɒnəkɪst/ *noun* a person who supports or believes in rule by a monarch

monarchy /ˈmɒnəki/ *noun* 1. rule by a king or queen ○ *The monarchy was overthrown in the revolution, and the king replaced by a president.* 2. a country ruled by a king or queen ○ *Belgium, Sweden and Britain are monarchies.*

Monday Club /ˈmʌndeɪ klʌb/ *noun* a club for right-wing members and supporters of the Conservative Party in Britain (NOTE: Their first meetings were held at lunchtime on Mondays.)

money /ˈmʌni/ *noun* coins or bank notes

Money Bill /ˈmʌni bɪl/ *noun* 1. a Bill which authorises expenditure from the Exchequer 2. a Bill which authorises the levy of taxes

money market /ˈmʌni ˌmɑːkɪt/ *noun* the business of lending and bor-rowing money carried on by the banks and other financial institutions

money supply /ˈmʌni səˌplaɪ/ *noun* the amount of money which exists in a country

monocracy /mɒnˈɒkrəsi/ *noun* a form of government in which one person rules alone

Monopolies Commission, Monopolies and Mergers Commission *noun* the British body which examines takeovers of one company by another, and mergers between companies to make sure that a monopoly is not being created

monopolisation /məˌnɒpəlaɪ ˈzeɪʃ(ə)n/, **monopolization** *noun* complete control of the trade in particular goods or services

monopoly /məˈnɒpəli/ *noun* a situation where one person or company has the complete control of trade in particular goods or the supply of a particular service ○ *to have the monopoly of alcohol sales* or *to have the alcohol monopoly* ○ *The company has the absolute monopoly of imports of French wine.* (NOTE: A more common US term is **trust**.)

Monroe doctrine /mʌnˈrəʊ ˌdɒktrɪn/ *noun* US the principle that the USA has an interest in preventing outside interference in the internal affairs of American states, especially from Europe (NOTE: So called because it was first proposed by President Monroe in 1823.)

moral majority /ˈmɒrəl məˈdʒɒrɪti/ *noun* in the USA, a group of people with conservative Christian beliefs and political opinions

moratorium /ˌmɒrəˈtɔːriəm/ *noun* a temporary stop to an activity, especially by official agreement ○ *The Conference called for a moratorium on killing seals.* (NOTE: The plural is **moratoria**.)

morning hour /ˈmɔːnɪŋ aʊə/ *noun* US the period at the beginning of each day's sitting of Congress, when members can make a short speech on any topic they choose

most-favoured nation /ˌməʊst ˌfeɪvəd 'neɪʃ(ə)n/ *noun* a country which is given the best trade terms by another country. Abbr **MFN** □ **most-favoured-nation clause** an agreement between two countries that each will offer the other the best possible terms in commercial contracts

Mother of Parliaments /ˌmʌðə əv 'pɑːləmənts/ *noun* the British Parliament at Westminster

motion /'məʊʃ(ə)n/ *noun* **1.** a proposal which will be put to a meeting for that meeting to vote on, e.g. a proposal to the House of Commons or Congress ○ *to propose* or *to move a motion* ○ *to speak against* or *for a motion* ○ *The meeting voted on the motion.* ◊ **subsidiary motion, substantive motion** □ **the motion was carried** or **defeated by 220 votes to 196** the motion was approved or not approved □ **to table a motion** to put forward a proposal for discussion □ **motion to suspend the rules** a motion to speed up the passage of a bill, by limiting debate on it and not allowing any amendments □ **motion to reconsider a vote** a motion at the end of a discussion of any bill, but especially one passed with a close vote, so that a second vote has to be taken to settle the matter **2.** an application to a judge in court, asking for an order in favour of the person making the application

move /muːv/ *verb* to ask a meeting to vote on a proposal ○ *She moved the proposal for new street lighting.* ○ *He moved that the accounts be agreed.* ○ *I move that the meeting adjourn for ten minutes.* (NOTE: The US term is **move for**: *Congressman Smith moved for a measure to be considered.*) □ **to move the previous question** to propose that the previous motion should be discussed again, so that the debate on the current question is dropped

movement /'muːvmənt/ *noun* **1.** a change, especially an improvement ○ *movements in the money markets* ○ *cyclical movements of trade* **2.** a group of people working towards the same

aim, though not necessarily members of a political party ○ *the British Labour Movement* ○ *He was the founder of the movement for the reunification of his country.* **3.** the process of changing place or position ○ *free movement of labour* **4.** a part of a military operation ○ *The satellites observed troop movements.* ○ *The forces closed in on two sides in a pincer movement.*

mover /'muːvə/ *noun* a person who proposes a motion ○ *The mover of this resolution has said that it is a matter of public safety.* □ **movers and shakers** the people who are powerful or influential in making things happen

MP /'em 'piː/ *abbreviation* Member of Parliament *or* military police (NOTE: The plural is **MPs**.)

MSP *abbreviation* Member of the Scottish Parliament (NOTE: The plural is **MSPs**.)

multilateral /ˌmʌltiˈlæt(ə)rəl/ *adjective* involving more than two countries, people or groups ○ *multilateral nuclear disarmament*

multilateralism /ˌmʌlti 'læt(ə)rəlɪz(ə)m/ *noun* the belief that a policy should only be followed by several countries acting together

multilaterally /ˌmʌltiˈlæt(ə)rəli/ *adverb* between more than two parties or countries ○ *The group of western nations agreed multilaterally to reduce import tariffs.*

multilateral nuclear disarmament /ˌmʌltiˈlæt(ə)rəl 'njuːkliə dɪs 'ɑːməmənt/ *noun* an agreement between several countries to stop making or holding nuclear weapons

multinational /ˌmʌltiˈnæʃ(ə)nəl/ *adjective* referring to several countries ○ *a multinational peacekeeping force* ■ *noun* a large company operating in several countries

multipartite /ˌmʌltiˈpɑːtaɪt/ *adjective* involving more than two political parties or countries

multiparty /ˌmʌltiˈpɑːti/ *adjective* where several political parties exist in the same country ○ *a multiparty de-*

mocracy ○ *Multiparty elections will be held next year.*

multiple voting /ˈmʌltɪp(ə)l ˈvəʊtɪŋ/ *noun* the illegal practice of voting in more than one constituency in an election

multiracialism /ˌmʌlti ˈreɪʃ(ə)lɪz(ə)m/ *noun* the practice of fully including people of various ethnic groups in all aspects of a society

municipal /mjuːˈnɪsɪp(ə)l/ *adjective* referring to a town which has its own local government ○ *The finance department supervises the collection of municipal taxes.* ○ *She works in the municipal offices.*

municipal bond /mjuːˌnɪsɪp(ə)l ˈbɒnd/ *noun* a financial investment offered by a city or other local government to the general public, usually to pay for improvements to public facilities

municipalise /mjuːˈnɪsɪpəlaɪz/ *verb* **1.** to bring something such as a public service or area of land under the control of a city or other locally governed area **2.** to give a city or other area responsibility for government in local matters

municipality /mjuːˌnɪsɪˈpælɪti/ *noun* a town or city with its own local government

municipal law /mjuːˈnɪsɪp(ə)l lɔː/ *noun* law which is in operation within a state. Compare **international law**

mutineer /ˌmjuːtɪˈnɪə/ *noun* a person who takes part in a mutiny

mutinous /ˈmjuːtɪnəs/ *adjective* likely to disobey orders ○ *mutinous backbenchers*

mutiny /ˈmjuːtɪni/ *noun* the refusal to obey the orders of somebody in a position of authority such as the officers in the army or navy ■ *verb* to refuse to obey the orders of somebody in authority

MWA *abbreviation* Member of the Welsh Assembly (NOTE: The plural is **MWAs**.)

N

NAFTA /'næftə/ *abbreviation* North American Free Trade Agreement

NALGO *abbreviation* National Association of Local Government Officers

name /neɪm/ *verb* to refer formally by name to a Member of Parliament who has behaved in a way regarded as unsuitable, which leads to that MP being unable to enter the House of Commons for a period as a punishment ○ *The Secretary of State was named in the divorce case.*

nanny state /'næni steɪt/ *noun* a system of government which provides everything for the citizens and tells the citizens how they should behave

Nat /næt/ *noun* a member of the National Party in Australia or New Zealand, or of the former National Party in South Africa, or a member of parliament belonging to the National Party

nation /'neɪʃ(ə)n/ *noun* a country and the people living in it. ◊ **nation state**

national /'næʃ(ə)nəl/ *adjective* referring to a particular country ■ *noun* a person who is a citizen of a state

national accounts /ˌnæʃ(ə)nəl ə'kaʊnts/ *plural noun* the record of a country's finances

National Anthem /ˌnæʃ(ə)nəl 'ænθəm/ *noun* a piece of music, usually with words which are sung to it, which is used to represent the nation officially and is played at official ceremonies

National Assembly /ˌnæʃ(ə)nə 'sembli/ *noun* the lower body of the legislature in many countries, including Benin, Botswana, Bulgaria, Burkina Faso, Cambodia, Central African Republic, Congo, Côte d'Ivoire, Cuba, Equatorial Guinea, France, Gabon, Guyana, Hungary, Kenya, South Korea, Kuwait, Laos, Lesotho, Mauritania, Mauritius, Namibia, Nicaragua, Pakistan, Quebec, Senegal, Seychelles, South Africa, Tanzania, Thailand, Togo and Vietnam

National Assembly for Wales /ˌnæʃ(ə)nəl əˌsembli fə' weɪlz/ *noun* the devolved government for Wales, made up of elected members, with the power to introduce secondary legislation in areas such as health and education in Wales

National Audit Office /ˌnæʃ(ə)nəl 'ɔːdɪt ˌɒfɪs/ *noun* an independent body, headed by the Comptroller and Auditor-General, which examines the accounts of government departments

National Congress /'næʃ(ə)nəl 'kɒngres/ *noun* the legislature in Ecuador and Venezuela

National Council /'næʃ(ə)nəl 'kaʊns(ə)l/ *noun* the upper house of the legislature in Namibia, Nepal and Slovakia

National Front /'næʃ(ə)nəl frʌnt/ *noun* a right-wing political group with racist opinions

National Guard /'næʃ(ə)nəl gɑːd/ *noun* in the USA, the state militia or volunteer army which can be called on to act on the orders of the federal government

National Guardsman /ˌnæʃ(ə)nəl 'gɑːdzmən/ *noun US* in the USA, a member of the National Guard

National Health Service /ˌnæʃ(ə)nəl 'helθ ˌsɜːvɪs/ *noun* a British organisation which provides medical services free of charge or at a low cost, to the whole population. Abbr **NHS**

National Institutes of Health /ˌnæʃ(ə)nəl ˌɪnstɪtjuːts əv 'helθ/ noun an agency of the US federal government that conducts and supports medical research and programmes designed to improve people's health. Abbr **NIH**

National Insurance /ˌnæʃ(ə)nəl ɪn'ʃʊərəns/ noun a British tax on income which pays for medical care, hospitals and unemployment benefits

National Insurance contributions /ˌnæʃ(ə)nəl ɪn'ʃʊərəns ˌkɒntrɪbjuːʃ(ə)nz/ plural noun money paid both by an employee and an employer to the National Insurance system

nationalisation /ˌnæʃ(ə)nəlaɪ'zeɪʃ(ə)n/, **nationalization** noun the act of taking control of a private industry by the state

nationalise /'næʃ(ə)nəlaɪz/, **nationalize** verb to put a private industry under state ownership and control

nationalised industry /ˌnæʃ(ə)nə ˌlaɪzd 'ɪndəstri/ noun a company which was once privately owned, but now belongs to the state

nationalism /'næʃ(ə)nəˌlɪz(ə)m/ noun **1.** the desire for political independence by people who have the same culture ○ Basque nationalism **2.** the feeling of great pride in one's country

nationalist /'næʃ(ə)nəlɪst/ noun **1.** a person who wants his or her ethnic group or country to be politically independent ○ a Welsh nationalist ○ the Scottish Nationalist Party **2.** a person who is very proud of his or her country or feels it is better than other countries

nationality /ˌnæʃə'nælɪti/ noun the legal state of being the citizen of a country □ **he is of United Kingdom nationality** he is a citizen of the United Kingdom □ **he has dual nationality** he is a citizen of two countries at the same time

National Party /ˌnæʃ(ə)nəl 'pɑːti/ noun a political party representing the interests of the nation

National Party of Australia /'næʃ(ə)nəl 'pɑːti əv ɒs'treɪliə/ noun in Australia, a conservative political party that has usually formed a coalition with the Liberal Party of Australia

National People's Congress /ˌnæʃ(ə)nəl ˌpiːpəlz 'kɒŋgres/ noun the legislature in China

Nationalrat /ˌnæʃə'nɑːlræt/ noun **1.** the lower house of the legislature in Austria **2.** the lower house of the federal legislature in Switzerland

National Security Council /'næʃ(ə)nəl sɪ'kjʊərəti 'kaʊns(ə)l/ noun in the United States, a council that decides on policies designed to maintain national security, consisting of the president, the secretary of state, the national security adviser, and senior military and intelligence officers. Abbr **NSC**

national socialism /'næʃ(ə)nəl 'səʊʃəlɪz(ə)m/ noun the ideology of the German Nazi Party, including national expansion, totalitarian government and racial purity

National Socialist Party /ˌnæʃ(ə)nəl 'səʊʃəlɪst ˌpɑːti/ noun a political party founded in Germany in 1919 and led by Adolf Hitler. Also called **Nazi Party**

National State Assembly /ˌnæʃ(ə)nəl steɪt ə'sembli/ noun the legislature in Sri Lanka

National Union of Civil and Public Servants /'næʃ(ə)nəl 'juːnjən əv 'sɪv(ə)l ən 'pʌblɪk/ noun a trade union representing civil servants replaced by the Public Services, Tax and Commerce Union. Abbr **NUCPS**

Nation of Islam /'neɪʃ(ə)n əv 'ɪzlɑːm/ noun a movement of African Americans who follow Islam and believe that Black Americans have Islamic origins. Abbr **NoI**

nation state /'neɪʃ(ə)n steɪt/ noun a country which is an independent political unit, usually formed of people with the same language and traditions ○ *The 19th century saw the rise of many European nation states.*

nationwide /ˌnæʃ(ə)nəˌlaɪzd ˈɪndəstri/ *adjective, adverb* across the whole of a country ○ *A nationwide opinion poll suggested that the Opposition is losing support in marginal constituencies.* ○ *They're gaining ground nationwide.*

native /ˈneɪtɪv/ *noun* **1.** a person who comes originally from a place or was born there ○ *She lives in London, but she is a native of Denmark.* **2.** an original inhabitant of a colony (*offensive*) ○ *The colonists captured the natives and sold them into slavery.* **3.** □ **to go native** to cease to represent the interests of the United Kingdom, and instead to start to believe in the policies of the country where you are working (*of officials*)

native land /ˈneɪtɪv lænd/ *noun* the country where someone was born

nativism /ˈneɪtɪvɪz(ə)m/ *noun* **1.** a policy, especially in the United States, of favouring the interests of native citizens of a country over those of immigrants **2.** a policy of protecting traditional and local cultures

NATO /ˈneɪtəʊ/ *abbreviation* North Atlantic Treaty Organization

natural-born subject /ˌnætʃ(ə)rəl bɔːn ˈsʌbdʒɪkt/ *noun* formerly, a person born in the UK or a Commonwealth country who was a British citizen by birth

naturalisation /ˌnætʃ(ə)rəlaɪ ˈzeɪʃ(ə)n/, **naturalization** *noun* the granting of the citizenship of a state to someone who has come into the country from abroad ○ *She has applied for naturalisation.* ○ *You must fill in the naturalisation papers.*

naturalise /ˈnætʃ(ə)rəlaɪz/, **naturalize** *verb* to make someone a citizen of another country

naturalised /ˈnætʃ(ə)rəlaɪzd/, **naturalized** *adjective* having become a citizen of another country ○ *He is a naturalised American citizen.*

natural right /ˌnætʃ(ə)rəl ˈraɪt/ *noun* a freedom which people ought to enjoy to have something or do something, and which is thought to be theirs simply because they are human beings

Nazi /ˈnɑːtsi/ *noun* a person who was a member of the Nazi Party

Nazi Party /ˈnɑːtsi ˈpɑːti/ *noun* same as **National Socialist Party**

Nazism /ˈnɑːtsɪz(ə)m/ *noun* the belief in racist and nationalist ideas and support for authoritarian government

NDPB *abbreviation* non-departmental public body

Near East /ˈnɪə ˈiːst/ *noun* the countries at the eastern end of the Mediterranean (NOTE: Now often called **the Middle East**.)

negative instrument /ˈnegətɪv ˈɪnstrʊmənt/ *noun* a form of Statutory Instrument which can be over-ruled by either House of Parliament

negotiate /nɪˈɡəʊʃieɪt/ *verb* □ **to negotiate with someone** to discuss a problem formally with someone, so as to reach an agreement ○ *The management refused to negotiate with the union.*

negotiating committee /nɪ ˈɡəʊʃieɪtɪŋ kəˌmɪti/ *noun* a group of representatives of management who discuss pay and hours of work with representatives of the workers

negotiation /nɪˌɡəʊʃiˈeɪʃ(ə)n/ *noun* a discussion between two people or two groups who disagree, intended to reach an agreement between them □ **to enter into negotiations, to start negotiations** to start discussing a problem □ **to resume negotiations** to start discussing a problem again, after talks have stopped for a time □ **to break off negotiations** to refuse to go on discussing a problem □ **to conduct negotiations** to negotiate

negotiator /nɪˈɡəʊʃieɪtə/ *noun* a person who tries to reach an agreement with someone

neighbour /ˈneɪbə/, **neighbouring state** *noun* a country which is next to another, sharing a common border

(NOTE: The US spelling is **neighbor** or **neighboring state**.)

nemine contradicente /ˌneminei ˌkɒntrædɪ'sentei/, **nem con** /ˌnem 'kɒn/ *Latin phrase meaning* 'with no one speaking against something': a phrase used to show that no one spoke against the proposal, although some may have abstained in the vote ○ *The motion was adopted nem con.* Compare **unanimous**

neo- /niːəʊ/ *prefix* meaning 'new' or 'in a new form' ○ *a neo-fascist movement* ○ *a neo-Nazi organisation*

neocolonialism /ˌniːəʊkə 'ləʊniəlɪz(ə)m/ *noun* a policy by which a strong country tries to influence or control weaker countries which are independent

neocon /'niːəʊkɒn/ *noun US* same as **neoconservative**

neoconservative /ˌniːəʊkən 'sɜːvətɪv/ *noun* someone who began to support conservative policies in the mid-1980s as a reaction to the social changes of the 1960s-70s

neofascism /ˌniːəʊ'fæʃɪz(ə)m/ *noun* **1.** modern support for Fascist beliefs **2.** the beliefs of white groups or movements that hold racist views, especially those involved in violence towards non-white people

neofascist /ˌniːəʊ'fæʃɪst/ *adjective* relating to neofascism ■ *noun* someone who has Fascist or white racist opinions

neo-Nazi /ˌniːəʊ 'nɑːtsi/ *noun* **1.** someone who supports Nazi beliefs **2.** a white person who has racist views, especially one involved in violence towards non-white people

net gain /ˌnet 'ɡeɪn/ *noun* the total number of seats gained in an election after subtracting the number of seats lost ○ *The government lost twenty seats and gained thirty one, making a net gain of eleven.*

neutral /'njuːtrəl/ *adjective* **1.** not taking sides in a dispute ○ *The conference agreed to refer the dispute to a neutral power.* ○ *The UN sent in neutral observers to observe the elections.*

2. referring to a country which refuses to take part in wars or which does not join in a war ○ *During the Second World War, Switzerland and Sweden remained neutral.* ○ *The navy was accused of having attacked neutral shipping.* ○ *Neutral states in the area have tried to bring an end to the war.* ■ *noun* a country which is neutral

neutralism /'njuːtrəlɪz(ə)m/ *noun* a policy of being neutral

neutrality /njuː'trælɪti/ *noun* being neutral

neverendum /ˌnevə'rendəm/ *noun* **1.** the practice of holding of referendums on the same subject on many occasions **2.** a referendum on a subject on which there have been referendums before

New Democratic Party /njuː ˌdemə'krætɪk 'pɑːti/ *noun* one of the main political parties in Canada, representing the interests of the working class

New Labour /ˌnjuː 'leɪbə/ *noun* the British Labour Party as it has developed since 1995, abandoning the principle of state ownership and moving towards a greater acceptance of a free-market economy

New Left /ˌnjuː 'left/ *noun* a political movement, mainly among students and intellectuals in the United States and Europe during the 1960s and 1970s, that wanted radical social and economic change

New National Party /ˌnjuː 'næʃ(ə)nəl ˌpɑːti/ *noun* in South Africa, a political party formed in 1998 when the National Party changed its name to distance itself from its apartheid policies in the past

New Right /ˌnjuː 'raɪt/ *noun* a conservative political movement that developed in the United States during the late 1960s, with a commitment to established religion, patriotism, and less control from government

news agency /'njuːz ˌeɪdʒənsi/ *noun* an office which distributes news to newspapers and television companies

newspeak /'njuːspiːk/ *noun* language that is designed to conceal the truth, especially when used by bureaucrats and politicians

NF *abbreviation* National Front

NGO *abbreviation* non-governmental organization

NIC /ˌen aɪ 'siː/ *abbreviation* National Insurance contributions

nihilism /'naɪhɪlɪz(ə)m/ *noun* **1.** the general rejection of accepted social practices and beliefs **2.** the belief that all authority is corrupt and must be rejected in order to establish a just society

Nimbyism /'nɪmbiːɪz(ə)m/ *noun* the practice of objecting to something such as a road, airport or housing being developed near where someone lives (NOTE: Nimby stands for 'not in my backyard'.)

NIO *abbreviation* Northern Ireland Office

NLF *abbreviation* National Liberation Front

no /nəʊ/ *noun* in the House of Commons, a vote against a motion ○ *The proposal received a resounding 'No' vote.* □ **the No lobby, the Noes lobby** the room in the House of Commons which MPs pass through when they vote against a motion □ **the Noes have it** the announcement that a motion has been defeated

No. 10 Downing Street, No. 10 ↓ **Number 10**

No. 11 Downing Street, No. 11 ↓ **Number 11**

nobility /nəʊ'bɪlɪti/ *noun* all noble families, taken as a group

noble /'nəʊb(ə)l/ *noun* a person from a family which has been given a title such as lord

nobleman /'nəʊb(ə)lmən/, **noblewoman** /'nəʊb(ə)lwʊmən/ *noun* a person who has a title such as lord or duchess

nod /nɒd/ *verb* to move the head forwards to show agreement ○ *When the chairman asked her if she would head the subcommittee, the treasurer nod-* ded. □ **the proposal went through on the nod** the motion was carried without any discussion and no formal vote □ **to nod through** to agree that an MP's vote is recorded, even if he or she has not personally gone through the voting lobby, e.g. when an MP is present in the Houses of Parliament but is too ill to go into the chamber

no-fly zone /ˌnəʊ 'flaɪ ˌzəʊn/ *noun* an area of sky which the military forces of other countries are ordered not to use. ◊ **exclusion zone**

NoI *abbreviation* Nation of Islam

Nolan Committee /'nəʊlən kə ˌmɪti/ *noun* same as **Committee on Standards in Public Life**

nomenklatura *noun* **1.** in Communist governments, the class consisting of the people holding positions of authority in the bureaucracy **2.** in Communist countries, the system for appointing people to senior positions in the bureaucracy, controlled by committees in the Communist Party

nominate /'nɒmɪneɪt/ *verb* to suggest someone or name someone for a job ○ *She was nominated as Labour candidate.* □ **to nominate someone to a post** to appoint someone to a post without an election □ **to nominate someone as proxy** to name someone to act for you, especially in a vote

nomination /ˌnɒmɪ'neɪʃ(ə)n/ *noun* **1.** the act of suggesting or naming someone for a job ○ *He was proposed for nomination as Labour candidate.* □ **nominations close at 10.00 a.m.** the last time for nominating someone is 10.00a.m. **2.** a person who has been nominated ○ *There were a number of nominations for the post of Deputy Leader.*

nominative /'nɒmɪnətɪv/ *adjective* appointed or suggested for election to an office or position. Abbr **nom.**

nominee /ˌnɒmɪ'niː/ *noun* a person who has been nominated ○ *She is the Party leader's nominee for the post.*

COMMENT: In the UK, a person who is nominated as a candidate for local or national elections, has to have the signatures of local residents as his or her sponsors, and, in the case of national elections, has to deposit a sum of money which is forfeited if not enough votes are received. In the United States, the executive (i.e. the President) nominates people to federal offices such as members of the Supreme Court or the cabinet, but these nominations are subject to confirmation by the Senate. Most nominations are accepted without discussion, but some are debated, and some are not confirmed. If the executive nominates someone to a federal post in one of the states without consulting the senators for that state, they can object to the nominee by saying that he is 'personally obnoxious' to them.

non-aggression /ˌnɒn əˈgreʃ(ə)n/ *noun* a policy of not using force against another country □ **a non-aggression treaty** a treaty between two countries who agree not to attack each other

nonaligned /ˌnɒnəˈlaɪnd/ *adjective* not formally associated with any major world power

noncooperation /ˌnɒnkəʊˌɒpə ˈreɪʃ(ə)n/ *noun* the practice of refusing to pay taxes or obey other laws as a protest

non-departmental public body /ˌnɒn ˌdiːpɑːtment(ə)l ˌpʌblɪk ˈbɒdi/ *noun* an organisation set up to carry out a specific role within government responsibilities, but which is not a government department or part of one. Abbr **NDPB**

non-governmental organisation /ˌnɒn ˌgʌv(ə)nment(ə)l ˌɔːgənaɪˈzeɪʃ(ə)n/ *noun* a pressure group or charity which is not fully funded by a government and which may work with the government on a local, national or international level. Abbr **NGO**

non-intervention /ˌnɒn ˌɪntə ˈvenʃ(ə)n/ *noun* a policy of not becoming involved in the internal affairs of another country ○ *The USA has followed a policy of non-intervention.*

non-proliferation treaty /ˌnɒn prəˌlɪfəˈreɪʃ(ə)n ˌtriːti/ *noun* an agreement to prevent the use of nuclear weapons spreading to countries which do not have them

non-resident /ˌnɒn ˈrezɪdənt/ *noun* a person who does not live in a place, or a company which is not officially based in a place ○ *He has a non-resident account with a French bank.* ○ *She was granted a non-resident visa.*

nonstate actor /ˌnɒnsteɪt ˈæktə/ *noun* a person or group whose actions are not controlled by a state or government, e.g. an international terrorist group

nonvoter /nɒnˈvəʊtə/ *noun* somebody who does not vote or is not eligible to vote

north /nɔːθ/ ◇ **the North 1.** the north of a country **2.** the developed countries of the world ○ *the North-South divide*

North American Free Trade Association /ˌnɔːθ əˌmerɪkən friː ˈtreɪd əˌsəʊsieɪʃ(ə)n/ *noun* the trade agreement between Canada, Mexico and the United States which allows goods to be taken from one country to another free of taxes. Abbr **NAFTA**

North Atlantic Treaty Organisation /ˌnɔːθ ətˌlæntɪk ˈtriːti ˌɔːgənaɪzeɪʃ(ə)n/ *noun* the alliance set up in 1949 to link various countries in a common political and military alliance to provide mutual defence in the case of attack by Communist countries. The members in 2004 were expanded by the inclusion of a number of the former Communist countries of the Warsaw Pact. The members are: Belgium, Bulgaria, Canada, Czech Republic, Denmark, Estonia, France, Germany, Greece, Hungary, Iceland, Italy, Latvia, Lithuania, Luxembourg, the Netherlands, Norway, Poland, Portugal, Romania, Slovakia, Slovenia, Spain, Turkey, the UK, and the USA. Abbr **NATO**

Northern Alliance /ˌnɔːð(ə)n ə ˈlaɪəns/ *noun* a loose grouping of Afghan military forces that ended Taliban rule in Afghanistan in 2001

Northern Ireland Assembly /ˌnɔːð(ə)n ˌaɪələnd əˈsembli/ *noun* the devolved elected representative body set up in 1999 in Belfast with limited powers to make laws for Northern Ireland (NOTE: The Northern Ireland Assembly has been unable to work effectively because of continued distrust between the political parties in Northern Ireland and has been suspended for longer than it has been in effective operation.)

Northern Ireland Executive /ˌnɔːð(ə)n ˈaɪələnd ɪgˌzekjʊtɪv/ *noun* the devolved government of Northern Ireland, suspended from 14 October 2002

Northern Ireland Office /ˌnɔːð(ə)n ˈaɪələnd ˌɒfɪs/ *noun* during devolution, a UK government department responsible for constitutional and security issues in Northern Ireland. Abbr **NIO**

North-South dialogue /ˌnɔːθ saʊθ ˈdaɪəlɒg/ *noun* discussions between the industrialised countries of the northern hemisphere and the developing countries of the southern hemisphere

North-South Divide /ˌnɔːθ saʊθ dɪˈvaɪd/ *noun* the political and economic differences between industrialised countries of the northern hemisphere and the developing countries of the southern hemisphere

Northstead /ˈnɔːθsted/ ♦ **Chiltern Hundreds**

note /nəʊt/ *noun* **1.** a brief piece of writing **2.** an official document with a particular purpose

notice /ˈnəʊtɪs/ *noun* **1.** a piece of written information ○ *The company receptionist pinned up a notice about the pension scheme.* **2.** the official passing of information to someone, especially warning that something may happen such as a that a contract is going to end, that a worker will leave his job or that a tenant must leave the property he or she is living in ○ *The Leader of the Opposition has given notice that he will seek an emergency debate on the economy.* ○ *The Minister asked for notice of the question.*

notice of motion /ˌnəʊtɪs əv ˈməʊʃ(ə)n/ *noun* a document telling the other party to a case that an application will be made to the court

notwithstanding /ˌnɒtwɪðˈstændɪŋ/ *adverb, preposition* without being affected by something ○ *The debate proceeded notwithstanding the objections of the Opposition members* or *the objections of Opposition members notwithstanding.* (NOTE: can be used before or after the phrase to which it refers)

nuclear deterrent /ˌnjuːkliə dɪˈterənt/ *noun* a nuclear weapon which it is hoped will prevent attacks from other countries because of fears that it will be used

nuclear disarmament /ˌnjuːkliə dɪsˈɑːməmənt/ *noun* the process of reducing or getting rid of nuclear weapons and/or the capacity to manufacture them

nuclear energy /ˌnjuːkliə ˈenədʒi/ *noun* electricity made using a nuclear process

nuclear-free zone /ˌnjuːkliə friː ˈzəʊn/ *adjective* an area where the people say they will not allow nuclear power stations or nuclear weapons to be placed

nuclear proliferation /ˌnjuːkliə prəˌlɪfəˈreɪʃ(ə)n/ *noun* the spread of nuclear weapons to countries who have previously not possessed them

nuclear test /ˌnjuːkliə ˈtest/ *noun* a test on a nuclear weapon

nuclear test ban /ˌnjuːkliə ˈtest ˌbæn/ *noun* a decision to stop the testing of nuclear weapons

nuclear war /ˌnjuːkliə ˈwɔː/ *noun* a war using nuclear weapons

NUCPS *abbreviation* National Union of Civil and Public Servants

null /nʌl/ *adjective* of no value □ **to render a decision null** to make a decision useless or to cancel a decision

nullification /ˌnʌlɪfɪˈkeɪʃ(ə)n/ *noun* the act of making something useless or of no value

nullify /ˈnʌlɪfaɪ/ *verb* to make something of no value or force

Number 10 /ˌnʌmbəˈ ten/ *noun* No 10, Downing Street, the official home of the Prime Minister of the United Kingdom (NOTE: It is used informally to refer to the Prime Minister) □ **he is hoping to move into Number Ten after the election** he is expecting to be elected Prime Minister

Number 11 /ˌnʌmbər ɪˈlevən/ *noun* No 11, Downing Street, the official home of the Chancellor of the Exchequer of the United Kingdom (NOTE: It is used informally to refer to the Chancellor of the Exchequer.) □ **he's set his sights on Number 11** he would like to become Chancellor of the Exchequer

numerical order /njuːˌmerɪk(ə)l ˈɔːdə/ *noun* the arrangement of records in order of their numbers ○ *The documents are filed in numerical order.*

nuncio /ˈnʌnsiəʊ/ *noun* an ambassador of the Pope

O

OAS *abbreviation* Organization of American States

oath of allegiance /ˌəʊθ əv ə'liːdʒəns/ *noun* **1.** a promise to be loyal or to obey the orders of a country or ruler **2.** an oath sworn by all MPs before they can take their seats in the House of Commons, unless they affirm instead. ◊ **affirm** □ **to take the oath** to swear allegiance to the Queen before taking a seat in the House of Commons as an MP ○ *after taking the oath, the new MP signs the test roll*

obedience /ə'biːdiəns/ *noun* the practice of doing what someone asks you to do ○ *Every citizen should show obedience to the laws of the state.* ○ *The army swore obedience to the president.*

objection /əb'dʒekʃən/ *noun* a statement of opposition to something

objector /əb'dʒektə/ *noun* a person who opposes something. ◊ **conscientious objector**

observer /əb'zɜːvə/ *noun* **1.** someone who is appointed to act as a witness to an important event such as an election, sometimes in another country, to see that it has been carried out fairly ○ *United Nations observers were stationed on the ceasefire line.* **2.** someone who attends a meeting to listen but not to take part ○ *Two official observers attended the meeting.* ○ *International observers were present during the general elections.*

obstruct /əb'strʌkt/ *verb* to get in the way or to stop something progressing ○ *MPs attempted to obstruct the passage of the Bill.*

obstruction /əb'strʌkʃən/ *noun* an act of preventing some actions from being taken ○ *The MPs were successful in their obstruction of the Bill.*

obstructive /əb'strʌktɪv/ *adjective* trying to prevent something deliberately ○ *MPs complained of the obstructive behaviour of some right-wingers.*

obtain /əb'teɪn/ *verb* to be a rule or to have a legal status ○ *a rule obtaining in international law* ○ *This right does not obtain in the House of Commons.*

occupation /ˌɒkjʊ'peɪʃ(ə)n/ *noun* an invasion of a country or place by an army, which then stays there to keep control □ **army of occupation** an army which invades a country and then stays there to keep control

occupy /'ɒkjʊpaɪ/ *verb* to invade a place or building or country and stay there ○ *The protesters occupied the radio station.* ○ *The enemy army occupied the south of the country.* □ **occupying forces** armed forces which invade a country and then stay there

Ofcom /'ɒfkɒm/ *noun* a regulatory body for the telecommunications and broadcasting industries

office /'ɒfɪs/ *noun* **1.** a British government department □ **the Home Office** the ministry dealing with the internal affairs of the country, including the police and the prisons **2.** a post or position ○ *She holds or performs the office of treasurer.* □ **high office** an important position or job □ **the high offices of state** the most important ministerial posts in the British government (the Prime Minister, the Foreign Secretary, the Chancellor of the Exchequer, the Home Secretary) **3.** the set of rooms where an organisation works or where business is done **4.** a room where someone works and does business

office holder /'ɒfɪs 'həʊldə/ *noun* an official in a government position

Office of Fair Trading /ˌɒfɪs əv feə 'treɪdɪŋ/ *noun* the British government department which protects consumers against unfair or illegal business

officer /'ɒfɪsə/ *noun* **1.** a person who has an official position, e.g. a person working in a local government department ○ *Detailing the expenditure will necessitate a high cost in officer time.* ○ *The report was drawn up by the officers on the instructions of the council.* ○ *The members ignored the advice of the officers.* ◊ **police officer 2.** a usually unpaid official of a club or society ○ *the election of officers of an association*

official /ə'fɪʃ(ə)l/ *adjective* **1.** done because it has been authorised by a government department or organisation ○ *on official business* ○ *He left official documents in his car.* ○ *She received an official letter of explanation.* **2.** done or approved by a director or by a person in authority ○ *This must be an official order – it is written on the department's notepaper.* □ **the strike was made official** the local strike was approved by the main trade union office ■ *noun* a person working in a central or local government department ○ *Airport officials inspected the shipment.* ○ *Government officials stopped the import licence.* ○ *The council members met with officials to discuss the implementation of the new policy.* (NOTE: In the UK, a distinction is made between an official, who is an appointed employee of the government, and elected representatives. In US English, even the President is an official.) □ **high official** an important person in a government department □ **minor official** a person in a low position in a government department

officialdom /ə'fɪʃ(ə)ldəm/ *noun* (*usually disapproving*) officials work-

ing together in a set way ○ *The whole plan has been obstructed by officialdom.*

officialese /əˌfɪʃə'liːz/ *noun* the language used in government documents, often regarded as difficult to understand

Official Journal /əˌfɪʃ(ə)l 'dʒɜːn(ə)l/ *noun* in the European Union, the published record of all the regulations and directives that have been produced

officially /ə'fɪʃ(ə)li/ *adverb* in an official way ○ *Officially he knows nothing about the problem, but unofficially he has given us a lot of advice about it.*

official mediator /əˌfɪʃ(ə)l 'miːdieɪtə/ *noun* the government official who tries to make the two sides in an industrial dispute agree

Official Receiver /əˌfɪʃ(ə)l rɪ 'siːvə/ *noun* the government official whose job is to deal with bankrupt companies

Official Report /ə'fɪʃ(ə)l rɪ'pɔːt/ *noun* the exact record of what is said and done in the House of Commons and House of Lords. ◊ **Hansard**

official secret /əˌfɪʃ(ə)l 'siːkrət/ *noun* a piece of information which is important to the state and which it is a crime for an official to tell someone who has no right to know about it

Official Secrets Act /əˌfɪʃ(ə)l 'siːkrəts ˌækt/ *noun* the Act of Parliament which makes it a crime for anyone to make public secret information relating to the state

Official Unionist Party /ə'fɪʃ(ə)l 'juːnjənɪst 'pɑːti/ *noun* same as **Ulster Unionist Party**

officio /ə'fɪʃɪəʊ/ ◆ **ex officio**

off licence /'ɒf ˌlaɪs(ə)ns/ *noun* **1.** a licence to sell alcohol to be drunk away from the place where it is bought **2.** a shop which sells alcohol to be taken away for drinking elsewhere

off-message /ˌɒf 'mesɪdʒ/ *adjective* not following the official policy of a political party or other organisation

OFSTED /'ɒfsted/ *noun* the government department that monitors educational standards in schools and colleges in England and Wales. Full form **Office for Standards in Education**

OHMS *abbreviation* On Her Majesty's Service

000 a statement saying how much income you have to the tax office

Oireachtas *noun* the national parliament of Ireland, consisting of the president and two chambers: the lower is the Dáil Eireann and the upper, the Seanad Eireann

Old Commonwealth /əʊld 'kɒmənwelθ/ *noun* the oldest members of the Commonwealth, e.g. Canada and Australia

Old Labour /əʊld 'leɪbə/ *noun* the British Labour Party, as it existed during most of the 20th century, supporting traditional socialist principles such as state ownership and opposition to a free market economy. Compare **New Labour**

oligarch /'ɒlɪgɑːk/ *noun* a member of an oligarchy

oligarchical /ˌɒlɪ'gɑːkɪk(ə)l/, **oligarchic** /ˌɒlɪ'gɑːkɪk/ *adjective* referring to an oligarchy

oligarchy /'ɒlɪgɑːki/ *noun* **1.** government by a small group of people **2.** a small ruling group ○ *The country is ruled by an oligarchy called the 'fifteen families'.* **3.** a state ruled by a small group

ombudsman /'ɒmbʊdzmən/ *noun* an official who investigates complaints by the public against government departments or other large organisations

COMMENT: There are in fact several ombudsmen: the main one is the Parliamentary Commissioner, but there are also others, such as the Health Service Commissioners, who investigate complaints against the Health Service, and the Local Commissioners or Local Government Ombudsmen who investigate complaints against local authorities. Although ombudsmen will make their recommendations to the department concerned, and may make their recommendations public, they has no power to enforce them. The Parliamentary Commissioner may only investigate complaints which are presented through an MP, but the Local Government Ombudsmen can be approached directly, or through a local councillor. A member of the public first brings the complaint to a councillor or MP, and if they cannot get satisfaction from the department against which the complaint is made, then the matter is passed to the Ombudsman.

one man one vote /ˌwʌn mæn ˌwʌn 'vəʊt/ *noun* the democratic principle that each person entitled to vote has a single vote, equal to all the others

one minute speech /ˌwʌn 'mɪnət ˌspiːtʃ/ *noun US* a short speech by a member of the House of Representatives on any subject at the beginning of the day's business

One-Nation Conservatism /ˌwʌn ˌneɪʃ(ə)n kən'sɜːvəˌtɪz(ə)m/ *noun* the belief that Conservatives should include every willing person in the life and opportunity of our country and get support from all classes by undertaking social reforms to help the working class

COMMENT: The One Nation Conservative tradition, with its emphasis on social justice, was started by Benjamin Disraeli. In his novel *Sybil* (1845) he had described the rich and the poor as 'Two nations between whom there is no intercourse and no sympathy; who are as ignorant of each other's habits, thoughts, and feelings, as if they were dwellers in different zones, or inhabitants of different planets; who are formed by a different breeding, are fed by different food, are ordered by different manners, and are not governed by the same laws'.

1922 Committee /ˌnaɪntiːn ˌtwenti 'tuː kəˌmɪti/ *noun* a committee formed of all backbench Conservative MPs in the House of Commons, who meet regularly and question ministers and other party leaders (NOTE: The equivalent in the Labour Party is the Parliamentary Labour Party (PLP).)

one-party state /ˌwʌn ˌpɑːti 'steɪt/ *noun* a country in which only one party is allowed to exist, although voters generally have a choice of candidates all from the same party

on-message /ˌɒn ˈmesɪdʒ/ *adjective* following the official policy of a political party or other organisation

OPEC /ˈəʊpek/ *n* an organisation of oil-producing countries. Full form **Organization of Petroleum Exporting Countries** (NOTE: The members are Algeria, Gabon, Indonesia, Iran, Iraq, Kuwait, Libya, Nigeria, Qatar, Saudi Arabia, the United Arab Emirates, and Venezuela.)

open door policy /ˈəʊpən dɔː ˈpɒlɪsi/ *noun* a trading policy by which a country allows free trade with all other countries

open-ended /ˌəʊpən ˈendɪd/ *adjective* with no fixed limit or restrictions to what has been agreed ○ *an open-ended agreement* (NOTE: The US term is **open-end**.)

open government /ˈəʊpən ˈɡʌv(ə)nmənt/ *noun* a system in which most decisions by government and most government records are available for any citizen to read

open hearing /ˌəʊpən ˈhɪərɪŋ/ *noun* a court case or meeting which is open to the public and to journalists

opening /ˈəʊp(ə)nɪŋ/ *noun* **1.** a ceremony to celebrate the start of a public event ○ *The Queen attends the State Opening of Parliament every year,* **2.** the act of making something open ■ *adjective* the first of several similar things ○ *the chairman's opening remarks* ○ *The opening speech from the Home Secretary was interrupted by Opposition shouts.*

open society /ˈəʊpən səˈsaɪəti/ *noun* a society in which people can say what they think freely and openly

opinion /əˈpɪnjən/ *noun* a belief or set of beliefs held by people about an issue

opinion poll /əˈpɪnjən pəʊl/ *noun* a study of the opinions of a small carefully chosen group of people, so as to guess the opinion of the whole population ○ *Politicians take very careful*

note of the opinion polls in the run-up to a general election.

opinion research /əˈpɪnjən rɪ ˈsɜːtʃ/ *noun* the study of the changing opinions of a population based on interviewing small representative groups

opponent /əˈpəʊnənt/ *noun* a person who is against you or who votes against what you propose ○ *The pro-nuclear group tried to discredit their opponents in the debate.*

oppose /əˈpəʊz/ *verb* to try to stop something happening ○ *A minority of committee members opposed the motion.* ○ *We are all opposed to the government's plan.* ○ *The Speaker opposed the opposition's application for an adjournment.*

opposed business /əˈpəʊzd ˈbɪznɪs/ *noun* matters for discussion in the House of Commons which an MP objects to

opposition /ˌɒpəˈzɪʃ(ə)n/ *noun* **1.** the action of trying to stop something or of not agreeing to something ○ *There was considerable opposition to the plan for reorganising the local boundaries.* ○ *The voters showed their opposition to the government by voting against the proposal in the referendum.* **2. Opposition** the largest political party which opposes the government ○ *The Opposition tried to propose a vote of censure on the Prime Minister.* ○ *The spokesman for the Opposition* or *the Opposition spokesman answered the Minister's allegations.* □ **Leader of the Opposition, Opposition Leader** the head of the largest political party opposing the government **3. Opposition** a group of parties which oppose the government

Opposition Day /ˌɒpəˈzɪʃ(ə)n deɪ/ *noun* a day on which a debate is held on a subject chosen by the Opposition

Opposition front bench /ˌɒpə ˈzɪʃ(ə)n frʌnt bentʃ/ *noun* **1.** the seats for the Opposition Shadow Cabinet **2.** the members of the Opposition Shadow Cabinet ○ *An Opposition front bench spokesman asked why the*

Government had been so slow in investigating the affair.

oppress /ə'pres/ *verb* to rule cruelly and unfairly, especially by limiting the personal freedom of the citizens ○ *The dictator has stayed in power by using the army and police force to oppress the people.*

oppression /ə'preʃ(ə)n/ *noun* cruel and unfair rule and control

oppressive /ə'presɪv/ *adjective* using cruel and unfair methods of government ○ *Under the dictator's oppressive regime, the ordinary citizens were afraid to speak out against the system.*

oppressor /ə'presə/ *noun* a ruler who governs in a cruel or unjust way ○ *The people rose in revolution to overthrow their oppressors.*

opt out /ˌɒpt 'aʊt/ *verb* to decide not to take part in a group, activity or agreement, or to stop taking part ○ *Under John Major the UK opted out of some provisions of the Maastricht Treaty such as the Social Chapter.*

opt-out /'ɒpt aʊt/ *noun* a decision or permission not to take part in something

Orange Order /'ɒrɪndʒ 'ɔːdə/ *noun* a Protestant organisation that strongly supports Protestantism in Ireland, especially Northern Ireland

order /'ɔːdə/ *noun* **1.** a general state of calm, where everything is working as planned. ◊ **law and order 2.** an official statement asking someone to do something □ **on the orders of someone** because someone has officially asked ○ *On the orders of the Chief Constable, the demonstrators dispersed.* **3.** the arrangement of records such as filing cards or invoices ○ *filed in date* or *alphabetical order* **4.** the arrangement of business in the House of Commons. ◊ **order of business, order of the day 5.** □ **to bring a meeting to order, to come to order** (*of a meeting*) to get a meeting back to discussing the agenda again after an interruption □ **Order! Order!** a call by the Speaker of the House of Commons

to bring the meeting to order **6.** a general social or political situation at a particular time ○ *a threat to the established order* ○ *a time of great changes to the existing social order* **7.** a request for goods to be supplied ○ *to give a supplier an order* or *to place an order with a supplier for military equipment* **8.** a document which allows money to be paid to someone ○ *She sent us an order on the Chartered Bank.*

Order Book /'ɔːdə bʊk/ *noun* a list showing the House of Commons' business for each day of the rest of the session of Parliament

Order in Council /ˌɔːdə ɪn 'kaʊns(ə)l/ *noun* a decision made by the Queen in Council, on the advice of her ministers, in an area which does not need the agreement of Parliament

order of business /ˌɔːdə əv 'bɪznɪs/ *noun* the timetable showing what the House of Commons has to do for that day

COMMENT: The normal order of business of the House of Commons begins with prayers, followed by messages from the Queen or official messages from foreign governments, motions for writs to hold by-elections, private business and Question Time, when ministers answer questions about the work of their departments. Following this, various matters can be discussed, including debate on motions and public Bills.

order of precedence /'ɔːdə əv 'presɪd(ə)ns/ *noun* the arrangement of things or people according to their importance ○ *The item on finance takes precedence over all other items on the agenda.*

order of the day /'ɔːdə əv ðɪ deɪ/ *noun* a matter which the House of Commons has decided will be discussed on an agreed day

order paper /ˌɔːdə 'peɪpə/ *noun* a piece of paper showing the timetable to be followed that day in the House of Commons ○ *As the Prime Minister rose to speak his supporters waved their order papers in great excitement.*

orders /'ɔːdəz/ *plural noun* secondary legislation made by ministers, under powers given by Act of Parliament, which still has to be approved by Parliament before coming into force

ordinance /'ɔːdɪnəns/ *noun* **1.** a law or rule made by an authority **2.** *US* a rule made by a town council which is effective only within the town

ordinarily /'ɔːd(ə)n(ə)rɪli/ *adverb* □ **ordinarily resident** usually resident in some country

ordinary resolution /ˌɔːd(ə)n(ə)ri ˌrezə'luːʃ(ə)n/ *noun* a matter or decision which can be agreed by a simple majority of those voting

organ /'ɔːgən/ *noun* **1.** an organisation that is responsible on behalf of a larger institution for a particular job **2.** the newspaper, magazine or other regular publication of a particular organisation, which gives official information ○ *the official organ of the association*

Organization of African Unity /ˌɔːgənaɪ'zeɪʃ(ə)n əv 'æfrɪkən 'juːnəti/ *noun* an organisation of African states, replaced in 2002 by the African Union

Országgyűlés *noun* the legislature in Hungary

OSCE *abbreviation* Organization for Security and Cooperation in Europe

OSD *abbreviation* Office of the Secretary of Defense

outcome /'aʊtkʌm/ *noun* the result ○ *We are waiting for the outcome of the enquiry.* ○ *The outcome of the debate was in doubt.*

outcry /'aʊtkraɪ/ *noun* a strong public protest

Outer House /'aʊtə haʊz/ *noun* a part of the Scottish Court of Session, formed of five judges

outgoing /aʊt'gəʊɪŋ/ *adjective* a person or group that is about to leave office ○ *the outgoing president*

outlaw /'aʊtlɔː/ *verb* to say that something is not allowed by law ○ *The government has proposed a bill to outlaw drinking in public.* ■ *noun* former-

ly, a person who was excluded from society as a punishment

outline planning permission /ˌaʊt(ə)laɪn 'plænɪŋ pə,mɪʃ(ə)n/ *noun* general permission to build a property on a piece of land, but not final because there are no details

outpoll /aʊt'pəʊl/ *verb* to receive more votes than an opponent in an election

outreach /'aʊtriːtʃ/ *noun* services or advice for members of the public who find travel difficult, provided outside a hospital or government offices in the places where people live

outvote /aʊt'vəʊt/ *verb* to defeat someone in a vote ○ *He was outvoted 3 to 1.*

Oval Office /ˌəʊvəl 'ɒfɪs/ *noun* the room in the White House which is the personal office of the President of the United States (NOTE: It is also used to mean the President in person: *The Oval Office was not pleased by the attitude of the Senate.*)

overall /ˌəʊvər'ɔːl/ *adjective* covering everything ○ *The Chief Executive has overall responsibility for running the council's affairs.*

overall majority /ˌəʊvərɔːl mə'dʒɒrɪti/ *noun* a majority of votes or seats, which is more than all the votes and seats of the opposition taken together ○ *The government had an overall majority of two.* ○ *After the election, the ruling coalition lost its overall majority.* Also called **straight majority**

overclass /'əʊvəklɑːs/ *noun* the governing or ruling class of a country

over-populated /'əʊvə 'pɒpjʊleɪtɪd/ *adjective* having too many people

overrepresent /ˌəʊvəreprɪ'zent/ *verb* to give more representation to a group than is reasonable based on its size ○ *The present system tends to overrepresent the majority party.* ○ *Males are overrepresented in the House of Commons.*

overriding interest /ˌəʊvəraɪdɪŋ 'ɪntrəst/ *noun* a more important con-

cern than any other ○ *National security is the overriding interest in this
case.*

overthrow *verb* /ˌəʊvə'θrəʊ/ to remove a government or leader suddenly from power ○ *The regime was overthrown in a military coup.* ■ *noun*
/'əʊvəθrəʊ/ the sudden removal of a
government or leader ○ *The army was
involved in the overthrow of the president.*

OVP *abbreviation* Office of the Vice
President

P

pacifism /ˈpæsɪfɪz(ə)m/ *noun* the belief that war is wrong

pacifist /ˈpæsɪfɪst/ *noun* a person who believes that war is wrong ■ *adjective* believing that war is wrong

pacify /ˈpæsɪfaɪ/ *verb* **1.** to make someone who is angry or upset feel happier ○ *The announcement was clearly intended to pacify angry residents.* **2.** to end war or fighting in a place and establish peaceful conditions

pack /pæk/ *verb* to fill a committee or other group with members who are sympathetic to your views ○ *The left-wing group packed the general purposes committee with activists.*

packaging /ˈpækɪdʒɪŋ/ *noun* a way of introducing someone or something to the public in order to create a favourable impression

pact /pækt/ *noun* an agreement between two parties or countries ○ *The countries in the region signed a non-aggression pact.* ○ *The two minority parties made an electoral pact not to oppose each other in agreed constituencies.*

page /peɪdʒ/ *verb* to send an electronic message to someone on a pager ■ *noun* in the US Congress, a High School student employed to support members and get work experience

pager /ˈpeɪdʒə/ *noun, noun* a small electronic device for receiving messages when a person cannot be contacted by phone, e.g. when they are in a meeting or in Parliament ○ *received a pager message* (NOTE: Pagers are a useful way of getting messages to people in the House of Commons and House of Lords discreetly and without making a noise.)

paid-up member /ˌpeɪd ʌp ˈmembə/ *noun* a person who has paid to be a member of a political party or other organisation

pair /peə/ *noun* an agreement between two MPs from opposite sides of the House of Commons not to vote on a motion, so allowing one of them to be away from the House during a vote if necessary ○ *She was not able to find a pair, so had to come back from Paris to attend the debate.* ■ *verb* to arrange for two MPs from opposite sides of the House of Commons to agree that if one of them is away from the House in an emergency the other one will not vote ○ *He was paired with John Smith.*

palace /ˈpælɪs/ *noun* **1.** a large house, especially one where a ruler or leader lives or used to live **2.** the royal family, especially the British royal family ○ *a Palace spokesman*

Palace of Westminster /ˌpæləs əv ˈwestmɪnstə/ *noun* the Houses of Parliament, together with the area round them

COMMENT: The Palace was the main home of the kings of England from the middle of the 11th century until 1512, by which time most governing and judicial functions took place there. After private chapels were abolished in 1547, the Royal Chapel of St Stephen within the Palace of Westminster was handed over to the Commons as a meeting place, until 1834 when most of the Palace was burned down. The present Houses of Parliament were built during the next 30 years. The chamber of the House of Commons was destroyed in a German air attack in 1941 and rebuilt after the Second World War.

palace revolution /ˈpælɪs ˌrevəˈluːʃ(ə)n/ *noun* a change of leader or ruler achieved by those who are already part of the ruling group

pamphlet /ˈpæmflət/ *noun* a small book, often about a political issue

pan- /pæn/ *prefix* covering all □ **pan-African**, **pan-American** covering all Africa or all America

Pan-African /ˌpæn ˈæfrɪkən/ *adjective* relating to all the nations of Africa

pantisocracy /ˌpæntɪsˈɒkrəsi/ *noun* a community in which everyone shares power and is equal

Papal Nuncio /ˌpeɪp(ə)l ˈnʌnsiəʊ/ *noun* an ambassador sent by the Pope to a country

paper /ˈpeɪpə/ *noun* **1.** a written report or proposal ○ *The Treasurer asked his deputy to write a paper on new funding.* ○ *The planning department prepared a paper for the committee on the possible uses of the site.* **2.** a newspaper **3.** an official document

paper tiger /ˈpeɪpə ˈtaɪɡə/ *noun* a person, organisation or country which appears to be strong and powerful but is in fact weak

parastatal /pærəˈsteɪt(ə)l/ *adjective* performing a function usually associated with a government under indirect government control ○ *a parastatal utility company*

Paris /ˈpærɪs/ ◆ **Treaty of Paris**

parish council /ˌpærɪʃ ˈkaʊnsəl/ *noun* the smallest unit of local government, representing a group of at least 200 people in a village or small town

parish meeting /ˌpærɪʃ ˈmiːtɪŋ/ *noun* a meeting which must be held once a year in a parish and which all electors in the parish may attend

parish pump politics /ˌpærɪʃ pʌmp ˈpɒlɪtɪks/ *noun* local politics, concerning only minor local issues

Parl. *abbreviation* **1.** Parliament **2.** parliamentary

parliament /ˈpɑːləmənt/ *noun* **1.** the elected group of representatives who form the legislative body which makes the laws of a country ○ *the Dáil or Irish parliament* □ **Mother of Parliaments** the British Parliament at Westminster **2. Parliament** in the UK, the body formed of the House of Commons and House of Lords. ◊ **Act of Parliament, Houses of Parliament** □ **to open Parliament** to start a new session of Parliament ○ *Te Queen opened the new Parliament yesterday.*

Parliament Act /ˈpɑːləmənt ækt/ *noun* an Act passed in 1911 that prevented the House of Lords from having the power to veto the financial proposals of the Commons and from holding up other legislation for more than two years. It also made the maximum length of a parliament five years.

parliamentarian /ˌpɑːləmenˈteəriən/ *noun* **1.** a member of one of the Houses of Parliament ○ *A delegation of British parliamentarians was invited to visit Canada.* **2.** one of two officials of the US Congress who attend all debates and advise on procedure: the House Parliamentarian and the Parliamentarian of the Senate

parliamentarianism /ˌpɑːləmenˈteəriənɪz(ə)m/ *noun* government of a country by a parliament

parliamentary /ˌpɑːləˈment(ə)ri/ *adjective* referring to parliament

parliamentary agent /ˌpɑːləment(ə)ri ˈeɪdʒ(ə)nt/ *noun* an expert, usually a lawyer, who advises people who are not MPs on how to get a Bill through Parliament

parliamentary calendar /ˌpɑːləment(ə)ri ˈkælɪndə/ *noun* a timetable of events in Parliament, with dates for discussion of each Bill

Parliamentary Commissioner /ˌpɑːləˌment(ə)ri kəˈmɪʃ(ə)nə/, **Parliamentary Commissioner for Administration** /ˌpɑːləment(ə)ri kə ˌmɪʃ(ə)nə fər ədmɪnɪˈstreɪʃ(ə)n/ *noun* the official who investigates complaints by the public against government departments. Also called **Ombudsman**

Parliamentary Commissioner for Standards /ˌpɑːləment(ə)ri kə

ˌmɪʃ(ə)nə fə 'stændədz/ *noun* an official whose job is to supervise the Register of Members' Interests and to advise the Committee on Standards and Privileges about issues relating to the MPs' code of conduct. Also called **Ombudsman**

parliamentary   counsel /ˌpɑːləment(ə)ri 'kaʊnsəl/, **parliamentary   draftsman** /ˌpɑːlə'ment(ə)ri 'drɑːftsmən/ *noun* a lawyer who is responsible for drawing up parliamentary Bills. Also called **parliamentary draftsman**

parliamentary   diary /ˌpɑːlə'ment(ə)ri 'daɪəri/ *noun* the list of days of the week, showing what business is to take place in Parliament on each day

parliamentary draftsman /ˌpɑːlə'ment(ə)ri 'drɑːftsmən/ *noun* same as **parliamentary counsel**

parliamentary etiquette /ˌpɑːlə'ment(ə)ri 'etɪket/ *noun* the formal rules of behaviour in Parliament

Parliamentary Labour Party /ˌpɑːləˌment(ə)ri ˌleɪbə 'pɑːti/ *noun* the group formed of all Labour Party members elected to Parliament. Abbr **PLP**

parliamentary   party /ˌpɑːlə'ment(ə)ri 'pɑːti/ *noun* the members of a political party who are also Members of Parliament

Parliamentary Private Secretary /ˌpɑːləˌment(ə)ri ˌpraɪvət 'sekrətri/ *noun* the most junior rank of minister, acting as a general helper to a particular Cabinet minister. Abbr **PPS**

Parliamentary   privilege /ˌpɑːləment(ə)ri 'prɪvɪlɪdʒ/ *noun* the right of a Member of Parliament or Member of the House of Lords to speak freely to the House without the possibility of being sued for slander

Parliamentary Secretary /ˌpɑːlə ˌment(ə)ri 'sekrətri/, **Parliamentary Under-Secretary** /ˌpɑːləˌment(ə)ri ˌʌndə 'sekrətri/ *noun* a government member such as an MP or a member of the House of Lords who works in a department headed by a Secretary of State or Minister of State (NOTE: To avoid confusion, they are called Parliamentary Under-Secretaries in departments where the head of the department is a Secretary of State.)

Parliamentary Secretary to the Treasury /ˌpɑːlə'ment(ə)ri 'sekrətri tə ðɪ 'treʒəri/ *noun* in the House of Commons, the Government Chief Whip. ◊ **Captain of the Honourable Corps of Gentleman-at-Arms**

parliamentary   sketch /ˌpɑːlə 'ment(ə)ri sketʃ/ *noun* a short humorous article in a newspaper on events that have recently taken place in Parliament

Parliamentary Under-Secretary /ˌpɑːləˌment(ə)ri ˌʌndə 'sekrətri/, **Parliamentary Under-Secretary of State** *noun* ♦ **Parliamentary Secretary**

parliamentary   year /ˌpɑːlə 'ment(ə)ri jɪə/ *noun* the year of a session of Parliament, running from the Opening of Parliament, usually in the autumn, until the recess usually in the following summer

participation /pɑːˌtɪsɪ'peɪʃ(ə)n/ *noun* the way in which people become involved in the political process by voting, campaigning, joining political parties and generally playing an active part in politics (NOTE: The low turnout in recent local and general elections has led people to express concerns about the level of participation in British politics.)

particularism /pə'tɪkjʊlərɪz(ə)m/ *noun* the policy of allowing political divisions within a country or federation to be self-governing, without regard to what effect this may have on the larger body

partisan /'pɑːtɪz(ə)n, ˌpɑːtɪ'zæn/ *noun* **1.** a person who supports a policy or political party strongly ○ *She's a partisan of the campaign for more women Members of Parliament.* **2.** an armed supporter of a political group which is fighting against the ruling government

partisan alignment /ˌpɑːtɪz(ə)n ə ˈlaɪnmənt/ *noun* the long-term connection between a person and a particular political party for which they regularly vote (NOTE: Partisan alignment seems to be in decline in most modern democracies.)

partisan dealignment /ˌpɑːtɪz(ə)n ˌdiəˈlaɪnmənt/ *noun* the way in which in recent years people have been less willing to vote regularly for a particular political party

partition /pɑːˈtɪʃ(ə)n/ *noun* the act of dividing up a country

party /ˈpɑːti/ *noun* a political group which joins together to gain representation and political power and which is united by common goals and ideas □ **the party line** the official policy of a political party, which must be followed by its members and supporters □ **to toe the party line** to say what the party expects you to say or not to have a different view from the official party policy ○ *He was expelled from the party for refusing to toe the party line.*

party headquarters /ˈpɑːti hed ˈkwɔːtəz/ *noun* the central office of a political party ○ *The leader called a meeting of the national committee at the party headquarters.*

party leader /ˌpɑːti ˈliːdə/ *noun* the head of a political party, who usually becomes head of government if the party wins power

COMMENT: Normally a party leader has a great deal of power when it come to making appointments and deciding policy. This power has increased in recent years as the influence of the party conference has declined. Party leaders must still consult widely among their colleagues before they make important decisions. In the end, they have been appointed by the party membership and can be dismissed by them if they get out of touch with party opinion.

party line /ˌpɑːti ˈlaɪn/ *noun* the official policy of a political party or other organisation

party list system /ˌpɑːti lɪst ˈsɪstəm/ *noun* an electoral system used for constituencies which have more than one representative, in which a voter votes for a list of candidates belonging to a particular party rather than for an individual candidate. Seats are then given to each party according to their share of the vote in that constituency and to each candidate according to the position they have been given by their party on the list. The next candidate on a party's list fills any vacancy that occurs in mid-term. Also called **list system** (NOTE: This system has been used for British elections to the European Parliament since1999.)

COMMENT: Under the list system, each party draws up a list of candidates, and the electors vote for the party list, not for individual candidates. The parliament is then formed of candidates from each party's list in proportion to the total number of votes which the party has received. British elections to the European Parliament are conducted under a party list system.

party man /ˈpɑːti mæn/ *noun* a man who is a loyal member or supporter of a political party

party person /ˈpɑːti ˈpɜːs(ə)n/ *noun* a loyal member or supporter of a political party

party political broadcast /ˈpɑːti pəˈlɪtɪk(ə)l ˈbrɔːdkɑːst/ *noun* a short television or radio programme in which a political party talks about political issues, especially during an election

party politics /ˌpɑːti ˈpɒlɪtɪks/ *noun* the situation where decisions are made or actions taken in line with the policies of a particular party, rather than independently or in the general interest

party woman /ˈpɑːti ˈwʊmən/ *noun* a woman who is a loyal member or supporter of a political party

pass /pɑːs/ *noun* a piece of paper allowing someone to go into a building or area ○ *You need a pass to enter the Ministry offices.* ○ *All members of staff must show a pass.* ■ *verb* **1.** to vote to make a law ○ *Parliament passed the Bill which has now become law.* ○ *The Congress passed the bill over the president's veto.* **2.** to approve something ○ *The Director of Finance has to pass an invoice before it is paid.* ○ *The loan has been passed by the council.* **3.** to be successful in an exam or test

passable /'pɑːsəb(ə)l/ *adjective* referring to proposed legislation that is likely to be passed or made law

passage /'pæsɪdʒ/ *noun* **1.** the process of passing through a system ○ *They tried to obstruct the Bill's passage through the House of Commons.* **2.** a piece of writing ○ *The censor removed several passages from the newspaper report.*

passive resistance /ˌpæsɪv rɪ'zɪst(ə)ns/ *noun* resistance to authority using peaceful methods such as demonstration or noncooperation rather than violence

passport /'pɑːspɔːt/ *noun* an official document with a photograph proving that you are a citizen of a country, which you usually have to show when you travel from one country to another (NOTE: Passports now contain biometric data on the holder as a means of preventing identity fraud and can be checked electronically.)

patent /'peɪtənt, 'pætənt/ *noun* official permission to be the only person to have the right to produce something which you have invented ■ *verb* to receive a patent

patented /'peɪtəntɪd, 'pætəntɪd/ *adjective* protected by a patent

patentee /ˌpeɪtən'tiː/ *noun* a person who has received a patent

Patent Office /'peɪt(ə)nt 'ɒfɪs/ *noun* the government office which issues patents

paternalism /pə'tɜːn(ə)lɪz(ə)m/ *noun* a style of government or management which limits individual choice and personal responsibility

patrial /'peɪtrɪəl/ *noun* **1.** ((*under the 1971 Immigration Act*)) a person who has the right to live in the United

Kingdom because he or she was born before 1 January 1983 and has a parent who was born in the UK **2.** ((*before the 1981 British Nationality Act*)) a person who had the right to live in the United Kingdom because he or she was born, adopted, registered or naturalised in the United Kingdom

patriarchal /ˌpeɪtri'ɑːk(ə)l/ *adjective* referring to a patriarchy

patriarchy /'peɪtrɪɑːki/ *noun* ruled or controlled by men

patriate /'peɪtrɪeɪt/ *verb* to transfer control to the home country ○ *The Canadian constitution was formally patriated in 1982.*

patriot /'pætrɪət/ *noun* a person who proudly supports his or her country

patriotic /ˌpætri'ɒtɪk/ *adjective* referring to patriotism ○ *It is every citizen's patriotic duty to learn the words of the National Anthem.*

patriotism /'pætrɪətɪz(ə)m/ *noun* the feeling of great pride and support for your country. Compare **chauvinism**

patronage /'pætrənɪdʒ/ *noun* the right to give government posts or honours to people ○ *The Prime Minister has considerable patronage.*

patronage secretary /ˌpætrənɪdʒ 'sekrət(ə)ri/ *noun* the official of the Prime Minister's staff who deals with giving people honours and government jobs

PAU *abbreviation* Pan American Union

pax /pæks/ *noun* a period of peace and stability under the influence of a particular powerful country or empire ○ *pax Brittanica*

Paymaster-General /'peɪˌmɑːstə 'dʒen(ə)rəl/ *noun* the government minister who heads the office that acts as paying agent for government departments

PC /ˌpiː 'siː/ *abbreviation* **1.** personal computer **2.** police constable **3.** politically correct **4.** privy council

PCP /ˌpiː siː 'piː/ *abbreviation* Progressive Conservative Party

PCS *abbreviation* Public and Commercial Services Union

PD *abbreviation* police department

peace /piːs/ *noun* **1.** the state of not being at war ○ *After six years of civil war, the country is now at peace.* ○ *The peace treaty was signed yesterday.* ○ *Both sides claimed the other side broke the peace agreement.* **2.** the state of being quiet or calm

'…there never was a good war or a bad peace' [*Benjamin Franklin*]

Peace Corps /ˈpiːs ˈkɔː/ *noun* a US government organisation that trains volunteers to work in developing countries on educational and agricultural projects

peaceful coexistence /ˌpiːsf(ə)l ˌkəʊɪgˈzɪstəns/ *noun* a situation where countries may be in complete disagreement, but exist together without threatening war

peace process /ˈpiːs ˌprəʊses/ *noun* the gradual establishment of peace by a process of negotiation between people who have been at war

Peel /piːl/, **Sir Robert** (1788–1850) prime minister of Great Britain (1834–35 and 1841–46) and, s Home Secretary (1822–27 and 1828–30), the person who created the London police force, later known as 'bobbies' or 'peelers'. He founded the modern Conservative Party and it won the 1841 election.

peer /pɪə/ *noun* **1.** a member of the House of Lords (NOTE: A peer is disqualified from standing for election to the House of Commons, but can renounce the peerage in order to be able to stand for election as an MP.) **2.** a person who is in the same group or rank as another ○ *a teacher well respected by her peers*

peerage /ˈpɪərɪdʒ/ *noun* **1.** all peers, taken as a group **2.** the position of being a peer ○ *Three new peerages were created in the New Year's Honours List.* ○ *He was elevated to the peerage in 1993.*

Peerages Act /ˈpɪərɪdʒɪz ækt/ *noun* an Act passed in 1963 that allowed hereditary peers to refuse their title for life. It also admitted female hereditary peers to the House of Lords and allowed the admittance of all Scottish Peers.

COMMENT: The Act was introduced because Tony Benn, a Labour MP, wanted to continue to be an MP after he inherited the title of Viscount Stansgate. At the time this status automatically disqualified him from continuing to be an MP although he was entitled to become a Member of the House of Lords.

peeress /ˈpɪərˈes/ *noun* a female member of the House of Lords

penal /ˈpiːn(ə)l/ *adjective* referring to punishment □ **penal code** a set of laws governing crime and its punishment

penal institution /ˈpiːn(ə)l ˌɪnstɪtjuːʃ(ə)n/ *noun* a place where criminals are kept, e.g. a prison

penalise /ˈpiːnəlaɪz/, **penalize** *verb* to punish someone for breaking a rule or law ○ *The government penalised councils for overspending.* ○ *The contractors were penalised for late delivery.*

penal system /ˌpiːn(ə)l ˈsɪstəm/ *noun* the system of punishments relating to different crimes

pending /ˈpendɪŋ/ *adverb* while waiting for ○ *Pending the council's decision, rates should be paid in the usual way.* ○ *Pending advice from our lawyers, we sent a simple letter of acknowledgement.*

Pentagon /ˈpentəgən/ *noun* the building used by Department of Defense in Washington (NOTE: The building has five sides, hence the name, which is also used to mean the Defense Department itself: *Pentagon officials stated that the supply of arms was illegal*; *Sources close to the Pentagon refused to comment on the story.*)

people /ˈpiːp(ə)l/ *plural noun* **1.** human beings seen as a group ○ *young people* ○ *old people* ○ *Thousands of people lined the streets to watch the procession.* ○ *Most people voted for* *the new constitution.* **2.** all the members of a nation ○ *the government of the people, by the people, for the people* ○ *The President promised to serve the people.* (NOTE: The plural **peoples** means 'members of several nations': *the peoples of southern Africa.*) □ **a man** or **woman of the people** a leader or politician who understands what is important to ordinary people ■ *noun* someone's business assistants and advisers ○ *Ask your people to contact me next week.*

People's Assembly /ˌpiːpəlz əˈsembli/ *noun* the legislature in Egypt

People's Bureau /ˌpiːpəlz ˈbjʊərəʊ/ *noun* the embassy of the Libyan Republic

People's Council /ˌpiːpəlz ˈkaʊnsəl/ *noun* the legislature in Syria

People's Party /ˌpiːpəlz ˈpɑːti/ *noun* the name given to some political parties, e.g. in Austria

people's republic /ˌpiːpəlz rɪˈpʌblɪk/ *noun* a Socialist or Communist republic

per /pɜː, pə/ *preposition* **1.** at a rate of **2.** out of ○ *The rate of imperfect items is about fifteen per hundred.* ○ *The birth rate has fallen to twenty per thousand.*

per capita /pə ˈkæpɪtə/ *adjective, adverb* for each person □ **average income per capita, per capita income** the average income of one person

per cent /pə ˈsent/ *adjective, adverb* out of each hundred or for each hundred ○ *Eighty per cent (80%) of crimes are solved.* (NOTE: It is usually written % after numbers.)

perestroika /ˌpereˈstrɔɪkə/ *noun* a period of political and economic reform that took place in the 1980s in the former Soviet Union

period /ˈpɪəriəd/ *noun* a particular length of time ○ *the post-war period*

periodic /ˌpɪəriˈɒdɪk/, **periodical** /ˌpɪəriˈɒdɪk(ə)l/ *adjective* happening regularly from time to time ○ *the periodic rise of extreme right-wing groups*

Permanent Secretary /ˌpɜːmənənt ˈsekrətri/ *noun* a chief civil servant in a government department or ministry (NOTE: The Canada term is **Deputy Minister**.)

COMMENT: Permanent Secretaries are appointed by the Prime Minister but are responsible to the Secretary of State in charge of the relevant department.

permit /ˈpɜːmɪt/ *noun* an official document which allows someone to do something □ **export permit, import permit** an official document which allows goods to be exported or imported

per procurationem /ˈpɜː prɒkjʊrætsɪˈəʊnəm/ *Latin phrase meaning* 'with the authority of.' Abbr **p.p.**

per se /ˈpɜː ˈseɪ/ *Latin phrase meaning* 'on its own' or 'by itself' ○ *Fixing the rates is not per se a matter for the Housing Committee, though they may wish to offer an opinion.*

persecute /ˈpɜːsɪkjuːt/ *verb* to treat someone cruelly or unfairly on political, religious or racial grounds

persecution /ˌpɜːsɪˈkjuːʃ(ə)n/ *noun* cruel or unfair treatment of someone on political, religious or racial grounds

person /ˈpɜːs(ə)n/ *noun* a human being

persona /pɜːˈsəʊnə/ *Latin word meaning* person □ **persona grata** a person who is acceptable to a government, used especially of foreign diplomats □ **persona non grata** a person who is not acceptable to a government, used especially of foreign diplomats ○ *The Military Attaché was declared persona non grata and asked to leave the country.*

personal allowances /ˌpɜːs(ə)n(ə)l əˈlaʊənsɪz/ *plural noun* the part of a person's income which is not taxed ○ *allowances against tax* or *tax allowances*

Personal Bill /ˈpɜːs(ə)nəl bɪl/ *noun* a private bill introduced into Parliament which refers to a single person and is the only way in which the person concerned can get justice, usually in matters of property

personal income /ˌpɜːs(ə)n(ə)l ˈɪnkʌm/ *noun* the income received by an individual person before tax is paid

personality cult /ˌpɜːsəˈnælɪti kʌlt/ *noun* intense popular feeling built around the character of a politician, usually a dictator

personal statement /ˈpɜːs(ə)n(ə)l ˈsteɪtmənt/ *noun* a statement made by an MP after Question Time, when he or she apologises to the House for something. Also called **personal explanation**

persuadable /pəˈsweɪdəb(ə)l/ *noun* a voter who is regarded as being willing to vote for a candidate if the right arguments are given

persuade /pəˈsweɪd/ *verb* to get people to do or believe what you want by using clever arguments ○ *After hours of discussion, they persuaded the proposer of the motion to accept the amendment.* ○ *We could not persuade the French negotiating team to sign the agreement.*

persuasive /pəˈsweɪsɪv/ *adjective* able to get people to do or believe what you want by using clever arguments ○ *He made a very persuasive speech against restoring the death penalty.*

pertain /pəˈteɪn/ *verb* to apply or exist in a particular instance

petition /pəˈtɪʃ(ə)n/ *noun* **1.** a written request signed by the people supporting it, asking those with power to do something ○ *They presented a petition with a million signatures to Parliament, asking for the law to be repealed.* ○ *The councillor presented two petitions which were referred to the appropriate committees.* **2.** a written request made to a court ■ *verb* to make an official request ○ *He petitioned the government for a special pension.* ○ *The marriage had broken down and the wife petitioned for divorce.*

COMMENT: Petitions to the House of Commons are written by hand, and have a set form of words. After a petition is presented in the House of Commons at the beginning of the day's business, it is said to 'lie upon the table' and is placed in a bag behind the Speaker's Chair.

petitioner /pəˈtɪʃ(ə)nə/ *noun* a person who puts forward a petition

petty bourgeois /ˌpeti ˈbʊəʒwɑː/ *adjective* referring to the lower middle class

petty bourgeoisie /ˌpeti bʊəʒwɑˈziː/ *noun* the lower middle class of small shopkeepers and minor civil servants (NOTE: The word **bourgeois** is used in radical or communist circles to refer to anyone who is a capitalist, or even to anyone who is not a communist.)

PFI *noun* a government scheme to encourage private companies to fund public capital projects such as the building of hospitals and schools. Full form **Private Finance Initiative**

photo opportunity /ˌfəʊtəʊ ˌɒpəˈtjuːnəti/ *noun* a planned opportunity for the media to photograph a politician or other public figure doing something, especially to produce favourable publicity

pink /pɪŋk/ *adjective* relating to political views that are slightly left-wing

Pitt /pɪt/, **William, 1st Earl of Chatham** (1708–78) As secretary of state (1756–61), he was the most powerful politician in Great Britain and effectively prime minister. He headed a new government from 1766 to 1768.

Pitt, William (1759–1806) Great Britain's youngest prime minister, at the age of 24. Great Britain's youngest prime minister, at the age of 24 (1783–1801), and returning for a second term (1804–06), during which period the Act of Union (1800(1783–1801)) incorporated Ireland into the United Kingdom.

place /pleɪs/ *noun* □ **the other place** or **another place** (*in the House of Commons*) the House of Lords

placeman /ˈpleɪsmən/ *noun* someone who receives a public office as a reward for services to a political party and uses it for personal greed or ambition

Plaid Cymru /ˌplaɪd ˈkʊmri/ *noun* the political party which supports independence for Wales (NOTE: The name means 'Party of Wales' in the Welsh language)

plank /plæŋk/ *noun* a main item of policy, or an important aspect of something ○ *A proposal to raise taxes is the central plank of the party's platform.*

planned /plænd/ *adjective* done according to a plan

planned economy /ˌplænd ɪˈkɒnəmi/ *noun* a system where the government plans all business activity

planner /ˈplænə/ *noun* a person who makes plans

planning /ˈplænɪŋ/ *noun* 1. the activity of organising how something should be done 2. the activity of organising how land and buildings are to be used

planning authority /ˈplænɪŋ ɔːˌθɒrəti/ *noun* the section of local government which gives permission for changes to be made to existing buildings or for new use of land

planning department /ˈplænɪŋ dɪˌpɑːtmənt/ *noun* the section of a local government office which deals with requests for planning permission

planning inquiry /ˈplænɪŋ ɪnˌkwaɪri/ *noun* a hearing before a government inspector relating to a decision of a local authority in planning matters

planning permission /ˈplænɪŋ pəˌmɪʃ(ə)n/ *noun* the official document allowing someone to build new structures on empty land or to alter existing buildings

platform /ˈplætfɔːm/ *noun* a set of policy proposals put forward by a candidate in an election

Plato /ˈpleɪtəʊ/ *noun* an Ancient Greek philosopher (c. 428–347 BC) whose 'Republic' is considered the greatest work of political philosophy (NOTE: Plato argued that the best form of government would be one where philosophers were rulers and where everyone learnt to accept their position in life.)

pleasure /ˈpleʒə/ ♦ **Her Majesty's pleasure**

plebiscite /ˈplebɪsaɪt/ *noun* a type of vote to decide an important issue, involving the eligible population of a town, region or country ○ *The province decided by plebiscite to lower the voting age to eighteen.*

COMMENT: There is no agreement on the difference between a referendum and a plebiscite, and the words seem to be largely interchangeable. Referendum is the more modern term, and the word plebiscite carries bad overtones of its use in the days of Fascism.

pledge /pledʒ/ *noun* a promise ○ *The voters were impressed by the opposition's pledge to reduce taxes.* □ **to fulfil an election pledge** to do what was promised before an election ■ *verb* to promise to do something ○ *The government has pledged not to raise taxes.* ○ *He pledged his support to the party leader.*

plenary session /ˈpliːnəri ˌseʃ(ə)n/ *noun* a meeting of all the members of a group ○ *The European Parliament met in plenary session.*

plenipotentiary /ˌplenɪpəˈtenʃəri/ *noun* a person given full power to act on behalf of a government in discussions with another country ○ *The treaty was signed by plenipotentiaries on behalf of the three governments.*

plenum /ˈpliːnəm/ *noun* a meeting at which all members of a group are present

PLO *abbreviation* Palestine Liberation Organization

PLP *abbreviation* Parliamentary Labour Party

pluralism /ˈplʊərəlɪz(ə)m/ *noun* a social system which has different political, ethnic or religious groups co-existing within it

pluralist state /ˌplʊərəlɪst ˈsteɪt/ *noun* a state which has different political, ethnic or religious groups co-existing within it and exerting influence over the government

plurality /pluə'rælɪti/ *noun* **1.** the number of votes which a candidate receives more than those for another candidate ○ *The candidate with a simple plurality wins the seat.* **2.** having more votes than another candidate (NOTE: [all senses] **Plurality** is more commonly used in US English.)

plural voting /'pluərəl 'vəʊtɪŋ/ *noun* formerly, a system of voting that allowed some people to vote more than once in an election or to vote in different constituencies

plutocracy /pluː'tɒkrəsi/ *noun* a system of rule by rich people

plutocrat /'pluːtəkræt/ *noun* a person who is a member of a plutocracy

PM *abbreviation* Prime Minister

pocket /'pɒkɪt/ *verb* ((of a US president)) to retain a bill without signing it in order to stop it becoming approved by Congress

pocket borough /ˌpɒkɪt 'bʌrə/ *noun* in Great Britain before the Reform Act of 1832, a political constituency whose representative in Parliament was chosen by one landowner or landowning family

pocket veto /ˌpɒkɪt 'viːtəʊ/ *noun* US the refusal by the President of the USA to sign a bill passed by Congress, which the President may use if the bill is given to him within ten days of the time when Congress adjourns and which Congress cannot override

COMMENT: The President's 'ordinary' veto gives the power to refuse to sign a bill into law. He must return his reasons for the veto within ten days. If Congress does not give him sufficient time to do this, that is if Congress gives him the bill less than ten days before the end of a session, the President can simply ignore the bill. This is called the pocket veto. While the 'ordinary' veto can be overturned by a two-thirds majority in both houses, the pocket veto cannot be overturned at all by Congress.

pogrom /'pɒgrəm/ *noun* a planned campaign of persecution or extermination of an ethnic group supported by a government (NOTE: The term was first used of the campaigns against the Jews in tsarist Russia.)

point /pɔɪnt/ *noun* a question or statement relating to a matter ○ *in answer to the points raised by the Opposition spokesman* ○ *There are two points to be considered.* ○ *The Chief Executive made the point that the day in question was a Sunday.* □ **to take someone's point** to agree that the point made by another speaker is correct ○ *I take your point but it has no bearing on the issue.* □ **point taken, I take your point** I agree that what you say is valid

point of fact /ˌpɔɪnt əv 'fækt/ *noun* a question which has to be decided regarding the facts of a case □ **in point of fact** really or actually

point of order /ˌpɔɪnt əv 'ɔːdə/ *noun* a question by one of the people taking part in a formal debate or meeting that relates to the way in which a meeting is conducted, in particular whether rules are being properly observed ○ *he raised an interesting point of order* ○ *on a point of order, Mr Smith asked the chairman to give a ruling on whether the committee could approve its own accounts*

COMMENT: To raise a point of order, someone may say: 'On a point of order, Mr. Chairman', and the Chairman should stop the discussion to hear what the person raising the point wishes to say.

polemic /pə'lemɪk/ *noun* a strong, often controversial argument against or, less often, in favour of something

polemics /pə'lemɪks/ *noun* the practice of arguing strongly for or against something

police /pə'liːs/ *noun* the official group of people who keep law and order in a country ○ *The police have cordoned off the town centre.* ■ *verb* **1.** to keep law and order in a place ○ *The President used the National Guard to police the capital.* **2.** to make sure that regulations or guidelines are carried out ○ *The department is carefully policing the way the guidelines are being followed.*

COMMENT: Under English law, the police are organised by area, each area functioning independently with its own police force. London, and the area round London, is policed by the Metropolitan Police Force under the direct supervision of the Home Secretary. Outside London, each police force is answerable to a local police authority, although day-to-day control of operations is vested entirely in the Chief Constable.

police authority /pə,liːs ɔːˈθɒrɪti/ noun the local committee which supervises the police force of an area

Police Commissioner /pə,liːs kəˈmɪʃ(ə)nə/ noun the highest rank in a police force

Police Complaints Board /pə,liːs kəmˈpleɪnts ,bɔːd/ noun a group which investigates complaints made by members of the public against the police

police constable /pəˈliːs ,kʌnstəb(ə)l/ noun in the United Kingdom, Canada, Australia, and New Zealand, a police officer of the lowest rank. Abbr **PC**

police force /pəˈliːs fɔːs/ noun a group of policemen organised in an area ○ The members of several local police forces have collaborated in the hunt for the terrorists. ○ The London police force is looking for more recruits.

police headquarters /pə,liːs hed ˈkwɔːtəz/ noun the main offices of a police force

police inspector /pə,liːs ɪnˈspektə/ noun the rank in the police force above sergeant and below chief inspector

policeman /pəˈliːsmən/ noun a man who is a member of a police force

police officer /pəˈliːs ,ɒfɪsə/ noun a member of a police force

COMMENT: Under English law, a police officer is primarily an ordinary citizen who has certain powers under common law and by statute.

police precinct /pə,liːs ˈpriːsɪŋ(k)t/ noun US a section of a town with its own police station

police protection /pə,liːs prəˈtekʃən/ noun the services of the police to protect someone who might be harmed

police sergeant /pə,liːs ˈsɑːdʒənt/ noun the rank in the police force above constable and below inspector

police state /pəˈliːs steɪt/ noun a country or system in which the government uses the police or army to control the people ○ After the coup, the generals were accused of operating a police state.

police station /pəˈliːs ,steɪʃ(ə)n/ noun the local office of a police force

policewoman /pəˈliːswʊmən/ noun a woman member of a police force

policing /pəˈliːsɪŋ/ noun the activity of keeping law and order in a place, using the police force ○ The council is debating the Chief Constable's policing methods.

policy /ˈpɒlɪsi/ noun a detailed plan of how something will be done ○ government policy on wages or government wages policy ○ the government's prices policy ○ the country's economic policy ○ Our policy is to submit all contracts to the legal department. ○ It is not the policy of the council to give grants for more than three years. □ **the government made a policy statement** or **made a statement of policy** the government declared in public what its plans were

policy committee /ˈpɒlɪsi kəˈmɪti/ noun a small group which discusses plans for the way in which something will be done

policy community /ˈpɒlɪsi kə ˈmjuːnɪti/, **policy network** noun the close relationship between government departments, pressure groups, local authorities, academics, think tanks and a wide variety of influences involved in developing policy

Politburo /ˈpɒlɪtbjʊərəʊ/ noun the Central Committee of a Communist Party (NOTE: In North Korea the Politburo is the governing group in the country.)

politic ♦ body politic

political /pə'lɪtɪk(ə)l/ *adjective* relating to the state, government, political parties or elections ○ *They are hoping for a political rather than a military solution to the crisis.*

political correctness /pə,lɪtɪk(ə)l kə'rektnəs/ *noun* the attempt to speak, write or act in a way that will avoid giving offence to groups such as people with disabilities, ethnic groups or women, who have often been referred to or treated in inappropriate ways in the past (*disapproving*) Abbr **PC**. ◊ **inclusive**

political crime /pə,lɪtɪk(ə)l 'kraɪm/ *noun* a crime committed for a political reason, e.g. assassination

political economy /pə,lɪtɪk(ə)l ɪ'kɒnəmi/ *noun* the study of ways in which economics and government policies affect each other

political editor /pə'lɪtɪk(ə)l 'edɪtə/ *noun* the chief journalist on a newspaper, or television or radio station who deals with political stories

political fund /pə'lɪtɪk(ə)l fʌnd/ *noun* the money which a trade union collects from its members to give to a political party

political levy /pə,lɪtɪk(ə)l 'levi/ *noun* the part of the subscription of a member of a trade union which the union then pays to support a political party

political life /pə'lɪtɪk(ə)l laɪf/ *noun* activities and work associated with especially national or international politics

'Never lose your temper with the press or the public is a major rule of political life' [*Christabel Pankhurst*]

politically correct /pə,lɪtɪkli kə'rekt/ *adjective* avoiding giving offence to groups such as people with disabilities, ethnic groups or women. Abbr **PC**

political officer /pə,lɪtɪk(ə)l 'ɒfɪsə/ *noun* a diplomat in a colony who is concerned mainly with the relations between his government at home and the administration in the colony or with the governments of the countries near the colony

political party /pə'lɪtɪk(ə)l ,pɑːti/ *noun* a group of people who try to achieve political power and who are united by common beliefs about how the country should be run

political prisoner /pə,lɪtɪk(ə)l 'prɪz(ə)nə/ *noun* a person kept in prison because he or she is an opponent of the political party in power. Also called **prisoner of state**

political refugee /pə,lɪtɪk(ə)l ,refjʊ'dʒiː/ *noun* a person who leaves a country because he or she is afraid of persecution for their political beliefs

politician /,pɒlɪ'tɪʃ(ə)n/ *noun* a person involved in politics, especially national or international politics □ **a full-time politician** a person whose job is in politics, as an elected representative

'…the most successful politician is he who says what everybody is thinking most often and in the loudest voice' [*Theodore Roosevelt*]

politicise /pə'lemɪk/ *verb* **1.** to introduce political opinions into the discussion of an issue of general public interest **2.** to make someone more aware of or active in politics

politicking /'pɒlɪtɪkɪŋ/ *noun* political campaigning or speech-making, especially when regarded as insincere or to someone's own advantage

politico /pə'lɪtɪkəʊ/ *noun* a politician, especially one regarded as ineffective, insincere or self-serving (*informal*)

politico- /pəlɪtɪkəʊ/ *prefix* political and ○ *politico-economic reasons for debt*

politics /'pɒlɪtɪks/ *noun* the theory and practice of governing a country □ **local politics** or **national politics** the practice of governing a local area, or of governing a country

'…politics is the art of the possible' [*R.A. Butler*]

polity /'pɒlɪti/ *noun* a particular form of government that exists within a state or an institution

poll /pəʊl/ *noun* **1.** the process of a political election. ◊ **exit poll, opinion poll, straw poll** □ **to go to the polls** to vote to choose a Member of Parliament or a local councillor □ **the polls opened an hour ago** the voting started officially an hour ago ◊ **the polls close at 10 o'clock** the voting ends at 10 o'clock **2.** the number of votes cast in an election ◊ *a low poll* ■ *verb* **1.** to receive a particular number or percentage of votes in an election ◊ *He polled only 123 votes in the general election.* ◊ *The centre parties polled 15% of the votes.* **2.** to ask a representative number of people their opinion and to hope to discover as a result what the whole population thinks. ◊ **opinion poll**

polling booth /'pəʊlɪŋ buːð/ *noun* a small enclosed space in a polling station, where the voter goes to mark his or her ballot paper in private. Also called **voting booth**

polling day /'pəʊlɪŋ deɪ/ *noun* the day of an election

polling station /'pəʊlɪŋ ˌsteɪʃ(ə)n/ *noun* a central public place such as a library or school where people of the surrounding area go to vote

pollster /'pəʊlstə/ *noun* an expert in designing, holding and understanding opinion polls

poll tax /'pəʊl tæks/ *noun* **1.** a tax paid at the same rate by each adult member of the population. Also called **community charge 2.** same as **community charge**

COMMENT: Nicknamed the poll tax after the hated 14th-century Poll Tax, which had been a major cause of the Peasants' Revolt, the community charge was first introduced in Scotland and later in England and Wales as a replacement for the former system of 'rates', a tax on the size of owned property. It was so unpopular that in 1990 there were violent protests and demonstrations against it, a large non-payment campaign, and large anti-government votes in local elections and by-elections. It had a big influence in Margaret Thatcher losing the leadership of the Conservative party and was later abolished.

polyarchy /'pɒliɑːki/ *noun* rule by many people

populace /'pɒpjʊləs/ *noun* the ordinary people in an area or country ◊ *The government has hidden its plans from the populace.*

popular /'pɒpjʊlə/ *adjective* **1.** liked by many people ◊ *This is our most popular model.* **2.** referring to people in general ◊ *a popular misconception about local government* ◊ *The policy has wide popular appeal.* **3.** suitable for most people who have no special or technical knowledge ◊ *a popular account of the cloning issue*

Popular Front /'pɒpjʊlə frʌnt/ *noun* **1.** a group of Socialist and Communist parties, formed in 1935 to fight fascism **2.** a left-wing organisation formed to fight a ruling government or colonial power

Popular Party /'pɒpjʊlə 'pɑːti/ *noun* a political party which claims to represent a large number of ordinary people

popular sovereignty /'pɒpjʊlə 'sɒvrɪnti/ *noun* in the United States, the doctrine that a government is subject to the will of the people

popular vote /ˌpɒpjʊlə 'vəʊt/ *noun* a vote of the majority of the people in a country □ **the president is elected by popular vote** the president is elected by a majority of all the voters in the country, as opposed to being elected by parliament

COMMENT: The President of the USA is elected by an electoral college, not by popular vote.

populated /'pɒpjʊleɪtɪd/ *adjective* where people live ◊ *a heavily populated area* or *a densely populated area*

population /ˌpɒpjʊ'leɪʃ(ə)n/ *noun* **1.** all the people who live in a place ◊ *Less than half the population bothered to vote in the last election.* **2.** the number of people living in a place ◊ *a city with a population of two million* or *with a 2 million population* ◊ *The population of Britain has fallen over the last few years.*

populism /'pɒlɪtɪkz(ə)m/ *noun* politics that considers the interests of ordinary people, as opposed to those of a privileged elite

populist /'pɒpjʊlɪst/ *adjective* designed to appeal to what most people are thought to want ○ *populist policies* ■ *noun* a politician who appeals to people by playing on their emotions and fears

populous /'pɒpjʊləs/ *adjective* where many people live ○ *The most populous area of the country is round the capital.*

pork /pɔːk/ *noun* government money and jobs awarded by politicians to their supporters or constituents to win their favour, especially when the strategy has failed

portcullis /pɔːt'kʌlɪs/ *noun* the emblem of both UK Houses of Parliament, in the form of a portcullis with a crown above it (NOTE: A portcullis is a heavy iron grid that was raised and lowered to protect the gateway of a castle.)

portfolio /pɔːt'fəʊliəʊ/ *noun* the particular job of a government minister ○ *He was offered the Defence portfolio.*

position paper /pə'zɪʃ(ə)n 'peɪpə/ *noun* a detailed report on a subject giving the official opinion and recommendations of a government or organisation

positive discrimination /ˌpɒzɪtɪv dɪskrɪmɪ'neɪʃ(ə)n/ *noun* the policy of giving more favourable treatment to members of groups who have often suffered from unfair treatment ○ *The council's policy of positive discrimination has ensured that more women are appointed to senior posts.*

positive vetting /ˌpɒzɪtɪv 'vetɪŋ/ *noun* the close investigation of a person who applies for a civil service job working with secret information

possession /pə'zeʃ(ə)n/ *noun* the situation of having something □ **how did the information come into his possession, how did he get possession of the information?** how did he

acquire the information? □ **the Committee was not in full possession of the facts** the Committee did not know everything about the matter □ **an MP in possession of the House** an MP who is speaking to the House of Commons, and so cannot be interrupted or stopped

postal ballot /'pəʊst(ə)l ˌbælət/ *noun* an election where the voters send their voting papers by post

postal vote /'pəʊst(ə)l vəʊt/ *noun* a vote made by sending in a voting paper by post

postbag /'pəʊstbæg/ *noun* the letters received by a well-known person, MP, newspaper, or TV or radio programme ○ *The postbag was full of complaints about the proposals for the new airport.* (NOTE: The US term is **mailbag**.)

posteriori ♦ a posteriori

POTUS /'pɒtəs/ *noun* full form **President of the United States** (*used in memos and internal documents by White House staff*)

power /'paʊə/ *noun* **1.** the strength or ability to do something **2.** the authority or legal right to do things or to make people do things ○ *the powers of a local authority in relation to children in care* ○ *the powers and duties conferred on the tribunal by the statutory code* ○ *The treasurer has no power to vary the order.* ○ *The President was granted wide powers under the new constitution.* **3.** a powerful country or state ○ *one of the important military powers in the region*

'Power tends to corrupt and absolute power corrupts absolutely.' [Lord Acton]

power base /'paʊə beɪs/ *noun* a group of voters or supporters providing the core of someone's political power or influence ○ *he has built up a power base in the unions*

power bloc /'paʊə blɒk/ *noun* a group of countries linked together as a powerful group

power broker /'paʊə 'brəʊkə/ *noun* a person or country that is able to use their influence to affect the policies and decisions of others

powerful /'pauəf(ə)l/ *adjective* having the power to influence or control what people do or think ○ *a powerful argument against military intervention in the area* ○ *The party has a powerful publicity department.*

powerless /'pauələs/ *adjective* having no power ○ *The government was powerless in the face of the campaign.*

power play /'pauə pleɪ/ *noun* the use of influence or threats to achieve something

power politics /ˌpauə 'pɒlɪtɪks/ *noun* the threat to use economic or military force by one powerful country to try to get other countries to do what it wants

p.p. on behalf of, or with the authority of (*used before a signature when signing a letter for someone else*) Full form **per procurationem**

PPP /ˌpiː piː 'piː/ *abbreviation* public private partnership

PPS *abbreviation* Parliamentary Private Secretary

PR *abbreviation* **1.** proportional representation **2.** public relations

Praesidium, Presidium *noun* the main committee of a governing Communist Party

pragmatic sanction /præg'mætɪk 'sæŋkʃən/ *noun* a decree issued by a sovereign that has the force of law

pray /preɪ/ *verb* to ask someone to do something ○ *Members pray that action may be taken.*

prayer /preə/ *noun* **1.** a request to the House of Commons to do something or not to do something **2.** a motion in the House of Commons asking the Crown to annul a statutory instrument **3.** a request to God

prayers /preəz/ *plural noun* an address to God, which begins each sitting of the Houses of Parliament

preamble /priːˈæmb(ə)l/ *noun* the first words in an official document such as a Bill before Parliament or

contract, introducing the document and setting out the main points in it

precautions /prɪ'kɔːʃ(ə)nz/ *plural noun* steps taken to prevent something unpleasant ○ *The company did not take proper fire precautions.* ○ *Staff must take precautions against theft.*

precedence /'presɪd(ə)ns/ *noun* the right to be first, because of being the most important

precedent /'presɪd(ə)nt/ *noun* something such as a judgment which has happened earlier, and which can show what should be done in the present case

precept /'priːsept/ *noun* an order asking for rates to be paid □ **the Metropolitan Police precept** part of the council tax paid in London which pays for the Metropolitan Police Force

precinct /'priːsɪŋkt/ *noun* **1.** an open area in a town around which there are shops or other buildings **2.** *US* an administrative district in a town (NOTE: The UK equivalent is **ward**.)

preclude /prɪ'kluːd/ *verb* to forbid or to prevent ○ *The High Court is precluded by statute from reviewing such a decision.* ○ *This agreement does not preclude a further agreement between the parties in the future.*

predecessor /'priːdɪsesə/ *noun* a person who has held a job before the present person ○ *He had to accept the treaty which his predecessor had signed.*

pre-empt /ˌpriː 'empt/ *verb* to act before someone else can act ○ *The President pre-empted the call for more democracy by suddenly announcing a general election.*

pre-emption /ˌpriː 'empʃən/ *noun* the right of first refusal to buy something before it is sold to someone else

preference /'pref(ə)rəns/ *noun* something which is liked or wanted more than other things □ **to have** or **show** or **express a preference for** to like something better than something else ○ *We have a clear preference for a diplomatic solution.* □ **in order of preference** arranged with your first choice first and your last choice last ○ *List the candidates in order of preference.* □ **personal preference** a feeling of liking or wanting something that is different for different people ○ *The choice of car is not just a matter of personal preference – there are environmental consequences to take into account.*

preferential duty /ˌprefərenʃ(ə)l ˈdjuːti/, **preferential tariff** *noun* a special low rate of tax

preferential treatment /ˌprefərenʃəl ˈtriːtmənt/ *noun* better treatment given to one person or group than to another without reasonable cause ○ *No-one should get preferential treatment on the housing list just because they are related to a councillor.*

preferential voting /ˌprefəˈrenʃəl ˈvəʊtɪŋ/ *noun* an electoral system used in some countries such as Australia, in which voters indicate their chosen candidates in order of preference

preferment /prɪˈfɜːmənt/ *noun* the process of giving someone an important job or a better job than they had before

prejudge /priːˈdʒʌdʒ/ *verb* to form an opinion about something or someone without having all the information

prejudice /ˈpredʒʊdɪs/ *noun* **1.** an unreasonable opinion about someone based on false ideas about their religion, race, gender or class **2.** harm done to someone ■ *verb* to harm someone or something ○ *The reports appeared to prejudice his chances of getting the appointment.*

prejudiced /ˈpredʒʊdɪst/ *adjective* based on prejudice ○ *The speakers were clearly prejudiced against foreigners.*

pre-legislative scrutiny /ˌpriː ˌledʒɪslətɪv ˈskruːtɪni/ *noun* the process of allowing MPs who have special knowledge of the subject of a Bill to make comments at an early stage, in a departmental Select Committee, before a bill is introduced into Parliament

preliminary /prɪˈlɪmɪn(ə)ri/ *adjective* happening at an early stage in a process

preliminary discussion /prɪ ˌlɪmɪn(ə)ri dɪˈskʌʃ(ə)n/, **preliminary meeting** *noun* a discussion or meeting which takes place before the main discussion or meeting starts

preliminary ruling /prɪˌlɪmɪn(ə)ri ˈruːlɪŋ/ *noun* a decision made by a court before its final judgement ○ *The preliminary ruling of the European Court of Justice was meticulously prepared and indicated that the case was going against the company.*

premier /ˈpremɪə/ *noun* **1.** the Prime Minister **2.** (*in a federal state*) the chief minister of a state or province as opposed to the Prime Minister of the Federal government. This applies to the States of Australia, the Provinces of Canada and also in China.

premiership /ˈpremɪəʃɪp/ *noun* the period when a Prime Minister governs ○ *during the premiership of Harold Wilson* (NOTE: In Canada and Australia, it is also used to refer to provincial or state premiers.)

premises /ˈpremɪsɪz/ *noun* a building and the land it stands on ○ *reviewing the local tax on business premises* ○ *licensed premises*

premium bonds /ˈpriːmɪəm bɒndz/ *plural noun* government bonds, part of a national savings scheme, which do not pay any interest but which give the owner the chance to win a weekly or monthly prize

prerogative /prɪˈrɒgətɪv/ *noun* a special right which someone has to do something

prerogative of mercy /prɪ ˌrɒgətɪv əv ˈmɜːsi/ *noun* a power used by the Home Secretary to reduce a sentence imposed by the courts on a criminal

prerogative order /prɪˌrɒgətɪv ˈɔːdə/, **prerogative writ** *noun* a command ordering a body to do its duty or not to do some act, or to hold an inquiry into its own actions

prerogative powers /prɪˌrɒgətɪv
'paʊəs/ *plural noun* the special powers used by a government, acting in
the name of the King or Queen, to do
something such as declare war, nominate ministers, without needing to ask
Parliament to approve the decision

presence /'prez(ə)ns/ *noun* being
present or being at a place when something happens ○ *The will was signed in
the presence of two witnesses.*

present /'prez(ə)nt/ *adjective* **1.**
happening now ○ *The present international situation means that police
have been put on the alert.* ○ *What is
the present address of the company?*
2. being there when something happens ○ *Only four Opposition MPs
were present when the vote was put.* ■
verb **1.** to give someone something ○
*The mayor presented certificates to
members of the public who had helped
in the rescue operations.* ○ *She was
presented with a watch on completing
twenty-five years' service with the
council.* **2.** to bring, send or show a
document □ **to present a petition** to
bring a petition before a meeting for
discussion ○ *Councillor Smith presented a petition requesting improvements to the hospital bus service.*

presentation /ˌprez(ə)n'teɪʃ(ə)n/
noun **1.** the process or a ceremony of
giving something to someone ○ *They
made him a presentation of a watch
after twenty-five years' service.* ○ *At a
presentation ceremony in the White
House, the President awarded the
Medal of Honor to three people.* **2.** a
talk, demonstration or exhibition to
explain something ○ *The developers
made a presentation of the proposed
new civic centre.* ○ *We have asked two
PR firms to make presentations of advertising campaigns aimed at tourists.*

preservation order /ˌprezə
'veɪʃ(ə)n ˌɔːdə/ *noun* a court order
which prevents a building from being
knocked down or a tree from being cut
down

preside /prɪ'zaɪd/ *verb* **1.** to be
chairman of a meeting ○ *to preside
over a meeting* ○ *The meeting was*

*held in the committee room, Mr Smith
presiding.* **2.** to be in control when
something happens ○ *The generals
presided over a period of economic
decline.* ○ *The finance minister presided over a run-down of the country's
gold reserves.*

presidency /'prezɪdənsi/ *noun* **1.**
the position of president ○ *The presidency of the European Union passes
from country to country every six
months.* **2.** the period when a president
is governing ○ *during Kennedy's presidency* or *during the Kennedy presidency*

president /'prezɪd(ə)nt/ *noun* **1.**
the head of a department, company or
court ○ *He was elected president of the
sports club.* ○ *A.B. Smith has been appointed president of the company.* **2.**
the head of a republic ○ *the President
of the United States* (NOTE: As a title
of a head of state, President can be
used with a surname: *President
Ford, President Wilson.* In the United
States, it is also often as a term of
address with Mr in front: *Mr President.*)

COMMENT: A president is the head of
state of a republic. It may be a ceremonial title, with some executive powers while the real power resides in the
Prime Minister, as in India. In other
states such as the USA, the President
is both head of state and head of government. The President of the USA is
elected by an electoral college, and
holds the executive power under the
United States constitution. The legislative power lies with Congress, and
the President cannot force Congress
to enact legislation, but can veto legislation which has been passed by Congress.

president-elect /ˌprezɪd(ə)nt ɪ
'lekt/ *noun* an elected or appointed
president who has not yet officially
started work in that role

presidential /ˌprezɪ'denʃəl/ *adjective* referring to a president of a country ○ *the US presidential elections* ○
*Three presidential candidates have
appeared on television.* ○ *The National Guard has surrounded the Presidential Palace.* □ **presidential gov-**

ernment a type of government where the head of the executive is a president

presidential-style /ˌprezɪ'denʃəl ˌstaɪl/ *adjective* working in a similar way to the United States presidency □ **presidential-style government** a type of government similar to that of the United States, where the President is not a member of the elected legislature □ **presidential-style campaign** an election campaign which concentrates on the person of the leader of the party, and not on the party's policies ○ *The Prime Minister was accused of running a presidential-style government* or *a presidential-style election campaign.*

President of the Board of Trade /ˌprezɪdənt əv ðə ˌbɔːd əv 'treɪd/ *noun* a title sometimes given to the minister in charge of the British Department of Trade, equivalent to a Minister of Commerce

President of the European Commission /ˌprezɪdənt əv ðə ˌjʊərəpiːən kə'mɪʃ(ə)n/ *noun* the chief executive of the European Union and head of the European Commission, elected for a five-year period

President of the Senate /ˌprezɪdənt əv ðə 'senət/ *noun* the person who chairs debates in the US Senate and has a casting vote, nominally the Vice-President of the USA, but usually a deputy, except when a casting vote is likely to be used

president pro tempore /ˌprezɪd(ə)nt prəʊ 'tempəreɪ/ *noun* a senator who takes the place of the Vice-President as chair of the Senate, or who appoints deputies to do so, when the Vice-President is not present

presidium *noun* another spelling of **Praesidium**

press /pres/ *noun* newspapers and magazines □ **in the press** in or mentioned by news publications ○ *The Minister has been in the press a lot recently.* ○ *He has been strongly criticised in the press for the decision.* □ **the local press** newspapers which are sold in a small area of the country □

the national press newspapers which are sold in all parts of the country ■ *verb* to ask for something again and again ○ *She pressed the Minister for a reply.* ○ *The Opposition pressed for a debate.*

press conference /'pres ˌkɒnf(ə)rəns/ *noun* a meeting where reporters from the news media are given news by politicians, the police or others, who answer the reporters' questions

Press Council /'pres ˌkaʊns(ə)l/ *noun* a body which hears complaints from the public about newspapers and attempts to get newspapers to report the news in a responsible way

press coverage /'pres ˌkʌv(ə)rɪdʒ/ *noun* reports about something by newspapers

press gallery /'pres ˌgæləri/ *noun* a part of the House of Commons, House of Lords or other council chamber, where journalists sit to report on debates

pressing /'presɪŋ/ *adjective* urgent ○ *There is a mass of pressing business for the committee to consider.*

press release /'pres rɪˌliːs/ *noun* a report about something which is sent to newspapers, television and radio stations by people involved so that they can get publicity for it

press secretary /'pres ˌsekrət(ə)ri/ *noun* a person employed by an organisation to spread favourable news stories about the organisation ○ *The information was communicated by the President's Press Secretary.*

pressure /'preʃə/ *noun* a force or strong influence to make someone change his or her opinions or course of action ○ *The army exerts strong political pressure on the President.* ○ *The Prime Minister gave in to pressure from the backbenchers.* ○ *The Whips applied pressure on the rebel MPs to vote with the government.*

pressure group /'preʃə gruːp/ *noun* a group of people with similar interests, who try to influence government policies

pressure politics /ˌpreʃə ˈpɒlɪtɪks/ *noun* the activity of attempting to change a government's policies by political discussion and influence

previous question /ˈpriːviəs ˈkwestʃ(ə)n/ *noun* **1.** in the House of Commons, a motion to stop a question being debated, so that a vote cannot be held on it **2.** in the House of Lords and US legislative bodies, a motion to put a question that will end a debate so that a vote on a bill can be taken immediately

price controls /ˈpraɪs kənˌtrəʊlz/ *noun* legal measures to prevent prices rising too fast

prima facie /ˌpraɪmə ˈfeɪʃi/ *Latin phrase meaning* 'on the face of it or as things seem at first'

primary /ˈpraɪməri/ *adjective* **1.** in the first place □ **of primary importance** extremely important, the most important of all ○ *The question is of primary importance to the security of the country.* **2.** the first of several stages ■ *noun US* a local election in which members of a political party choose candidates for an election (NOTE: In the USA, primaries are held in some states to choose a candidate for the presidency in advance of the nominating conventions.)

COMMENT: In the USA, primaries are held in some states to choose a candidate for the presidency in advance of the nominating conventions.

Prime Minister /ˌpraɪm ˈmɪnɪstə/ *noun* the head of a government ○ *the Australian Prime Minister* or *the Prime Minister of Australia*

COMMENT: The title Prime Minister is used in most countries to indicate the head of the government, except in countries, such as the USA, where the President is head of government as well as the head of state. The British Prime Minister is not the head of state, but the head of government. The Prime Minister is usually the leader of the party which has the majority of the seats in the House of Commons, and forms a cabinet of executive ministers who are either MPs or members of the House of Lords.

Prime Ministerial /ˌpraɪm ˌmɪnɪˈstɪəriəl/ *adjective* referring to a Prime Minister □ **Prime Ministerial government** a form of government where a Prime Minister is the head of government

Prime Minister's Questions /ˌpraɪm ˌmɪnɪstəz ˈkwestʃənz/ *noun* the period, currently of 30 minutes on Wednesdays, when MPs ask questions the Prime Minister directly

primus inter pares /ˌpraɪməs ɪn ˈtɜː peəs/ *Latin phrase meaning* 'first among equals': used sometimes to refer to the office of Prime Minister, implying that all ministers are equal, and the Prime Minister is simply the most important of them (NOTE: There is a great deal of discussion over the question of whether the Prime Minister is merely first among equals or whether in recent years the Prime Minister has become more like a president who dominates the Cabinet.)

prince /prɪns/ *noun* **1.** a male member of a royal family, usually the son of a king or queen ○ *one of the Saudi royal princes* **2.** the title of the ruler of a small country such as Cambodia or Monaco (NOTE: spelt with a capital letter when used as a title: *Prince Charles*; *Prince Abdullah*)

prince consort /ˌprɪns ˈkɒnsɔːt/ *noun* **1.** **Prince Consort** the title given to Prince Albert, the husband of Queen Victoria (1837–1901) **2.** the title given to the husband of a ruling queen ○ *When Queen Victoria reigned as queen, her husband, Albert, was Prince Consort.*

princedom /ˈprɪnsdəm/ *noun* a small country ruled by a prince

Prince of Wales /ˌprɪns əv ˈweɪlz/ *noun* the title of the eldest son of the king or queen of England

princess /prɪnˈses/ *noun* a female member of a royal family, especially the daughter of a king or queen, or the wife of a prince

Princess Royal /ˌprɪnˈses ˈrɔɪəl/ *noun* the title given to the eldest daughter of a king or queen (NOTE: spelt with a capital letter as a title: *Princess Anne*; *the Princess of Wales*)

principal /'prɪnsɪp(ə)l/ *noun* **1.** a person who is responsible for something, especially person who is in charge of a company or person who commits a crime **2.** a person or company which is represented by an agent ○ *The agent has come to London to see her principals.* **3.** money invested or borrowed on which interest is paid ○ *to repay principal and interest* ■ *adjective* most important ○ *The principal shareholders asked for a meeting.* ○ *The country's principal products are paper and wood.* Compare **principle**

principality /ˌprɪnsɪ'pælɪti/ *noun* a country ruled by a prince ○ *the Principality of Monaco* ◊ **co-principality** (NOTE: The state of Andorra is in fact a co-principality, as it is governed by two princes; in Britain, 'the Principality' is the name given to Wales.)

principle /'prɪnsɪp(ə)l/ *noun* a basic point or general rule

prioritise /praɪ'ɒrɪˌtaɪz/ *verb* **1.** to put some things that need to be done first and do them before others **2.** to put the things you have to do in an order of importance

priority /praɪ'ɒrɪti/ *noun* something which is more important than other things □ **order of priority** an order in which things are arranged, where the most important comes first ○ *let us deal with the points on the agenda in order of priority* □ **the government has got its priorities wrong** the government is giving importance to things that are not regarded as important

priority area /praɪ'ɒrɪti 'eəriə/ *noun* a part of the country to which government must give extra money because of its needs

prisoner of conscience /'prɪz(ə)nə əv 'kɒnʃəns/ *noun* a person who has been put in prison because of his or her beliefs

prisoner of state /'prɪz(ə)nə əv steɪt/ *noun* same as **political prisoner**

prisoner of war /ˌprɪz(ə)nə əv 'wɔː/ *noun* a member of the armed forces captured by the enemy in time of war. Abbr **POW**

prison visitor /ˌprɪz(ə)n 'vɪzɪtə/ *noun* a member of a board of visitors appointed by the Home Secretary to visit, inspect and report on conditions in prisons

private /'praɪvət/ *adjective* **1.** belonging to a single person, not a company or the state **2.** not public, limited to a small group ○ *The discussions between the minister and his civil servants must remain private if they are to be of any value*

Private Bill /'praɪvət bɪl/, **Private Act** *noun* a Bill or Act of Parliament relating to a particular person or institution

Private Calendar /'praɪvət 'kælɪndə/ *noun US* the list of Private Bills to be discussed in the House of Representatives

Private Finance Initiative /ˌpraɪvət 'faɪnæns ɪˌnɪʃətɪv/ *noun* full form of **PFI**

private member /'praɪvət 'membə/ *noun* an ordinary backbench MP who is not a member of the Government or on the Opposition front bench

Private Member's Bill /ˌpraɪvət 'membəz ˌbɪl/ *noun* a Bill which is drawn up and introduced to Parliament by an ordinary Member of Parliament, not by a government minister

Private Secretary /ˌpraɪvət 'sekrətri/ *noun* a civil servant attached personally to a Secretary of State or Prime Minister, who acts as the link between the minister and the department

private sector /'praɪvət ˌsektə/ *noun* all companies and businesses which are owned by shareholders or individuals, not by the state. Compare **public sector**

private sitting /ˈpraɪvət ˈsɪtɪŋ/ *noun* an occasion when Parliament meets without any members of the public being present and without written records or recordings being made. Private sittings occur rarely.

privatisation /ˌpraɪvətaɪˈzeɪʃ(ə)n/, **privatization** *noun* the action of privatising a state-owned industry

privatise /ˈpraɪvətaɪz/, **privatize** *verb* to sell a state-owned industry to private shareholders, usually to members of the public

privilege /ˈprɪvɪlɪdʒ/ *noun* **1.** a special advantage attached to a position or office ○ *The office of Mayor carries privileges, such as the use of the mayoral car and driver.* ○ *One of the privileges of the job is being able to use the company helicopter.* **2.** protection from the law given in some circumstances to particular individuals like Members of Parliament in UK or the President in USA □ **breach of parliamentary privilege** speaking in a defamatory way about Parliament or about a Member of Parliament □ **Crown privilege** right of the Crown or of the government not to have to produce documents in court **3.** *US* order of priority □ **motion of the highest privilege** a motion which will be discussed first, before all other motions

privileged /ˈprɪvɪlɪdʒd/ *adjective* protected by privilege

privileged communication /ˌprɪvɪlɪdʒd kəˌmjuːnɪˈkeɪʃ(ə)n/ *noun* a letter which could be libellous but which is protected by privilege, e.g. a letter from a client to his lawyer

privileged meeting /ˌprɪvɪlɪdʒd ˈmiːtɪŋ/ *noun* a meeting where what is said will not be repeated to other people

privileged questions /ˌprɪvɪlɪdʒd ˈkwestʃ(ə)ns/ *plural noun US* the order of priority of motions to be discussed

Privy Council /ˌprɪvi ˈkaʊnsəl/ *noun* a body of senior advisers who advise the Queen on some matters, mainly formed of members of the cab-

inet and former members of the cabinet. It never meets as a group, but three Privy Councillors need to be present when the Queen signs Orders in Council.

Privy Councillor /ˌprɪvi ˈkaʊnsələ/ *noun* a member of the Privy Council

Privy Purse /ˈprɪvi pɜːs/ *noun* **1.** the official who manages the personal finances of the British monarch **2.** the allowance from public funds given to the British monarch to cover personal expenses

Privy Seal /ˈprɪvi siːl/ *noun* **1.** a seal that used to be attached to documents authorised by the British king or queen **2.** same as **Lord Privy Seal**

PRO *abbreviation* Public Record Office

pro- /prəʊ/ *prefix* meaning in favour of ○ *a pro-abortion lobby* ○ *the president is very pro-British* ○ *Public opinion is not pro-European.*

proactive /prəʊˈæktɪv/ *adjective* prepared to take the initiative in doing things, rather than reacting to events as they happen ○ *The Leader of the Opposition said that the government minister should have been far more proactive in his approach to the problem.*

procedural /prəˈsiːdʒərəl/ *adjective* referring to procedure □ **procedural problem, procedural question** an issue or difficulty relating to correct procedure ○ *The debate lasted two hours because councillors argued over procedural problems.*

procedural motion /prəˈsiːdʒərəl ˌməʊʃ(ə)n/ *noun* a proposal to allow something to happen under the rules of procedure ○ *The chairman moved a procedural motion so that the committee could discuss the next business.*

procedure /prəˈsiːdʒə/ *noun* the way in which something is usually done ○ *to follow the proper procedure*

proceedings /prəˈsiːdɪŋz/ *plural noun* **1.** using a court to settle a legal dispute **2.** an event

proceeds /'prəʊsiːdz/ *plural noun* the money which results from selling something

process /prəʊ'ses/ *noun* a series of things which are done in order to achieve something ■ *verb* to deal officially with a document or request

processing /'prəʊsesɪŋ/ *noun* **1.** the sorting of information ○ *processing of information or of figures* **2.** moving slowly in a procession

proclamation /ˌprɒklə'meɪʃ(ə)n/ *noun* an official public statement ○ *the proclamation of a state of emergency*

proconsul /'prəʊkɒnsəl/ *noun* **1.** a governor or administrator of a colony or other dependency **2.** a senior administrator in a country under the control of an invader's armed forces, whose job is to restore essential services, establish a new government and restore normal life for the population as quickly as possible

Procurator Fiscal /ˌprɒkjʊreɪtə 'fɪsk(ə)l/ *noun* (*in Scotland*) the law officer who decides whether a criminal should be prosecuted

prodemocracy /ˌprəʊdɪ'mɒkrəsi/ *adjective* supporting a democratic system of government

profit /'prɒfɪt/ *noun* the money which results from a successful business

profiteer /ˌprɒfɪ'tɪə/ *noun* a person who makes too much profit, especially when goods are in short supply

profiteering /ˌprɒfɪ'tɪərɪŋ/ *noun* making too much profit

progovernment /prəʊ 'ɡʌv(ə)nmənt/ *adjective* **1.** supporting a government currently in power **2.** supporting a strong government influence on society

programme /'prəʊɡræm/; *US* /'prəʊɡræm/ *noun* a plan of action, especially a party's plan of political or legislative action (NOTE: The US spelling is **program.**) □ **the government's legislative programme** the bills which the government plans to put before the House

progress *noun* /'prəʊɡres/ movement forwards □ **motion to report progress** a motion to adjourn a meeting of the House of Commons sitting as a committee until a later date, similar to the motion for adjournment of the debate ■ *verb* /prəʊ'ɡres/ to move forwards ○ *The government is progressing towards the completion of its legislative programme.*

progressive /prə'ɡresɪv/ *adjective* in favour of new, usually left-wing ideas

Progressive /prə'ɡresɪv/ *adjective* belonging to or associated with a progressive political party ■ *noun* a member of a progressive political party

Progressive Conservative Party /prəʊˌɡresɪv kən'sɜːvətɪv ˌpɑːti/ *noun* one of the main political parties in Canada

Progressive Democrats /prə ˌɡresɪv 'deməkræts/ *plural noun* a political party in the Republic of Ireland

Progressive Party /prəʊ'ɡresɪv 'pɑːti/ *noun* a South African national political party that merged with part of the United Party in 1977 to form the Progressive Federal Party

progressive tax /prə'ɡresɪv tæks/ *noun* a tax which becomes higher as someone's salary increases, e.g. income tax

progress report /'prəʊɡres rɪ ˌpɔːt/ *noun* a document which describes what progress has been made

proletarian /ˌprəʊlə'teəriən/ *adjective* referring to the working class ○ *a proletarian movement for government reform* □ **the proletarian revolution** in Marxist theory, the stage when the proletariat overthrows a capitalist society

proletariat /ˌprəʊlə'teəriət/ *noun* the working class, especially manual and industrial workers and their families □ **the urban proletariat** working people who live in towns □ **dictatorship of the proletariat** in Marxist theory, the period after a revolution when the Communist Party takes control until a classless society develops

promote /prə'məʊt/ *verb* **1.** to introduce a new Bill into Parliament **2.** to give someone a more important job ○ *He was promoted from deputy to sales manager.* **3.** to advertise **4.** to encourage something to grow ○ *The United Nations hopes to promote better understanding between countries with different systems of government.* ○ *The government's campaign to promote increased prosperity in urban centres.*

promoter /prə'məʊtə/ *noun* a person who introduces a new Bill into Parliament

propaganda /ˌprɒpə'gændə/ *noun* (*usually as criticism*) statements which describe the policies or actions of a government in a way which persuades people to believe they are true and correct ○ *The people have grown used to not believing government propaganda.* ○ *The leader of the opposition denounced the council's advertising campaign as simple propaganda.*

propaganda radio /ˌprɒpə'gændə 'reɪdiəʊ/ *noun* radio broadcasts aimed at changing people's political ideas

propaganda war /ˌprɒpə'gændə wɔː/ *noun* a fight between two parties or governments, using radio or television or newspapers, to publicise their ideas and to try to persuade people to believe them

propagandist /ˌprɒpə'gændɪst/ *noun* a person who issues propaganda

proportion /prə'pɔːʃ(ə)n/ *noun* a part of a total ○ *A proportion of the pretax profit is set aside for contingencies.* ○ *Only a small proportion of our sales comes from retail shops.*

proportional representation /prə,pɔːʃ(ə)n(ə)l ˌreprɪzen'teɪʃ(ə)n/ *noun* a system of electing representatives where each political party is given the number of places which is directly related to the number of votes cast for the party. Abbr **PR**

proposal /prə'pəʊz(ə)l/ *noun* a suggestion, thing suggested ○ *to make a proposal* or *to put forward a proposal* □ **to lay a proposal before the House** to introduce a new Bill before Parliament for discussion

propose /prə'pəʊz/ *verb* to suggest that something should be done ○ *The Bill proposes that any party to the proceedings may appeal.* Compare **second** □ **to propose a motion** to ask a meeting to vote for a motion and explain the reasons for this

proposer /prə'pəʊzə/ *noun* a person who introduces a motion or suggests that something should be done ○ *Each candidate needs a proposer and seconder.* ○ *Mr Smith is the proposer of the vote of thanks, but who is seconding him?* Compare **seconder**

proposition /ˌprɒpə'zɪʃ(ə)n/ *noun* **1.** a proposal or suggestion that can be discussed or formally debated **2.** a suggested law or change to a law that people can vote for or against (*US*)

prorogation /ˌprəʊrə'geɪʃ(ə)n/ *noun* the ending by the Queen of a session of Parliament

prorogue /prə'rəʊg/ *verb* ((*of the Queen*)) to end a session of Parliament ○ *Parliament was prorogued for the summer recess.*

proscribe /prəʊ'skraɪb/ *verb* to ban or forbid □ **a proscribed political party** a political party which has been banned

Prospect /'prɒspekt/ *noun* a trade union representing engineers and scientists. It was formed in 2001 by the merger of IPMS (The Institute of Professional, Managers and Specialists) and EMA (the Engineers and Managers Association).

prospective candidate /prə,spektɪv 'kændɪdeɪt/ *noun* a person who may be chosen as candidate for a constituency

protected country /prə,tektɪd 'kʌntri/ *noun* an independent country which is defended by another, more powerful, country

protective treaty /prə,tektɪv 'triːti/ *noun* an agreement by which one country agrees to defend another smaller country

protector /prə'tektə/ *noun* a person or country which defends others

protectorate /prə'tekt(ə)rət/ *noun* **1.** a country which is being protected or governed by another more powerful country ○ *a British protectorate* **2.** □ **the Protectorate** period from 1653 – 1658 when Oliver Cromwell was Lord Protector

pro tempore *Latin phrase meaning* for a time. ◊ **president pro tempore**

protest *noun* /'prəʊtest/ a statement or action to show that you do not approve of something ○ *to make a protest against high prices* □ **in protest at** showing that you do not approve of something ○ *the staff occupied the offices in protest at the low pay offer* ■ *verb* /prə'test/ □ **to protest against something** to say that you do not approve of something ○ *the retailers are protesting against the ban on imported goods*

protester /prə'testə/ *noun* a person who protests ○ *Protesters marched to Downing Street.*

protest march /'prəʊtest mɑːtʃ/ *noun* a demonstration where protesters walk as a group through the streets

protest strike /'prəʊtest straɪk/ *noun* a refusal to work in protest at a particular grievance

protocol /'prəʊtəkɒl/ *noun* **1.** a first version of what has been agreed in negotiations between countries ○ *The negotiators signed the protocol of the treaty.* **2.** a list of things which have been agreed **3.** the correct behaviour between ambassadors and the officials of different governments, or in any other formal proceedings

provide /prə'vaɪd/ *verb* **1.** to give or supply something **2.** to allow that something will happen

provided that /prə'vaɪdɪd ðæt/, **providing** /prə'vaɪdɪŋ/ *conjunction* on condition that ○ *The committee will decide on the planning application next week provided (that) or providing the architect's report is received in time.* (NOTE: In legal documents, the form **provided always that** is often used.)

province /'prɒvɪns/ *noun* **1.** a large administrative division of a country ○ *the ten provinces of Canada* ○ *The premier of the Province of Alberta.* **2.** an area of a country away from the capital city □ **in the provinces** in the country outside London **3.** □ **the Province** Northern Ireland

provincial /prə'vɪnʃəl/ *adjective* referring to a province ○ *a provincial governor* ○ *The company is based in the provincial capital.* ■ *noun* a person from the country, not the capital

provincial police /prə,vɪnʃəl pə 'liːs/ *noun* a Canadian police force that operates within a province but not in urban areas, which have their own police forces

provision /prə'vɪʒ(ə)n/ *noun* **1.** a legal condition □ **the provisions of a Bill** conditions listed in a Bill before Parliament **2.** money put aside in accounts in case it is needed in the future ○ *The council has made a £2m provision for bad debts.*

provisional /prə'vɪʒ(ə)n(ə)l/ *adjective* temporary, not final or permanent ○ *provisional budget* ○ *They wrote to give their provisional acceptance of the contract.*

Provisional /prə'vɪʒ(ə)n(ə)l/ *noun* a member of an unofficial group in the Irish Republican Army

provisionally /prə'vɪʒ(ə)nəli/ *adverb* not finally ○ *The contract has been accepted provisionally.* ○ *He was provisionally appointed director.*

proviso /prə'vaɪzəʊ/ *noun* a condition in a contract ○ *We are signing the contract with the proviso that the terms can be discussed again in six months' time.* (NOTE: The proviso usually begins with the phrase '**provided always that**'.)

provocateur /prɒvɒkə'tɜː/ ♦ **agent**

provost /'prɒvəst/ *noun* the leading elected official in a Scottish town, with a position similar to that of a mayor in England

prowar /prəʊˈwɔː/ *adjective* supporting war in general, a specific war, or the policy of going to war in a specific situation

proxy /ˈprɒksi/ *noun* **1.** a document which gives someone the power to act on behalf of someone else ○ *to sign by proxy* **2.** a person who acts for someone else, especially by voting as they instruct, e.g. at a meeting or in an election ○ *to act as proxy for someone*

proxy vote /ˈprɒksi vəʊt/ *noun* a vote made by proxy

PS /ˌpiː ˈes/ *abbreviation* **1.** Permanent Secretary **2.** private secretary

PSBR *abbreviation* Public Sector Borrowing Requirement

psephologist *noun* a person who makes a study of elections and voting patterns

psephology *noun* the study of elections and voting patterns

PSNI *abbreviation* Police Service of Northern Ireland

PTA *abbreviation* Passenger Transport Authority *or* Parent Teacher Association

PTC *abbreviation* Public Services, Tax and Commerce Union

public /ˈpʌblɪk/ *adjective* **1.** referring to all the people in general **2.** referring to the government or the state **3.** taking place in front of many people, as opposed to in private ○ *a public appearance by a member of the Royal Family* ○ *the public opening of the new park* □ **in public** in a way that allows many people hear or see something ○ *He never comments on these matters in public.* ■ *noun* □ **the public**, **the general public** the people in general ◇ **public administration 1.** means by which government policy is carried out **2.** people responsible for carrying out government policy

Public Accounts Committee /ˌpʌblɪk əˈkaʊnts kəˌmɪti/ *noun* a select committee of the House of Commons which examines the spending of each department, including such matters as whether the department was en-

titled to spend the money in question, and whether the spending was a waste of money

public affairs /ˈpʌblɪk əˈfeəz/ *plural noun* political issues that affect people generally

Public and Commercial Services Union /ˈpʌblɪk ən kəˈmɜːʃ(ə)l ˈsɜːvɪsɪz ˈjuːnjən/ *noun* a trade union representing employees of government departments and agencies, with over 250,000 members. It was formed in 1998 with the merger of the PCS (Public Services, Tax and Commerce Union) and the IRSF (Inland Revenue Staff Federation). Abbr **PCS**

Public Bill /ˌpʌblɪk ˈbɪl/ *noun* a Bill referring to a matter applying to the public in general which is introduced in Parliament by a government minister

public corporation /ˈpʌblɪk ˌkɔːpəˈreɪʃ(ə)n/ *noun* in the United Kingdom, an organisation set up by the government to run a state-owned enterprise such as the BBC, and whose chairman and governors are appointed by a government minister

public domain /ˌpʌblɪk dəʊˈmeɪn/ *noun* **in the public domain** referring to information which is available to the public

public enquiry /ˈpʌblɪk ɪŋˈkwaɪri/ *noun* another spelling of **public inquiry**

public expenditure /ˌpʌblɪk ɪk ˈspendɪtʃə/ *noun* the money spent by local or central government

public eye ◇ **in the public eye** well-known because of appearing frequently in the media ◇ **out of the public eye** not seen in the media as much as before

public figure /ˌpʌblɪk ˈfɪgə/ *noun* a person who is well-known, often through the media, especially a politician

public finance /ˌpʌblɪk ˈfaɪnæns/ *noun* the raising of money by governments through taxes or borrowing and the spending of it

public funds /ˌpʌblɪk 'fʌndz/ *plural noun* the government money available for spending

public gallery /'pʌblɪk 'gæləri/ *noun* an area where members of the public can sit to listen to debates in a council chamber or the House of Commons or House of Lords

public health /ˌpʌblɪk 'helθ/ *noun* the general health of a community and the measures taken to protect it

public image /ˌpʌblɪk 'ɪmɪdʒ/ *noun* the way in which someone or an organisation is regarded by the public, even if this is not a true picture ○ *The ecological disaster has given oil companies a bad public image.*

public inquiry /'pʌblɪk ɪn'kwaɪəri/ *noun* an official investigation to find out exactly what went wrong in a particular situation, led by a judge or other experienced person appointed by the government

public interest /ˌpʌblɪk 'ɪntrəst/ *noun* **1.** the right of the public to know about something which affects them □ **in the public interest** for the benefit of the public ○ *The newspaper claimed that the publication of the details was in the public interest.* **2.** general interest by people in something ○ *There was little public interest in the proposed scheme.*

public life /'pʌblɪk laɪf/ *noun* the kind of work and activities in politics, education, religion and business that lead to someone being well-known ○ *After his wife's accident, he decided to retire from public life.*

public monopoly /ˌpʌblɪk mə'nɒpəli/ *noun* a situation where the state is the only supplier of a product or service. Also called **state monopoly**

public office /'pʌblɪk 'ɒfɪs/ *noun* a position in a government department ○ *She has held public office for twenty years.*

public opinion /ˌpʌblɪk ə'pɪnjən/ *noun* what most people think about something

public order /ˌpʌblɪk 'ɔːdə/ *noun* a situation where the general public is calm and well behaved

public ownership /ˌpʌblɪk 'əʊnəʃɪp/ *noun* a situation in which an industry or business is owned by the state ○ *The company has been put into state ownership.* Also called **state ownership**

public policy /ˌpʌblɪk 'pɒlɪsi/ *noun* political plans affecting the general good of all the people

public private partnership /'pʌblɪk 'praɪvət 'pɑːtnəʃɪp/ *noun* a partnership between government and private companies to provide services and infrastructure traditionally provided by the public sector. Abbr **PPP**

public prosecutor /ˌpʌblɪk 'prɒsɪkjuːtə/ *noun* a government official who brings charges against criminals. In the UK this is the Director of Public Prosecutions.

Public Record Office /'pʌblɪk rɪ'kɔːd 'ɒfɪs/ *noun* a UK institution which stores official documents after they are made available to the public, usually 30 years after they were created. Abbr **PRO**

public relations /ˌpʌblɪk rɪ'leɪʃ(ə)nz/ *noun* keeping good links between an organisation or a group and the public so that people know what the group is doing and approve of it. Abbr **PR**

public relations department /ˌpʌblɪk rɪ'leɪʃ(ə)nz dɪˌpɑːtmənt/ *noun* the section of an organisation which deals with relations with the public

public relations officer /ˌpʌblɪk rɪ'leɪʃ(ə)nz ˌɒfɪsə/ *noun* an official who deals with relations with the public

public sector /'pʌblɪk ˌsektə/ *noun* industries and services which are owned by the state ○ *A report on wage rises in the public sector* or *on public sector wage settlements.* Compare **private sector**

Public Sector Borrowing Requirement /'pʌblɪk 'sektə 'bɒrəʊɪŋ rɪ'kwaɪəmənt/ *noun* the amount of money which a government has to borrow

public servant /ˌpʌblɪk 'sɜːvənt/ *noun* someone who works for the government or a government organisation, or someone holding an elected position in government

public service /ˌpʌblɪk 'sɜːvɪs/ *noun* **1.** work in a government job or in an organisation controlled by government ○ *a long career in public service* **2.** an essential service that is provided by government such as education or healthcare, or a service that benefits the public in general such as transport

Public Services, Tax and Commerce Union *noun* a British trade union representing civil servants. Abbr **PTC**

public spending /ˌpʌblɪk 'spendɪŋ/ *noun* the money spent by the government and government organisations

public transport /ˌpʌblɪk 'trænspɔːt/ *noun* transport such as buses, trains which is used by any member of the public

public utility /'pʌblɪk juː'tɪlɪti/ *noun* a company that provides gas, electricity or water

public works /ˌpʌblɪk 'wɜːks/ *plural noun* projects such as road or school building or the renewal of sewers that are undertaken by government for the community

pure democracy /ˌpjʊə dɪ'mɒkrəsi/ *noun* a form of democracy in which the people exercise direct power instead of through representatives they have elected to govern on their behalf

purge /pɜːdʒ/ *verb* to remove opponents or unacceptable people from a group or from their jobs ○ *The activists have purged the party of moderates* or *have purged the moderates from the party.* ○ *The new regime purged the senior military officers within a few days of taking control.*

pursuant to /pə'sjuːənt tə/ *adverb* relating to or concerning ○ *matters pursuant to Article 124 of the EU treaty* ○ *pursuant to the powers conferred on the local authority* ○ *pursuant to Standing Order No. 61*

pursue /pə'sjuː/ *verb* to continue with discussion or debate ○ *We shall pursue this matter at our next meeting.*

pursuit /pə'sjuːt/ *noun* the process of trying to achieve something

'...all men...are endowed by their Creator with certain unalienable rights; that among these are life, liberty, and the pursuit of happiness' [*US Declaration of Independence*]

purview /'pɜːvjuː/ *noun* within the limits that a law, organisation or person is responsible for or deals with ○ *It is within the purview of the Finance Committee to review the council's expenditure.*

put /pʊt/ *verb* □ **to put a proposal to someone** to ask someone to consider a suggestion □ **to put a proposal to the vote** to ask a meeting to vote for or against a proposal □ **to move that the question be put** to ask that a meeting should vote immediately on a proposal without further discussion

put down /ˌpʊt 'daʊn/ *verb* **1.** to stop or crush a rebellion ○ *The Prime Minister ordered the army to put down the revolt.* **2.** to suggest that a motion should be debated in a meeting ○ *He put down a motion criticising the government for its foreign policy.* **3.** to write something in an account book ○ *to put down a figure for expenses*

put forward /ˌpʊt 'fɔːwəd/ *verb* to propose or suggest that something should be done ○ *Mr John Smith's name has been put forward as a candidate for Treasurer.* ○ *The government has put forward ten pieces of legislation for the next session.* ○ *He put forward the suggestion that council meetings should be held on Saturdays.*

put in /ˌpʊt 'ɪn/ *verb* to place inside

put off /ˌpʊt 'ɒf/ *verb* to arrange for something to take place later than planned ○ *The hearing was put off for* two weeks. ○ *He asked if we could put the visit off until tomorrow.*

put on /ˌpʊt 'ɒn/ *verb* to place on □ **to put an item on the agenda** to list an item for discussion at a meeting □ **to put an embargo on trade** to forbid trade

put out /ˌpʊt 'aʊt/ *verb* to send out ○ *to put work out to freelance workers* ○ *We put all our typing out to a bureau.*

putsch /pʊtʃ/ *noun* an armed attack on a government by people trying to overthrow it

PW *abbreviation* Policewoman

Q

QMV *abbreviation* qualified majority voting

qua /kwɑː/ *conjunction* as, or acting as ○ *a decision of the Lord Chancellor qua head of the judiciary*

Quai d'Orsay /ˌkaɪ ˈdɔːsaɪ/ *noun* the street by the river Seine in Paris, where the French Foreign Ministry has its offices (NOTE: often used to refer to the Foreign Ministry itself, or to its policies)

qualification /ˌkwɒlɪfɪˈkeɪʃ(ə)n/ *noun* a limitation or exception to what has been said or written ○ *the minister said that the new rules would apply immediately but with the qualification that cars more than ten years old would be exempt*

qualified majority vote /ˈkwɒlɪfaɪd məˈdʒɒrɪti vəʊt/ *noun* the voting system used in most cases on the Council of Ministers of the European Union by which more than a simple majority of votes is required to reach agreement (NOTE: The effect of using the qualified majority vote is to remove the national veto on change but not to make change as easy to achieve as it would be if a simple majority were required.)

qualify /ˈkwɒlɪfaɪ/ *verb* **1.** to achieve the examination result or the skills needed to do a job **2.** to limit in some way **3.** to change or to amend

quango /ˈkwæŋɡəʊ/ *noun* a group of people appointed by a government with powers to deal with problems, but largely independent of government control. Full form **quasi-autonomous non-governmental organization** (NOTE: The plural is **quangos.**)

quarter /ˈkwɔːtə/ *noun* **1.** a period of three months **2.** a section of a town ○ *the old Turkish quarter*

quarter day /ˈkwɔːtə deɪ/ *noun* a day at the end of a three month period, when rents should be paid

COMMENT: In England the quarter days are 25th March (Lady Day), 24th June (Midsummer Day), 29th September (Michaelmas Day) and 25th December (Christmas Day).

Quartet /kwɔːˈtet/ *noun* an international group of representatives from the United States, the European Union, the Russian Federation and the United Nations that meets regularly to encourage a peace process between Israel and the Palestinian Authority

quash /kwɒʃ/ *verb* to overturn a decision, or to make something not exist ○ *The appeal court quashed the verdict.* ○ *She applied for judicial review to quash the order.*

quasi- /kweɪzaɪ/ *prefix* almost or which seems like ○ *a quasi-official body* ○ *a quasi-judicial investigation*

queen /kwiːn/ *noun* **1.** a female ruler ○ *the queen of the Netherlands* **2.** the wife of a king (NOTE: [all senses] written with a capital letter when used as a title: *Queen Elizabeth II*)

Queen Mother /ˈkwiːn ˈmʌðə/ *noun* a woman who is the mother of a King or Queen

Queen's Messenger /ˌkwiːnz ˈmesɪndʒə/ *noun* a diplomat who carries messages from Britain to British embassies. Also called **King's Messenger**

Queen's Speech /ˌkwiːnz ˈspiːtʃ/ *noun* a speech written by the government and delivered by the Queen at the opening of a session of Parliament which outlines the government's plans for the next year

quell /kwel/ *verb* to keep under control ○ *Mounted police were brought in to quell the riots.*

query /'kwɪəri/ *noun* question ○ *The Chief Secretary to the Treasury had to answer a mass of queries from MPs.* ■ *verb* to ask a question about something or to suggest that something may be wrong ○ *The opposition spokesman queried the statements made by the Cabinet Office officials.*

question /'kwestʃ(ə)n/ *noun* **1.** words which need an answer ○ *MPs asked the minister questions about the Swiss bank accounts.* ○ *She said she wished to put three questions to the Permanent Secretary.* ○ *The managing director refused to answer questions about redundancies.* ○ *The market research team prepared a series of questions to test the public's attitude to the government's record on law and order.* ◊ **written question 2.** a problem ○ *He raised the question of the cost of the lawsuit.* ○ *The main question is that of time.* ○ *The tribunal discussed the question of redundancy payments.* **3.** a matter or motion to be discussed by Parliament □ **to put the question** to ask MPs to say whether they agree with the motion or not □ **question negatived** a motion not carried or agreed to in a meeting ■ *verb* **1.** to ask questions ○ *The inspectors questioned the Minister's staff for four hours.* ○ *She questioned the chairman about the council's investment policy.* **2.** to ask or to suggest that something may be wrong ○ *MPs questioned the reliability of the confidential report.* ○ *The leader of the council questioned the result of the opinion poll.*

question of personal privilege /ˌkwestʃ(ə)n əv ˌpɜːs(ə)n(ə)l 'prɪvɪlɪdʒ/ *noun US* a matter referring to a member of Congress, which is usually given priority over other matters

question of privilege /ˌkwestʃ(ə)n əv 'prɪvɪlɪdʒ/ *noun* a matter which refers to the House or a member of it

Question Time /'kwestʃ(ə)n taɪm/ *noun* the period in the House of Commons and the European Parliament when members can put questions to ministers about the work of their departments

quid pro quo /ˌkwɪd prəʊ 'kwəʊ/ *Latin phrase meaning* 'one thing for another': action done in return for something done or promised

Quirinal *noun* one of the seven hills of Rome, where the Italian government has its offices (NOTE: used as a term for the Italian government)

quisling /'kwɪzlɪŋ/ *noun* a person who gives their support to the enemy of their country (NOTE: From the name of the Norwegian collaborator with the Nazis, Vidkun Quisling.)

quorate /'kwɔːreɪt/ *adjective* having enough people present at a meeting for the meeting to be held ○ *The resolution was invalid because the shareholders' meeting was not quorate.* ◊ **inquorate**

quorum /'kwɔːrəm/ *noun* the smallest number of people who have to be present at a meeting to make it valid

COMMENT: In the House of Commons, the quorum is 40 MPs; 30 peers are needed for a quorum in the House of Lords. In the US Congress, a majority of members must be present, that is, 51 in the Senate and 218 in the House of Representatives.

quota /'kwəʊtə/ *noun* a fixed amount of something which is allowed to be sold or bought or obtained

quota system /'kwəʊtə ˌsɪstəm/ *noun* a plan which limits the number of people or of goods or of money which can be used or brought into a country or taken out of a country

quotation /kwəʊ'teɪʃ(ə)n/ *noun* words taken out of a speech or a book

q.v., quod vide *Latin phrase meaning* 'which see' used to refer to another document ○ *A similar case appears in the agenda for the Social Services Committee (q.v.).*

R

rabble /'ræb(ə)l/ *noun* the ordinary people regarded as inferior

rabble-rouser /'ræb(ə)l ˌraʊzə/ *noun* a politician who encourages an angry crowd to take violent action

rabble-rousing /'ræb(ə)l 'raʊzɪŋ/ *adjective* encouraging people to take violent action ○ *a rabble-rousing speech*

race /reɪs/ *noun* **1.** a competition or test to see who is the best at doing something ○ *The race is on for the Democratic presidential nomination.* **2.** a group of people who share the same language, history or culture, or who are different from other groups in terms of their physical appearance

race relations /ˌreɪs rɪ'leɪʃ(ə)nz/ *plural noun* the relations between people of different racial groups

racial /'reɪʃ(ə)l/ *adjective* referring to different ethnic groups

racial discrimination /ˌreɪʃ(ə)l dɪsˌkrɪmɪ'neɪʃ(ə)n/ *noun* unfair treatment of someone because of their ethnic background

racial prejudice /ˌreɪʃ(ə)l 'predʒʊdɪs/ *noun* feelings of dislike for someone because of their ethnic background ○ *They investigated the claims of racial prejudice against the Housing Committee chairman.*

racial profiling /ˌreɪʃ(ə)l 'prəʊfaɪlɪŋ/ *noun* the practice by some police of stopping and questioning members of specific ethnic groups more often than others without reasonable cause

racial segregation /ˌreɪʃ(ə)l ˌsegrɪ'geɪʃ(ə)n/ *noun* the practice of keeping different races apart

racism /'reɪsɪz(ə)m/, **racialism** /'reɪʃ(ə)lɪz(ə)m/ *noun* a belief in racist ideas ○ *The minority groups have accused the council of racism in their allocation of council houses.*

racist, racialist (*usually as criticism*) actions based on racist ideas ■ *adjective* /'reɪsɪst/; /'reɪʃ(ə)lɪst/ believing that people from other ethnic groups are different and should receive different and usually worse treatment ■ *noun* /'reɪsɪst/; /'reɪʃ(ə)lɪst/ a person with racist ideas

radical /'rædɪk(ə)l/ *adjective* **1.** extreme or involving great change ○ *The problem of overcrowding is so great, that only a radical solution can solve it.* ○ *The new leader has started a radical rethink of the party's policies.* **2.** concerned with the most important or basic parts of something ■ *noun* **1.** a person who believes that a complete change should be made to society to reduce social problems **2.** **Radical** a member or supporter of a Radical Party

radicalise /'rædɪkəlaɪz/ *verb* to adopt politically radical views, or encourage someone to do this

radicalism /'rædɪkəlɪz(ə)m/ *noun* the political ideas of radicals

Radical Party /'rædɪk(ə)l 'pɑːti/ *noun* a political party in favour of great or rapid change in society

raise /reɪz/ *verb* **1.** to increase or to make higher ○ *The government has raised the penalties for drug smuggling.* ○ *The company raised its dividend by 10%.* **2.** to ask a meeting to discuss a question ○ *to raise a question* or *a point at a meeting* ○ *in answer to the point of order raised by Mr*

Smith □ **to raise an objection** to say that you object to something ○ *The opposition members of the Committee raised a series of objections to the wording of the statement.* **3.** to obtain money ○ *The council is trying to raise the capital to fund its housing programme.* ○ *The government hopes to raise the money by extra taxation.* ○ *Where will she raise the money from to start up her business?* ■ *noun US* an increase in salary ○ *He asked the boss for a raise.* (NOTE: The UK term is **rise.**)

raison d'état /ˌreɪzɒn deɪ'tæ/ *noun* a strong reason that is believed to justify political or diplomatic action that might otherwise be rejected (NOTE: Raison d'état is open to criticism because it can be used to justify acts such as the abolition of individual rights if the general good of the people seems to require it at the time.)

raison d',tat /ˌraɪzɒn deɪ'tæ/ *noun* the reason for a political action, which says that an action is right because it is for the common good

> COMMENT: Raison d',tat is open to criticism because it can be used to justify acts such as the abolition of individual rights, if the general good of the people may seem to require it at the time.

Raj /rɑːdʒ/ *noun* the period of British government of India

Rajya Sabha *noun* the upper house of Parliament in India. Compare **Lok Sabha**

rally /'ræli/ *noun* a mass political meeting

ram /ræm/ *verb* to force the passage of a bill, usually against strong objections

rank /ræŋk/ *noun* a level or grade in an army or other organisation ○ *In the Foreign Service, the rank of secretary is lower than that of ambassador.* ○ *He was promoted to the rank of Chief Superintendent.* ■ *verb* to be level with

rapprochement /ræ'prɒʃmɒŋ/ *French word meaning* 'coming closer', a situation where two states become friendly after a period of unfriendliness ○ *Political commentators have noted the rapprochement which has been taking place since the old president died.*

rate /reɪt/ *noun* **1.** a measurement of something **2.** the cost of something ■ *verb* **1.** to estimate the size or value of something **2.** to be worthy of something

rate of inflation /ˌreɪt əv ɪn'fleɪʃ(ə)n/ *noun* a percentage increase in prices over a period of one year. Also called **inflation rate**

rates /reɪts/ *plural noun* until 1989 in Scotland and 1990 in England and Wales, local taxes on the size of owned property

ratification /ˌrætɪfɪ'keɪʃ(ə)n/ *noun* official approval of something which has already been agreed ○ *The Chair of Finance asked the committee for ratification of his decision.*

ratify /'rætɪfaɪ/ *verb* to approve officially something which has already been agreed ○ *The treaty was ratified by Congress.* ○ *The ceasefire agreement has to be ratified by all the parties involved.* ○ *Although the directors had acted without due authority, the company ratified their actions.*

re /riː/ *preposition* about or concerning or referring to ○ *re your inquiry of May 29th* ○ *re: Smith's memorandum of yesterday* ○ *re: the agenda for the AGM* □ **in re** concerning or in the case of ○ *in re Jones & Co. Ltd*

reaction /ri'ækʃən/ *noun* **1.** an action taken in reply to or as a result of something else ○ *The reaction of the minister has been to attack the Opposition parties.* **2.** extreme conservatism or opposition to any reform ○ *The slogan of the Socialists was 'Defeat the Forces of Reaction'.*

reactionary /ri'ækʃən(ə)ri/ *adjective, noun* holding extreme conservative views, being opposed to all reform ○ *The newspaper is becoming more and more reactionary.* ○ *As he grew older, the President's policies became reactionary.*

reading /'riːdɪŋ/ *noun* one of the three stages of discussion of a Bill in Parliament

COMMENT: First Reading is the formal presentation of the Bill when the title is read out; Second Reading is the stage when printed copies of the Bill are available and it is explained by the Minister proposing it, there is a debate and a vote is taken; the Bill is then discussed in Committee and at the Report Stage; Third Reading is the final discussion of the Bill in the whole House of Commons or House of Lords.

read out /ˌriːd 'aʊt/ *verb* to remove someone formally from membership of a political party or other group

Reagan /'reɪgən/, **Ronald** (1911–2004) 40th president of the United States (1981–89), during which period relations with the former Soviet Union greatly improved

Reaganomics /ˌreɪgə'nɒmɪks/ *noun* the free-market economic approach of US president Ronald Reagan, involving cuts in taxes and social spending together with removal of controls on domestic markets

realign /riːə'laɪn/ *verb* to form new alliances or associations, or cause people or groups to do this

realignment /ˌriːə'laɪnmənt/ *noun* **1.** a change in the relationship between political parties or between countries in an alliance ○ *a basic realignment of parties on the left* ○ *a realignment of Caribbean states* ○ *The General Election of 1997 produced an important realignment in British politics, when the long period of Conservative dominance which had lasted since 1979 was brought to an end by a Labour landslide victory.* **2.** the process of making a change in a system, so that different parts are in a different relationship to each other □ **a currency realignment** a change in the international exchange rates

realm /relm/ *noun* **1.** an area ruled by a king or queen **2.** a particular area of interest or activity ○ *the political realm*

Realpolitik /reɪ'ɑːlpɒlitiːl/ *German word meaning* politics based on real and practical considerations and not on theoretical or moral principles

rebate /'riːbeɪt/ *noun* an amount of money which is officially returned to someone, reducing the amount that has to be paid ○ *a tax rebate*

rebel /'reb(ə)l/ *noun* a person who fights against the government or against people in authority ○ *Anti-government rebels have taken six towns.* ○ *Rebel ratepayers have occupied the town hall.* ■ *verb* to fight against authority (NOTE: **rebelling – rebelled**)

rebellion /rɪ'beljən/ *noun* a fight against the government or against those in authority ○ *The army has crushed the rebellion in the southern province.*

rebellious /rɪ'beljəs/ *adjective* fighting against authority

rebut /rɪ'bʌt/ *verb* to reply to a point made by someone in a debate or argument ○ *She attempted to rebut the assertions made by the Opposition spokesman.*

rebuttal /rɪ'bʌt(ə)l/ *noun* the act of rebutting something

recall /rɪ'kɔːl/ *noun* **1.** asking someone to come back ○ *MPs are asking for the recall of Parliament to debate the crisis.* ○ *After his recall, the Ambassador was interviewed at the airport.* **2.** *US* the system of ending the period in office of an elected official early, following a popular vote ■ *verb* **1.** to ask someone to come back ○ *MPs are asking for Parliament to be recalled to debate the financial crisis.* ○ *The witness was recalled to the committee room.* □ **to recall an ambassador** to ask an ambassador to return to his or her country, usually as a way of breaking off diplomatic relations **2.** to remember ○ *The witness could not recall having seen the papers.*

receipt /rɪ'siːt/ *noun* a document showing that someone has paid for something or that someone has taken delivery of something ■ *verb* to stamp or to sign a document to show that it has been received or to stamp an invoice to show that it has been paid

receive /rɪ'siːv/ *verb* to accept a report officially ○ *It was resolved that the reports of the subcommittees be received.*

receiver of wrecks /rɪˌsiːvər əv 'reks/ *noun* the official of the Department of Trade and Industry who deals with legal problems of wrecked ships within his or her area

receiving /rɪ'siːvɪŋ/ *noun* the act of taking something which has been delivered

recess /rɪ'ses/ *noun* 1. the period when Parliament or another body is not sitting ○ *During August, Parliament is in recess.* ○ *The council's last meeting before the summer recess will be on 23rd July.* 2. (*in Congress*) the period when the chamber does not meet, but is not adjourned ■ *verb* (*of the US Senate*) not to meet, but without adjourning ○ *The Senate recessed at the end of the afternoon.*

reciprocal /rɪ'sɪprək(ə)l/ *adjective* involving two countries or people or organisations in an agreement to give equal amounts of help to each other

reciprocal trade /rɪˌsɪprək(ə)l 'treɪd/ *noun* trade between two countries, where each agrees to buy goods from the other ○ *The two countries signed a reciprocal trade agreement.*

reciprocate /rɪ'sɪprəkeɪt/ *verb* to do the same thing to someone as he or she has just done to you ○ *The President offered to free political prisoners if the rebels would reciprocate by freeing their hostages.*

reciprocity /ˌresɪ'prɒsɪti/ *noun* an arrangement which applies when two people, countries or organisations give an equal amount of help to one another

recognise /'rekəgnaɪz/, **recognize** /'rekəgˌnaɪz/ *verb* to approve something as being legal □ **to recognise a government** to say that a government which has taken power in a foreign country is the legal government of that country □ **to recognise a trade union**

to accept that a union can act on behalf of staff ○ *although all the staff had joined the union, the management refused to recognise it*

recognition /ˌrekəg'nɪʃ(ə)n/ *noun* the formal acceptance by one country of the independent and legal status of another

recommendation /ˌrekəmen'deɪʃ(ə)n/ *noun* 1. a suggestion that something should be done ○ *The government is acting on the recommendations of the Royal Commission.* ○ *The subcommittee forwarded a recommendation for two new computers to the Finance Committee.* ○ *The Council will consider the recommendation of the subcommittee that the budget be revised.* 2. a statement that someone or something is good ○ *We appointed her on the recommendation of her former employer.* 3. in the European Union, a piece of advice about how to do something, which is not compulsory but which people are encouraged to adopt.
◊ **decision, directive, regulations**

recommit /ˌriːkə'mɪt/ *verb US* to send a bill back to the committee which reported it, for further discussion

recommittal /ˌriːkə'mɪt(ə)l/ *noun* a decision to send a bill back to a committee for further discussion

reconvene /ˌriːkən'viːn/ *verb* to meet again ○ *The committee has adjourned, and will reconvene tomorrow morning.*

record /rɪ'kɔːd/ *noun* 1. a report of something which has happened, especially an official report of a court action ○ *The chairman signed the minutes as a true record of the last meeting.* □ **off the record** unofficially or in private ○ *he made some remarks off the record about the rising crime figures in the borough* 2. a description of what has happened in the past ○ *the clerk's record of service* or *service record* ○ *the company's record in industrial relations* 3. a result which is much better or much worse than earlier results ■ *adjective* same as **record-breaking** ○ *record profits* ○ *record* *losses* ■ *verb* to note or to report ○ *The company has recorded another year of increased sales.* ○ *Your complaint has been recorded and will be investigated.* ○ *The Government recorded another defeat over the Opposition.*

record-breaking /ˈrekɔːdbreɪkɪŋ/ *adjective* much better or worse than any others before

recorded vote /rɪˌkɔːdɪd ˈvəʊt/ *noun US* a vote in Congress, where each member's vote is counted and listed

records /ˈrekɔːdz/ *plural noun* documents which give information ○ *The names of customers are kept in the company's records.* ○ *We find from our records that our invoice number 1234 has not been paid.*

recount *noun* /ˈriːkaʊnt/ a second count of the votes cast in an election, usually done because there was a very close result when they were first counted ○ *The vote was very close, so the loser asked for a recount.* ○ *After three recounts, Edward Jones was declared the winner by eleven votes.* ■ *verb* /riːˈkaʊnt/ to count again

recurrent /rɪˈkʌrənt/ *adjective* happening again and again ○ *recurrent items of expenditure*

red /red/ *noun* the colour used to represent Socialist or Communist Parties ■ *plural noun* □ **the Reds** (*usually as criticism*) Communists ■ *adjective* Communist, referring to a Communist Party

red box /ˌred ˈbɒks/ *noun* same as **despatch box 1**

redeploy /ˌriːdɪˈplɔɪ/ *verb* to make better use of people or equipment, by moving them to another job or place ○ *The council is proposing to redeploy staff from other departments to make up the staff vacancies in the Finance Department.*

redeployment /ˌriːdɪˈplɔɪmənt/ *noun* the process of using staff or equipment in other places

Red Flag /ˌred ˈflæg/ *noun* **1.** the symbol of international Communism

2. a song sung by communists and socialists

redistribute /ˌriːdɪˈstrɪbjuːt/ *verb* to share out again ○ *In some forms of proportional representation, the votes cast for the losing candidates at the first count are redistributed among the main candidates to ensure an election.*

redistribution /riːˌdɪstrɪˈbjuːʃən/ *noun* **1.** the process of sharing something out in a different way □ **redistribution of wealth** the process of taxing people with more money to make improvements in the lives of poorer people **2.** the action of changing Parliamentary constituencies or electoral districts to make them more representative in the light of population changes

redistrict /riːˈdɪstrɪkt/ *verb* to change the boundaries of electoral districts in an area in order to allow for changes in population

red line /ˌred ˈlaɪn/ *noun* an essential component or concession in a series of negotiations, especially negotiations on the European Constitution ○ *set out red line issues, relating to tax, foreign policy and defence policy* ○ *We have well-established red lines and we are succeeding in maintaining them.*

red tape /ˌred ˈteɪp/ *noun* the rules which slow down administrative work ○ *The application was held up for several months by red tape.*

reduced /rɪˈdjuːst/ *adjective* lower ○ *New businesses pay a reduced rate of tax.*

redundant /rɪˈdʌndənt/ *adjective* no longer used or employed

re-elect /ˌriː ɪˈlekt/ *verb* to elect again ○ *The sitting member was re-elected with an increased majority.*

re-election /ˌriː ɪˈlekʃən/ *noun* electing someone again ○ *The committee has opposed the automatic re-election of the chairman.*

referee /ˌrefəˈriː/ *noun* **1.** a person who can give a report on someone's character or ability or speed of work ○ *to give someone's name as referee* ○ *She gave the name of her boss as a ref-*

eree. ○ *When applying please give the names of three referees.* **2.** a person to whom a problem is passed for a decision ○ *The question of maintenance payments is with a court-appointed referee.*

reference /'ref(ə)rəns/ *noun* **1.** passing a problem to a committee or expert for an opinion **2.** mentioning or dealing with ○ *with reference to your letter of May 25th* ○ *The minister made no reference to the new agreement with the United States.* **3.** the numbers or letters which make it possible to find a document which has been filed ○ *our reference: PC/MS 1234* ○ *Thank you for your letter (reference 1234).* ○ *Please quote this reference in all correspondence.* ○ *When replying please quote reference 1234.* **4.** a written report on someone's character or ability ○ *to write someone a reference* or *to give someone a reference* ○ *to ask applicants to supply references* **5.** a person who reports on someone's character or ability ○ *to give someone's name as reference* ○ *Please use me as a reference if you wish.*

referendum /ˌrefə'rendəm/ *noun* a type of vote, where a whole population is asked to vote on a single question or a number of related questions ○ *The government decided to hold a referendum on the abolition of capital punishment.* Compare **plebiscite** (NOTE: The plural is **referenda** or **referendums**.)

referral /rɪ'fɜːrəl/ *noun* the act of passing a topic or problem on to someone else to decide ○ *the referral of the complaint to the subcommittee* ○ *the referral of a bill to the relevant committee*

refer to /rɪ'fɜː'tuː/ *verb* **1.** to mention or to deal with or to write about something ○ *referring to the court order dated June 4th* ○ *We refer to your letter of May 26th.* ○ *He referred to an article which he had seen in 'The Times'.* **2.** to pass a problem on to someone else to decide ○ *to refer a· question to a committee* ○ *The report*

stands referred to the Finance Committee. ○ *We have referred your complaint to the tribunal.* **3.** □ **'refer to drawer'** words written on a cheque which a bank refuses to pay

reflag /riː'flæg/ *verb* to change the place of registration of a ship, so that she flies a different flag

reform /rɪ'fɔːm/ *noun* a change made to something to make it better ○ *the need for reform of the benefit system* ○ *The reform in the legislation was intended to make the tribunal procedure more straightforward.* ◊ **electoral reform** ■ *verb* to change something to make it better ○ *The group is pressing for the health service to be reformed.*

reformer /rɪ'fɔːmə/ *noun* a person who tries to change society or an organisation to make it better ○ *a prison reformer*

refugee /ˌrefjʊ'dʒiː/ *noun* a person who has left a country because of war, or political or religious persecution

refund *noun* /'riːfʌnd/ money paid back ■ *verb* /rɪ'fʌnd/ to pay back money ○ *to refund the cost of postage* ○ *Travelling expenses will be refunded to witnesses giving evidence to the tribunal.* ○ *All money will be refunded if the goods are not satisfactory.*

refusenik /rɪ'fjuːznɪk/ *noun* someone who refuses to cooperate with something, especially because of the principles they hold

regal /'riːg(ə)l/ *adjective* **1.** like a king or queen **2.** suitable for a king or queen

regency /'riːdʒənsi/ *noun* the period of government by a regent □ **the Regency** the period between 1811 and 1820 when Britain was ruled by the Prince of Wales in place of his father, King George III, who was insane

regent /'riːdʒənt/ *noun* a person who governs in place of a king or queen, usually when the king or queen is a child or is ill

regicide /'redʒɪsaɪd/ *noun* **1.** the killing of a king or queen **2.** a person who has killed a king or queen

regime /reɪ'ʒiːm/ *noun* **1.** a government, especially a strict or cruel government ○ *the eventual overthrow of the regime* **2.** a system or style of government ○ *Under a military regime, civil liberties may be severely curtailed.* **3.** a system of rules for doing something ○ *changes in the tax regime*

regime change /reɪ'ʒiːm tʃeɪndʒ/ *noun* **1.** a change in a country's government made by force by another power **2.** a change in leadership, e.g. of a country or political party

regimen /'redʒɪmən/ *noun* a government or style of government

region /'riːdʒən/ *noun* a large area of a country ○ *a mountainous region* ○ *the Highland regions of Scotland*

regional /'riːdʒ(ə)nəl/ *adjective* referring to a region

Regional Council /ˌriːdʒ(ə)nəl 'kaʊns(ə)l/ *noun* a unit of local government in Scotland, covering a very large area of the country

Regional Development Plan /ˌriːdʒ(ə)nəl dɪ'veləpmənt plæn/ *noun* a government scheme to bring industry and jobs to a poor area

Regional government /'riːdʒ(ə)nəl 'gʌv(ə)nmənt/ *noun* a form of local government which covers a wide area and groups together smaller units of administration (NOTE: In 2002 the Labour government announced that it would develop regional government in England in those areas which support its introduction.)

regionalise /'riːdʒ(ə)nəlaɪz/ *verb* **1.** to divide an area into administrative regions **2.** to transfer something to a regional administration ○ *plans to regionalise the fire service*

regionalism *noun* the policy of dividing a political territory into areas with separate administrations

register of electors /ˌredʒɪstər əv ɪ'lektəz/ *noun* same as **electoral register**

Register Office /ˌredʒɪstə 'ɒfɪs/ *noun* an office where records of births, marriages and deaths are kept and where civil marriages are performed

Register of Members' Interests /ˌredʒɪstə əv ˌmembəz 'ɪntrəsts/ *noun* the book showing the special interests, sponsorship and employment of MPs

registrar /ˌredʒɪ'strɑː/ *noun* a person responsible for keeping an official list of names

Registrar-General /ˌredʒɪstrɑː 'dʒen(ə)rəl/ *noun* an official who is responsible for register offices and the registering of births, marriages and deaths

Registrar of Births Marriages and Deaths *noun* a local government official who registers births, marriages and deaths in an area

Registrar of Companies /ˌredʒɪstrɑː əv 'kʌmp(ə)niz/ *noun* an official who keeps a record of companies, the details of their directors and their financial state

registration /ˌredʒɪ'streɪʃ(ə)n/ *noun* the process of drawing up an official list of names

Registration Officer /ˌredʒɪ'streɪʃ(ə)n 'ɒfɪsə/ *noun* an official who draws up the register of electors in each constituency

regnant /'regnənt/ *adjective* ruling or reigning

regulate /'regjʊˌleɪt/ *verb* **1.** to change something so that it works well or is correct **2.** to use rules or laws to ensure that a particular industry or activity works well □ **government-regulated price** a price which is imposed by the government

regulation /ˌregjʊ'leɪʃ(ə)n/ *noun* the act of making sure that something will work well by using laws or rules ○ *the regulation of trading practices*

regulations /ˌregjʊ'leɪʃ(ə)nz/ *plural noun* **1.** rules made by organisations, clubs or councils, which have to be followed by their members ○ *According to council regulations, the outgoing chairman cannot stand for re-election.* ○ *The manufacturer had not applied the new government regu-*

lations on standards for electrical goods. ○ *Safety regulations which apply to places of work.* ○ *Regulations concerning imports and exports are explained in this booklet.* **2.** in the European Union, rules or laws made by the Council of Ministers or Commission which apply directly to all Member States. ◊ **decision, directive, recommendation**

regulatory /ˈregjʊlət(ə)ri/ *adjective* having powers to control an industry and to ensure that it operates fairly and safely ○ *The independent radio and television companies are supervised by a regulatory body.* ○ *Complaints are referred to several regulatory bodies.*

reign /reɪn/ *noun* the period of time when someone is king or queen ○ *an Act dating back to the reign of Queen Victoria* ■ *verb* **1.** to be king or queen ○ *Queen Victoria reigned for 64 years.* □ **the reigning monarch** the king or queen at the time **2.** to be the most important feature ○ *Chaos reigned in the capital for several days after the revolution.* ○ *It was half an hour before peace reigned again in the council chamber.*

reins /reɪnz/ *noun* the leather strings attached to a horse's head, to allow the rider to control it □ **to take up the reins of government** to begin to rule □ **he holds the reins of power** he is the ruler of the country

relate /rɪˈleɪt/ *verb* to link something to something else ○ *the law which relates to drunken driving*

related /rɪˈleɪtɪd/ *adjective* connected or linked or being of the same family ○ *offences related to drugs* or *drug-related offences*

relating to /rɪˈleɪtɪŋ tuː/ *adverb* referring to or connected with ○ *documents relating to the application*

relation /rɪˈleɪʃ(ə)n/ *noun* □ **to enter into relations with someone** to start discussing a business deal with someone □ **to break off relations with someone** to stop dealing with someone

relationship /rɪˈleɪʃ(ə)nʃɪp/ *noun* **1.** a connection or link with something or someone else ○ *What is the relationship between inflation and the cost-of-living?* ○ *There is no relationship between the two decisions.* **2.** the way in which two or more people act towards each other ○ *The relationship between the two councillors had been difficult for some time.*

release /rɪˈliːs/ *noun* **1.** setting someone free or allowing someone to leave prison **2.** allowing secret documents to become public ○ *the release of Cabinet papers after thirty years* ■ *verb* **1.** to free someone or something or to allow someone to leave prison ○ *to release goods from customs* ○ *The president released the opposition leader from prison.* ○ *The customs released the goods against payment of a fine.* **2.** to make something public ○ *Cabinet papers are released after thirty years.* ○ *The company released information about the new mine in Australia.* ○ *The government has refused to release figures for the number of unemployed women.*

Remembrance /rɪˈmembrəns/ *noun* remembering

Remembrance Day /rɪˈmembrəns deɪ/, **Remembrance Sunday** *noun* 11th November or the nearest Sunday, when the people killed in war are remembered

Remembrancer /rɪˈmembrənsə/ *noun* a British official of the Exchequer who collects debts owed to the Crown. Also called **Queen's Remembrancer, King's Remembrancer**

remit /ˈriːmɪt/ *noun* an area of responsibility given to someone ○ *This department can do nothing on the case as it is not part of* or *beyond our remit.*

remittance /rɪˈmɪt(ə)ns/ *noun* money which is sent ○ *Please send remittances to the treasurer.* ○ *The family lives on a weekly remittance from their father in the USA.*

rent controls /'rent kən‚trəʊlz/ *plural noun* the government regulation of rent

reopen /riː'əʊpən/ *verb* to start discussions again or to start investigating a case again ○ *The government has decided to reopen negotiations with the rebels.* ○ *The hearing reopened on Monday afternoon.*

Rep. *abbreviation* **1.** Representative **2.** Republic **3.** Republican

repatriate /riː'pætrieɪt/ *verb* to send someone away from the country he or she is living in and back to their country of birth, sometimes by force ○ *If terrorism increases, the government may be forced to repatriate foreigners living in the area.*

repatriation /riː‚pætri'eɪʃ(ə)n/ *noun* sending someone back to his or her country of birth ○ *The repatriation of the refugees will take months.*

repeal /rɪ'piːl/ *noun* passing a law to abolish or do away with an earlier law or custom so that it is no longer in force ○ *MPs are pressing for the repeal of the Immigration Act.* ■ *verb* to abolish or to do away with a law or custom ○ *The Bill seeks to repeal the existing legislation.*

reply /rɪ'plaɪ/ *noun* **1.** an answer ○ *in reply to your letter of the 24th* ○ *the company's reply to the takeover bid* ○ *There was no reply to my letter or to my phone call.* **2.** an opposing view given in a discussion or debate ■ *verb* **1.** to answer ○ *to reply to a letter* ○ *The company has replied to the takeover bid by offering the shareholders higher dividends.* **2.** to give an opposing view in a discussion or debate ○ *The Foreign Secretary opened for the Government and the shadow Foreign Secretary replied for the Opposition.* ◇ **right of reply 1.** the right of someone to answer claims made by an opponent ○ *he demanded the right of reply to the newspaper allegations* **2.** the right of the mover of a motion to reply to the arguments of someone who has attacked the motion

report /rɪ'pɔːt/ *noun* **1.** a statement describing what has happened or describing what the present situation is ○ *to make a report or to present a report or to send in a report* ○ *The court heard a report from the probation officer.* ○ *The chairman has received a report from the insurance company.* **2.** an official document from a committee set up by the government to investigate something ○ *The committee has issued a report on the problems of inner city violence.* ○ *The Director of Social Services has prepared a report on children in care.* **3.** a document in which a committee of the House of Commons or Congress explains the discussions which have been held about a bill which has been given to it to examine, and contains the amendments which the committee has proposed should be made to the bill ■ *verb* **1.** to make a statement describing something ○ *The council officers reported on the progress of the development plan.* ○ *He reported the damage to the insurance company.* ○ *We asked the bank to report on his financial status.* **2.** □ **to report a bill** (*of a committee*) to send a bill back to the main chamber with amendments and comments **3.** to go to a place or to attend ○ *to report for an interview* ○ *Please report to our London office for training.*

reporter /rɪ'pɔːtə/ *noun* an official who makes a written record of the proceedings of a legislature

reporting restrictions /rɪ‚pɔːtɪŋ rɪ'strɪkʃ(ə)ns/ *plural noun* limits on the information about a case which can be made public in newspapers or on radio or television

Report Stage /rɪ'pɔːt steɪdʒ/ *noun* the stage in the discussion of a Bill in the House of Commons, where the amendments to the bill proposed at Committee Stage are debated by the whole House of Commons

represent /‚reprɪ'zent/ *verb* **1.** to be the elected representative of an area in Parliament or on a council ○ *He represents one of the northern industrial constituencies.* **2.** to act on behalf of someone ○ *The defendant is represented by her solicitor.* **3.** to describe or to show ○ *He was represented as a man of great honour.*

representation /ˌreprɪzen ˈteɪʃ(ə)n/ *noun* **1.** a statement, especially a statement made to persuade someone to enter into a contract **2.** being represented by a lawyer **3.** a system where the people of a country elect representatives to a parliament which governs the country

Representation of the People Act /ˌreprɪzenteɪʃ(ə)n əv ðə ˈpiːp(ə)l ˌækt/ *noun* an Act of Parliament which states how elections must be organised

representative /ˌreprɪˈzentətɪv/ *noun* **1.** a person elected to represent a group of people ○ *The legislature is made up of representatives elected by secret ballot.* **2.** *US* a member of the lower house of Congress □ **House of Representatives** lower house of the American Congress **3.** a diplomat who acts on behalf of a government ○ *The British representative in the area.* **4.** a person who represents another person or group of people ○ *The court heard the representative of the insurance company.*

repress /rɪˈpres/ *verb* to rule in a dictatorial way by preventing opposition through limiting basic freedoms ○ *Dictators try to repress opposition to their regimes.*

repression /rɪˈpreʃ(ə)n/ *noun* dictatorial rule involving the restriction of free speech and of political opposition ○ *The country is recovering from twenty years of repression.*

repressive /rɪˈpresɪv/ *adjective* using repression ○ *The civil rights demonstrators complained about the government's repressive methods.*

reprisal /rɪˈpraɪz(ə)l/ *noun* the taking of property or people by force from another country as a punishment

Repub. *abbreviation* **1.** Republic **2.** Republican

republic /rɪˈpʌblɪk/ *noun* a state which is not a monarchy, but which is

governed by elected representatives headed by a President ○ *Singapore was declared a republic in 1965* ○ *Most republics have Presidents as head of state.*

republican /rɪˈpʌblɪkən/ *adjective* **1.** referring to a republic **2.** believing in the idea of a republic ○ *Some members of the Opposition have republican sympathies.*

Republican /rɪˈpʌblɪkən/ *noun* **1.** a member or supporter of a Republican Party, especially in the USA **2.** a person who believes in a republic as the best form of government

republicanise /rɪˈpʌblɪkənaɪz/ *verb* to make a country into a republic

republicanism /rɪˈpʌblɪkənɪz(ə)m/ *noun* **1.** the belief that an electorate should have the power in a country **2.** the theory and principles of republican government

Republicanism /rɪˈpʌblɪkənɪz(ə)m/ *noun* **1.** support for the Republican Party in the United States **2.** support for the idea of uniting Northern Ireland politically with the Republic of Ireland

Republican Party /rɪˈpʌblɪkən ˈpɑːti/ *noun* one of the two main political parties in the USA, which supports business and freedom, and opposes liberalism

requisition /ˌrekwɪˈzɪʃ(ə)n/ *verb* **1.** to demand or request formally ○ *A special meeting was requisitioned by six members.* **2.** to take private property into the temporary ownership of the state for the state to use ○ *The army requisitioned all the trucks to carry supplies.*

rescind /rɪˈsɪnd/ *verb* to annul or to cancel officially a law or contract ○ *to rescind a contract* or *an agreement* ○ *The committee rescinded its earlier resolution on the use of council premises.*

rescission /rɪˈsɪʒ(ə)n/ *noun* **1.** the cancellation of a contract or law **2.** *US* a section of an appropriation bill which cancels money previously appropriated but not spent

reserve /rɪ'zɜːv/ *noun* money or other things which are set aside for future use □ **a country's foreign currency reserves, gold reserves** a country's reserves in currencies of other countries or in gold ■ *verb* to put aside for future use

reshuffle /riː'ʃʌf(ə)l/ *noun* the changing of positions, especially those of Cabinet ministers ○ *In the reshuffle, the Secretary of State for Education was moved to the Home Office.* ■ *verb* to change the positions of Cabinet ministers ○ *The President is expected to reshuffle his Cabinet soon.*

residence /'rezɪd(ə)ns/ *noun* **1.** the place where someone lives ○ *The crowd gathered outside the Governor's residence.* ○ *She has a country residence where she spends her weekends.* ○ *The Prime Minister has two official residences: Number 10, Downing Street in London, and Chequers in the country.* **2.** the act of living or operating officially in a country

residence permit /'rezɪd(ə)ns ˌpɜːmɪt/ *noun* an official document allowing a foreigner to live in a country ○ *He has applied for a residence permit.* ○ *She was granted a residence permit for one year.*

Residency /'rezɪd(ə)nsi/ *noun* the house where a colonial governor lives

resident /'rezɪd(ə)nt/ *noun* **1.** a person or company living or operating in a place ○ *Fire broke out in the council flats and the residents were brought out as quickly as possible.* ○ *The warden of the hostel looks after the residents.* ○ *British residents in the country are advised to leave as soon as possible.* **2.** the title of a diplomat of lower rank than an Ambassador, living in a foreign country **3.** the governor of a colony ■ *adjective* living or based in a country ○ *The company is resident in France for tax purposes.* □ **person ordinarily resident in the UK** a person who normally lives in the UK

resident commissioner /'rezɪd(ə)nt kə'mɪʃ(ə)nə/ *noun* in the United States, a representative from a

dependency who is allowed to speak but not vote in the House of Representatives

residuary /rɪ'zɪdjuəri/ *adjective* remaining

residuary body /rɪ'zɪdjuəri ˌbɒdi/ *noun* a body set up to administer the ending of a local authority, when it has been abolished, and to manage those of its functions which have not been given over to other authorities

resign /rɪ'zaɪn/ *verb* to leave a job ○ *He resigned from his post as treasurer.* ○ *He has resigned with effect from July 1st.* ○ *She resigned as Education Minister.*

COMMENT: MPs are not allowed to resign their seats in the House of Commons. If an MP wants to leave the House, he has to apply for an office of profit under the Crown, such as the Stewardship of the Chiltern Hundreds, which will disqualify him or her from membership of the House of Commons.

resignation /ˌrezɪg'neɪʃ(ə)n/ *noun* the act of giving up a job ○ *The newspaper published the Minister's letter of resignation and the Prime Minister's reply.* ○ *He wrote his letter of resignation to the chairman.*

resilience /rɪ'zɪliəns/ *noun* the ability of government to respond to a difficult situation in a way that prevents it from becoming a crisis

resist /rɪ'zɪst/ *verb* to fight against something or not to give in to something ○ *Parents are resisting the local authority's attempt to close the school.* ○ *The party moderates were unable to resist the takeover by the extremists.* ○ *The President's bodyguard resisted the attempted coup.*

resistance /rɪ'zɪstəns/ *noun* **1.** an action which shows that people are opposed to something ○ *There was a lot of resistance from the local residents to the new plan.* ○ *The Home Secretary's proposal met with strong resistance from the probation service.* ○ *After the coup, there were still pockets of resistance in some parts of the country.* **2.** a group which fights secretly against an enemy occupying a country ○ *He was in the French Resistance during the war.* □ **resistance fighters** armed soldiers who are fighting against a government or an occupying enemy

resolution /ˌrezə'luːʃ(ə)n/ *noun* **1.** a decision taken by one of the Houses of Parliament or Congress to show their opinion of something **2.** a decision taken at the United Nations **3.** a decision taken at a meeting ○ *The conference passed a resolution condemning the use of force by the police.* ○ *The resolution from the platform was defeated by a large majority.* □ **extraordinary resolution, special resolution** a resolution such as one to change the articles of an organisation, which usually requires a larger majority of votes than an ordinary resolution ○ *the special resolution presented to the conference requires a two-thirds majority to be passed*

resource /rɪ'zɔːs/ *verb* to give money to ○ *The nurseries are well resourced and are full of modern equipment.*

respect /rɪ'spekt/ *noun* the honour shown to someone in authority

responsible /rɪ'spɒnsɪb(ə)l/ *adjective* being answerable or accountable to someone or some group of people for the job you perform ◇ **responsible for 1.** to blame for ○ *the government is responsible for the collapse of the economy* **2.** being in charge of or in control of ○ *the committee chairman was found to be the person responsible for leaks to the press* ○ *Ministers are responsible for the actions of their officials* ○ *the caretaker is responsible for the security of the building* ○ *she is responsible for twenty junior office staff*

responsible government /rɪ ˌspɒnsɪb(ə)l 'gʌv(ə)nmənt/ *noun* a form of government which acts as the people wish, and which is accountable to Parliament and through it to the people for its actions

res publica /ˌreɪz 'pʊblɪkə/ *noun* the state as a concept

restitution /ˌrestɪ'tjuːʃ(ə)n/ *noun* **1.** the return of property which has been illegally obtained ○ *The court ordered the restitution of assets to the company.* **2.** payment for damage or loss to the people who have suffered as the result of an action for which you are responsible

restrictive practices /rɪˌstrɪktɪv 'præktɪsɪz/ *plural noun* attempts by workers to prevent employers from making them work in such a way as to deprive other workers of jobs

result /rɪ'zʌlt/ *verb* to happen because of something else

résumé /'rezjʊmeɪ/ *noun* **1.** the summary of a piece of writing ○ *A r,sum, of the debate was published in yesterday's paper.* **2.** *US* the summary of a person's life story showing important details of education and work experience (NOTE: The UK term is **curriculum vitae** or **CV.**)

retiral /rɪ'taɪərəl/ *noun US, & Scottish* same as **retirement**

retire /rɪ'taɪə/ *verb* **1.** to stop work and take a pension ○ *She retired with a £6,000 pension.* ○ *The chairman of the company retired at the age of 65.* ○ *The shop is owned by a retired policeman.* **2.** to make an employee stop work and take a pension ○ *They decided to retire all staff over 50 years of age.* **3.** to come to the end of an elected term of office ○ *The treasurer retires after six years.* ○ *Two retiring directors offer themselves for re-election.* **4.** to go away from a court for a period of time ○ *The magistrates retired to consider their verdict.* ○ *The jury retired for four hours.*

retirement /rɪ'taɪəmənt/ *noun* the act of retiring from work

retirement age /rɪ'taɪəmənt eɪdʒ/ *noun* the age at which people stop work. In the UK this is usually 65.

retirement pension /rɪ'taɪəmənt ˌpenʃən/ *noun* a regular payment which someone receives when they reach the age to stop work

retract /rɪ'trækt/ *verb* to withdraw a statement because it was wrong ○ *The* minister was forced to retract her statement about the Leader of the Opposition.

retroactive /ˌretrəʊ'æktɪv/ *adjective* taking effect from a particular time in the past, rather from the present ○ *They received a pay rise retroactive to last January.*

retroactively /ˌretrəʊ'æktɪvli/ *adverb* going back to a time in the past

retrospective /ˌretrəʊ'spektɪv/ *adjective* taking effect from a particular time in the past, rather than from the present □ **with retrospective effect** applying to a past period ○ *the tax ruling has retrospective effect*

retrospective legislation /ˌretrəʊspektɪv ˌledʒɪ'sleɪʃ(ə)n/ *noun* an Act of Parliament which applies to a specified period before the Act was passed

retrospectively /ˌretrəʊ'spektɪvli/ *adverb* in a retrospective way ○ *The ruling is applied retrospectively.*

return /rɪ't3ːn/ *noun* **1.** going back or coming back **2.** sending back **3.** □ **to make a return to the tax office**, **to make an income tax return** to send a statement of income to the tax office **4.** the election of an MP **5.** the profit or income from money invested ■ *verb* **1.** to send something back, or go back **2.** to say or do something similar to something that has been said to you or done for you ○ *She helped me with my report and I was later able to return the favour.* ○ *The visitor returned our greeting and bowed slightly.* **3.** to elect an MP for a constituency ○ *She was returned with an increased majority.*

returning officer /rɪ'tɜːnɪŋ ˌɒfɪsə/ *noun* an official, usually a High Sheriff or mayor, who superintends a parliamentary election in a constituency, receives the nominations of candidates and announces the result of the vote

COMMENT: When a writ for an election is issued, the returning officer for each constituency must give notice of the election, and candidates may be nominated up to eight days after the writs are issued.

reunification /ˌriːjuːnɪfɪ'keɪʃ(ə)n/ *noun* the process of being united again after being separated or divided ○ *the reunification of Germany*

reunify /riː'juːnɪfaɪ/ *verb* to unite again after being separated ○ *reunified Germany*

revanche *noun* a policy of regaining lost territory

revenue /'revənjuː/ *noun* money earned or income ○ *The purpose of the bill is to raise revenue by imposing a sales tax on luxury goods.* ○ *The tax provides less than half the council's revenue.*

revenue expenditure /ˌrevənjuː ɪk'spendɪtʃə/ *noun* the day-to-day costs of a local council, including the wages of the staff and the cost of maintaining the buildings (NOTE: no plural in UK English; US English uses **expenditures.**)

revenue officer /'revənjuː ˌɒfɪsə/ *noun* a person working in a government tax office

revenue tariff /'revənjuː 'tærɪf/ *noun* a tax designed to produce public revenue

review /rɪ'vjuː/ *noun* **1.** a general examination of something ○ *The education officer presented the annual review of teaching staff.* ○ *The coroner asked for a review of police procedures.* **2.** a magazine ■ *verb* to examine something generally ○ *A committee has been appointed to review civil service salaries.* ○ *The council has reviewed its housing policy and decided to make no major changes.*

revisionism /rɪ'vɪʒ(ə)nɪz(ə)m/ *noun* changing or trying to change the principles on which a political party is based (*used as criticism*) ○ *The former Party leader was accused of revisionism.*

revisionist /rɪ'vɪʒ(ə)nɪst/ *adjective, noun* a person who wants to change a party's principles

revocable /'revəkəb(ə)l/ *adjective* possible to cancel or overturn

revocation /ˌrevəʊ'keɪʃ(ə)n/ *noun* the cancelling of a permission, right, agreement or offer

revoke /rɪ'vəʊk/ *verb* to cancel a permission, right, agreement or offer ○ *to revoke a clause in an agreement* ○ *The treaty on fishing rights has been revoked.*

revolt /rɪ'vəʊlt/ *noun* an act of opposition or rebellion against authority ○ *The whips are trying to quell the revolt in the party.* ○ *The revolt in the army was put down by the President's bodyguard.* □ **in revolt against** rebelling against ○ *the farmers were in revolt against the tax collectors* ■ *verb* to rebel against or oppose an authority ○ *Seventy MPs revolted and voted against the Government.* ○ *The President's bodyguard revolted and the revolt spread to other parts of the army.*

revolution /ˌrevə'luːʃ(ə)n/ *noun* **1.** an armed rising against a government or state or the entire social system ○ *The government was overthrown by a revolution led by the head of the army.* **2.** a period of social change, where the previous way of life changes radically

revolutionary /ˌrevə'luːʃ(ə)n(ə)ri/ *adjective* **1.** referring to a revolution ○ *Revolutionary troops surrounded the President's Palace.* **2.** very new and different ○ *The minister has proposed a revolutionary new system of collecting tax.* ■ *noun* a person who takes part in a revolution ○ *The palace was surrounded by revolutionaries.*

Revolutionary War /ˌrevə'luːʃ(ə)n(ə)ri wɔː/ *noun* the American War of Independence

revolutionise /ˌrevə'luːʃənaɪz/ *verb* **1.** to introduce revolutionary ideas to people **2.** to bring about a revolution in a country **3.** to completely change the way something is considered or done ○ *The Internet revolutionised public access to information.*

rider /'raɪdə/ *noun* **1.** an additional clause to a contract or report **2.** *US* a clause attached to a bill, which may have nothing to do with the subject of the bill, but which the proposer hopes to get passed into law more easily in this way

riding /'raɪdɪŋ/ *noun* **1.** (*in Yorkshire*) an administrative section of the county of Yorkshire, now no longer used **2.** (*in Canada*) a constituency or area of the country represented by an MP

rig /rɪg/ *verb* to arrange an election dishonestly so that a particular candidate wins ○ *The Opposition claimed that the election had been rigged.* ◊ **ballot-rigging**

right /raɪt/ *noun* **1.** something that a person is legally or morally allowed to have or do ○ *the right to life* ○ *The Minister has the right to be heard by the House.* ○ *She has a right to the property.* ○ *The staff have a right to know what the company is doing.* **2.** people who are political conservatives or whose ideas and beliefs are conservative ○ *The right have opposed the increases in government spending.* ○ *Members on the right of the party oppose the new manifesto.* □ **a move to the right** a move to support more conservative policies ○ *the centre party has shown a noticeable move to the right in recent years*

COMMENT: The division of political parties and political ideas into left, right and centre dates from the French Revolution when deputies in the National Assembly sat on the left or right of the chamber according to their views. It was easiest to apply these labels when socialist (left) parties faced conservative (right) parties in the middle years of the twentieth century. Some commentators say the old divisions of left and right are less and less relevant in the modern world, but they continue to be used.

rightful /'raɪtf(ə)l/ *adjective* legally or morally correct

Right Honourable /ˌraɪt 'ɒn(ə)rəb(ə)l/ *noun* a title given to members of the Privy Council (NOTE: usually written **Hon.**: *the Hon. Member; the Rt. Hon. William Smith, M.P.*)

rightist /'raɪtɪst/ *adjective* right-wing ■ *noun* a person with right-wing views

right of abode /ˌraɪt əv əˈbəʊd/ *noun* the right to live in a country

right-of-centre /ˌraɪt əv ˈsentə/ *adjective* relating to political views that are slightly right-wing

right of establishment /ˌraɪt əv ɪˈstæblɪʃmənt/ *noun* the right of a citizen of a Member State of the European Union to live and work in any EU country

right of petition /ˌraɪt əv pəˈtɪʃ(ə)n/ *noun* the right of any citizen of the European Union to forward an official complaint to the European Parliament. Any citizen of a Member State of the EU can present a petition, either personally or as the representative of a group.

right to strike /ˌraɪt tə ˈstraɪk/ *noun* the general right of workers to stop working as a means of protest

right wing /ˌraɪt ˈwɪŋ/ *noun* the part of a country, party or group which is more conservative than the rest ○ *the right wing of the Conservative Party*

right-wing /ˌraɪt ˈwɪŋ/ *adjective* favouring the right or conservative policies ○ *a right-wing newspaper* ○ *Right-wing politicians have plotted to bring down the government.*

right-winger /ˌraɪt ˈwɪŋə/ *noun* a person who supports a conservative point of view

Riigikogu *noun* the legislature in Estonia

Riksdag *noun* the legislature in Sweden

ringleader /ˈrɪŋliːdə/ *noun* a person who organises something dishonest or illegal

riot /ˈraɪət/ *noun* violent actions by large numbers of people in public ○ *Riots broke out when the government tried to increase the price of bread.* ■ *verb* to take part in a riot ○ *The street was blocked by rioting students.*

rioter /ˈraɪətə/ *noun* a person who takes part in a riot

rioting /ˈraɪətɪŋ/ *noun* the activity of being involved in a riot ○ *Rioting broke out when the price rises were announced.*

riotous /ˈraɪətəs/ *adjective* disorderly, as in a riot ○ *The crowd engaged in riotous behaviour.*

riot police /ˈraɪət pəˌliːs/ *noun* a police force with special equipment to deal with riots

ripple effect /ˈrɪp(ə)l ɪˈfekt/ *noun* a series of effects or consequences that result from a single event

rise /raɪz/ *noun* **1.** an increase or growth in height ○ *a rise in the crime rate* or *in inflation* or *in interest rates* **2.** an increase in salary (NOTE: The US term is **raise.**) ■ *verb* **1.** to move upwards or to become higher ○ *Prices are rising faster than inflation.* ○ *The rate of companies going into receivership has risen by 15%.* **2.** to stop sitting ○ *The House rose at 12.15 a.m.* ○ *The court will rise at 5 p.m.* **3.** to rebel against authority ○ *The southern states rose against the government.*

rising /ˈraɪzɪŋ/ *noun* a small rebellion ○ *The government acted swiftly to put down the rising in the university town.* ◊ **uprising**

robocall /ˈrəʊbəʊkɔːl/ *noun* a telephone call made using a recorded voice, used in election campaigning and marketing

rod /rɒd/ *noun* a stick that indicates someone's official office or authority. ◊ **Black Rod**

roll /rəʊl/ *noun* a list of names (NOTE: From the fact that they used to be written on a long sheet which was stored rolled up.)

rollcall /ˈrəʊlkɔːl/ *noun* reading out a list of names to see if everyone is present □ **yea-and-nay rollcall** *US* a vote in Congress, where names are read out and each member says how he or she is voting

Rome /rəʊm/ ◆ **Treaty of Rome**

Roosevelt /ˈruːzəvelt/, **Franklin D.** (1882–1945) the 32nd president of the United States, he served longer than any other president (1933–45)

rostrum /ˈrɒstrəm/ *noun* a high desk where a member stands to speak to an assembly or meeting ○ *The representative of one of the Civil Service unions was at the rostrum when the interruption occurred.* (NOTE: The plural is **rostra**.)

rotten borough /ˌrɒt(ə)n ˈbʌrə/ *noun* a political constituency with few electors but the same right to elect a representative as a constituency with many more people, especially in England before 1832. ◊ **pocket borough**

round /raʊnd/ *noun* a series of discussions ○ *The next round of negotiations will be held in London.*

round table conference /ˌraʊnd ˌteɪb(ə)l ˈkɒnf(ə)rəns/ *noun* a discussion held by people sitting at a round table, showing that each party at the meeting is of equal status with the rest ○ *The government is trying to get the rebel leaders to come to the conference table.*

Rousseau, Jean-Jacques /ˈruːsəʊ/ *noun* the French philosopher (1712–78) whose book 'The Social Contract' (1762) justified democracy but seemed also to put the individual under the complete control of a democratic government. The opening lines of 'The Social Contract' are: *Man is born free and everywhere he is in chains.*

royal /ˈrɔɪəl/ *adjective* referring to a king or queen ■ *noun* a member of a royal family

Royal Assent /ˌrɔɪəl əˈsent/ *noun* the signing of a Bill by the monarch, the ceremonial final stage by which a Bill becomes law as an Act of Parliament (NOTE: No monarch has refused to give the Royal Assent for three hundred years)

Royal Canadian Mounted Police /ˈrɔɪəl kəˈneɪdiən ˈmaʊntɪd pə ˈliːs/ *noun* a police force that operates throughout Canada except in cities and provinces with their own police forces. Abbr **RCMP**

Royal Commission /ˌrɔɪəl kə ˈmɪʃ(ə)n/ *noun* a group of people given the job by the government of examining and reporting on a major problem

Royal Duke /ˈrɔɪəl djuːk/ *noun* a prince of the royal house who has been given the title of Duke (NOTE: The wife of a **duke** is a **duchess**.)

Royal Family /ˌrɔɪəl ˈfæm(ə)li/ *noun* the family of a king or queen

royalist /ˈrɔɪəlɪst/ *noun* a person supporting rule by a king or queen

Royal pardon /ˌrɔɪəl ˈpɑːd(ə)n/ *noun* a pardon, given very rarely by the monarch on the advice of the elected government, by which a person found guilty of a crime is forgiven and need not serve a sentence

Royal prerogative /ˌrɔɪəl prɪ ˈrɒgətɪv/ *noun* the set of powers which have been transferred in the course of the last 300 years from the British Crown to the Prime Minister, including the right to declare war, make peace, appoint Cabinet ministers, create government departments, appoint bishops, give honours and titles, and dissolve parliament (NOTE: the royal prerogative is now only used on the advice of the elected government)

Royals /ˈrɔɪəlz/ *plural noun* members of a royal family (*informal*)

royalty /ˈrɔɪəlti/ *noun* members of a royal family ○ *Special security measures are taken if royalty is present.* (NOTE: can take singular or plural verb)

RSFSR *abbreviation* Russian Soviet Federated Socialist Republic

Rt Hon. *abbreviation* Right Honourable

rubber stamp /ˌrʌbə ˈstæmp/ *noun* a stamp made of hard rubber, cut to form letters, used to print something on a document, often to show that the document has been approved ■ *verb* to approve of something automatically, without much thought ○ *The council rubber stamped the decisions of the President.*

rule /ruːl/ *noun* **1.** the way in which a country is governed ○ *The country has had ten years of military rule.* **2.** a statement or order which says how things should be done, e.g. an order governing how members vote in Parliament or Congress ○ *The debate followed the rules of procedure used in the British House of Commons.* **3.** *US* a special decision made by the Rules Committee which states how a particular bill should be treated in the House of Representatives ■ *verb* **1.** to govern a country ○ *The country is ruled by a group of army officers.* ○ *The dictator ruled the country for thirty years.* **2.** to give an official decision ○ *The Speaker ruled that the question was out of order.* ○ *The commission of inquiry ruled that the company was in breach of contract.* **3.** to be in force or to be current ○ *prices which are ruling at the moment*

rule of law /ˌruːl əv ˈlɔː/ *noun* the principle of government, that all persons, organisations and the government itself are equal before and answerable to the law and that no person should be punished without a trial

ruler /ˈruːlə/ *noun* a person who governs or controls a country or part of a country

ruling /ˈruːlɪŋ/ *adjective* **1.** in power or in control ○ *the ruling Democratic Party* ○ *The actions of the ruling junta have been criticised in the press.* **2.** the most important ○ *The ruling consideration is one of cost.* ○ *We will invoice at ruling prices.* ■ *noun* a decision

made by a judge, arbitrator or the chairman of a meeting ○ *The MPs disputed the Speaker's ruling.* ○ *According to the ruling of the court, the contract was illegal.*

run /rʌn/ *verb* **1.** to control or manage ○ *He ran the department while the chief was away.* ○ *The question is: who is really running the country, the President or his wife?* **2.** to offer yourself as a candidate in an election ○ *He is running for president.* ○ *He had no hope of winning the nomination, so he decided not to run.*

running mate /ˈrʌnɪŋ meɪt/ *noun* a person who stands for election at the same time as another candidate for a different office, and voters have to vote for both together, e.g. the candidates for Vice-President and President of the USA

runoff /ˈrʌnɒf/ *noun* an election held after an earlier one that produced no clear winner

run-up /ˈrʌn ʌp/ *noun* □ **run-up to an election** the period before an election ○ *In the run-up to the General Election, opinion polls were forecasting heavy losses for the government.*

rural /ˈrʊərəl/ *adjective* referring to the countryside, as opposed to the towns ○ *An MP representing a rural constituency.* ○ *The party has to win the rural vote.*

S

S2P *abbreviation* state second pension

safe /seɪf/ *adjective* not in danger

safeguard /ˈseɪfgɑːd/ *noun* protection ○ *The proposed legislation will provide a safeguard against illegal traders.* ■ *verb* to protect ○ *The embassy acted to safeguard the interests of the tourists.*

safe seat /ˌseɪf ˈsiːt/ *noun* a seat where the Member of Parliament has a large majority and is not likely to lose the seat at an election

safety /ˈseɪfti/ *noun* the position of not being in danger

Sale of Goods Act /ˌseɪl əv ˈɡʊdz ˌækt/ *noun* an Act of Parliament which regulates the selling of things which can be moved ○ *The law relating to the sale of goods is governed by the Sale of Goods Act 1979.*

sales tax /ˈseɪlz tæks/ *noun* a tax paid on things which are sold

sanction /ˈsæŋkʃən/ *noun* **1.** official permission to do something ○ *You will need the sanction of the local authority before you can knock down the old office block.* ○ *The payment was made without official sanction.* **2.** a punishment for an act which goes against what is accepted behaviour ■ *verb* to approve officially or to give official permission ○ *The council sanctioned the expenditure of £1.2m on the development plan.*

satellite state /ˈsætəlaɪt steɪt/ *noun* a country which is economically or politically dependent on another

sceptre /ˈseptə/ *noun* a ceremonial stick used as a symbol of the authority of a monarch

schedule /ˈʃedjuːl/ *noun* **1.** a plan of things that need to be done and of when they should be done **2.** an additional section of documents attached to a Bill before Parliament or to the agenda or minutes of a meeting, or to a contract ○ *schedule of markets to which a contract applies* ○ *see the attached schedule* or *as per the attached schedule* ○ *the schedule before referred to* **3.** a list ○ *The schedule of charges is revised annually.* ■ *verb* **1.** to list officially ○ *scheduled prices* or *scheduled charges are subject to change without notice* ○ *The house is scheduled as an ancient monument.* **2.** to plan the time when something will happen ○ *The building is scheduled for completion in May.*

Schedule A /ˌʃedjuːl ˈeɪ/ *noun* the section of the Finance Acts under which tax is charged on income from land or buildings

Schedule B /ˌʃedjuːl ˈbiː/ *noun* the section of the Finance Acts under which tax is charged on income from woodlands

Schedule C /ˌʃedjuːl ˈsiː/ *noun* the section of the Finance Acts under which tax is charged on profits from government stock

Schedule D /ˌʃedjuːl ˈdiː/ *noun* the section of the Finance Acts under which tax is charged on income from trades, professions, interest and other income which does not come from employment

Schedule E /ˌʃedjuːl ˈiː/ *noun* the section of the Finance Acts under which tax is charged on wages, salaries and pensions

Schedule F /ˌʃedjuːl 'ef/ *noun* the section of the Finance Acts under which tax is charged on income from dividends

scheme /skiːm/ *noun* a plan, policy, or programme carried out by a government or business ○ *a road-widening scheme*

Schengen Agreement *noun* an agreement between some countries in the European Union and associated states, abolishing internal border controls over the movement of people and goods between member countries (NOTE: The countries are: Austria, Belgium, Denmark, France, Finland, Germany, Greece, Iceland, Italy, Luxembourg, the Netherlands, Norway, Portugal, Spain and Sweden. Schengen is a village in Luxembourg.)

Schröder /'ʃrəʊdə/, **Gerhard** (*b.* 1944) leader of the Social Democratic Party, and chancellor of Germany (1998–)

Scotland Yard /ˌskɒtlənd 'jɑːd/ *noun* the headquarters of the Metropolitan Police in London, from which national criminal investigations are coordinated. Full form **New Scotland Yard**

Scot Nat /ˌskɒt 'næt/ *noun* same as **Scottish Nationalist**

Scottish Executive /'skɒtɪʃ ɪg'zekjʊtɪv/ *noun* the devolved government of Scotland. ◊ **Scottish Parliament**

Scottish Executive Development Department /'skɒtɪʃ ɪg'zekjʊtɪv dɪ'veləpmənt dɪ'pɑːtmənt/ *noun* a department of the Scottish Executive, responsible for planning, building control and housing, social justice, and economic advice. Abbr **SEDD**

Scottish Executive Education Department /'skɒtɪʃ ɪg'zekjʊtɪv ˌedjʊ'keɪʃ(ə)n dɪ'pɑːtmənt/ *noun* a department of the Scottish Executive, responsible for education at school level, social services, culture, sport, and tourism. Abbr **SEED**

Scottish Executive Environment and Rural Affairs Department *noun* a department of the Scottish Executive, responsible for agriculture, rural development, food, and fisheries. Abbr **SEERAD**

Scottish Executive Health Department /'skɒtɪʃ ɪg'zekjʊtɪv helθ dɪ'pɑːtmənt/ *noun* a department of the Scottish Executive, responsible for health and ambulance services. Abbr **SEHD**

Scottish Executive Justice Department /'skɒtɪʃ ɪg'zekjʊtɪv 'dʒʌstɪs dɪ'pɑːtmənt/ *noun* a department of the Scottish Executive, responsible for all aspects of the legal system and the police

Scottish Nationalist /'skɒtɪʃ 'næʃ(ə)nəlɪst/ *noun* a member or supporter of the Scottish National Party ■ *adjective* relating to the Scottish National Party

Scottish National Party /'skɒtɪʃ 'næʃ(ə)nəl 'pɑːti/ *noun* a Scottish political party that advocates full political independence for Scotland. Abbr **SNP**

Scottish Parliament /'skɒtɪʃ 'pɑːləmənt/ *noun* the devolved elected representative body set up in 1999 in Edinburgh with limited powers to make laws for Scotland

Scott Report /'skɒt rɪˌpɔːt/ *noun* the document produced in 1996 by the enquiry headed by Lord Justice Scott which revealed that ministers had concealed information from Parliament and had allowed three business men to be unjustly put on trial for selling arms to Iraq (NOTE: The Scott Report contained very damaging information about how government ministers had behaved, but no minister resigned as a result, largely because the ministers responsible were no longer in the jobs they had held when the events occurred.)

SCPS *abbreviation* Society of Civil and Public Servants

scrutineer /ˌskruːtɪ'nɪə/ *noun* someone whose job is to monitor the counting of votes at an election and see that it happened correctly. ◊ **observer**

SDLP *abbreviation* Social Democratic and Labour Party

SDP *abbreviation* Social Democratic Party

seal /siːl/ *noun* **1.** a piece of wax or red paper attached to a document to show that it is legally valid. ◊ **Great Seal 2.** a piece of paper or metal or wax attached to close something, so that it can be opened only if the paper or metal or wax is removed or broken ○ *The seals on the ballot box had been tampered with.* ■ *verb* **1.** to close something tightly **2.** to attach a seal or to stamp something with a seal ○ *The customs sealed the shipment.*

sealed   instrument /ˌsiːld ˈɪnstrʊmənt/ *noun* a document which has been signed and sealed

Seanad Éireann *noun* the upper house of the legislature in Ireland (NOTE: The lower house is the Dail Éireann.)

seat /siːt/ *noun* **1.** a chair ○ *Seats have been placed on the platform for the members of the council.* ○ *Opposition MPs left their seats and walked out of the chamber in protest.* **2.** membership of the House of Commons or being a Member of Parliament ○ *He lost his seat in the general election.* **3.** a constituency ○ *This is a safe Tory seat.* **4.** membership of a committee ○ *Marginal seats showed a swing away from the government.*

COMMENT: In the British House of Commons, the seats are arranged in rows facing each other across the chamber, with the table in between the front benches and the Speaker's chair at the end. In other legislative chambers (as in the French National Assembly), the seats are arranged in a semi-circle facing the rostrum with the seat of the President of the Assembly behind it.

secede /sɪˈsiːd/ *verb* to withdraw from a nation, state, organisation or alliance and become independent ○ *The American colonies seceded from* *Great Britain in 1776 and formed the USA.*

secession /sɪˈseʃ(ə)n/ *noun* the act of seceding

secessionism /sɪˈseʃənɪz(ə)m/ *noun* a policy of withdrawal from a nation, state, organisation or alliance

secessionist /sɪˈseʃ(ə)nɪst/ *noun* a person who is in favour of secession ■ *adjective* of a country which has seceded or wishes to secede ○ *a secessionist state*

second /ˈsekənd/ *verb* □ **to second a candidate** to formally support a candidate wishing to stand for an office who has already been proposed by someone else ○ *The name of Ms Brown has been proposed for the post of treasurer, who is willing to second her?* □ **to second a motion** to speak in support of a motion after it has been presented by someone else, but before a vote is taken ○ *The motion is proposed by Mr Smith, seconded by Mrs Jones.*

secondarily /ˌsekənˈdeərɪli/ *adverb* in second place

secondary /ˈsekənd(ə)ri/ *adjective* **1.** second in importance ○ *Mr Smith raised a further objection, which he said was of secondary importance to the first.* **2.** at a second stage

second ballot /ˌsɪkɒnd ˈbælət/ *noun* the electoral system used in France and other countries, in which if a candidate does not get 50% of the votes on the first vote, a second vote is held a short time later, with the lowest candidate or candidates removed from the list, so the voters must give one of the remaining candidates more than 50% of the votes

second chamber /ˌsɪkɒnd ˈtʃeɪmbə/ *noun* the upper house in a legislative assembly with two chambers, e.g. the British House of Lords

second-class citizen /ˌsɪkɒnd klɑːs ˈsɪtɪz(ə)n/ *noun* a person who does not have the same rights, privileges or opportunities as the rest of the population

seconder /'sekəndə/ *noun* a person who supports a proposal made by someone else ○ *Mr Brown has been proposed by Mr Jones, and Miss Smith is his seconder.* ○ *The motion could not be put, because the proposer could not find a seconder for it.*

Second Reading /ˌsekənd 'riːdɪŋ/ *noun US* the detailed debate on a Bill in the House of Commons, or House of Lords in the UK, or in the House of Representatives or Senate in USA (NOTE: Bills are given three 'readings' in both chambers in both USA and UK (as in many other legislatures). The second reading is usually the occasion for a major, detailed debate.)

secret agent /ˌsiːkrət 'eɪdʒənt/ *noun* someone who spies for a government or organisation

secretariat /ˌsekrɪ'teəriət/ *noun* an important office and the officials who work in it, usually headed by a Secretary or Secretary-General ○ *the United Nations secretariat* ○ *the Commonwealth secretariat*

secretary /'sekrət(ə)ri/ *noun* **1.** a person who types letters or files documents or arranges meetings for someone ○ *the Minister's secretary and personal assistant* ○ *My secretary deals with visitors.* ○ *His secretary phoned to say he would be late.* **2.** the Secretary of State or member of the government in charge of a department ○ *the Education Secretary* ○ *the Foreign Secretary* **3.** a senior civil servant **4.** an official of a company or society

Secretary for Defense /ˌsekrətri fə dɪ'fens/ *noun* the government minister in charge of the armed forces in the USA. Also called **Defense Secretary**

Secretary-General /ˌsekrətri 'dʒen(ə)rəl/ *noun* the main administrator in a large organisation such as the United Nations or a political party ○ *The main power in the country is held by the Secretary-General of the ruling party.*

Secretary of State /ˌsekrət(ə)ri əv 'steɪt/ *noun* **1.** a member of the government in charge of a department ○ *the Secretary of State for Education and Skills* **2.** *US* the senior member of the government in charge of foreign policy. See also notes at **foreign, minister 3.** (*in Canada*) a government minister with general responsibilities for publications, broadcasting and the arts

COMMENT: The uses of the words **Secretary** and **Secretary of State** are confusing: **1.** In the UK, a Secretary of State is the head of a government department, usually a Cabinet Minister. Other members of the government, though not in the Cabinet, are Parliamentary Secretaries or Parliamentary Under-Secretaries of State, who are junior ministers in a department. Finally the Parliamentary Private Secretary is a minister's main junior assistant in Parliament **2.** In the USA, the Secretary of State is the person in charge of the Department of State, which is concerned with foreign policy. The equivalent in most other countries is the Foreign Minister (Foreign Secretary in the UK). Other heads of department in the US government are called simply Secretary: Secretary for Defense or Defense Secretary **3.** In the British Civil Service, a government department is headed by a Permanent Secretary, with several Deputy Secretaries and Under-Secretaries. They are all government employees and are not MPs. Also a civil servant is a minister's Private Secretary, who is attached to the minister personally, and acts as his link with the department. The British Civil Service formerly used the titles Permanent Secretary, Deputy Secretary, Assistant Secretary and Principal Secretary as grades, but these have now been replaced by a system of numbers (G1, G2, G3, etc.) **4.** Both in the UK and USA, the word Secretary is used in short forms of titles with the name of the department. So, the Secretary of State for Education and Skills in the UK, and the Secretary for Education in the USA are both called Education Secretary for short. In the USA, the word Secretary can be used before a surname: Secretary Smith.

Secretary of State for Defence /ˌsekrətri əv steɪt fə dɪ'fens/ *noun* the government minister in charge of the armed forces in the United Kingdom. Also called **Defence Secretary**

Secretary of the Treasury /ˌsekrət(ə)ri əv ðə ˈtreʒəri/, **Secretary to the Treasury** noun US the senior member of the government in charge of financial affairs. Also called **Treasury Secretary**

Secretary to the Cabinet /ˈsekrətri tə ði ˈkæbɪnət/ noun same as **Cabinet Secretary**

Secretary to the Senate /ˌsekrətri tə ðə ˈsenət/ noun US the head of the administrative staff in the Senate

secret ballot /ˌsiːkrət ˈbælət/ noun an election where the voters vote in secret

Secret Intelligence Service /ˈsiːkrət ɪnˈtelɪdʒəns ˈsɜːvɪs/ noun a British government agency concerned with obtaining information about other countries which may be of use to the government's defence, security, economy and foreign services

secret police /ˌsiːkrət pəˈliːs/ noun in dictatorships or totalitarian regimes, the organisation which works in secret spying on people in order to stop opposition

secret service /ˌsiːkrət ˈsɜːvɪs/ noun the government service which spies on other countries and on citizens of its own country suspected of wanting to rebel

sectarian /sekˈteəriən/ adjective relating to relations between religious groups or denominations, especially when the groups hold rigidly to a set of doctrines and are intolerant of other views

section /ˈsekʃən/ noun a part of an Act of Parliament or law ○ She does not qualify for a grant under section 2 of the Act.

sectionalism /ˈsekʃənəlɪz(ə)m/ noun concern for the interests of one group or area in preference to other areas

secularism /ˈsekjʊlərɪz(ə)m/ noun the belief that religion and religious bodies should have no official part in public life or in running public institutions, especially schools

Securities and Exchange Commission /sɪˈkjʊərətiz ən ɪksˈtʃeɪndʒ kəˈmɪʃ(ə)n/ noun an agency of the US government set up to control financial transactions and protect investors against bad practices. Abbr **SEC**

security /sɪˈkjʊərɪti/ noun **1.** safety from harm, damage or attack ○ Our passengers' security is of great importance to us. ◊ **social security 2.** the feeling of being safe in a situation, or the degree to which someone feels safe □ **security of employment, job security** a feeling by a worker that he has the right to keep his job until he retires □ **security of tenure** the right to keep a position or rented accommodation, provided that specific conditions are met

security clearance /sɪˈkjʊərɪti ˈklɪərəns/ noun the process of making sure that a person is acceptable for work in a government department where secret documents are kept

Security Council /sɪˈkjʊərɪti ˌkaʊnsəl/ noun the permanent ruling body of the United Nations, with the responsibility for preserving international peace

COMMENT: The Security Council has fifteen members, five of which (USA, Russia, UK, France and China) are permanent members, the other ten being elected by the General Assembly for periods of two years. The five permanent members each have a veto over the decisions of the Security Council.

Security Service /sɪˈkjʊərəti ˈsɜːvɪs/ noun a British government agency concerned with national security, in particular counter-terrorism and counter-espionage. ◊ **MI5**

Security Services /sɪˈkjʊərəti ˈsɜːvɪsɪz/ plural noun the government organisations which protect the country against the activities of enemies such as spies and terrorists

securocrat /sɪˈkjʊərəkræt/ noun a senior military, police or intelligence officer with power to influence government policy

SEDD *abbreviation* Scottish Executive Development Department

sedition /sɪˈdɪʃ(ə)n/ *noun* the use of words or actions that are intended to lead to revolution or an armed uprising against the state

seditious /sɪˈdɪʃəs/ *adjective* referring to sedition

SEED *abbreviation* Scottish Executive Education Department

SEERAD *abbreviation* Scottish Executive Environment and Rural Affairs Department

segregate /ˈsegrɪgeɪt/ *verb* to separate or keep apart, especially to keep different races in a country apart ○ *Single-sex schools segregate boys from girls.*

segregation /ˌsegrɪˈgeɪʃ(ə)n/ *noun* the practice of keeping ethnic, racial, religious, or gender groups separate, especially by enforcing the use of separate facilities such as schools and usually discriminating against a minority group

segregationist /ˌsegrɪˈgeɪʃənɪst/ *adjective, noun* supporting a policy of segregation

SEHD *abbreviation* Scottish Executive Health Department

Seimas *noun* the legislative body in Lithuania

seizure /ˈsiːʒə/ *noun* the act of taking possession of something ○ *The court ordered the seizure of the shipment* or *of the company's funds.*

Sejm *noun* the lower house of the legislature in Poland

Select Committee /sɪˌlekt kəˈmɪti/ *noun* **1.** (*in the House of Commons*) a special committee with members representing various political parties, which examines the work of a government department or a particular problem in the House of Commons (NOTE: There are also a smaller number of Select Committees in the House of Lords) **2.** (*in Congress*) a committee set up for a special purpose, usually to investigate something

COMMENT: The main non-departmental Select Committees are: the Committee of Privileges which considers breaches of parliamentary privilege; the Committee of the Parliamentary Commissioner which considers the reports of the Ombudsman; the Public Accounts Committee which examines government expenditure. The departmental select committees are: Culture, Media and Sport; Defence; Education and Skills; Environment and Rural Affairs; Health; Home Affairs; International Development; Northern Ireland Affairs; Science and Technology; Scottish Affairs; Trade and Industry; Transport, Local Government and the Regions; Treasury; Welsh Affairs; and Work and Pensions.

self-determination /ˌself dɪtɜːmɪˈneɪʃ(ə)n/ *noun* the free choice by the people of a country as to which country should govern them ○ *Countries with powerful neighbours have to fight for the right to self-determination.*

self-government /self ˈgʌv(ə)nmənt/, **self-rule** /ˌself ˈruːl/ *noun* the control of a country by its own government, free from foreign influence

semi-autonomous /ˌsemi ɔːˈtɒnəməs/ *adjective* ruled partly by its own local government and partly by national government or another country or region

Sen. *abbreviation* **1.** senate **2.** senator

senate /ˈsenət/ *noun* the upper house of a legislative body ○ *France has a bicameral system: a lower house or Chamber of Deputies and a upper house or Senate.*

COMMENT: The senate is the upper house of the legislature in many countries, including Antigua, Argentina, Australia, Belgium, Bolivia, Brazil, Canada, Chile, Colombia, Congo, Czech Republic, Dominican Republic, France, Italy, Jamaica, Mauritania, Mexico, Paraguay, the Philippines, Poland, Romania, South Africa, Spain, Thailand, Trinidad and Tobago, the USA, Uruguay, Venezuela.

Senate /ˈsenət/ *noun* **1.** the upper house of the American Congress (NOTE: The US Senate has 100 members, each state electing two senators by popular vote. Bills may be introduced in the Senate, with the exception of bills relating to finance. The Senate has the power to ratify treaties and to confirm presidential appointments to federal posts.) **2.** the upper chamber of the federal parliament of Canada, made up of 104 senators appointed by the ruling government **3.** the upper house of the federal parliament of Australia, made up of 76 members, 12 from each state plus two each from the Northern Territory and Australian Capital Territory

senator /ˈsenətə/ *noun* the member of a senate (NOTE: written with a capital letter when used as a title: *Senator Jackson*)

senatorial /ˌsenəˈtɔːriəl/ *adjective* referring to a senate or to senators

senatorial courtesy /ˌsenəˌtɔːriəl ˈkɜːtəsi/ *noun* the polite way in which members of the US Senate behave towards one another during their debates and discussions

Senned *noun* the devolved elected representative body set up in Wales in 1999. English **Welsh Assembly**

separationist *noun, adjective* same as **separatist**

separation of powers /ˌsepəreɪʃ(ə)n əv ˈpaʊəs/ *noun* the system in which the power in a state is separated between the legislative body which passes laws, the judiciary which enforces the law, and the executive which runs the government

COMMENT: In the USA, the three parts of the power of the state are kept separate and independent: the President does not sit in Congress; Congress cannot influence the decisions of the Supreme Court, etc. In the UK the legislative and executive powers are fused, because of our parliamentary system of government which means that the executive is always part of the legislature. The government or executive is responsible to Parliament and can be dismissed by it on a Vote of No Confidence. There has also been a partial fusion of powers in the UK between the legislature and judiciary because the law lords sit in the House of Lords, but by reforms introduced in 2003–4, this will stop and a completely independent Supreme Court will be set up. In the USA, members of government are not members of Congress, though their appointment has to be approved by Senate; in the UK, members of government are usually Members of Parliament, although some are members of the House of Lords.

separatism /ˈsep(ə)rətɪz(ə)m/ *noun* the belief that a part of a country should become separate and independent from the rest

separatist /ˈsep(ə)rətɪst/ *adjective* referring to separatism ○ *The rise of the separatist movement in the south of the country.* ■ *noun* a person who believes that part of the country should become separate and independent

sergeant /ˈsɑːdʒənt/ *noun* a police officer of a rank above constable. Abbr **Sgt, Sergt**

sergeant at arms /ˈsɑːdʒənt ət ˈɑːmz/ *noun* someone with the job of keeping order in a legislative body or court of law

Serjeant at Arms /ˈsɑːdʒənt ət ˈɑːmz/ *noun* an official of the House of Commons who keeps order in the House, makes sure that no one enters the chamber of the House unless invited to do so, and removes members if asked to do so by the Speaker (NOTE: The spelling **Sergeant at Arms** is used in the US House of Representatives.)

serve /sɜːv/ *verb* **1.** to spend time as a member of a committee or as Member of Parliament ○ *He served six years on the Foreign Relations Committee.* ○ *She has served two terms as chairman.* **2.** to deal with a customer **3.** to do a type of work

service /ˈsɜːvɪs/ *noun* □ **civil service** the organisation and personnel which administer a country under the direction of the government

session /'seʃ(ə)n/ *noun* **1.** a meeting, or the time when a meeting is held ○ *The morning session* or *the afternoon session will be held in the conference room.* □ **opening session, closing session** the first part or last part of a conference **2.** the period when Parliament is meeting, usually about 12 months long ○ *The government is planning to introduce the Bill at the next session of Parliament.* ○ *The first session of the new Parliament opened with the reading of the Queen's Speech.*

COMMENT: The Parliamentary session starts in October with the Opening of Parliament and the Queen's Speech. It usually lasts until August. In the USA, a new congressional session starts on the 3rd of January each year.

sessional /'seʃən(ə)l/ *adjective* referring to a session

sessional Select Committee /,seʃ(ə)n(ə)l sɪ,lekt kə'mɪti/ *noun* a Select Committee set up at the beginning of each session of parliament ○ *the Select Committee on Defence* or *the Defence Select Committee*

sessions /'seʃ(ə)nz/ *plural noun* a court

set aside /,set ə'saɪd/ *verb* to decide not to apply a decision ○ *The arbitrator's award was set aside on appeal.*

set forth /,set 'fɔːθ/ *verb* to put down in writing ○ *The argument is set forth in the document from the European Court.*

set out /,set 'aʊt/ *verb* **1.** to put down in writing ○ *The claim is set out in the enclosed document.* ○ *The figures are set out in the tables at the back of the book.* **2.** to try to do something ○ *The Government has set out to discredit the Opposition.*

settle /'set(ə)l/ *verb* **1.** to go to live in a new area, often abroad ○ *In the 18th century, thousands of people left the country to settle in North America.* **2.** to put an end to an argument ○ *The decision of the arbitration board settled the dispute.* ○ *The matter was set-*tled by an agreement to change the working hours.*

settlement /'set(ə)lmənt/ *noun* **1.** a group of homes built in a new area ○ *a British settlement on the coast of India* **2.** an agreement which ends a dispute between people or between countries ○ *The Department for Education reached a settlement with the teachers' union.*

settler /'set(ə)lə/ *noun* a person who goes to colonise a country ○ *Settlers built up colonies along the banks of the river.*

shadow /'ʃædəʊ/ *adjective* to follow or to watch

Shadow Cabinet /,ʃædəʊ 'kæbɪnət/ *noun* the senior members of the Opposition who cover the areas of responsibility of the actual Cabinet, and will form the Cabinet if their party is elected to government ○ *the shadow Minister for the Environment* ○ *the shadow spokesman on energy matters*

shadow senator /'ʃædəʊ 'senətə/ *noun* a non-voting representative of the District of Columbia in the US Senate

shanty town /'ʃænti taʊn/ *noun* an area of badly built houses around a large city where poor people live

shareholder /'ʃeəhəʊldə/ *noun* a person who owns shares in a company

sheikh /ʃeɪk/ *noun* a leader or prince in an Arab country

sheikhdom /'ʃeɪkdəm/ *noun* a state or area ruled by a sheikh ○ *Many of the Gulf sheikhdoms export oil.*

Sheriff /'ʃerɪf/ *noun* same as **High Sheriff**

Sheriff Court /'ʃerɪf kɔːt/ *noun* a court presided over by a sheriff

sheriffdom /'ʃerɪfdəm/ *noun* a district in Scotland with a Sheriff Court

shire /'ʃaɪə/ *noun* a county in the United Kingdom, used in county names such as Buckinghamshire and Berkshire □ **the shires** the rural counties in the centre of England ○ *the Tory Party is very strong in the shires* ○ *we* *have to make sure that we do not lose the support of the shire voters*

shire county /ˈʃaɪə ˈkaʊnti/ *noun* a county that is not based on a metropolitan area

shortcoming /ˈʃɔːtˈkʌmɪŋ/ *noun* a fault in somebody's character or in a plan or organisation ○ *The government plan has many shortcomings.*

short title /ˌʃɔːt ˈtaɪt(ə)l/ *noun* the usual brief name by which an Act of Parliament is known

short title clause /ˌʃɔːt ˈtaɪt(ə)l ˌklɔːz/ *noun* a section in a Bill which gives the short title by which the Act will be known

show of hands /ˌʃəʊ əv ˈhændz/ *noun* an informal vote that involves counting the hands raised by people to show support for or rejection of a proposal

shroud-waving /ˈʃraʊd ˌweɪvɪŋ/ *noun* the deliberate use of distressing events or statistics to make more of an issue or gain political advantage

shuttle diplomacy /ˈʃʌt(ə)l dɪ ˌpləʊməsi/ *noun* diplomatic negotiations by an official who travels frequently between the countries involved

SI *abbreviation* statutory instrument

signatory /ˈsɪɡnət(ə)ri/ *noun* a person who signs a contract, or a country which signs a treaty or convention ○ *You have to get the permission of all the signatories to the agreement if you want to change the terms.* ○ *Britain is a signatory to the Geneva Convention.*

sine die /ˌsiːni ˈdiːeɪ/ *Latin phrase meaning* 'without a day'

sine qua non /ˌsɪni kwɑː ˈnɒn/ *Latin phrase meaning* 'without which not': condition without which something cannot work ○ *Agreement by the management is a sine qua non of all employment contracts.*

single ballot /ˈsɪŋɡ(ə)l ˈbælət/ *noun* an election where only one round of voting is held

single chamber /ˌsɪŋɡ(ə)l ˈtʃeɪmbə/ *noun* a legislature with only one chamber, as in New Zealand and Nebraska. ◊ **unicameral**

Single European Act /ˈsɪŋɡ(ə)l ˌjʊərəˈpiːən ˌeɪ siː ˈtiː/ *noun* a treaty of the European Union signed in 1987 which aimed to create a free internal market in labour, goods, and services by 1992

Single Market /ˈsɪŋɡ(ə)l ˈmɑːkɪt/, **Single European Market** *noun* the European Union considered as a free trade area, with no tariff barriers between its member states

single transferable vote /ˌsɪŋɡ(ə)l trænsˈfɜːrəb(ə)l vəʊt/ *noun* a proportional voting system where each voter votes for the candidates in order of preference, and this vote is transferred to the next preference candidate if the first choice is not elected. A calculation based on the total votes is made to show how many votes, or what quota, a candidate needs to be elected. Candidates with more than this electoral quota of first preference votes are automatically elected, and their second preference votes are passed to other candidates, and so on until the full number of candidates have the required quota and so are elected. Abbr **STV** (NOTE: It is used for the European Parliament, and in Northern Ireland for district councils.)

sinking fund /ˈsɪŋkɪŋ fʌnd/ *noun* a sum of money saved by a government regularly from taxation and used to pay off its debts

Sinn Féin /ˌʃɪn ˈfeɪn/ *noun* a nationalist Irish republican party

Sir /sɜː/ *noun* the title given to a baronet or knight (NOTE: The title is always used with the man's Christian name, and in a formal address, with the surname as well: *Good morning, Sir George*; *May I introduce Sir George Carey?*; *Sir George and Lady Carey attended the dinner.*)

sit /sɪt/ *verb* **1.** to meet ○ *No one can enter the Council Chamber when the committee is sitting.* ○ *The court sat from eleven to five o'clock.* **2.** to be an

MP ○ *She sat for a London constituency for ten years.* ○ *The sitting MP was re-elected with a comfortable majority.* **3.** □ **to sit on the bench** to be a magistrate

sit-down strike /'sɪt daʊn ˌstraɪk/ *noun* a form of industrial action in which workers refuse to leave their workplace until their demands are listened to

sit-in /'sɪt ɪn/ *noun* a form of protest in which people occupy a building or public place and refuse to leave until their demands are listened to

sitting /'sɪtɪŋ/ *noun* a meeting of Parliament or of a court or of a tribunal

COMMENT: Parliamentary sittings start at 2.30 p.m. on Mondays, Tuesdays and Wednesdays; at 11.30 a.m. on Thursdays; and at 9.30 a.m. on Fridays. They continue until business is completed, which is expected to be no later that 10.30 p.m on the first three days, and earlier on Thursday and Friday. Occasionally there are all-night sessions when very important or controversial matters are debated. These hours may seem strange, but they are needed to allow committee and constituency work to take place at other times. Before 1997 the hours were even later, but were changed as part of the modernisation policies of the Labour government.

sketch /sketʃ/ *noun* ♦ **parliamentary sketch**

sketch-writer /'sketʃ ˌraɪtə/ *noun* a journalist who writes parliamentary sketches

slander /'slɑːndə/ *verb* the crime of using spoken words to harm someone by saying things which are untrue about them

slate /sleɪt/ *noun* a list of candidates for a position ○ *the Democratic slate in the state elections*

slavocracy /ˌsleɪˈvɒkrəsi/ *noun* a ruling group consisting of owners of slaves, or rule by owners of slaves

sleaze /sliːz/ *noun* political activity of a dishonest or disreputable sort, usually involving bribery and corruption (NOTE: In the 1990s various politicians were accused of sleaze, for example by taking free holidays and payments from prominent business men.)

sleeper /'sliːpə/ *noun* a spy who lives an ordinary life often for many years before starting spying activities

sleeper cell /'sliːpə sel/ *noun* a group of trained terrorists who live ordinary lives while waiting for instructions to commit a terrorist act

slip law /'slɪp lɔː/ *noun US* a law published for the first time after it has been approved, printed on a single sheet of paper, or as a small separate book

slogan /'sləʊgən/ *noun* a short phrase which shows the beliefs of a party, used to attract voters ○ *The party's slogan is 'More Power to the People'.* ○ *The party campaigned under the slogan 'Responsibility and Trust'.*

SLP *abbreviation* Scottish Labour Party

slum /slʌm/ *noun* a crowded dirty area of a town where poor people live ○ *The children were brought up in the slums of Glasgow.*

slum clearance /'slʌm ˌklɪərəns/ *noun* the organised demolishing of slum areas to replace them with modern blocks of flats

smoke-filled room /ˌsməʊk fɪld 'ruːm/ *noun* a room where deals are made in private (NOTE: The image is of participants who have spent a long time there discussing and smoking.)

snap /snæp/ *adjective* sudden or unexpected ○ *The Prime Minister called a snap election.* ○ *The Committee will discuss the matter fully and will not reach a snap decision.*

SNP *abbreviation* Scottish National Party

SO *abbreviation* standing order

soapbox /'səʊpbɒks/ *noun* a wooden box used to stand on by a public speaker

soapbox oratory /'səʊpbɒks 'ɒrət(ə)ri/ *noun* a form of public speaking which is aimed at attracting the general public in a simple, direct way

social /'səʊʃ(ə)l/ *adjective* referring to society in general ○ *The government dealt carefully with many of the social problems of the day.*

social assistance /'səʊʃ(ə)l ə'sɪst(ə)ns/ *noun* same as **social security**

Social Chapter /'səʊʃ(ə)l ˌtʃæptə/ *noun* a section of the Maastricht Treaty on European Union (1993) which commits Member States to reducing unemployment, improving working conditions, discussions between management and workers, and removing discrimination

social class /ˌsəʊʃ(ə)l 'klɑːs/ *noun* a group of people who have some position in society

Social Credit /'səʊʃ(ə)l 'kredɪt/ *noun* a system of monetary reform, founded in Canada

social democracy /ˌsəʊʃ(ə)l dɪ'mɒkrəsi/ *noun* a belief that changes should be made to the structure of society to produce greater equality, with a mixed economy where there is some state involvement in industry and welfare but also a strong free market, and in addition a political system based on democratic freedom

social democrat /ˌsəʊʃ(ə)l 'deməkræt/ *noun* **1.** a person who believes in social democracy **2. Social Democrat** a person who supports or belongs to a Social Democratic Party ○ *The Social Democrats are in the majority in some areas of the country.*

Social Democratic /'səʊʃ(ə)l ˌdemə'krætɪk/ *adjective* referring to a Social Democratic Party

Social Democratic and Labour Party /'səʊʃ(ə)l ˌdemə'krætɪk ən 'leɪbə 'pɑːti/ *noun* a political party in Northern Ireland, many of whose supporters want to unite Northern Ireland and the Republic of Ireland peacefully. Abbr **SDLP**

Social Democratic Party /'səʊʃ(ə)l demə'krætɪk 'pɑːti/ *noun*

a political party which is in favour of social democracy

social exclusion /ˌsəʊʃ(ə)l ɪk'skluːʒ(ə)n/ *noun* lack of the benefits enjoyed by most members of society, because of factors such as poverty, social or ethnic background or disability

social housing /'səʊʃ(ə)l 'haʊzɪŋ/ *noun* housing provided by organisations such as local authorities or housing associations for renting cheaply to people who cannot afford to buy their own homes or rent privately

social insurance /ˌsəʊʃ(ə)l ɪn'ʃʊərəns/ *noun* state insurance based on compulsory contributions that gives some income to unemployed and retired people

socialism /'səʊʃəlɪz(ə)m/ *noun* the belief that in a state the means of production, distribution and exchange should be controlled by the people, that the people should be cared for by the state and that wealth should be shared equally

Socialist /'səʊʃəlɪst/ *adjective* **1.** in favour of socialism **2.** referring to or supporting a Socialist Party ■ *noun* **1.** a person who believes in socialism **2.** a person who supports or is a member of a Socialist Party

Socialist Party /'səʊʃəlɪst ˌpɑːti/ *noun* a political party such as those in France, Spain and Portugal, which follows socialist policies and beliefs

Socialist Workers Party /ˌsəʊʃəlɪst 'wɜːkəz ˌpɑːti/ *noun* a British political party that opposes capitalism

social ownership /ˌsəʊʃ(ə)l 'əʊnəʃɪp/ *noun* a situation where an industry is nationalised and run by a board appointed by the government

social security /ˌsəʊʃ(ə)l sɪ'kjʊərɪti/ *noun* money or help provided by the government to people who need it ○ *He lives on social security payments.*

social services /ˌsəʊʃ(ə)l 'sɜːvɪsɪz/ *noun* a department of a local or national government which provides services such as health care, advice, and money for people who need help

social worker /ˈsəʊʃ(ə)l ˌwɜːkə/ noun a person who works in a social services department, visiting and looking after people who need help

society /səˈsaɪəti/ noun 1. a group of people who live together and have the same laws and customs ○ British society has changed since the Second World War. ○ All Western societies have the same social problems. (NOTE: not used with **the**) 2. an organisation of people with the same interests or jobs ○ a political society ○ a debating society ○ the Society of Education Officers

socio-economic /ˈsəʊʃɪəʊiːkə ˈnɒmɪk/ adjective referring to social and economic conditions ○ The socio-economic system in capitalist countries. □ **socio-economic groups** groups in society divided according to income and position

socio-political /ˌsəʊʃɪəʊ pə ˈlɪtɪk(ə)l/ adjective combining social and political matters

Solicitor-General /səˌlɪsɪtə ˈdʒen(ə)rəl/ noun one of the law officers, a Member of the House of Commons and deputy to the Attorney-General

Solicitor-General for Scotland /səˌlɪsɪtə ˌdʒen(ə)rəl fə ˈskɒtlənd/ noun a junior law officer in Scotland

solidarity /ˌsɒlɪˈdærɪti/ noun an expression of unity between people with common interests

source /sɔːs/ noun 1. a person who gives someone, especially a journalist, some information ○ The information had come from a usually reliable source. 2. the origin from which something comes ○ energy from renewable sources ○ You must declare income from all sources to the Inland Revenue. □ **at source** referring to a system of removing tax or other payments from someone's income before the income is paid ○ income taxed at source ○ maintenance payments deducted at source

South /saʊθ/ noun 1. a region of a country, e.g. the part of the USA to the south of Washington 2. □ **the South** the less industrialised countries of the world, mainly in the southern hemisphere

sovereign /ˈsɒvrɪn/ noun a title given to the king or queen ○ The sovereign's head appears on coins and stamps. ■ adjective having complete freedom to govern itself

sovereign state /ˌsɒvrɪn ˈsteɪt/ noun an independent country which governs itself

sovereigntist /ˈsɒvrɪntɪst/ noun a supporter of sovereignty for Quebec

sovereignty /ˈsɒvrɪnti/ noun the power to govern independently □ **to have sovereignty over a territory** to have power to govern a territory ○ Two neighbouring states claimed sovereignty over the offshore islands. □ **the sovereignty** or **supremacy of Parliament** the right of Parliament to make or undo laws

sovereignty association /ˈsɒvrɪnti əˌsəʊsiˈeɪʃ(ə)n/ noun a proposed economic and political association between a sovereign Quebec and the rest of Canada

soviet /ˈsəʊviət/ noun 1. an elected local, regional or national council used to govern the USSR before the fall of communism which began in 1989 2. □ **the Supreme Soviet** the legislative body of Tajikistan ■ adjective referring to the former Soviet Union

Soviet Union /ˈsəʊviət ˈjuːnjən/ noun the former Union of Soviet Socialist Republics (USSR), now split into the Russian Federation and various independent states, some of which joined the Russian Federation in the Commonwealth of Independent States (CIS)

Speaker /ˈspiːkə/ noun a person who acts as chairman of a meeting of a parliament □ **discussions held behind the Speaker's chair** informal discussions between representatives of opposing political parties meeting on neutral ground away from the floor of the House

COMMENT: In the House of Commons, the Speaker is an ordinary Member of Parliament chosen by the other members; the speaker in the House of Lords is the Lord Chancellor. Plans announced in 2003–4 will lead to the abolition of the office of Lord Chancellor and a new chairman for the House of Lords will need to be chosen. In the US Congress, the Speaker of the House of Representatives is an ordinary congressman, elected by the other congressmen; the person presiding over meetings of the Senate is usually the Vice-President.

Speaker's Chaplain /ˌspiːkəz ˈtʃæplɪn/ *noun* a clergyman who reads prayers at the beginning of each sitting of the House of Commons

special agent /ˌspeʃ(ə)l ˈeɪdʒənt/ *noun* 1. a person who does secret work for a government 2. a person who represents someone in a particular matter

Special Branch /ˈspeʃ(ə)l brɑːnʃ/ *noun* the branch of the UK police force that specialising in political security and is the executive arm of the government intelligence agencies

special committee /ˈspeʃ(ə)l kə ˈmɪti/ *noun* a committee set up by Congress to investigate something

special constable /ˌspeʃ(ə)l ˈkʌnstəb(ə)l/ *noun* in the United Kingdom, someone who acts as a volunteer police officer, especially when a large police force is necessary as for large public events

special interest group /ˌspeʃ(ə)l ˈɪntrəst ˌgruːp/ *noun* people who try to influence government to support the industry or particular concerns that they belong to or support

specialise /ˈspeʃəlaɪz/, **specialize** *verb* to concentrate on one particular subject or area of activity

special session /ˌspeʃ(ə)l ˈseʃ(ə)n/ *noun US* a session of Congress called in an emergency by the President to discuss an important matter when Congress is not normally in session

special sessions /ˌspeʃ(ə)l ˈseʃ(ə)ns/ *plural noun* a court hearing called to meet an unusual emergency

speech /spiːtʃ/ *noun* 1. speaking or ability to talk 2. a talk given in public ○ *to make a speech in Parliament* ○ *counsel's closing speech to the jury* ○ *The Chancellor's Budget Speech lasted two hours.*

speech of acceptance /ˌspiːtʃ əv əkˈseptəns/ *noun* a speech made by someone agreeing to take a job, e.g., after being chosen to stand as a candidate for Parliament. Also called **acceptance speech**

sphere of influence /ˌsfɪə əv ˈɪnfluəns/ *noun* an area of the world where one country plays a leading role over other states ○ *Some Latin American states fall within the USA's sphere of influence.*

spin /spɪn/ *noun* an interpretation of information that is intended to guide public opinion in a particular direction

spin doctor /ˈspɪn ˌdɒktə/ *noun* a person who gives political information to journalists expressed in a way that is good for the party or government by which he or she is employed ○ *There is nothing new in politics about using spin doctors apart from the name.*

spinmeister /ˈspɪnmeɪstə/ *noun* same as **spin doctor**

spiritual /ˈspɪrɪtʃuəl/ *adjective* referring to religious matters

splendid isolation /ˌsplendɪd ˌaɪsəˈleɪʃ(ə)n/ *noun* a policy where a country refuses to join with other countries in treaties

splinter group /ˈsplɪntə gruːp/ *noun* a small group which breaks away from a main political party, or other organisation

spoils of war /ˌspɔɪlz əv ˈwɔː/ *plural noun* the goods or valuables taken by an army from an enemy

spoils system /ˈspɔɪlz ˌsɪstəm/ *noun* in the USA, the way in which the senior civil servants and appointments to the federal bureaucracy are temporary appointments made by the newly elected President (NOTE: The alternative system is the merit system, by which the majority of US civil servants are now appointed.)

spoilt ballot paper /ˌspɔɪlt ˈbælət ˌpeɪpə/ *noun* a voting form which has not been filled in correctly by the voter and therefore cannot be counted

spokesman /ˈspəʊksmən/ *noun* a man who speaks in public on behalf of a group ○ *A White House spokesman denied the news report.* ○ *A government spokesman in the House of Lords revealed that discussions had been concluded on the treaty.* (NOTE: The plural is **spokesmen**.)

spokesperson /ˈspəʊksˌpɜːs(ə)n/ *noun* a person who speaks in public on behalf of a group

spokeswoman /ˈspəʊksˌwʊmən/ *noun* a woman who speaks in public on behalf of a group (NOTE: The plural is **spokeswomen**.)

sponsor /ˈspɒnsə/ *noun* **1.** a person or group such as a trade union which pays money towards the expenses of an MP or candidate **2.** an MP who introduces a Bill in the House of Commons ■ *verb* **1.** to support the expenses of an MP or candidate □ **to sponsor an MP** to pay part of the election expenses of an MP, and contribute to his or her local party's funds. For this the MP is expected to represent the sponsor's interests in Parliament. **2.** to propose a Bill in the House of Commons

sponsorship /ˈspɒnsəʃɪp/ *noun* the act of sponsoring ○ *Sponsorship of two MPs cost the company several thousand pounds.*

spy /spaɪ/ *noun* a person who watches, listens or investigates secretly to get information about another country, or a rival organisation ○ *Half the embassy staff are spies.* ○ *The government asked the military attaché to leave the country, as they had evidence that he was a spy.* ■ *verb* **1.** to watch, listen to, or investigate another country or rival organisation secretly to get information **2.** to see □ **I spy strangers** formerly, used by an MP

who wanted a debate to take place in private

spying /ˈspaɪɪŋ/ *noun* the action of a spy ○ *She was sentenced to death for spying for the enemy.*

spymaster /ˈspaɪmɑːstə/ *noun* a man in charge of spies

Square Mile /ˌskweə ˈmaɪl/ *noun* the City of London, the British financial centre

SSN *abbreviation* Social Security Number

SSP *abbreviation* state second pension

Stalin /ˈstɑːlɪn/, **Joseph** (1879–1953) general secretary of the Soviet Communist Party (1922–53) and ruler of the former Soviet Union as a dictator after 1930. He removed political opponents in a series of purges and causing nationwide famine with his collectivist agricultural policy. After World War II, he extended Soviet control over most of Eastern Europe.

Stalinism /ˈstɑːlɪnɪz(ə)m/ *noun* a political system based on the centralised authority of the Communist party and an oppressive totalitarian state, as in the former Soviet Union under Stalin

stalking horse /ˌstɑːkɪŋ ˈhɔːs/ *noun* a candidate who stands election only to conceal the potential candidacy of someone else, to divide the opposition, or to determine how strong the opposition is

stand /stænd/ *noun* **1.** a determined position on some issue ○ *The government's stand against racial prejudice.* ○ *The police chief criticised the council's stand on law and order.* **2.** the position of a member of Congress on a question, either for or against ■ *verb* **1.** to offer yourself as a candidate in an election ○ *He stood as a Liberal-Democrat candidate in the General Election.* ○ *He is standing against the present deputy leader in the leadership contest.* ○ *She was persuaded to stand for parliament.* ○ *He has stood for office several times, but has never been elected.* (NOTE: The US term is

run.) 2. to exist or to be in a state ○ *The House stands adjourned.* ○ *The report stood referred to the Finance Committee.*

standard of living /ˌstændəd əv ˈlɪvɪŋ/ *noun* the quality of personal home life, measured by things such as the amount of food or clothes bought, or size of the family car

standard rate /ˈstændəd reɪt/ *noun* the basic rate of income tax which is paid by most taxpayers or basic rate of Value Added Tax which is paid on most goods and services

standards officer /ˈstændədz ˌɒfɪsə/ *noun* ♦ **trading standards officer**

stand down /ˌstænd ˈdaʊn/ *verb* to say you no longer wish to be considered as a candidate in an election ○ *The wife of one of the candidates is ill and he has stood down.*

Ständerat /ˈstendəraːt/ *noun* the States Council, the upper house of the legislature in Switzerland

stand in for /ˌstænd ˈɪn fɔː/ *verb* to take the place of someone ○ *Mr Smith is standing in for the chairman who is away on holiday.*

standing /ˈstændɪŋ/ *adjective* permanent ■ *noun* reputation ○ *the financial standing of a company* ◇ **standing committee 1.** permanent committee which always examines the same problem **2.** committee of Members of Parliament which examines in detail Bills which are not passed to other committees ▶ ◇ (all senses) **ad hoc**

standing orders /ˌstændɪŋ ˈɔːdəz/ *plural noun* the rules governing the way in which a meeting or a debate in Parliament or a local council is run

standing vote /ˈstændɪŋ vəʊt/ *noun US* a vote in the House of Representatives, where members stand up to be counted

standstill agreement /ˈstændstɪl əˌɡriːmənt/ *noun* an agreement that things should remain as they are, e.g. one between a creditor country and a debtor country that needs extra time to repay its debt

Star Chamber /ˈstɑː ˌtʃeɪmbə/ *noun* **1.** a royal court which in the past tried cases without a jury **2.** a cabinet committee which examines the spending proposals of government departments

Star-spangled Banner /ˌstɑː ˌspæŋɡld ˈbænə/ *noun* a national anthem of the USA. Compare **Hail to the Chief**

START *abbreviation* Strategic Arms Reduction Talks

state /steɪt/ *noun* **1.** an independent country **2.** the political system of a country represented by its government (NOTE: The state is the permanent embodiment of the political system. The members of the government hold the power of the state during their term in office.) □ **offence against the State** an act of attacking the lawful government of a country **3.** a semi-independent section of a federal country such as the USA **4.** a condition ○ *The Prime Minister is due to make a speech on the state of the economy.* ○ *In his state of the EU address, the President said that only by working together could the countries of the union tackle the problem of unemployment.* ■ *verb* to say clearly ○ *The document states that all revenue has to be declared to the tax office.*

state capital /ˌsteɪt ˈkæpɪt(ə)l/ *noun* the main town in a state or province. Also called **provincial capital**

state capitalism /ˌsteɪt ˈkæpɪt(ə)lɪz(ə)m/ *noun* an economic system in which the state has control of capital and the means of production

State Capitol /ˌsteɪt ˈkæpɪt(ə)l/ *noun* the building in the main city of a state, where the state legislature meets

State Chamber /ˌsteɪt ˈtʃeɪmbə/ *noun* the lower house of the legislature in Slovenia

state-controlled /ˈsteɪt kənˌtrəʊld/ *adjective* run by the state ○ *state-controlled television*

State Council /ˌsteɪt ˈkaʊns(ə)l/ *noun* the upper house of the legislature in Slovenia

State Department /ˈsteɪt dɪ ˌpɑːtmənt/ *noun* the US government department dealing with relations between the USA and other countries ◊ See note at **foreign**

State Duma /ˌsteɪt ˈduːmə/ *noun* the lower house of the legislature in Russia

State enterprise /ˌsteɪt ˈentəpraɪz/ *noun* a company run by the state ○ *The bosses of State industries are appointed by the government.*

statehood /ˈsteɪthʊd/ *noun* the status of a state in a federal union, especially the United States ○ *The states are listed in date of statehood.*

statehouse /ˈsteɪthaʊs/ *noun* a building in a US state capital in which its state legislature meets

stateless person /ˌsteɪtləs ˈpɜːs(ə)n/ *noun* a person who is not a citizen of any state

state line /ˌsteɪt ˈlaɪn/ *noun* the official boundary between two US states

statement /ˈsteɪtmənt/ *noun* **1.** saying something clearly □ **to make a statement to the House** (*of a Member of Parliament*) to tell the House of Commons that you have done something wrong or to explain your actions to the House **2.** a written document containing information

state of emergency /ˌsteɪt əv ɪ ˈmɜːdʒənsi/ *noun* a dangerous or difficult situation such as a natural disaster, a war or a revolution, during which the government has to take special measures to control the country □ **the government declared a state of emergency** the government decided that the situation was so dangerous that they had to take special measures to control the country

State of the Union message /steɪt əv ðə ˌjuːnjən ˈmesɪdʒ/ *noun* an annual speech by the President of the USA which sums up the political situation in the country

State Opening of Parliament /ˌsteɪt ˌəʊp(ə)nɪŋ əv ˈpɑːləmənt/ *noun* the ceremony when the Queen opens a new session of Parliament and reads the Queen's Speech which has been written for her by the government

State-owned /ˌsteɪt ˈəʊnd/ *adjective* owned by the State

state school /ˈsteɪt skuːl/ *noun* a school paid for with public money

state second pension /ˌsteɪt ˌsekənd ˈpenʃən/ *noun* an additional pension paid by the government to supplement the basic state pension, based on an employee's earnings and National Insurance contributions

state secret /ˌsteɪt ˈsiːkrət/ *noun* a piece of information that is supposed to be known only to authorised people

States-General /ˌsteɪts ˈdʒen(ə)rəl/ *noun* the legislative body in the Netherlands, equivalent to Parliament or Congress

statesman /ˈsteɪtsmən/ *noun* an important and respected political leader or representative of a country ○ *Several statesmen from Western countries are meeting to discuss defence problems.* (NOTE: The plural is **statesmen.**)

statesmanlike /ˈsteɪtsmənlaɪk/ *adjective* wise and skilful, like a good political leader

statesmanship /ˈsteɪtsmənʃɪp/ *noun* the ability of being a good political leader

state socialism /ˌsteɪt ˈsəʊʃəlɪz(ə)m/ *noun* a system in which the state controls the major industries and banks and plans economic and social welfare for the benefit of all citizens

States of the Union /ˌsteɪts əv ðə ˈjuːnjən/ *plural noun* the states joined together to form the United States of America

statesperson /ˈsteɪtspɜːs(ə)n/ *noun* a senior politician who plays an important role in government or international affairs and is widely respected for integrity

states' rights /ˌsteɪts 'raɪts/ *plural noun* the powers and rights not granted by the US Constitution to the federal government and not forbidden to the states by the Constitution

state trooper /ˌsteɪt 'truːpə/ *noun* a member of the highway patrol police of a US state

state visit /ˌsteɪt 'vɪzɪt/ *noun* a ceremonial visit paid by a head of state to another country

statism /'steɪtɪz(ə)m/ *noun* the theory that economic and political power should be controlled by a central government

statistics /stə'tɪstɪks/ *plural noun* information shown in the form of numbers ○ *She asked for the birth statistics for 1992.* ○ *Council statistics show that the amount of rented property in the borough has increased.* ○ *Government trade statistics show that exports to the EU have fallen over the last six months.*

status /'steɪtəs/ *noun* **1.** importance or position in society **2.** the legal position of a country, a person or a group

statute /'stætʃuːt/ *noun* an established written law, especially an Act of Parliament

statute-barred /ˌstætʃuːt 'bɑːd/ *adjective* a court case which cannot be brought because it is too long since the event in dispute occurred under the Statute of Limitations

statute book /'stætʃuːt bʊk/ *noun* all laws passed by Parliament which are still in force ○ *The Act is still on the statute book, and has never been repealed.*

statutes at large /ˌstætʃuːts ət 'lɑːdʒ/ *plural noun US* a printed list of acts passed in each session of Congress

statutorily /'stætʃʊt(ə)rɪli/ *adverb* by act of parliament □ **a statutorily protected tenant** a tenant protected by law

statutory /'stætʃʊt(ə)ri/ *adjective* fixed by act of parliament ○ *There is a statutory period of probation of thir-*teen weeks. ○ *The authority has a statutory obligation to provide free education to all children.* ○ *Powers conferred on an authority by the statutory code.*

statutory books /ˌstætʃʊt(ə)ri 'bʊks/ *plural noun* the official registers which a company must keep, e.g. the register of shareholders and the minute books of board meetings

statutory declaration /ˌstætʃʊt(ə)ri ˌdeklə'reɪʃ(ə)n/ *noun* **1.** a statement made to the Registrar of Companies that a company has complied with specific legal conditions **2.** a declaration signed and witnessed for official purposes

statutory duty /ˌstætʃʊt(ə)ri 'djuːti/ *noun* a duty which someone must perform and which is laid down by act of parliament

statutory holiday /ˌstætʃʊt(ə)ri 'hɒlɪdeɪ/ *noun* a holiday which is fixed by act of parliament

statutory instrument /ˌstætʃʊt(ə)ri 'ɪnstrʊmənt/ *noun* an order which has the force of law, made by a minister under powers granted by an Act of Parliament. Abbr **SI**

statutory undertakers /ˌstætʃʊt(ə)ri ˌʌndə'teɪkəz/ *plural noun* bodies formed by act of parliament and having legal duties to provide services such as gas, electricity, water

stealth tax /'stelθ tæks/ *noun* a new tax or tax increase that is introduced in a way that allows it to be relatively unnoticed by the public, or an additional charge that is effectively, though not officially, a tax

steering committee /'stɪərɪŋ kəˌmɪti/ *noun* a committee which works out the agenda for discussion by a main committee or conference, and so can influence the way the main committee or conference works

stenographer /stə'nɒɡrəfə/ *noun* an official person who can write in shorthand and so take records of what is said in Parliament or in court

step down /ˌstep ˈdaʊn/ *verb* to resign ○ *He stepped down as Chair of the Finance Committee.*

step up /ˌstep ˈʌp/ *verb* to increase ○ *The government has stepped up its grants to small businesses.* (NOTE: **stepping – stepped**)

Stewardship of the Chiltern Hundreds /ˌstjuːədʃɪp əv ðə ˌtʃɪltən ˈhʌndrədz/ *noun* a nominal government position, which disqualifies a person from being a Member of Parliament (NOTE: If an MP wishes to resign, he or she is said to 'take the Chiltern Hundreds' in order to do so)

stipulate /ˈstɪpjʊleɪt/ *verb* to state firmly that something particular must be done ○ *The government stipulated that the applicants should take a means test.*

Stormont /ˈstɔːmɒnt/ *noun* a large house in Belfast, where the Northern Ireland Assembly and executive meets

Storting /ˈstɔːtɪŋ/ *noun* the legislative body in Norway

straight majority /ˌstreɪt məˈdʒɒrɪti/ *noun* more than half the votes. Also called **overall majority**

straight ticket /ˈstreɪt ˌtɪkɪt/ *noun* a vote for all the candidates put forward by a political party

stranger /ˈstreɪndʒə/ *noun* a visitor to Parliament who is allowed into the public gallery or the press gallery to watch the debates. ◊ **private sitting**

COMMENT: Formerly, an MP who wanted a debate to take place in private could call out 'I Spy Strangers'. Since 1998 the procedure has been replaced by one based on the motion 'that the House sit in private'.

strangers' gallery /ˈstreɪndʒəz ˌɡæləri/ *noun* a gallery from which members of the public may observe the business of a legislature, especially in the British House of Commons

strategic /strəˈtiːdʒɪk/ *adjective* based on a long-term plan of action

strategic planning /strəˌtiːdʒɪk ˈplænɪŋ/ *noun* planning for the future long-term work of a government or other organisation

strategy /ˈstrætədʒi/ *noun* a long-term plan of action ○ *The Opposition's electoral strategy was to attack the government's record on unemployment.*

straw poll /ˌstrɔː ˈpəʊl/ *noun* an unofficial vote or expression of opinion used to discover the likely result of an election or the trend of opinion regarding an issue ○ *A straw poll among members of staff shows the government is in the lead.*

strike /straɪk/ *noun* **1.** a refusal by workers to work, as a protest **2.** □ **to come out on strike, to go on strike** to stop working, as a protest ○ *the local government workers are on strike for higher pay* □ **to take strike action** to stop working, as a protest □ **strike ballot, strike vote** a vote by employees to decide if a strike should be held □ **strike call** a demand by a union for a strike ■ *verb* **1.** to stop working, as a protest ○ *to strike for higher wages* or *for shorter working hours* ○ *to strike in protest against bad working conditions* **2.** to remove a word from a text or a name from a list □ **to strike from the record** to remove words from the written minutes of a meeting because they are incorrect or offensive ○ *the chairman's remarks were struck from the record* □ **to strike out the last word** *US* a way of getting permission of the chair to speak on a question, by moving that the last word of the amendment or section being discussed should be deleted

strongman /ˈstrɒŋmæn/ *noun* a powerful leader who rules by force

STUC *abbreviation* Scottish Trades Union Congress

stuff /stʌf/ *verb* to put invalid ballot papers into a ballot box to affect the result of an election

stump /stʌmp/ *verb* to campaign for election to a public office

STV *abbreviation* single transferable vote

sub- /sʌb/ *prefix* meaning less important

sub-clause /ˌsʌb ˈklɔːz/ *noun* part of a section in a Bill being considered by Parliament

subcommittee /ˈsʌbkəmɪti/ *noun* a committee which is formed to advise a larger committee ○ *The Schools Subcommittee makes recommendations to the Education Committee.*

subject /ˈsʌbdʒɪkt/ *noun* **1.** what something is concerned with ○ *The subject of the report was poverty in the inner cities.* **2.** a person who is a citizen of a country, especially one with a king or queen ○ *She is a British subject.* ○ *British subjects do not need visas to visit European Union countries.* ■ *adjective* □ **subject peoples** races ruled by another power

subject to /sʌbˈdʒekt tuː/ *adjective* **1.** depending on □ **the contract is subject to government approval** the contract will be valid only if it is approved by the government □ **subject to contract** not legal until a contract has been signed ○ *The sale is agreed, subject to contract.* **2.** under ■ *verb* to make someone suffer something ○ *He was subjected to torture.* ○ *The MP subjected the committee to a boring list of figures.*

sub judice /ˌsʌb ˈdʒuːdɪsi/ *Latin phrase meaning* 'under the law': being considered by a court, and so not to be mentioned in the media or in Parliament ○ *The papers cannot report the case because it is still sub judice.*

submit /səbˈmɪt/ *verb* to ask for something to be considered by a committee or meeting ○ *She submitted six planning applications to the committee.*

subpoena /səˈpiːnə/ *noun* a court order telling someone to appear before a Parliamentary Committee or a court of law ■ *verb* to order someone to appear before a parliamentary committee or a court of law ○ *She was subpoenaed to appear before the Commons committee on Defence.*

subscribe /səbˈskraɪb/ ◇ **to subscribe to something 1.** to sign something, showing that you agree to it **2.** to support a policy or proposal

sub-section /ˈsʌb ˌsekʃən/ *noun* a part of a section of a document such as an Act of Parliament ○ *You will find the information in sub-section 3 of Section 47.*

subsidiarity /səbˌsɪdiˈærɪti/ *noun* (*in the EU*) the principle that decisions should be taken at the lowest possible effective level

subsidiary motion /səbˌsɪdiəri ˈməʊʃ(ə)n/ *noun* a motion which is related to another motion, e.g. a motion to adjourn discussion of the other motion

subsidise /ˈsʌbsɪdaɪz/, **subsidize** *verb* to give money to an organisation to help it continue to work ○ *The youth theatre is subsidised by the council.* ○ *The government has refused to subsidise the construction work.*

subsidy /ˈsʌbsɪdi/ *noun* money given by a government to an organisation to help it continue to work ○ *The club relies on council subsidies for its finance.*

substantive /ˈsʌbstəntɪv/ *adjective* real or actual

substantive motion /səbˌstæntɪv ˈməʊʃ(ə)n/ *noun* the main motion under discussion rather than a subsidiary one

substitute /ˈsʌbstɪtjuːt/ *noun* **1.** a person or thing which takes the place of someone or something else ○ *The Mayor was ill so she sent the Deputy Mayor as substitute.* **2.** *US* a motion introduced in place of the business being discussed, which has the effect of killing the original motion ■ *verb* to put in the place of something else ○ *He proposed to amend the motion by deleting the words 'the Council' in line three and substituting 'the Council Officers'.* ○ *Please substitute 'school' for 'college' on page 4.*

suburb /ˈsʌbɜːb/ *noun* an area on the edge of a city or town, which is mainly used for houses and not shops or offices ○ *a residential suburb*

subversion /səbˈvɜːʃ(ə)n/ *noun* secret acts intended to bring down a government or political system ○ *The government stated that the power of the State was being undermined by enemy subversion.*

subversive /səbˈvɜːsɪv/ *adjective* acting secretly to bring down a government or political system ○ *The police are investigating subversive groups in the student organisations.* ■ *noun* a person who acts secretly to bring down a government or political system ○ *The police have arrested several known subversives.*

subvert /səbˈvɜːt/ *verb* to act secretly to bring down a government or political system ○ *She was accused of trying to subvert the State.*

succeed /səkˈsiːd/ *verb* to follow, especially to take the place of someone who has retired or died ○ *George V succeeded his father Edward VII.* ○ *Mrs Jones is expected to succeed Mr Smith as Chair.* □ **to succeed to a title** to become a peer by inheriting the title from someone who has died

succession /səkˈseʃ(ə)n/ *noun* acquiring property or title from someone who has died

succession state /səkˈseʃ(ə)n steɪt/ *noun* a nation that was formerly part of another larger nation

successor /səkˈsesə/ *noun* a person who takes over from someone ○ *Mr Smith's successor as chairman will be Mr Jones.*

suffrage /ˈsʌfrɪdʒ/ *noun* the right to vote in elections

suffragette /ˌsʌfrəˈdʒet/ *noun* a woman who campaigned for women to be given the right to vote in the early part of the 20th century

suffragist /ˈsʌfrədʒɪst/ *noun* a supporter of the right to vote being given to a particular group such as women or all people above a particular age

suggest /səˈdʒest/ *verb* to put forward a proposal ○ *The chairman suggested (that) the next meeting should be held in October.* ○ *We suggested Mr Smith for the post of treasurer.*

suggestion /səˈdʒestʃən/ *noun* a proposal or idea which is put forward ○ *The Committee voted to accept the suggestion from the Secretary that meetings should start at 2.30 in future.*

sultan /ˈsʌltən/ *noun* an hereditary ruler of an Arab country

Sultanate /ˈsʌltəneɪt/ *noun* an Arab country ruled by a sultan

summit /ˈsʌmɪt/ *noun* **1.** the top of a mountain **2.** *also* **summit conference** a meeting between heads of state, especially the heads of powerful states ○ *The summit conference or summit meeting was held in Geneva.* ○ *The matter will be discussed at next week's summit of the EU leaders.*

summiteer /ˌsʌmɪˈtɪə/ *noun* someone taking part in a summit conference

summitry /ˈsʌmɪtri/ *noun* diplomacy as carried on in summit meetings

superintendent /ˌsuːpərɪnˈtendənt/ *noun* in the United Kingdom and Canada, a police officer of a rank above inspector, and in the United States a police officer of high rank, especially the head of a police department

superpower /ˈsuːpəpaʊə/ *noun* a very large state, with great economic strength, large armed forces and great influence in world politics

superpower diplomacy /ˈsuːpəpaʊə dɪˈpləʊməsi/ *noun* discussions between the leaders of very powerful countries

superstate /ˈsuːpəsteɪt/ *noun* a very large powerful country, especially one created by the union or federation of a number of nations or states

supplemental /ˌsʌplɪˈmentəl/ *adjective* additional to something

supplementary questions /ˌsʌplɪˌment(ə)ri ˈkwestʃ(ə)ns/ *plural noun* questions asked by an MP or councillor after a main written question has been answered, used to try to catch a Minister or council committee chairman by surprise or to embarrass him or her. Also called **supplementaries**

supply /sə'plaɪ/ *noun* **1.** the amount of something which is available to be used **2.** the stock of something which is needed ○ *The factory is running short of supplies of coal.* ○ *Supplies of coal have been reduced.* **3.** the act of providing something

Supply Bill /sə'plaɪ bɪl/ *noun* a parliamentary Bill voting tax to provide money for government use

Supply Days /sə'plaɪ ˌdeɪz/ *plural noun* days allocated in each session of Parliament for discussion of tax and other financial matters. Also called **allotted days**

support /sə'pɔːt/ *noun* agreement or encouragement ○ *The chairman has the support of the committee.* ■ *verb* **1.** to give money to help ○ *The government is supporting the computer industry to the tune of $2m per annum.* ○ *We hope the banks will support us during the expansion period.* **2.** to encourage or to agree with ○ *She hopes the other members of the committee will support her.* ○ *The electorate will not support another increase in income tax.*

supporter /sə'pɔːtə/ *noun* a person who agrees with and encourages someone ○ *Socialist supporters or supporters of the Socialist party were very pleased with the result.*

support price /sə'pɔːt praɪs/ *noun* in the European Union, the price at which a government will buy farm produce to stop the price from falling

suppress /sə'pres/ *verb* to use violent means to stop opposition to a government or the publication of views which support opposition to a government ○ *The peasants' revolt was suppressed by the army.*

supranational /ˌsuːprə'næʃ(ə)nəl/ *adjective* referring to an organisation which has power over national governments

supremacy /sʊ'preməsi/ *noun* being in an all-powerful position □ **the supremacy of Parliament** the situation of the British Parliament which can both pass and repeal laws

supreme /sʊ'priːm/ *adjective* most powerful or important

Supreme Council /sʊ'priːm 'kaʊns(ə)l/ *noun* the legislature in the Ukraine

Supreme Court /sʊ'priːm 'kɔːt/ **Supreme Court (of Judicature)** the highest court in England and Wales, consisting of the Court of Appeal and the High Court of Justice ■ *noun* the highest federal court in the USA and other countries

Supreme Kenges *noun* the legislative body in Kazakhstan

Supreme People's Assembly /sʊ'priːm ˌpiːpəlz ə'sembli/ *noun* the legislature in North Korea

Supreme Soviet /sʊ'priːm 'səʊviət/ *noun* the legislative body of Tajikistan

surgeon general /ˌsɜːdʒən 'dʒen(ə)rəl/ *noun* the chief public health officer of the United States, or the chief public health officer of some individual states (NOTE: The Surgeon General is roughly the equivalent of the UK Chief Medical Officer.)

surrender /sə'rendə/ *verb* **1.** to give in to an enemy ○ *The town surrendered to the guerrilla forces.* **2.** to hand over something to someone ○ *He surrendered his seal of office.*

survive /sə'vaɪv/ *verb* **1.** to live longer than another person ○ *He survived his wife.* ○ *She is survived by her husband and three children.* **2.** to continue to exist after something has happened ○ *The club will not survive all these changes.* ○ *The government survived the vote of no confidence.*

suspension /sə'spenʃən/ *noun* **1.** the act of stopping something for a time ○ *suspension of a sitting* **2.** a punishment by which someone has to leave a place for a time ○ *the suspension of an MP for unparliamentary behaviour* (NOTE: When an MP is 'named' by the Speaker for doing something against the rules of the House, the House will vote to suspend him. Suspension is normally for five days, though it may be for longer if the MP is suspended twice in the same session of Parliament.)

Sussex Drive /ˌsʌsɪks ˈdraɪv/ *noun* the address of the official residence of the Prime Minister of Canada

suzerain /ˈsuːzərən/ *noun* a ruler or nation that controls a dependent nation's international affairs but allows it to control its internal affairs

swear /sweə/ *verb* to promise that what you will say will be the truth ○ *She swore to tell the truth.* □ **'I swear to tell the truth, the whole truth and nothing but the truth'** the words used when a witness takes the oath in court

swear in /ˌsweə ˈɪn/ *verb* to make someone formally promise specific things before taking up a position ○ *He was sworn in as a Privy Councillor.*

swearing-in /ˌsweərɪŋ ˈɪn/ *noun* an act of making someone formally promise specific things before taking up a position ○ *Five hundred guests attended the swearing-in of the President.*

swing /swɪŋ/ *noun* a percentage change in votes from one election to another ○ *A 10% swing away from the government* or *to the Opposition.* ○ *He needs a 5% swing to recapture the seat which he lost at the last election.*

swinging voter /ˈswɪŋɪŋ ˈvəʊtə/ *noun* ANZ same as **floating voter**

swing voter /swɪŋ ˈvəʊtə/ *noun US* a person who does not vote for the same political party on all occasions, or whose voting behaviour is unpredictable

SWP *abbreviation* Socialist Workers Party

sympathiser /ˈsɪmpəθaɪzə/ *noun* a person who agrees in general with the policies of a political party, without being a party member ○ *The government is formed of communists and communist sympathisers.*

syndic /ˈsɪndɪk/ *noun* in some European countries, a government official, especially a civil magistrate

syndicalism /ˈsɪndɪkəlɪz(ə)m/ *noun* a type of socialism, where property and control of industry is in the hands of the trade unions in each industry

syndicate /ˈsɪndɪkət/ *noun* in some European countries, the office of a government official, especially a civil magistrate

system /ˈsɪstəm/ *noun* **1.** the arrangement or organisation of things which work together ○ *The British legal system has been taken as the standard for many other legal systems.* **2.** a particular way of doing things

T

table /'teɪb(ə)l/ *noun* **1.** a piece of furniture for sitting at **2.** the long table in the centre of the House of Commons between the two front benches. The Serjeant at Arms places the mace on the table when the business of the House begins. The two despatch boxes which the main speakers from either party talk across are also on the table. **3.** □ **to let a bill lie on the table** *US* not to proceed with discussion of a bill, but to hold it over to be debated later **4.** a list of numbers or facts set out in a list ■ *verb* to put written information on the table before or during a meeting, making them available to everyone at the meeting ○ *The report of the finance committee was tabled.* ◇ **to lay a bill on the table** *US* **1.** to present a bill to the House of Commons for discussion **2.** to kill debate on a bill in the House of Representatives

tactical /'tæktɪk(ə)l/ *adjective* done as part of a short-term plan to try to achieve success

tactical voting /ˌtæktɪk(ə)l 'vəʊtɪŋ/ *noun* a way of voting, which aims not at voting for the candidate you want to win, but at voting in such a way as to prevent the candidate whom you do not want to win from being elected (NOTE: In a case where the three candidates A, B and C, have 47%, 33% and 20% of the vote according to an opinion poll, C's supporters might all vote for B, to prevent A winning.)

take out /ˌteɪk 'aʊt/ *verb* to remove

take over /ˌteɪk 'əʊvə/ *verb* **1.** to take control of something such as a factory or organisation ○ *During the uprising, the rebels took over the Post Office and radio station.* ○ *The party has been taken over by an activist group.* **2.** to start to do a job in place of someone else ○ *The new leader of the party takes over on May 1st.* ○ *Ambassador Brown took over from Ambassador Green last April.* **3.** to replace something

Taliban /'tælɪbæn/ *plural noun* a strict Islamic group that ruled Afghanistan from 1996 until 2001

talk /tɔːk/ *plural noun* formal discussions between two or more groups to bring about agreement on an issue

talking shop /'tɔːkɪŋ ʃɒp/ *noun* a place where people talk, but not much action takes place ○ *The Council Chamber is just a talking shop.*

talk out /ˌtɔːk 'aʊt/ *verb* to go on talking in a debate, so that the time runs out before the vote can be taken ○ *The bill was talked out and so fell.*

Tammany Hall /ˌtæməni 'hɔːl/ *noun* the very powerful Democratic Party Committee in New York

Tammany Hall politics /ˌtæməni ˌhɔːl 'pɒlɪtɪks/ *noun* the use of bribery and violence to achieve political control especially in a big city, so-called after the Tammany Hall Society in late 19th century and early 20th century in New York

Tánaiste *noun* the Deputy Prime Minister in the Republic of Ireland

Taoiseach /'tiːʃək/ *noun* the Prime Minister of the Republic of Ireland

target /'tɑːgɪt/ *verb* to aim an attack or criticism at somebody or something ○ *The terrorists targeted military and political figures.* ○ *The advertising campaign is targeting floating voters.*

tariff /'tærɪf/ *noun* a tax on goods brought into or taken out of a country

task force /'tɑːsk fɔːs/ *noun* **1.** a group organised for a special purpose ○ *a government task force on inner-city problems* **2.** in the European Union, a group which organises work affecting more than one Directorate-General

tax /tæks/ *noun* **1.** money taken by the government or by an official body to pay for government services □ **excess profits tax** a tax on profits which are higher than what is thought to be normal **2.** □ **basic rate tax** the lowest rate of income tax □ **to levy a tax, to impose a tax** to make a tax payable ○ *the government has imposed a 15% tax on petrol* □ **to lift a tax** to remove a tax □ **tax allowances, allowances against tax** part of one's income which a person is allowed to earn and not pay tax on ■ *verb* to make someone pay a tax or to put a tax on something ○ *to tax businesses at 50%* ○ *income is taxed at 27%* ○ *These items are heavily taxed.* ◇ **tax deductions** *US* **1.** money removed from a salary to pay tax **2.** business expenses which can be claimed against tax ◇ **tax exemption** *US* **1.** being free from payment of tax **2.** the part of income which a person is allowed to earn and not pay tax on

taxable /'tæksəb(ə)l/ *adjective* possible to tax □ **taxable items** items on which a tax has to be paid □ **taxable income** income on which a person has to pay tax

taxation /tæk'seɪʃ(ə)n/ *noun* the act of taxing

tax avoidance /'tæks ə,vɔɪd(ə)ns/ *noun* trying legally to reduce the amount of tax to be paid

tax code /'tæks kəʊd/ *noun* a number given to someone to show the amount of income tax he or she must pay

tax concession /'tæks kən,seʃ(ə)n/ *noun* allowing less tax to be paid

tax-deductible /,tæks dɪ'dʌktɪb(ə)l/ *adjective* money deducted from the amount of income tax someone has to pay for some reason

tax deductions /'tæks dɪ,dʌkʃnz/ *US* money removed from a salary to pay tax

tax-exempt /,tæks ɪg'zempt/ *adjective* not subject to tax

tax-free /,tæks 'friː/ *adjective* on which tax does not have to be paid

taxing officer /,tæksɪŋ 'ɒfɪsə/ *noun* a person appointed by the House of Commons to assess the charges made by a Parliamentary agent

tax inspector /'tæks ɪn,spektə/ *noun* an official whose job is to assess the amount of tax that should be paid by a person or organisation and make sure the tax is paid. Also called **inspector of taxes**

taxpayer /'tækspeɪə/ *noun* a person or company which has to pay tax ○ *basic taxpayer* or *taxpayer at the basic rate* ○ *corporate taxpayers*

tax point /'tæks pɔɪnt/ *noun* **1.** the time when goods are supplied and when a tax such as Value Added Tax may be charged **2.** the time at which a tax begins to be applied

tax return /'tæks rɪ,tɜːn/ *noun* a completed tax form, with details of income and allowances. Also called **tax declaration**

tax schedules /'tæks ,ʃedjuːlz/ *plural noun* the six types of income as classified in the Finance Acts for British tax

tax year /'tæks ,jɪə/ *noun* the twelve month period on which taxes are calculated. In the UK this is 6th April to 5th April of the following year.

TD *abbreviation* Teachta Dala

Teachta Dala /,tɪæxtə 'dælə/ *noun* a member of the Irish Dail

technical /'teknɪk(ə)l/ *adjective* referring to a small point of procedure or of law ○ *The motion was rejected on a technical point.*

technicality /,teknɪ'kælɪti/ *noun* a small detail in the law, especially one which seems unfair ○ *The Appeal Court rejected the appeal on a technicality.*

technocrat /'teknəkræt/ *noun* an expert in engineering or science who has political or industrial power

teller /'telə/ *noun* **1.** a member who counts the votes in the House of Commons or House of Representatives **2.** a worker in a bank

COMMENT: When a division is called in the House of Commons, the Speaker appoints four MPs as tellers, two for the motion and two against. They do not vote, but check the other MPs as they pass through the division lobbies.

tem /tem/ ♦ **pro tempore**

temporal /'temp(ə)rəl/ ♦ **Lords**

tendency /'tendənsi/ *noun* a group within a political party which tries to push the party in a particular direction politically but which still remains fundamentally loyal to the party (NOTE: A faction may try to break away from a political party, while a tendency will avoid pushing its opposition to others in the party too far.)

tender /'tendə/ *noun* a document offering to do work or supply goods at a certain specified cost ■ *verb* to make an offer in the form of a tender

tenderer /'tendərə/ *noun* a person or company which tenders for work ○ *The company was the successful tenderer for the project.*

10 Downing Street /ˌten 'daʊnɪŋ ˌstriːt/ *noun* the house of the Prime Minister, where the Cabinet meets and which is the centre of the executive branch of the British government

Ten Minute Rule /ten 'mɪnɪt ruːl/ *noun* a standing order in the House of Commons, where an ordinary MP can introduce a Bill with a short speech ○ *The Bill was proposed under the Ten Minute Rule.*

tense /tens/ *adjective* a potentially dangerous situation ○ *The situation in the area is still tense.* ○ *As the situation became more tense, the Defence Department sent troops to nearby bases.*

tension /'tenʃən/ *noun* a period when relations between states are difficult and they may take action against each other ○ *The Security Council resolution is aimed at reducing tension in the area.* ○ *The attack on the ship increased tension in the area.* ○ *The debate in council showed the tension between the two factions.*

term /tɜːm/ *noun* **1.** a period of time ○ *the term of a lease* ○ *to have a loan for a term of fifteen years* ○ *during her term of office as manager* ○ *The term of the loan is fifteen years.* □ **medium-term** for a period of one or two years **2.** the length of a Parliament before new elections are called ○ *The autumn* or *winter term starts in September.* **3.** part of a university or college or school year

term limits /tɜːm 'lɪmɪts/ *noun* in the USA, a restriction on the number of times an elected official can hold office (NOTE: The US President is restricted to two terms, but efforts to impose term limits on other federal politicians have failed.)

territorial /ˌterɪ'tɔːriəl/ *adjective* referring to land □ **territorial claims** claims to own land which is part of another country □ **territorial waters** sea water near the coast of a country, which is part of the country and governed by the laws of that country □ **outside territorial waters** in international waters, where a single country's jurisdiction does not run

territorialise /ˌterɪ'tɔːriəlaɪz/ *verb* to increase the size of a country by adding a territory or territories to it

territorialism /terɪ'tɔːriəlɪzm/ *noun* a social system in which landowners have most control

territorial waters /ˌterɪtɔːriəl 'wɔːtəz/ *plural noun* the area of sea around a country's coast that is under the control of that country

territory /'terɪt(ə)ri/ *noun* an area of land ruled by a government ○ *Their government has laid claim to part of our territory.*

terror /'terə/ ◇ **Reign of Terror 1.** a period of repression and violence, when people live in a continual state of fear **2.** the period during the French Revolution when the Jacobins under Robespierre were all-powerful (1793–94)

terrorism /'terərɪz(ə)m/ *noun* the use of acts of public violence to achieve political change

terrorist /'terərɪst/ *adjective, noun* trying to achieve political change by acts of public violence ○ *The government has had to face a series of terrorist attacks on post offices and police stations.* ○ *Three terrorists seized the Minister and held him hostage.*

test ban /'test bæn/ *noun* an agreement between countries to stop testing some or all nuclear weapons

test roll /'test rəʊl/ *noun* a book in which each MP signs his or her name after taking the oath at the beginning of a new Parliament

textbook /'tekstbʊk/ *noun* a book which is used for studying

thalassocracy /ˌθælə'sɒkrəsi/ *noun* naval or commercial supremacy over a large area of sea

Thatcher /'θætʃə/, **Margaret, Baroness Thatcher of Kesteven** (*b.* 1925) the first woman prime minister of Great Britain (1979–90)

Thatcherism /'θætʃərɪz(ə)m/ *noun* the political policies and style of government of Margaret Thatcher, including privatisation, monetarism and lack of support for trade unions

there- /ðeə/ *prefix* that thing (NOTE: The following words formed from **there-** are frequently used in government and legal documents.)

thereafter /ðeər'ɑːftə/ *adverb* after that

therefor /ðeə'fɔː/ *adverb* for that

therefore /'ðeəfɔː/ *adverb* as a result of that

therefrom /ðeə'frʌm/ *adverb* from that

therein /ðeər'ɪn/ *adverb* in that

thereinafter /ˌðeərɪn'ɑːftə/ *adverb* afterwards mentioned in that document

thereinbefore /ˌðeərɪnbɪ'fɔː/ *adverb* before mentioned in that document

thereinunder /ˌðeərɪn'ʌndə/ *adverb* mentioned under that heading

thereof /ðeər'ɒv/ *adverb* of that

thereto /ðeə'tuː/ *adverb* to that

theretofore /ˌðeətʊ'fɔː/ *adverb* before that time

therewith /ðeə'wɪð/ *adverb* with that

think tank /'θɪŋk tæŋk/ *noun* a group of experts, academics and politicians who discuss important political, economic and social problems and suggest how they should be solved. Their suggestions are sometimes adopted by government, which may set up similar groups of its own. ○ *Professor Smith is a member of the government's economic think tank.*

third estate /ˌθɜːd ɪ'steɪt/ *noun* the common people

third force /ˌθɜːd 'fɔːs/ *noun* a group that acts to bring two opposing political groups or parties together

third party /ˌθɜːd 'pɑːti/ *noun* **1.** any person other than the two main parties involved in a contract or some business **2.** (*in a two-party system*) another political party, beside the main two

COMMENT: In UK the third party is the Liberal Democratic Party, although in Scotland this role is sometimes challenged by the Scottish National Party. In the USA any small party apart from the Republican or Democratic Parties is called a third party.

Third Reading /ˌθɜːd 'riːdɪŋ/ *noun* the final discussion and vote on a Bill in Parliament

Third Reich /ˌθɜːd 'raɪx/ *noun* the Nazi regime in Germany between 1933 and 1945

Third Republic /ˌθɜːd rɪ'pʌblɪk/ *noun* the French system of government set up after Napoleon III's reign, lasting until 1940

Third Way /,θɜːd 'weɪ/ *noun* a political policy that is neither Socialist nor Conservative, but combines aspects of free-market capitalism with egalitarian social aims

Third World /,θɜːd 'wɜːld/ *noun* a way of referring to developing countries in Africa, Asia and Latin America. ◊ **Fourth World** (NOTE: This description was relevant when there was a 'free' world led by America and a communist world led by Russia, but is now less useful since the fall of communism. It is also considered offensive by some.)

three line whip /,θriː laɪn 'wɪp/ *noun* strict instructions to the MPs in each political party to attend parliament and vote on a particular bill as their party whips tell them. This is done by underlining the matter three times on a piece of paper or 'whip' which is given to each MP in the party.

throne /θrəʊn/ *noun* a special chair for a king or queen

throw out /,θrəʊ 'aʊt/ *verb* **1.** to reject a proposal or refuse to accept it ◊ *The proposal was thrown out by the planning committee.* ◊ *The board threw out the draft contract submitted by the union.* **2.** to get rid of something ◊ *We threw out the old telephones and put in a computerised system.* ◊ *The AGM threw out the old board of directors.* (NOTE: **throwing – threw – has thrown**)

ticket /'tɪkɪt/ *noun US* a party's list of candidates for election to political office ◊ *He ran for governor on the Republican ticket.*

title /'taɪt(ə)l/ *noun* **1.** the right to hold goods or property ◊ *She has no title to the property.* **2.** a document proving a right to hold a property ◊ *She has a good title to the property.* **3.** a name given to a person in a job ◊ *He has the title 'Chief Executive'.* **4.** a name given to someone to show that they have received an honour or are a member of the nobility ◊ *He inherited his title from his uncle.* **5.** the name of a bill which comes before Parliament or name of an Act of Parliament □ **short title** the usual title of an Act of Parliament

titled /'taɪt(ə)ld/ *adjective* referring to a person with a title

titular /'tɪtjʊlə/ *adjective* holding a title ◊ *He is the titular head of state.*

tokenism /'təʊkənɪz(ə)m/ *noun* appointing a woman or someone from a minority group to a job just to avoid being criticised for being prejudiced

topple /'tɒp(ə)l/ *verb* to bring down or to make a government lose power or a person lose his or her position ◊ *The scandal toppled the minister.* ◊ *The smaller parties voted together and succeeded in toppling the government.*

Tory /'tɔːri/ *adjective* referring to a Conservative Party ■ *noun* a member or supporter of a Conservative Party (NOTE: used of the British Conservative Party, but also of other Conservatives, as in Canada)

totalitarian /təʊ,tælɪ'teəriən/ *adjective* (*often as criticism*) having total power and not allowing any opposition or any personal freedom ◊ *a totalitarian state* ◊ *the totalitarian regime of the junta*

totalitarianism /təʊ,tælɪ'teəriənɪz(ə)m/ *noun* (*usually as criticism*) a political system in which the state has total power over the citizens ◊ *Many extreme right-wing or left-wing governments have been accused of practising totalitarianism.*

town /taʊn/ *noun* a place where people live and work, with houses and other buildings

Town Clerk /,taʊn 'klɑːk/ *noun* the term used in the past for the most important permanent official of the administration of a town, working under the instructions of the town council. The official is now usually referred to as the Chief Executive.

town council /,taʊn 'kaʊnsəl/ *noun* the representatives elected to run a town

town councillor /ˌtaʊn ˈkaʊns(ə)lə/ *noun* a member of a town council

township /ˈtaʊnʃɪp/ *noun* **1.** (*in North America*) a small town which is a local government centre **2.** (*in South Africa*) a town outside the main urban areas

townspeople /ˈtaʊnzpiːp(ə)l/, **townsfolk** *noun* people who live in a town

town-twinning /ˈtaʊn ˌtwɪnɪŋ/ *noun* ♦ **twinning**

TPV *abbreviation* Temporary Protection Visa

trade /treɪd/ *noun* the business of buying and selling □ **export trade**, **import trade** the business of selling to other countries or buying from other countries ■ *verb* to buy and sell or to carry on a business ○ *to trade with another country* ○ *to trade on the Stock Exchange* ○ *The company has stopped trading.* ○ *He trades under the name or as 'Eeziphitt'.*

trade agreement /ˈtreɪd əˌgriːmənt/ *noun* an international agreement between countries over trade

trade deficit /ˈtreɪd ˌdefɪsɪt/ *noun* the amount by which a country imports more goods than it exports

Trade Descriptions Act /ˌtreɪd dɪ ˈskrɪpʃənz ækt/ *noun* an Act of Parliament which limits the way in which goods can be described so as to protect consumers from buying goods which have been given false descriptions

trademark /ˈtreɪdmɑːk/, **trade mark** /treɪd mɑːk/, **trade name** /ˈtreɪd neɪm/ *noun* a particular name, design or symbol which a company or maker uses for its product, has been registered by the maker, and which cannot be used by anyone else ○ *You cannot call your beds 'Softn'kumfi' – it is a registered trademark.*

Trades Union Congress /ˌtreɪdz ˈjuːnjən ˌkɒŋgres/ *noun* the central organisation for all British trade unions. Abbr **TUC** (NOTE: Although **Trades Union Congress** is the official name for the organisation, **trade union** is more common than **trades union**.)

trade union /ˌtreɪd ˈjuːnjən/, **trades union** /ˌtreɪdz ˈjuːnjən/ *noun* an organisation which represents workers who are its members in discussions with management about pay and conditions of work. Also called **trades union**. US term **labor union**

trade unionist /ˌtreɪd ˈjuːnjənɪst/, **trades unionist** *noun* a member of a trade union

Trading Standards Department /ˌtreɪdɪŋ ˈstændədz dɪˌpɑːtmənt/ *noun* a department of a council which deals with weighing and measuring equipment used by shops, and other consumer matters

trading standards officer /ˌtreɪdɪŋ ˈstændədz ˌɒfɪsə/ *noun* the official in charge of a council's Trading Standards Department

traitor /ˈtreɪtə/ *noun* a person who betrays his or her country, especially by giving secret information to the enemy

transact /trænˈzækt/ *verb* to do business with someone

transaction /trænˈzækʃən/ *noun* **1.** a piece of business done between companies or people **2.** the process of doing something

transcript /ˈtrænskrɪpt/ *noun* a written record of a spoken discussion or debate ○ *The Committee's report gives a full transcript of the evidence presented to it.* ○ *Transcripts of cases are available in the Supreme Court Library.*

transferable vote /træns ˈfɜːrəb(ə)l vəʊt/ *noun* a vote that will be given to a voter's second choice if the first-choice candidate receives too few votes to continue in the selection process

transitional period /træn ˈzɪʃ(ə)nəl ˈpɪəriəd/ *noun* the period during which new Member States of the European Union are allowed to introduce EU laws gradually, because introducing them immediately might cause difficulties

transnational /trænz'næʃ(ə)nəl/ *adjective* going beyond the borders of one state

transparency /træns'pærənsi/ *noun* an open and honest way of acting when making decisions, e.g. being open to the public about the actions of government or the European Union

treason /'triːz(ə)n/ *noun* the crime of betraying one's country, usually by helping the enemy in time of war ○ *She was accused of treason.* ○ *Three men were executed for treason.* ○ *The treason trial lasted three weeks.*

treasonable /'triːz(ə)nəb(ə)l/ *adjective* considered as treason ○ *He was accused of making treasonable remarks.*

Treasurer /'treʒərə/ *noun* the finance minister in the US federal government and in each of the state governments

treasurer's report /ˌtreʒərəz rɪ 'pɔːt/ *noun* a document from the treasurer of an organisation to explain the financial state of the organisation to its members

Treasury /'treʒəri/ *noun* the government department which deals with the country's finances □ **Secretary to the Treasury, Treasury Secretary** *US* the member of the government in charge of finance

COMMENT: In most countries, the government's finances are the responsibility of the Ministry of Finance, headed by the Finance Minister. In the UK, the Treasury is headed by the Chancellor of the Exchequer.

Treasury Bench /'treʒəri bentʃ/ *noun* the front bench in the House of Commons where the government ministers sit

Treasury Bill /'treʒəri bɪl/ *noun* a bill of exchange which does not give any interest and is sold by the government at a discount

treasury bonds /'treʒəri bɒndz/ *plural noun* the documents given to people who lend money to the govern-

ment of the USA, which promise repayment and interest on certain dates

Treasury counsel /ˌtreʒəri 'kaʊnsəl/ *noun* a lawyer who works in the Central Criminal Court on behalf of the Director of Public Prosecutions

Treasury Solicitor /ˌtreʒəri sə 'lɪsɪtə/ *noun* in England, the lawyer who is head of the government's legal department

treaty /'triːti/ *noun* **1.** a written legal agreement between countries ○ *The treaty was signed but never ratified.* ○ *The minister negotiated a commercial treaty* or *a cultural treaty with the French.* **2.** an agreement between individual persons

Treaty of Accession /ˌtriːti əv ək 'seʃn/ *noun* the treaty by which a new Member State joins the European Union, e.g. the treaty by which the UK joined the European Community in 1973

Treaty of Maastricht /ˌtriːti əv 'mɑːstrɪxt/ *noun* the treaty which established the European Union in 1993 on the basis of the European Economic Community set up in 1957. Also called **Treaty on European Union**

Treaty of Paris /ˌtriːti əv 'pærɪs/ *noun* the treaty which established the European Coal and Steel Community in 1951

Treaty of Rome /ˌtriːti əv 'rəʊm/ *noun* the treaty which established the European Economic Community and the European Atomic Energy Community in 1957, and which is the basis of the European Union established in 1993. ◊ **Maastricht Treaty**

trend /trend/ *noun* the general way things are going ○ *a downward trend in inflation* ○ *There is a trend away from old-fashioned party politics.* ○ *The report points to upwards trends in reported cases of international terrorism.*

TRH *abbreviation* Their Royal Highnesses

triarchy /'traɪɑːki/ *noun* government by three people or by three institutions

tribunal /traɪˈbjuːn(ə)l/ *noun* **1.** a court, especially a specialist court outside the judicial system which examines special problems and makes judgments **2.** a court set up, under English law, by the British government to judge or investigate a specific matter

Tribune group /ˈtrɪbjuːn gruːp/ *noun* a group of Labour MPs who support left-wing policies

tribute /ˈtrɪbjuːt/ *noun* a payment made by one ruler or state to another more powerful one

tricolour /ˈtreʒəri bɒnd/ *noun* a flag with three bands of colours like the French flag

trilateral /traɪˈlæt(ə)rəl/ *adjective* involving three states ○ *trilateral negotiations*

trilateralism /traɪˈlæt(ə)rəlɪz(ə)m/ *noun* relations or discussions between three nations, areas or groups

Trimble /ˈtrɪmb(ə)l/, **David** (*b.* 1944) leader of the Ulster Unionist Party (1995–), he had an important role in the peace negotiations that led to the Good Friday peace agreement in Northern Ireland (1998), for which he shared the Nobel Peace Prize (1998). He was first minister of the Northern Irish Assembly (1999–2002) until its suspension.

tripartism /traɪˈpɑːtɪz(ə)m/ *noun* division into three groups

tripartite /traɪˈpɑːtaɪt/ *adjective* formed of three groups or political parties

triplicate /ˈtrɪplɪkət/ *noun* a document with three copies

triumvirate /ˌtrɪˈʌmvɪrət/ *noun* a group of three men, especially three leaders running a country together

troika /ˈtrɔɪkə/ *noun* **1.** a group of three leaders running a country or a party (NOTE: It was originally used with reference to Russia, but now used for three leaders in any country.) **2.** in the European Union, a three-member group consisting of the country which is the current president, together with the previous president and the next one (*EU*)

trooper /ˈtruːpə/ *noun* a member of a mounted police unit

Trotskyism /ˈtrɒtskiɪz(ə)m/ *noun* a communist political theory opposed to Lenin and Stalin's belief in a strong, centralised Russian Communist Party, but in favour of continuous world revolution to prevent power being taken away from the people

Trotskyite /ˈtrɒtskiaɪt/ *noun* a person who supports the ideas of Trotskyism (NOTE: also informally called a **Trot**)

trouble /ˈtrʌb(ə)l/ *noun* □ **troubles** riots or disturbances

trust /trʌst/ *verb* to believe that someone will do something they have promised

trustee /trʌˈstiː/ *noun* **1.** a person who has charge of money or property in trust or a person who is responsible for a family trust ○ *the trustees of the pension fund* **2.** a country appointed by the United Nations to administer another country

trusteeship /trʌˈstiːʃɪp/ *noun* the position of being a trustee ○ *The territory is under United Nations trusteeship.*

tsarism /ˈsɑːrɪz(ə)m/ *noun* government by an emperor who has absolute power

TUC *abbreviation* Trades Union Congress

turncoat /ˈtɜːnkəʊt/ *noun* someone who abandons or betrays a group or cause and joins its opponents

turn down /ˌtɜːn ˈdaʊn/ *verb* to refuse ○ *The Speaker turned down the Opposition's request for an emergency debate.* ○ *The bank turned down their request for a loan.* ○ *The application for a licence was turned down.*

turn out /ˌtɜːn ˈaʊt/ *verb* **1.** to go to vote ○ *Voters turned out in thousands to vote for their sitting MP.* **2.** to throw out a government ○ *The ruling party was turned out in the election.* ○ *Vote for the Opposition and help to turn the government out!*

turnout /'tɜːnaʊt/ *noun* the number of people who vote in an election as a proportion of those who are qualified to vote but do not do so ○ *There was a very low turnout (only 26%) at the municipal elections.* ○ *In general elections, the turnout is usually higher than in local elections.* ○ *We can expect a very high turnout in this constituency.*

turnover /'tɜːnəʊvə/ *noun* the total amount of money a business receives for selling its goods or services in a year

Tweede Kamer *noun* the lower house of the States-General in the Netherlands

twin /twɪn/ *verb* to make a special arrangement between a town in one country and one of similar size or situation in another, involving visits between the two places

twinning /'twɪnɪŋ/ *noun* a special arrangement between a town in one country and one of similar size or situation in another country involving visits between the two places ○ *The district council's town-twinning com-* *mittee decided that Epping should be twinned with Eppingen in Germany.*

two-party system /ˌtuː ˌpɑːti 'sɪstəm/ *noun* the political system in many countries where there are only two large political parties, with the result that any smaller party finds it impossible to get enough votes to form a government

tyrannical /tɪ'rænɪk(ə)l/, **tyrannous** *adjective* cruel and unjust ○ *The people rose up against the tyrannical dictator.*

tyrannise /'tɪrənaɪz/ *verb* to govern a people or community with extreme cruelty and harshness

tyranny /'tɪrəni/ *noun* **1.** (*usually as criticism*) the use of force and fear to rule a country ○ *To arrest so many students on minor charges was an act of tyranny.* **2.** (*usually as criticism*) a government system which uses force and fear to rule

tyrant /'taɪrənt/ *noun* a ruler who rules by force and fear (*used as criticism*)

tzarism /'sɑːrɪz(ə)m/ *noun* another spelling of **tsarism**

U

UDA *abbreviation* Ulster Defence Association

UDI *abbreviation* Unilateral Declaration of Independence

UDR *abbreviation* Ulster Defence Regiment

UK *abbreviation* United Kingdom

UKIP /'juːkɪp/ *abbreviation* United Kingdom Independence Party

Ulster Unionist Party /'ʌlstə 'juːnjənɪst 'pɑːti/ *noun* the largest and most moderate of the Northern Ireland parties committed to the maintenance of the union with the UK. Also called **Official Unionist Party**

ultra /'ʌltrə/ *noun* a person who holds extreme political views, especially extreme conservative views

ultranationalism /ˌʌltrə'næʃ(ə)nə ˌlɪz(ə)m/ *noun* extreme nationalism

ultrapatriot /ˌʌltrə'pætriət/ *noun* someone who is extremely or excessively patriotic

ultraroyalist /ˌʌltrə'rɔɪəlɪst/ *noun* someone who is a very strong supporter of royalism

ultra vires /ˌʌltrə 'vaɪriːz/ *Latin phrase meaning* 'beyond its powers'

Uluk Kenesh *noun* the legislative body in Kyrgyzstan

UN *abbreviation* United Nations

unaligned /ˌʌnə'laɪnd/ *adjective* not associated with any major world power or any political party

un-American /ˌʌnə'laɪn/ *adjective* disloyal to the United States

unanimity /ˌjuːnə'nɪmɪti/ *noun* being completely in agreement

unanimous /juː'nænɪməs/ *adjective* where everyone votes in the same way ○ *There was a unanimous vote* against the proposal. ○ *They reached unanimous agreement.*

unanimous consent /juː ˌnænɪməs kən'sent/ *noun* the agreement to a motion in Congress without a vote because everyone agrees

unanimously /juː'nænɪməsli/ *adverb* with everyone agreeing ○ *The proposals were adopted unanimously.* ○ *The House voted unanimously to condemn the action by the rebels.*

unavoidably /ˌʌnə'vɔɪdəbli/ *adverb* in a way which cannot be avoided ○ *The hearing was unavoidably delayed.*

Uncle Sam /ˌʌŋk(ə)l 'sæm/ *noun* a personification of the government of the United States, shown as a tall thin white man with a white beard, wearing red and white striped trousers, a blue tail coat, and a stovepipe hat with a band of stars

unconstitutional /ˌʌnkɒnstɪ 'tjuːʃ(ə)n(ə)l/ *adjective* not allowed by the rules or laws of a country or organisation ○ *The chairman ruled that the meeting was unconstitutional.* ○ *The Appeal Court ruled that the action of the Attorney-General was unconstitutional.*

uncontested /ˌʌnkən'testɪd/ *adjective* not opposed or defended ○ *He was elected Secretary in an uncontested election.*

uncontroversial /ˌʌnkɒntrə'vɜːʃl/ *adjective* not causing disagreement

undemocratic /ˌʌndemə'krætɪk/ *adjective* not democratic ○ *Everyone must agree that the first-past-the-post system is undemocratic, because a candidate can be elected who has only a minority of the votes cast.*

under /ˈʌndə/ *preposition* **1.** lower than or less than ○ *The interest rate is under 10%.* ○ *Under 20% of MPs voted in the division.* ○ *Children under the age of 18 cannot vote.* **2.** controlled by or according to ○ *regulations under the Police Act* ○ *Under the terms of the agreement, the goods should be delivered in October.* ○ *She does not qualify under section 2 of the 1979 Act.*

undercover agent /ˌʌndəkʌvə ˈeɪdʒənt/ *noun* a spy or policeman working in secret

undermentioned /ˌʌndə ˈmenʃ(ə)nd/ *adjective* mentioned lower down in a document

underrepresent /ˌʌndərepriˈzent/ *verb* to give fewer elected representatives to the members of a group or people in an area than they ought to have ○ *Women are underrepresented in the House of Commons.* ○ *The present system tends to underrepresent minority parties.*

undersecretary /ˌʌndə ˈsekrɪt(ə)ri/ *noun* **1.** a secretary who ranks just below a chief secretary in a government or organisation **2.** a government minister who works for the secretary of state of a government department

undersheriff /ˈʌndəˌʃerɪf/ *noun* a person who is second to a High Sheriff

undesirable alien /ˌʌndɪzaɪrəb(ə)l ˈeɪliən/ *noun* a person who is not a citizen of a country, and who the government considers should not be allowed to stay in that country ○ *She was declared an undesirable alien and deported.*

undischarged bankrupt /ˌʌndɪstʃɑːdʒd ˈbæŋkrʌpt/ *noun* a person who has been declared bankrupt because they owe more money than they can repay, and has not been released from that state by repaying the money (NOTE: a bankrupt cannot become or remain as an MP)

undue influence /ˌʌndjuː ˈɪnfluəns/ *noun* wrongful pressure put on someone which prevents that person from acting independently ○ *The government was accused of putting undue influence on the board of the nationalised industry.*

unelectable /ˌʌnɪˈlektəb(ə)l/ *adjective* certain to be defeated if standing as a candidate for public office, e.g. because of extreme opinions on controversial issues

unemployed /ˌʌnɪmˈplɔɪd/ *adjective, noun* with no paid work, without a job

unemployment /ˌʌnɪmˈplɔɪmənt/ *noun* the fact of people not having jobs ○ *The unemployment figures* or *the figures for unemployment are rising.*

unemployment benefit /ˌʌnɪm ˈplɔɪmənt ˌbenɪfɪt/ *noun* the money paid by the government to someone who is unemployed

unenforceable /ˌʌnɪnˈfɔːsəb(ə)l/ *adjective* impossible to apply or make people accept

UNESCO /juːˈneskəʊ/ *noun* a United Nations agency that promotes international collaboration on culture, education, and science. Full form **United Nations Educational, Scientific, and Cultural Organization**

unfederated /ʌnˈfedəreɪtɪd/ *adjective* not being or belonging to a federation

UNHCR *abbreviation* United Nations High Commission for Refugees

uni- /juːni/ *prefix* meaning single

unicameral /ˌjuːniˈkæmərəl/ *adjective* of a legislature, having only one chamber or house. ◊ **bicameral**

COMMENT: Unicameral legislatures exist in many countries and states, including Denmark, Ecuador, Estonia, Finland, Gabon, Greece, Guatemala, Honduras, Hungary, Iceland, Israel, Kenya, Latvia, Lebanon, Lithuania, Malta, Mongolia, Morocco, Nebraska, New Zealand, Panama, Sweden and Turkey.

UNICEF /ˈjuːnɪsef/ *noun* a United Nations agency that works for the protection and survival of children around the world. Full form **United Nations Children's Fund**

UNIDO /ˌjuːˈniːdəʊ/ *abbreviation* United Nations Industrial Development Organization

unilateral /ˌjuːnɪˈlæt(ə)rəl/ *adjective* on one side only or done by one party only ○ *They took the unilateral decision to cancel the contract.*

Unilateral Declaration of Independence /ˌjuːnɪˌlæt(ə)rəl ˌdeklə-ˌreɪʃ(ə)n əv ˌɪndɪˈpendəns/ *noun* an act whereby a colony announces that it is independent without the agreement of the country to which it belongs. Abbr **UDI**

unilateral disarmament /ˌjuːnɪ-ˈlæt(ə)rəl dɪsˈɑːməmənt/, **unilateral nuclear disarmament** /ˌjuːnɪ-ˌlæt(ə)rəl ˌnjuːkliə dɪsˈɑːməmənt/ *noun* removing all nuclear weapons from a country, even if other countries keep theirs

unilateralism /ˌjuːnɪ-ˈlæt(ə)rəlɪz(ə)m/ *noun* the support for a policy of unilateral nuclear disarmament

unilaterally /ˌjuːnɪˈlæt(ə)rəli/ *adverb* by one party only ○ *They cancelled the contract unilaterally.*

union /ˈjuːnjən/ *noun* **1.** a state of being joined or the act of joining ○ *We support the union of the environmental pressure groups into a federation.* **2.** a group of independent states or organisations which have joined together into a federation **3.** the group of states which formed the United States of America **4.** a trade union **5.** a club or organisation for people with similar interests

Union /ˈjuːnjən/ *noun* **1.** the United States of America **2.** the union of Great Britain and Northern Ireland since 1920

Union Calendar /ˌjuːnjən ˈkælɪndə/ *noun* a list of bills for debate in the House of Representatives which deal with finances

unionised /ˈjuːnjənaɪzd/, **unionized** *adjective* a company where the members of staff belong to a trade union

Unionism /ˈjuːnjənɪz(ə)m/ *noun* **1.** loyalty to the federal union during the Civil War in the United States **2.** support or advocacy since 1920 for the union between Northern Ireland and Great Britain

unionist /ˈjuːniənɪst/ *noun* **1.** a member of a trade union **2.** a person who supports a political union of states or parties

Union Jack /ˌjuːnjən ˈdʒæk/, **Union Flag** /ˈjuːnjən flæg/ *noun* the national flag of the United Kingdom

Union Territory /ˈjuːnjən ˈterətri/ *noun* a territory in India ruled directly by the central government

UNISON /ˈjuːnɪsən/ *noun* the UK's largest trade union (over 1.3 million members), representing people working in public services and utilities. It was formed in 1993 when three major public sector unions, National Association of Local Government Officers (NALGO), National Union of Public Employees (NUPE) and Confederation of Health Service Employers (COHSE), merged.

unitary authority /ˈjuːnɪt(ə)ri ɔːˈθɒrɪti/ *noun* an administrative unit in Great Britain responsible for all local government services in its area, replacing a former system of two tiers of local government

United Kingdom /juːˌnaɪtɪd ˈkɪŋdəm/ *noun* an independent country, formed of England, Wales, Scotland and Northern Ireland ○ *He came to the UK to study.* ○ *Does she have a UK passport?* ○ *Is he a UK citizen?* ◊ **British Isles**. Abbr **UK**

United Kingdom Independence Party /juːˌnaɪtɪd ˌkɪŋdəm ˌɪndɪˈpendəns ˌpɑːti/ *noun* a right-wing party committed to withdrawing Britain from the European Union and opposed to immigration. Abbr **UKIP**

United Nations /juːˌnaɪtɪd ˈneɪʃ(ə)nz/ *noun* an organisation of nations that was formed in 1945 to promote peace, security, and international cooperation. Abbr **UN**

United States Code /juː,naɪtɪd steɪts 'kəʊd/ *noun* a book containing all the permanent laws of the USA, arranged in sections according to subject, and revised from time to time

United States of America /juː,naɪtɪd steɪts əv ə'merɪkə/ *noun* an independent country, a federation of states (originally thirteen, now fifty) in North America. Abbr **USA**

> COMMENT: The federal government (based in Washington D.C.) is formed of a legislature (the Congress) with two chambers (the Senate and House of Representatives), an executive (the President) and a judiciary (headed by the Supreme Court). Each of the fifty states making up the USA has its own legislature and executive (the Governor) as well as its own legal system and constitution.

universal franchise /,juːnɪvɜːs(ə)l 'fræntʃaɪz/, **universal suffrage** /,juːnɪvɜːs(ə)l 'sʌfrɪdʒ/ *noun* the right to vote of all adult members of the population

unlawful /ʌn'lɔːf(ə)l/ *adjective* against the law, illegal ○ *unlawful trespass on property* ○ *unlawful sexual intercourse*

unlawfully /ʌn'lɔːfəli/ *adverb* illegally or in an illegal way ○ *He was charged with unlawfully carrying firearms.*

UNMOVIC *abbreviation* United Nations Monitoring, Verification, and Inspection Commission

UNO *abbreviation* United Nations Organization

unopposed /,ʌnə'pəʊzd/ *adjective* having no one voting against ○ *The Bill had an unopposed second reading in the House.*

unparliamentary /ʌn,pɑːlə'ment(ə)ri/ *adjective* not suitable for Parliament

> COMMENT: Various terms of abuse are considered unparliamentary, in particular words which suggest that an MP has not told the truth. In a recent exchange in the House of Commons, a Member called others 'clowns' and 'drunks'; the Deputy Speaker said: 'Order. That is unparliamentary language, and I must ask the hon. Member to withdraw'. Another recent example occurred when an MP said: 'if the hon. Member were honest, I suspect that he would have to do the same'. *Mr. Speaker:* 'Order. All hon. Members are honest.'.

unparliamentary language /,ʌnpɑːlə,ment(ə)ri 'læŋgwɪdʒ/ *noun* words used in Parliament which are considered to be rude, and which the Speaker may ask the MP to withdraw

unperson /'ʌnpɜːsən/ *noun* someone, especially a public figure, whose existence is not acknowledged officially, often because they have opposed an authoritarian government

unpledged /ʌn'pledʒd/ *adjective* not having promised support for something, e.g. not having promised a vote to a particular candidate in an election

unpolitical /,ʌnpə'lɪtɪk(ə)l/ *adjective* not interested in politics or having no political preference ○ *The protest group is entirely unpolitical.*

unpolled /ʌn'pəʊld/ *adjective* **1.** not having taken part in a survey of public opinion **2.** not having cast a vote at an election **3.** not included in a list of electors

unreported /,ʌnrɪ'pɔːtɪd/ *adjective* **1.** not reported to the police ○ *There are thousands of unreported cases of theft.* **2.** not reported in the Law Reports ○ *Counsel referred the judge to a number of relevant unreported cases.*

unrest /ʌn'rest/ *noun* publicly expressed unhappiness or protest about something by many people, sometimes developing into violent behaviour ○ *Waves of political unrest troubled the country.*

UNRRA *abbreviation* United Nations Relief and Rehabilitation Administration

UNRWA *abbreviation* United Nations Relief and Works Agency

unseat /ʌn'siːt/ *verb* to make a sitting MP lose his seat in an election ○ *She only needs a small swing to have a good chance of unseating the present MP.*

UNSF *abbreviation* United Nations Special Fund for Economic Development

unwritten /ʌnˈrɪt(ə)n/ *adjective* not written or codified in a single document (NOTE: The British Constitution is described as unwritten because it is not contained in a single codified document but is to be found written in numerous different documents and is in some areas dependent on custom)

upcoming /ˈʌpkʌmɪŋ/ *adjective* about to take place soon ○ *the upcoming general elections*

upfront /ʌpˈfrʌnt/ *adjective* **1.** immediate or made in advance ○ *The shop asked for an upfront payment of £100.* **2.** being clear and honest about something, not trying to conceal anything ○ *The minister said she would be upfront about the difficulties facing the government.*

upheaval /ʌpˈhiːv(ə)l/ *noun* a sudden and violent change in a social or political system

upper chamber /ˈʌpə ˈtʃeɪmbə/ *noun* one of the two parts of a parliament that has two chambers, e.g. the British House of Lords or the American Senate. ◊ **lower chamber**

upper class /ˈʌpə klɑːs/ *noun* the richest or most influential people in a society

upper house /ˈʌpə haʊz/ *noun* the more important or older of the two houses or chambers in a bicameral system ○ *After being passed by the legislative assembly, a bill goes to the upper house for further discussion.* Also called **upper chamber** (NOTE: The House of Lords is sometimes described as the upper house in the UK, but has far less power than the House of Commons)

upper middle class /ˌʌpə ˈmɪd(ə)l klɑːs/ *noun* the richer half of the middle section in society, consisting of rich professional and business people

uprising /ˈʌpraɪzɪŋ/ *noun* an attempt to overthrow a government or state by armed force, a rebellion ○ *The left-wing uprising was crushed by the army.*

upset /ˈʌpset/ *noun* an unexpected result, e.g. in an election

urban /ˈɜːbən/ *adjective* referring to a town or city □ **urban decay** the condition where a part of a town becomes old or dirty or ruined, because businesses and wealthy families have moved away from it □ **urban redevelopment, urban renewal** rebuilding old parts of a town to build modern houses and new factories and offices

urban guerrilla /ˈɜːbən ɡəˈrɪlə/ *noun* someone who carries out violent acts in cities to advance a political cause

US, USA *abbreviation* United States of America

USAID /ˌjuː es ˈeɪd/ *noun* a US government agency that provides humanitarian aid and assistance for development to other countries. Full form **United States Agency for International Development**

USS /ˌjuː es ˈes/ *abbreviation* United States Senate

usual channels /ˌjuːʒʊəl ˈtʃæn(ə)lz/ *noun* the way in which much parliamentary business is agreed on in private by the whips and senior MPs of the various parties rather than in open debate

usurp /juːˈzɜːp/ *verb* to take and use a right which is not yours, especially to depose a king or queen and become king or queen yourself ○ *Henry IV usurped the throne from Richard II.* ○ *The councils complained that the new Education Bill would usurp their powers.*

usurpation /ˌjuːzɜːˈpeɪʃ(ə)n/ *noun* taking and using a right which is not yours, especially deposing a king or queen and becoming king or queen yourself

usurper /juːˈzɜːpə/ *noun* a person who usurps power ○ *The army killed the usurper and placed the king back on his throne again.*

utopia /juːˈtəʊpiə/ *noun* an imaginary political state where everything is as good as it could be, which gives people something to aim to achieve. Compare **dystopia** (NOTE: Sir Thomas More published his description of a perfect state in *Utopia* in 1516. The word means 'nowhere' or 'the perfect place' in Greek depending on its spelling)

utopian /juːˈtəʊpiən/ *adjective* perfect, and also difficult to achieve ○ *His utopian ideal of a state was impossible to put into practice.*

utopian socialism /juːˌtəʊpiən ˌsəʊʃəˈlɪz(ə)m/ *noun* a form of socialism based on the belief that a socialist society can be brought about by peacefully persuading those in power to accept it

U-turn /ˈjuː tɜːn/ *noun* a change of policy to do exactly the opposite of what was done before ○ *The Opposition was surprised at the Government's U-turn on defence expenditure.* ○ *The council did a U-turn and passed the development plan for the town centre.*

UU *abbreviation* Ulster Unionist

V

vacant seat /ˈveɪkənt siːt/ *noun* a constituency which has no MP at the moment ○ *The seat became vacant when Mr Smith was made a life peer.*

vacation /vəˈkeɪʃ(ə)n/ *noun* **1.** the period when the courts, or the universities are closed for their holidays **2.** *US* a holiday or period when people are not working

valid /ˈvælɪd/ *adjective* **1.** acceptable because it is true or reasonable ○ *That is not a valid argument* or *excuse.* **2.** possible to use lawfully ○ *ticket which is valid for three months* ○ *The contract is not valid if the signing of it has not been witnessed.* ○ *He was carrying a valid passport.*

valorem /vəˈlɔːrəm/ ♦ **ad valorem**

Value Added Tax /ˌvæljuː ædɪd ˈtæks/ *noun* a tax on goods and services, added as a percentage to the price. Abbr **VAT**

variation /ˌveəriˈeɪʃ(ə)n/ *noun* the amount by which something changes

VAT /ˌviː eɪ ˈtiː, væt/ *abbreviation* Value Added Tax

VAT declaration /ˈvæt dekləˌreɪʃ(ə)n/ *noun* a statement made by a company to say what VAT it has collected

VC *abbreviation* vice chancellor

venue /ˈvenjuː/ *noun* a place for a meeting ○ *The venue for next year's party conference will be Brighton.*

verbatim /vɜːˈbeɪtɪm/ *adjective, adverb* in the exact words ○ *Hansard provides a verbatim account of the proceedings of the House of Commons.*

versa /ˈvɜːsə/ ♦ **vice versa**

vest /vest/ *verb* to transfer to someone a legal right or duty or the legal ownership and possession of land ○ *The property was vested in the trustees.* (NOTE: you vest something **in** or **on** someone)

vested interest /ˌvestɪd ˈɪntrəst/ *noun* a personal reason for wanting something to happen

vet /vet/ *verb* to examine someone carefully to see if they are suitable for a job ○ *All applications are vetted by the Home Office.*

veto /ˈviːtəʊ/ *noun* the right to refuse to allow something to be accepted or to become law ○ *The President has the power of veto over Bills passed by Congress.* ○ *The UK used its veto in the Security Council.* ■ *verb* to refuse to allow something not to be accepted or to become law ○ *The resolution was vetoed by the president.* ○ *The council has vetoed all plans to hold protest marches in the centre of town.* (NOTE: The plural is **vetoes**.)

COMMENT: In the United Nations Security Council, each of the five permanent members has a veto. In the USA, the President may veto a bill sent to him by Congress, provided he does so within ten days of receiving it. The bill then returns to Congress for further discussion, and the President's veto can be overridden by a two-thirds majority in both the House of Representatives and the Senate.

vice /vaɪs/ *Latin word meaning* 'in the place of' ○ *was present: Councillor Smith (vice Councillor Brown)*

vice- /vaɪs/ *prefix* a deputy or second in command ○ *He is the vice-chairman of an industrial group.* ○ *She was appointed to the vice-chairmanship of the committee.*

vice chancellor /ˌvaɪs ˈtʃɑːns(ə)lə/ *noun* a deputy for the chancellor of a country

vice-consul /ˌvaɪs ˈkɒnsəl/ *noun* an officer who acts as the deputy for the official representing a country's commercial interest in another country

vicegerent /ˈvaɪsˌgerənt/ *noun* a deputy appointed to act on the authority of a ruler or magistrate, especially in administrative duties

vice-president /ˌvaɪs ˈprezɪd(ə)nt/ *noun* an official of a rank below a president, who can take the president's place if necessary ○ *When President Kennedy was assassinated, Vice-President Johnson became president.*

COMMENT: In the USA, the Vice-President is the president (i.e. the chairman) of the Senate. He also succeeds a president if the president dies in office (as Vice-President Johnson succeeded President Kennedy).

viceregal /ˌvaɪsˈriːg(ə)l/ *adjective* referring to a viceroy ○ *The reception was held at the Viceregal Palace.*

viceregent /ˌvaɪsˈriːdʒənt/ *noun* a deputy for the regent of a country

vicereine /ˈvaɪsren/ *noun* the wife of a viceroy

viceroy /ˈvaɪsrɔɪ/ *noun* a person who represents a king or queen in a colony ○ *In the nineteenth century, India was ruled by viceroys.*

viceroyalty /ˌvaɪsˈrɔɪəlti/ *noun* **1.** the office, term of office, or authority of a viceroy **2.** an area that is governed by a viceroy

vice versa /ˈvaɪsi ˈvɜːsə/ *Latin phrase meaning* 'reverse position': the other way round

videlicet /ˈvɪdiːlɪset/ *Latin word meaning* 'that is' or 'namely' (NOTE: usually abbreviated to **viz.**: *the Education Committee has three subcommittees, viz. Schools, Further Education and Training*)

village /ˈvɪlɪdʒ/ *noun* a group of houses and shops in a country area, smaller than a town

violate /ˈvaɪəleɪt/ *verb* to break a rule or a law ○ *The council has violated the planning regulations.* ○ *The action of the government violates the international treaty on commercial shipping.*

violation /ˌvaɪəˈleɪʃ(ə)n/ *noun* the act of breaking a rule ○ *The number of traffic violations has increased.* ○ *The court criticised the violations of the treaty on human rights.*

VIP *abbreviation* very important person ○ *Seats have been arranged for the VIPs at the front of the hall.*

virement /ˈvaɪəmənt/ *noun* the transfer of money from one account to another or from one section of a budget to another ○ *The council may use the virement procedure to transfer money from one area of expenditure to another.*

virtute officio /vɜːˈtuːteɪ ɒˈfɪsɪəʊ/ *Latin phrase meaning* 'by virtue of his office'

visa /ˈviːzə/ *noun* a special document or special stamp in a passport which allows someone to enter a country ○ *You will need a visa before you go to the USA.* ○ *He filled in his visa application form.*

viscount /ˈvaɪkaʊnt/ *noun* a member of the peerage, ranking between an earl and a baron

viscountess /ˈvaɪkaʊntes/ *noun* a woman who is the wife of a viscount, or who holds the rank of viscount

vital statistics /ˌvaɪt(ə)l stəˈtɪstɪks/ *plural noun* figures dealing with births, marriages and deaths in a district

viz ♦ **videlicet**

voice vote /ˈvɔɪs vəʊt/ *noun* a vote in Congress where the members shout Aye (Yes) or No

voluntarism /ˈvɒləntərɪz(ə)m/ *noun* the belief that the process of collective bargaining or the organisation of trade unions should be interfered with by government

voluntary services /ˈvɒlənt(ə)ri ˈsɜːvɪsɪz/ *plural noun* organisations which give free services or help to people

vote /vəʊt/ *noun* 1. marking a paper or holding up your hand, to show your opinion or to show who you want to be elected □ **to take a vote on a proposal, to put a proposal to the vote** to ask people present at a meeting to say if they agree or do not agree with the proposal □ **the French President is elected by popular vote** he is elected by a majority vote of all the people in France 2. the right to vote in elections ○ *Women were given the vote in 1928.* 3. the total number of votes cast □ **the vote was up on the last election** more votes were cast this time than the time before ■ *verb* to show an opinion by marking a paper or by holding up your hand at a meeting ○ *The meeting voted to close the factory.* ○ *52% of the members voted for Mr Smith as Chairman.* □ **to vote for a proposal, to vote against a proposal** to say that you agree or do not agree with a proposal □ **he was voted into the chair** he was elected chairman

vote-catcher /vəʊt ˈkætʃə/ *noun* same as **vote-winner**

vote down /ˌvəʊt ˈdaʊn/ *verb* to defeat a motion or proposal by voting against it ○ *The proposal was voted down.*

vote in /ˌvəʊt ˈɪn/ *verb* □ **to vote someone in** to elect someone ○ *the Tory candidate was voted in*

voteless /ˈvəʊtləs/ *adjective* without the right to choose or express a political opinion by voting

vote of confidence /ˌvəʊt əv ˈkɒnfɪd(ə)ns/ *noun* a vote in which voters show their approval of the leadership of a party or policy

vote of no confidence /ˌvəʊt əv nəʊ ˈkɒnfɪd(ə)ns/ *noun* same as **con-**fidence vote ○ *After the Commons passed a vote of no confidence in the government, the Prime Minister called a general election.*

vote out /ˌvəʊt ˈaʊt/ *verb* □ **to vote someone out** to make someone lose an election ○ *the government was voted out of office within a year*

voter /ˈvəʊtə/ *noun* a person who votes or is eligible to vote ○ *Voters stayed away from the polls because of the bad weather.*

voter alienation /ˈvəʊtə ˌeɪliə ˈneɪʃ(ə)n/ *noun* the feeling of many voters that, since voting does not produce the changes in their lives that they want, they have no motivation to vote

voter apathy /ˈvəʊtə ˈæpəθi/ *noun* lack of interest in voting in local and national elections, especially when one party regularly has a large majority or when people feel they have little influence in influencing decisions that affect their lives

vote through /ˌvəʊt ˈθruː/ *verb* to vote to accept ○ *The proposal was voted through by a large majority.*

vote-winner /ˈvəʊt ˈwɪnə/ *noun* a policy or strategy that will win many votes in an election

voting /ˈvəʊtɪŋ/ *noun* the act of making a vote

voting card /ˈvəʊtɪŋ kɑːd/, **voting paper** /ˈvəʊtɪŋ ˌpeɪpə/ *noun* the paper on which the voter puts a cross to show for whom he or she wants to vote

voting patterns /ˈvəʊtɪŋ ˌpætənz/ *plural noun* the tendency of voters to vote in a particular way

voting rights /ˈvəʊtɪŋ raɪts/ *plural noun* the rights of shareholders to vote at company meetings

W

Wag the Dog syndrome /ˌwæg ðə ˈdɒg ˌsɪndrəʊm/ *noun* a situation in which a US president uses military attacks on other nations to draw intense public and media scrutiny away from a personal scandal

waive /weɪv/ *verb* to give up a legal right ○ *He waived his claim to the estate.*

waiver /ˈweɪvə/ *noun* a situation in which someone gives up a legal right to something ○ *If you want to work without a permit, you will have to apply for a waiver.*

Wales Office /ˈweɪlz ˌɒfɪs/ *noun* a UK government department responsible for representing Welsh interests within the government of the United Kingdom (NOTE: The Welsh name is **Swyddfa Cymru.**)

war /wɔː/ *noun* the situation where one country fights another ○ *The two countries are at war.*

war crime /ˈwɔː kraɪm/ *noun* an illegal action committed by someone during a period of armed conflict ○ *A number of former Nazis were brought to trial for war crimes committed during the Second World War.*

ward /wɔːd/ *noun* **1.** a division of a town or city for administrative purposes. ◊ **electoral ward 2.** a child protected by a guardian or by a court

warden /ˈwɔːd(ə)n/ *noun* **1.** a person who is in charge of an institution ○ *The block of flats have a warden who helps elderly residents.* **2.** a person who sees that rules are obeyed

ward heeler /ˈwɔːd ˌhiːlə/ *noun* a person who does minor tasks for a local politician

wardship /ˈwɔːdʃɪp/ *noun* being in charge of a child or the power of a court to take on itself the rights and responsibilities of parents in the interests of a child (NOTE: no plural)

war on terror /ˌwɔː ɒn ˈterə/ *noun* the struggle against international terrorism which President Bush declared following the attacks on New York and Washington of 11 September 2001 ○ *Critics of the President were quick to point out that the problem with a war on terror is that you never know when you have won it.*

warring /ˈwɔːrɪŋ/ *adjective* fighting ○ *the warring factions on the town council*

Washington /ˈwɒʃɪŋtən/, **George** (1732–99) the first president of the United States

watchdog /ˈwɒtʃdɒg/, **watchdog body** /ˈwɒtʃdɒg ˌbɒdi/ *noun* a body which watches something, especially government departments, or businesses, to see that regulations are being obeyed ○ *The Post Office Users Council acts as a watchdog.*

Ways and Means /ˌweɪz ən ˈmiːnz/ ♦ **Chairman of Ways and Means** ■ *noun* in the United States, a legislative committee in charge of methods of raising money for government

Ways and Means resolution /ˌweɪz ən ˈmiːnz ˌrezəluːʃ(ə)n/ *noun* a Supply Bill, especially the annual budget proposals

WDA *abbreviation* Welsh Development Agency

weapons of mass destruction /ˌwepənz əv ˌmæs dɪsˈtrʌkʃən/ *noun* armaments which can kill large numbers of people, e.g., nuclear, biological and chemical weapons. Abbr **WMD**

Weber, Max /'veɪbə/ *noun* the German philosopher (1864–1920) who contributed most to the study of sociology (NOTE: Weber is famous for analysing authority into three forms: charismatic, traditional and rational.)

weights and measures department /ˌweɪts ən 'meʒəz dɪ ˌpɑːtmənt/ *noun* a council department dealing with weighing and measuring machines used in shops, and other consumer matters (NOTE: usually called the **Trading Standards Department**)

welfare /'welfeə/ *noun* the health, comfort and safety of a person, animal, or group ○ *It is the duty of the juvenile court to see to the welfare of children in care.*

welfare state /ˌwelfeə 'steɪt/ *noun* a state which spends a large amount of money to make sure that its citizens all have adequate housing, education, public transport and health services

Welsh Assembly /ˌwelʃ ə'sembli/ ♦ **National Assembly for Wales**

West /west/ *adjective, adverb, noun* **1.** one of the directions on the Earth's surface, the direction facing the setting sun **2.** a region of a country, as opposed to the East **3.** □ **the West** the democratic countries of Europe and North America, as opposed to the former Communist countries

Western European Union /ˌwestən ˌjʊərəpiːən 'juːnjən/ *noun* a union formed in 1954 with the aim of harmonising defence and security in the region, now including Belgium, France, Germany, Greece, Italy, Luxembourg, the Netherlands, Portugal, Spain and the United Kingdom as full members, and Bulgaria, the Czech Republic, Denmark, Estonia, Hungary, Iceland, Ireland, Latvia, Lithuania, Norway, Poland, Romania, the Slovak Republic and Turkey as associate members. Abbr **WEU**

West Lothian question /ˌwest 'ləʊtiən ˌkwestʃən/ *noun* the question that sets out a major issue of devolved government in the UK, that of the justice of allowing Westminster MPs representing Scottish constituencies to vote on issues affecting England and other parts of the UK, when non-Scottish MPs cannot vote on equivalent Scottish issues that are dealt with by the Scottish Assembly

Westminster /'westmɪnstə/ *noun* **1.** a borough in London, where the Houses of Parliament are **2.** the British parliament or parliamentary system

West Wing /'west wɪŋ/ *noun* the US president's senior staff and advisers

wet /wet/ *noun* a Conservative politician whose policies are regarded as more liberal than the mainstream of conservative opinion

WEU *abbreviation* Western European Union

whatever /ˌwɒtsəʊ'evə/, **whatsoever** *adjective* of any sort, at all ○ *There is no substance whatsoever in the report.* ○ *The police found no suspicious documents whatsoever.* ○ *There is nothing whatsoever to suggest that she intends to leave the country.* (NOTE: always used after a noun and after a negative)

wheeling and dealing /ˌwiːlɪŋ ən 'diːlɪŋ/ *noun* discussions and bargaining between political parties or groups or members of a committee to obtain a general agreement for something ○ *After some wheeling and dealing, the subcommittee members were selected.* ♦ **horse-trading**

whereas /weər'æz/ *conjunction* taking into consideration that ○ *whereas the contract between the two parties stipulated that either party may withdraw at six months' notice*

whereby /weə'baɪ/ *adverb* by which ○ *a deed whereby ownership of the property is transferred*

wherein /weər'ɪn/ *adverb* in which ○ *a document wherein the regulations are listed*

whereof /weər'ɒv/ *adverb* of which

whereon /weər'ɒn/ *adverb* on which ○ *land whereon a dwelling is constructed*

wheresoever /ˌweəsəʊ'evə/ *adverb* in any place where ○ *the insurance covering jewels wheresoever they may be kept*

Whig /wɪg/ *noun* the old name for a member of a political party which later became the Liberal Party in Britain, and is now called the Liberal Democratic Party

whip /wɪp/ *noun* **1.** an MP who controls the attendance of other MPs of his party in the House of Commons or Lords, and who tries to makes sure that all MPs vote as their party wants **2.** the instructions given by a whip to other MPs, telling them which business is on the agenda and underlining items where a vote may be taken

COMMENT: A party may decide to withdraw the Whip from an MP as a punishment for opposing it in some way. This prevents the MP from being involved in the party's activities in the parliament, although they remain as an MP and usually sit as an Independent until the Whip is restored to them.

whip in /ˌwɪp 'ɪn/ *verb* to keep the members of a political party in line with the party's aims

Whitehall /'waɪthɔːl/ *noun* a street in London, where several ministries have their offices (NOTE: used to refer to the Government or more particularly to the civil service: *Whitehall sources suggest that the plan will be adopted*; *there is a great deal of resistance to the idea in Whitehall*)

White House /ˌwaɪt 'haʊs/ *noun* the building in Washington D.C., where the President of the USA lives and works (NOTE: also used to mean the President himself, or the US government: *White House officials disclaimed any knowledge of the letter*;

the White House press secretary has issued a statement)

White Paper /ˌwaɪt 'peɪpə/ *noun* a report issued by the government as a statement of government policy on a particular problem, often setting out proposals for changes to legislation for discussion before a Bill is drafted. Compare **Green Paper**

winding up /ˌwaɪndɪŋ 'ʌp/ *noun* **1.** the ending of a meeting ○ *In his winding-up speech the Home Secretary warned the Commons of the seriousness of the situation.* **2.** the closing of a company and selling its assets

wind up /ˌwaɪnd 'ʌp/ *verb* **1.** to end a meeting or a debate ○ *She wound up the meeting with a vote of thanks to the committee.* ○ *The Home Secretary wound up for the government.* **2.** to close a company and sell its assets

wing /wɪŋ/ *noun* a group within a political party or movement that has distinct beliefs, especially either of two broad groupings, one more conservative, the other more liberal in its views

WMD *abbreviation* weapons of mass destruction

woman police constable /ˌwʊmən pəˌliːs 'kʌnstəb(ə)l/ *noun* in the United Kingdom, Canada, Australia, and New Zealand, a woman police officer of the lowest rank. Abbr **WPC**

women's suffrage /ˈwɪmɪnz 'sʌfrɪdʒ/ *noun* the right of women to vote in elections

wonk /wɒŋk/ *noun* an expert in matters of policy, especially in government, the economy, or diplomacy ○ *a policy wonk*

Woolsack /'wʊlsæk/ *noun* the seat of the Lord Chancellor in the House of Lords (NOTE: the Lord Chancellor is unlikely to sit for much longer on the Woolsack since proposals introduced in 2003–4 will abolish his office)

COMMENT: It is really a large cushion stuffed with wool, dating from the time when the wool trade was very important.

wording /'wɜːdɪŋ/ *noun* a series of words ○ *Did you understand the wording of the contract?* (NOTE: no plural)

Workers' Revolutionary Party /ˌwɜːkəz ˌrevəˈluːʃ(ə)n(ə)ri ˌpɑːti/ *noun* a Marxist political party in the United Kingdom

working class /ˌwɜːkɪŋ ˈklɑːs/ *noun* the people in low-paid jobs

World Bank /ˌwɜːld ˈbæŋk/ *noun* a specialised agency of the United Nations that guarantees loans to member nations for reconstruction and development (NOTE: The official name is **International Bank for Reconstruction and Development**.)

World Trade Organization /'wɜːld ˈtreɪd ɔːgənaɪˈzeɪʃn/ *noun* the international treaty which aims to try to reduce restrictions in trade between countries, and which replaced GATT. Abbr **WTO**

COMMENT: Formed on 1st January 1995 to replace the General Agreement on Tariffs and Trade (GATT).

world war /ˌwɜːld ˈwɔː/ *noun* a war involving several countries on each side, with fighting taking place in many parts of the world

WPC *abbreviation* woman police constable

writ /rɪt/ *noun* **1.** a legal document which begins an action in the High Court ○ *He issued writs for libel in connection with allegations made in a Sunday newspaper.* **2.** the legal document ordering that an election or a by-election should be held □ **to move a**

writ to propose in the House of Commons that a by-election should be held

write in /ˌraɪt ˈɪn/ *verb US* to vote for a candidate whose name does not appear on the ballot paper, by writing the candidate's name on it

write-in /'raɪt ɪn/ *noun* **1.** a vote cast in an election by adding someone's name to the ballot paper **2.** a candidate added to a ballot paper by a voter

write-in candidate /ˌraɪt ɪn ˈkændɪdeɪt/ *noun* a candidate whose name has been written by the voters on their ballot papers

writ of summons /ˌrɪt əv ˈsʌmənz/ *noun* notice from the Lord Chancellor asking a peer to attend the House of Lords

written answer /'rɪt(ə)n ˈɑːnsə/ *noun* a formal reply to a question put in writing to a Minister

written question /'rɪt(ə)n ˈkwestʃ(ə)n/ *noun* a question presented to a Minister in writing, usually dated two days after it is presented and answered within seven days of that date. If an answer is needed by an earlier date the question receives priority and is known as a 'question for answer on a named day', indicated by the letter N in the Order Book. However the answer may simply be that the Minister will answer the question as soon as possible.

WRP *abbreviation* Worker's Revolutionary Party

WTO *abbreviation* World Trade Organization

XYZ

xenophobe /ˈzenəfəʊb/ *noun* a person who hates foreigners

xenophobia /ˌzenəˈfəʊbiə/ *noun* the hatred of foreigners

xenophobic /ˌzenəˈfəʊbɪk/ *adjective* showing hatred of foreigners

yah-boo politics /ˌjɑː ˈbuː ˌpɒlɪtɪks/ *plural noun* politics in which parties automatically criticise and reject any idea put forward by an opposing party, regardless of its merits

Yang di-Pertuan Agong /ˈjæŋ dɪ ˈpɜːtwæn ˈægɒŋ/ *noun* the title given to the head of state of the Malaysian Federation, who is elected for five years by the rulers of the thirteen states which make up the federation

Yard /jɑːd/ *noun* same as **Scotland Yard**

YC *abbreviation* Young Conservative

yea and nay /ˌjeɪ ən ˈneɪ/ *noun* old forms of 'yes' and 'no' □ **yea and nay vote** a vote in a legislature where members say 'yes' or 'no'

zero-rated /ˌzɪərəʊ ˈreɪtɪd/ *adjective* having a Value Added Tax rate of 0%

zero-rating /ˈzɪərəʊ ˌreɪtɪŋ/ *noun* rating an item at 0% Value Added Tax

zionism /ˈzaɪənɪz(ə)m/ *noun* the belief that the Jewish people should have a homeland, and that Israel's independence and security should be defended

zionist /ˈzaɪənɪst/ *noun* a supporter of the belief that the Jewish people should have a homeland and that Israel's independence and security should be defended ■ *adjective* referring to zionism

zone /zəʊn/ *verb* to order that land in a district shall be used only for one type of building ○ *The land is zoned for industrial use.*

zoning /ˈzəʊnɪŋ/ *noun* an order by a local council that land shall be used only for one type of building (NOTE: no plural)

SUPPLEMENTS

Legislative Procedure in the United Kingdom

Legislative Procedure in the European Union

Legislative Procedure in the United States of America

United Kingdom Court Structure

United States of America Federal Court Structure

The United Kingdom: Members of the Cabinet

Prime Ministers of Great Britain

Structure of A British Government Department:
The Department of Trade and Industry

Kings and Queens of England

The United States of America: Members of the Cabinet

Presidents of the United States of America

Legislative procedure in the United Kingdom

Green Paper Stage	a paper discussing the issues surrounding the proposed bill (optional)
White Paper Stage	a paper stating current policy on the issues surrounding the proposed bill (optional)
Draft Bill Stage	the wording of the Bill is drafted
First Reading	the Bill is presented formally in Parliament, usually in the House of Commons, as a reading with no debate or decision
Second Reading	the Bill is read again to the House and a debate takes place
Committee stage	a standing committee (a committee of about 18 house members, more for long or complicated bills) debates whether each clause and schedule of the Bill should be kept or dropped
Report Stage	the whole house looks at the amendments proposed by the standing committee and propose and debate any of their own
Third Reading Stage	the whole redrafted Bill is read once more in the House and briefly discussed
Lords Approval Stage	the House of Lords takes the Bill and goes through the same procedure from First to Third Reading, debating any amendments. The Lords and Commons agree on a final text
Royal Assent Stage	royal approval is given and the Bill becomes a statute (Act of Parliament)

Important Note: The Parliament Act

The entire process must take place in one Session of Parliament, meaning that a Bill may not be passed purely because it has run out of time. This means that the House of Lords may 'kill' a Bill they don't wish to pass (for example the Hunting Bill 2002) by taking an overly long time to discuss it. In this case the Parliament Act means that the Bill can be reintroduced and passed in the following Session *without* the approval of the Lords, with the following conditions:

1.	The Lords had enough time to debate it before the end of the session (at least one month).

2.	The wording of the Bill has not changed since the last presentation.

3.	One year has passed since the Bill was given its Second Reading in the Commons.

Private Members' Bills go through the same procedure from First Reading. However, there is intense competition for the little Parliamentary time available for considering these. Unless the Bill is completely uncontroversial it is likely to be formally objected to at some stage and therefore dropped; otherwise it is more or less 'nodded through' without much debate.

Legislative procedure in the European Union

Proposal	the European Commission drafts the text of a Bill
First Reading	the European Parliament submits the Bill to a committee reading and a report is prepared with suggested amendments
Common Position	the European Council either accepts the amended Bill or suggests its own amendments (NB this is the first point at which the Bill can be passed)
Recommendation	a further committee assessment is undertaken of the Council's proposed amendments at Parliament and a recommendation given
Second Reading	Parliament debates the committee's report and vote by absolute majority whether to accept the Council's amendments and on further amendments of their own
Amended proposal	the Commission looks at Parliament's second reading decisions and drafts an amended proposal for the Council, who vote whether to accept or modify it (this is the second point at which the Bill can be passed)
Conciliation committee	a committee of members from both the Council and Parliament meet to agree on a joint text
Third Reading	Parliament meets to finally discuss whether to adopt the Bill as law. If no mutual agreement can be reached the Bill will lapse.

Legislative procedure in the United States of America

Introduction	the draft Bill is submitted to the House without reading or debate (any time while the House is in session)
Referral to Committee	the Bill is published and assigned an identification number, then sent to the appropriate committee (of 19) according to its subject
Committee Action 1	relevant offices and departments give their input, reports are prepared on the validity of the Bill and committee meetings are held
Committee Action 2	a public hearing may be held before a subcommittee with the questioning of witnesses and the attendance of interested parties
Markup	the subcommittee prepares a report on the hearing with any relevant amendments to the Bill
Final Committee Action	the full committee reads and amends the Bill and either reports it back favourably to the House, tables it or discharges it (thereby preventing it from progressing any further), or reports it back without recommendation (rare)
House Floor Consideration	the committee report is debated in the House and any further amendments voted on
Resolving Differences	the Bill is sent to the Senate for consideration and an identical version is agreed on by both bodies, possibly with the help of a mediating committee
Final Step	the Bill is approved (signed) by the President and becomes a Law

United Kingdom court structure

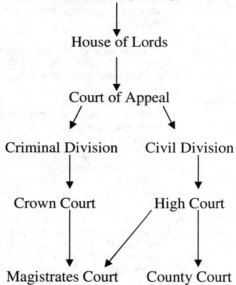

United States of America Federal court structure

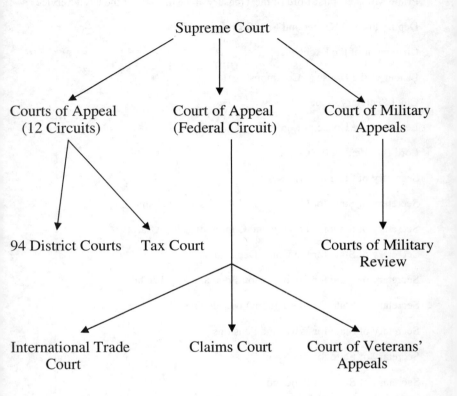

The United Kingdom: Members of the Cabinet

Prime Minister, First Lord of the Treasury and Minister for the Civil Service

Deputy Prime Minister and First Secretary of State

Chancellor of the Exchequer

Leader of the House of Commons

Chief Secretary to the Treasury

Leader of the House of Lords

Lord President of the Council

Secretary of State for Wales

Secretary of State for Constitutional Affairs (Lord Chancellor)

Secretary of State for Foreign and Commonwealth Affairs

Secretary of State for the Home Department

Secretary of State for Environment, Food and Rural Affairs

Secretary of State for International Development

Secretary of State for Work and Pensions

Secretary of State for Transport

Secretary of State for Scotland

Secretary of State for Health

Secretary of State for Northern Ireland

Secretary of State for Defence

Secretary of State for Trade and Industry

Secretary of State for Education and Skills

Secretary of State for Culture, Media and Sport

Parliamentary Secretary to the Treasury (Government Chief Whip)

Prime Ministers of Great Britain

Tony Blair (Labour)
1997 – Present
John Major (Conservative)
1990 – 1997
Margaret Thatcher (Conservative)
1979 – 1990
James Callaghan (Labour)
1976 – 1979
Harold Wilson (Labour)
1974 – 1976
Edward Heath (Conservative)
1970 – 1974
Harold Wilson (Labour)
1964 – 1970
Sir Alec Douglas-Home
(Conservative)
1963 – 1964
Harold Macmillan (Conservative)
1957 – 1963
Sir Anthony Eden (Conservative)
1955 – 1957
Winston Churchill (Conservative)
1951 – 1955
Clement Attlee (Labour)
1945 – 1951
Winston Churchill (Conservative)
1940 – 1945
Neville Chamberlain (Conservative)
1937 – 1940
Stanley Baldwin (Conservative)
1935 – 1937
J Ramsey Macdonald (Coalition)
1931 – 1935
J Ramsey Macdonald (Labour)
1929 – 1931
Stanley Baldwin (Conservative)
1924 – 1929
J Ramsey MacDonald (Labour)
1924
Stanley Baldwin (Conservative)
1923 – 1924
A Bonar Law (Conservative)
1922 – 1923
David Lloyd George (Liberal)
1916 – 1922

H H Asquith (Liberal)
1908 – 1916
Sir Henry Campbell-Bannerman
(Liberal)
1905 – 1908
A J Balfour (Conservative)
1902 – 1905
Marquess of Salisbury
(Conservative)
1895 – 1902
Earl of Rosebery (Liberal)
1894 – 1895
W E Gladstone (Liberal)
1892 – 1894
Marquess of Salisbury
(Conservative)
1886 – 1892
W E Gladstone (Liberal)
1886
Marquess of Salisbury
(Conservative)
1885 – 1886
W E Gladstone (Liberal)
1880 – 1885
Benjamin Disraeli (Conservative)
1874 – 1880
W E Gladstone (Liberal)
1868 – 1874
Benjamin Disraeli (Conservative)
1868
Earl of Derby (Conservative)
1866 – 1868
Earl Russell (Liberal)
1865 – 1866
Viscount Palmerston (Liberal)
1859 – 1865
Earl of Derby (Conservative)
1858 – 1859
Viscount Palmerston (Liberal)
1855 – 1858
Earl of Aberdeen (Conservative)
1852 – 1855
Earl Of Derby (Conservative)
1852
Lord John Russell (Whig)
1846 –1852

Sir Robert Peel (Tory)
1841 – 1846

Viscount Melbourne (Whig)
1835 – 1841

Sir Robert Peel (Tory)
1834 – 1835

Duke of Wellington (Tory)
1834

Viscount Melbourne (Whig)
1834

Earl Grey (Whig)
1830 – 1834

Duke of Wellington (Tory)
1828 –1830

Viscount Goderich (Tory)
1827 – 1828

George Canning (Tory)
1827

Earl of Liverpool (Tory)
1812 – 1827

Spencer Perceval (Tory)
1809 – 1812

Duke of Portland (Tory)
1807 – 1809

Lord Grenville (Whig)
1806 – 1807

William Pitt (Tory)
1804 – 1806

Henry Addington (Tory)
1801 – 1804

William Pitt (Tory)
1783 – 1801

Duke of Portland (Tory)
1783

Earl of Shelburne (Whig)
1782 – 1783

Marquess of Rockingham (Whig)
1782

Lord North (Tory)
1770 – 1782

Duke of Grafton (Whig)
1768 – 1770

Earl of Chatham (Whig)
1766 – 1768

Marquess of Rockingham (Whig)
1765 – 1766

George Grenville (Whig)
1763 – 1765

Earl of Bute (Tory)
1762 – 1763

Duke of Newcastle (Whig)
1757 – 1762

Duke of Devonshire (Whig)
1756 – 1757

Duke of Newcastle (Whig)
1754 – 1756

Henry Pelham (Whig)
1743 – 1754

Earl of Wilmington (Whig)
1742 – 1743

Sir Robert Walpole (Whig)
1721 – 1742

Structure of a British Government Department: The Department of Trade and Industry

Minister
Secretary of State for Trade and Industry
Ministers of State
Minister for E-Commerce and Competitiveness
        Private Secretary
Minister of State (Trade)
        Private Secretary
Minister of State for Industry and the Regions
        Private Secretary
Minister for Women and Equality
        Private Secretary
Minister of State for International Trade and Investment
        Private Secretary

Parliamentary Under-Secretaries of State
Minister for Employment Relations, Competition and Consumers
        Private Secretary
Parliamentary Under-Secretary of State for Science and Innovation
        Private Secretary
Parliamentary Under-Secretary of State for Small Business and Enterprise
        Private Secretary

Officials
Permanent Secretary
        Private Secretary

Directorates
Director General for the Business Group
Director General for the Innovation Group
Director General for the Energy Group
Director General for the Fair Markets Group
Director General for the Services Group
Director General for the Legal Services Group

Office of Science and Technology
Head of the Office of Science and Technology
Chief Scientific Adviser
Director of Transdepartmental Science and Technology
Director General of Research Councils
Director of the Science and Engineering Base Group

Strategy Unit
Director of Strategy
Chief Economic Adviser
Director General of Economics

UK Trade and Investment
Group Chief Executive of UK Trade and Investment
Chief Executive
Deputy Chief Executive
Corporate Strategy and Communications Group

Kings and Queens of England since 1066

House of Windsor
Elizabeth II
Head of the
Commonwealth
1952 – Present
George VI
1936 – 1952
Edward VIII
1936
George V
1910 – 1936

House of Saxe-Coburg
Edward VII
1901 – 1910

House of Hanover
Victoria
1837 – 1901
William IV
1830 – 1837
George IV
1820 – 1830
George III
1760 – 1820
George II
1727 – 1760
George I
1714 – 1727

House of Stuart
Anne
1702 – 1714
William III
1694 – 1702

Mary II & William III
1689 – 1694
James II
1685 – 1688
Charles II
1660 – 1685
The Commonwealth
1649 – 1659
Charles I
1625 – 1649
James I
1603 – 1625

House of Tudor
Elizabeth I
1558 – 1603
Mary I
1553 – 1558
Jane
1553 (reigned for 14 days)
Edward VI
1547 – 1553
Henry VIII
1509 – 1547
Henry VII
1485 – 1509

House of York
Richard III
1483 – 1485
Edward V
1483
Edward IV
1461 – 1483

House of Lancaster
Henry VI
1422 – 1461
Henry V
1413 –1422
Henry IV
1399 – 1413

House of Plantagenet
Richard II
1377 – 1399
Edward III
1327 – 1377
Edward II
1307 – 1327
Edward I
1272 – 1307
Henry III
1216 – 1272
John
1199 – 1216
Richard I
1189 – 1199
Henry II
1154 – 1189

House of Normandy
Stephen
1135 – 1154
Henry I
1100 – 1135
William II
1087 – 1100
William I
1066 – 1087

The United States of America: Members of the Cabinet

The President of the United States

The Vice-President of the United States

Secretary of State

Secretary of the Treasury

Secretary of Defense

Secretary of Commerce

Attorney-General

Secretary of the Interior

Secretary of Agriculture

Secretary of Labor

Secretary of Health and Human Services

Secretary of Housing and Urban Development

Secretary of Transportation

Secretary of Energy

Secretary of Education

Secretary of Veterans' Affairs

Ambassador to the United Nations

US Trade Representative

Administrator, Environmental Protection Agency

Director, Office of Management and Budget

National Security Adviser

White House Chief of Staff

Presidents of the United States of America

George W Bush (Republican)
2001 – Present
William Clinton (Democrat)
1993 – 2001
George Bush (Republican)
1989 – 1993
Ronald Reagan (Republican)
1981 – 1989
Jimmy Carter (Democrat)
1977 – 1981
Gerald Ford (Republican)
1974 – 1977
Richard M Nixon (Republican)
1969 – 1974
Lyndon B Johnson (Democrat)
1963 – 1969
John F Kennedy (Democrat)
1961 – 1963
Dwight D Eisenhower (Republican)
1953 – 1961
Harry S Truman (Democrat)
1945 – 1953
Franklin D Roosevelt (Democrat)
1933 – 1945
Herbert Hoover (Republican)
1929 – 1933
Calvin Coolidge (Republican)
1923 – 1929
Warren Harding (Republican)
1921 – 1923
Woodrow Wilson (Democrat)
1913 – 1921
William H Taft (Republican)
1909 – 1913
Theodore Roosevelt (Republican)
1901 – 1909
William McKinley (Republican)
1897 – 1901
Grover Cleveland (Democrat)
1893 – 1897
Benjamin Harrison (Republican)
1889 – 1893
Grover Cleveland (Democrat)
1885 – 1889
Chester Arthur (Republican)
1881 – 1885

James Garfield (Republican)
1881
Rutherford Hayes (Republican)
1877 – 1881
Ulysses S Grant (Republican)
1869 – 1877
Andrew Johnson (Republican)
1865 – 1869
Abraham Lincoln (Republican)
1861 – 1865
James Buchanan (Democrat)
1857 – 1861
Franklin Pierce (Democrat)
1853 – 1857
Millard Fillmore (Whig)
1850 – 1853
Zachary Taylor (Whig)
1849 – 1850
James Polk (Democrat)
1845 – 1849
John Tyler (Whig)
1841 – 1845
William Harrison (Whig)
1841
Martin Van Buren (Democrat)
1837 – 1841
Andrew Jackson (Democrat)
1829 – 1837
John Quincy Adams
(Democrat – Republican)
1825 – 1829
James Monroe
(Democrat – Republican)
1817 – 1825
James Madison
(Democrat – Republican)
1809 – 1817
Thomas Jefferson
(Democrat – Republican)
1801 – 1809
John Adams (Federalist)
1797 – 1801
George Washington (Federalist)
1789 – 1797